T0289498

Historical Evidence
and Argument

Historical Evidence and Argument

DAVID HENIGE

THE UNIVERSITY OF WISCONSIN PRESS

This book was published with the support of the Anonymous Fund
for the Humanities of the University of Wisconsin–Madison

The University of Wisconsin Press
1930 Monroe Street
Madison, Wisconsin 53711

www.wisc.edu/wisconsinpress/

3 Henrietta Street
London WC2E 8LU, England

Library of Congress Cataloging-in-Publication Data
Henige, David P.
Historical evidence and argument / David Henige.
        p.   cm.
Includes bibliographical references and index.
ISBN 0-299-21410-9 (cloth: alk. paper)
1. History—Methodology.   2. History—Philosophy.   I. Title.
        D16.H45   2006
    901—dc22   2005010203

To

JAN

and

JAN

Those who doubt most always err least.
Samuel Richardson, *Pamela*

What to believe, in the course of his reading, was Mr. Boffin's
chief literary difficulty indeed; for some time he was divided
in his mind between half, all, or none; at length, when he
decided, as a moderate man, to compound with half, the
question still remained, which half? And that stumbling-block
he never got over.
Dickens, *Our Mutual Friend*

We do not deal in belief where evidence is available.
Janet Neel, *O Gentle Death*

I am contented and happy and therefore not a good historian.
Goethe, *Sorrows of Young Werther*

CONTENTS

x   ❖   Contents

ACKNOWLEDGMENTS

Sigmund Freud would have said "aha!" but I think it all began early. Unconsciously (I imagine) following Robert Ingersoll's dictum that "[t]he child should be taught to investigate, not to believe," my mother wasted no time in enjoining the three of us that a jaundiced eye is all too often the most reliable of optics, and a host of experiences ever since have vindicated her view. By the same token, she was no less adamant that any skepticism be routinely tested, and that we should never fail to allow ourselves, if necessary, to be provisionally persuaded by the preponderance of evidence in whatever direction. As noticed below, I was ingenuousness personified at first, but eventually I found that it was seldom particularly necessary or profitable to believe unreservedly at any point in the process. I thank her then for setting me on the right track while I was still too young to suppose that I knew better, and thereby helping to save me from countless moments of chagrined disabusal.

In his "Ulysses" Tennyson wrote that "I am a part of all that I have met." Slightly exaggerated perhaps, but the fact remains that I have accumulated sizeable debts over the years, in part through being assimilated by the thoughts and attitudes of those with whom I have interacted. Some of these were more important, some more prolonged than others, and I cannot escape offering thanks—in some cases yet again.

I doubt whether any other ambiance than the one in which I have worked for these many years would have allowed me to paint with such broad strokes. The General Library System of the University of Wisconsin–Madison offers the ideal—even idyllic—asylum for the terminally inquisitive. Here curiosity is raised daily, but the same opportunities permit it to be quenched with gratifying efficiency; the real task is keeping up with opportunities there are constantly thrown up in virtually every direction. I have probably failed at this, but the fun is in the trying, and I confess happily to using and overusing, even abusing, the myriad opportunities shamelessly—and very gratefully too.

Even so, the lamentable state of library budgets these days, pitted against the unrelenting proliferation and increasing cost of information, make it impossible to rely entirely on local resources for any research initiative of a broadly comparative nature. And so, for the umpteenth time over the past thirty-five years, I find it necessary—but undeniably pleasurable—to thank the staff of Memorial Library's Interlibrary Loan Department for their continuing staunch support. Indeed, I cannot be grateful enough for their contributions over the years; their generous policy in acquiring materials enables me—and other users—to secure items for no higher purpose than to check the accuracy and context of quotations, whether transcribed by myself or by others.

In particular I want to thank Ken Frazier, the Director of the General Library System, for fostering an atmosphere that accepts that scholarship works best when all the boundaries are osmotic. At the same time the overall collegial atmosphere within Memorial Library itself has made using its rich materials a process that has been both extraordinarily efficient and congenial. It is hardly a wonder that over the years I have come to appreciate more and more the serendipitous circumstances into which I happen to have fallen.

Bruce Fetter and Jan Vansina both read rather longer versions of this work and offered advice that I was happy to take in terms of shortening and rationalizing the presentation of what, after all, is a disparate set of arguments. David Conrad and an anonymous reader offered the kinds of detached observations on the penultimate—but nearly ultimate—version that an author cannot produce, but also cannot prosper without. I especially appreciate Paul Irwin's really thorough exegesis of an earlier, less digested, version, reminding me once again what a loss his career path has been to African historiography. Phyllis Holman Weisbard read the entire manuscript at a late date in the process and brought to my attention several deficiencies that I had lost sight of through overfamiliarity, as well as offered some suggestions for including materials. I regret now that I did not give her an earlier crack at the text.

Camera-ready formatted pages were prepared by Jeff Kaufmann, who has done the same for *History in Africa*, a journal I edit, for several years. Jeff's technical skills and reliability—the second unquestionably rarer than the first—have helped relieve me of potentially large dollops of anxiety, allowing me to transfer these to other arenas.

Thinking back, I realize that an important catalyst that turned my face toward the road called method was a course in historical methodology that I took from J. Carroll Moody nearly forty years ago. Subsequent experience has taught me that very few academics want to bother teaching such a course, but Carroll Moody either was an exception or just managed to fool me. Either way, it was an experience from which I have clearly benefited.

The homonymous dedication hardly speaks for itself, so let me add a few thoughts. In different but complementary ways, both Jan Behn and Jan Vansina have provided support and encouragement over a very long period of time through this and other enterprises, not least by occasionally questioning my goals, or at least the ways by which I sought to achieve them. In what follows, readers will recognize the virtues and opportunities I see in such ceaseless dialectic and will understand my appreciation for being afforded it as my thinking progressed.

1

DECLAIMING THE ENDTIME

Who wants to fix a limit for the human mind? Who wants to
assert that everything which is knowable in the world is
already known?

No evidence, Cordelia, but a deep certainty.

I

As the second millennium clocked down, a flurry of writing on "the end of history" appeared. This proved millennarian not only in timing, but in outlook. The end was nigh, not because historians had gone as far with the available evidence as they could, but because there *was* no farther to go. The past had been effectively conquered.[1] The notion engendered some sport, then faded away. However brief its efflorescence, the incident reminds us how easy it is to proclaim victory, even when we are not sure who the enemy is.

The episode mirrored earlier occasions, less millennarian in timing, but more widely embraced. Many remain certain that ours is a unique creation, despite adverting possibilities too large to contemplate. What keeps these visions alive is an egocentric belief that time and space revolve around us, that we are the acme of all that has gone before, and the omphalos of a boundless yet centered universe. Less apocalyptic versions include the notion that we have at our disposal, or at least within reach, all that is required to answer almost any question we might care to ask, and it seems easy enough to accept this premise when those questions are about the past.

II

James Mill prefaced his history of India by assuring his readers that "I have performed the business of research, with a labour, and patience, which it would not be easy to surpass. And I believe there is no point, of great importance, involved in the History of India, which the evidence I have adduced is not sufficient to determine."[2] Later the very influential Lord Acton proclaimed his own version of the "end of history" when he unflinchingly pronounced that "[n]early all the evidence that will ever appear is accessible now."[3]

Just a few years earlier Charles-Victor Langlois and Charles Seignobos had said much the same: "[t]he quantity of existing documents, if not of known documents, *is given.* Despite all the procedures taken nowadays, time continually diminishes [this quantity]. *It will never increase* . . . When all the documents are known and have undergone procedures rendering them usable, the work of scholarship will be finished."[4] They were especially sanguine about the sources for classical antiquity. "No doubt the day will come when *all* the documents relating to the history of the ancient world will have been edited and critically treated. [Then] there will be no room in the field of classical antiquity for textual criticism (restitution) or source criticism (provenance)."[5] Even the most cursory glance at the *Année Philologique* or *Medioevo Latino,* where studies of texts and textual cruxes are listed every year by the hundreds, should quickly disabuse any who might wish that this prognosis had been correct.

III

When these historians pontificated, they joined a chorus of similar comment from other fields, whose practitioners also saw themselves as climaxing centuries of progress, but not necessarily as heralding further advances. Speaking before the British Medical Association, an eminent British surgeon cataloged recent progress, but declined to anticipate more: ". . . the very success in the past has made further progress in the future difficult, if not impossible; and the surgeon of the future must be content to be the follower of his predecessor. . . That the final limits of surgery have been reached in the direction of all that is manipulative and mechanical there can, I venture to think, be little doubt. . . We have reached, in many of our most important operations, the final limit to which surgery can be carried."[6]

Other scientists of the day thought the same. A pre-eminent physicist observed that "[t]his characteristic of modern experiments—that they consist principally of measurements,—is so prominent, that the opinion seems to have got abroad, that in a few years all the great physical constants will have been approximately estimated, and that the only occupation which will then be left to men of science will be to carry on these measurements to another place of decimals."[7] Even Albert Michelson, who had just helped demonstrate that previous theories of the speed of light were wrong, wrote that "[t]he more important fundamental laws and facts of physical science have all been discovered, and these are now so firmly established that the possibility of their ever being supplanted in consequence of new discoveries is exceedingly remote."[8] These observers, and many others, could not fail to recognize the great rate of recent progress, but used it only to project a stagnant future. This allowed them to place themselves at the very pinnacle of historical progress, even if this meant turning a purblind eye to the implications of the very progress they were witnessing.[9]

Nor was the motif limited to recent times. In the first century Sextus Julius Frontinus declared that "[l]aying aside also all considerations of works and engines of war, the invention of which has long since reached its limit, and for the improvement of which I see no further hope . . ."[10] Several orders of destructive weaponry magnitude later, it is almost unimaginable that any expert in the field could have thought along these lines at any time in the past.

Even when nirvana is not proclaimed outright, there is often a feeling that it can be achieved, even if not quite yet. The historical literature is larded with anticipations of this, several of which are noticed later in this work. For instance, a prominent protagonist in the debate over the historicity of early monarchical Israel wrote in 1996 that "the debate in this area is almost at an end."[11] Since the author was among those arguing against historicity, no one should have been more sure than he that he was wrong; in fact, the debate has escalated in scope, vitriol, and intensity since then, and shows no signs of abating.

IV

To be fair, it is not at all easy to imagine ourselves to be in the midst of time rather than at its climax. Change is often imperceptible even when real, but it is the case, for instance, that the earth's geology keeps grinding along at about the pace that it has maintained for millions, if not billions, of years. Rivers get larger, river get smaller, canyons grow deeper and mountains grow higher, the flora and fauna change mysteriously, but like the hour hand on a clock, it all happens too slowly to be observed, even if it can sometimes be measured when it *is* noticed.

At the end of an earlier century, Louis Leroy expressed more wonderment than certainty, as he viewed the kaleidoscopic changes that marked his time: "All the mysteries of God and the secrets of nature are not discovered at one time. The greatest things are difficult and long in comming . . . How many have bin first knowen and found out in this age? I say new lands, new seas, new formes of men, manners, lawes, and customes; new diseases and new remedies; new waies of the Heavens, and of the Ocean, never before found out; and new starres seen. Yea, and how many remaines to be knowen by our posteritie?"[12] The premise throughout the present work is that Leroy was far more right to wonder about this than Acton, Erichsen, Michelson, and so many others were not to.

2

TRAVELING HOPEFULLY

*Pardon me asking this, Charlie, but does he have any . . . you
know . . . evidence?*

*Accept all the evidence, and explain it by mistakes, alliances,
coups, counter-coups, alternative names, alternative sequences
of kings, double dating, different intercalary months in rival
jurisdictions, and so on. Most scholars have taken one or more
of these approaches, and the possibilities are infinite.*

I

When Srinavasa Ramanujan burst onto the world of mathematics in 1914, his work was recognized as brilliant, but also criticized as inchoate. He often provided solutions without step-by-step preliminaries. Nonetheless, his results survived testing so well that mathematicians came to accept that many solutions for which he provided no apparent basis would eventually prove to be valid.[1] Students learn that in algebra and geometry answers can be less important than the steps which lead to the answer, and a right answer without the right process might earn a failing grade. In the study of history, the process is no less important since answers can seldom be checked independently, are merely probable rather than certain, and derive their degree of probability partly from the process itself.

II

No one of us is without an ideology, however termed, whether or not conscious, whether or not declared, whether or not shared. As a word, and certainly as a notion, "ideology" has always been around, but recently has taken on more pervasive connotations. Here I treat ideology as a quasi-systematic ensemble of beliefs, attitudes, and aims that underpin the way we argue, the evidence we use and how we use it, and the ways we hope to influence others.[2] In this sense a strongly-held ideology is an effective facilitator in all we do. Despite its historically sinister, if not odious, associations—we prefer to use it only to describe our adversaries' points of view—in fact each of us marches through life equipped with a succession of usually not-well-defined ideologies. These might change over time, sometimes radically, but *en gros* they are what sustains us even through such changes.

My own relevant ideology is that experience tends increasingly to make us more cautious, skeptical, even cynical, and that the more experience we are able to muster, the greater the degree to which this is likely to happen. But this is true only if we maintain open minds not suffocated by a set of beliefs proclaiming closure and embraced as a whole, but for which the tangible evidence is exiguous or even non-existent.

All things considered, I cannot pretend to understand why similar minatory experiences affect people in different ways, especially since I argue that one cannot consult a large body of historical evidence without encountering problematic issues. In short, I cannot understand why all historians do not eventually transmute into some breed of skeptic. It might that some are posessed of a larger leaven of we-shall-overcome feelings than others, that they hold to lesser standards of proof or persuasion, or that they are unusually prone to give greater value to congenial material.

III

It is impossible from this distant perspective to sympathize with Acton's confident outburst or those of his various contemporaries, or to know what these authors expected the practical consequences to be. Presumably historians were to be content with working and reworking available evidence about the past or look to more contemporary topics. What accounts for these hilariously wrong predictions? A strikingly arrogant view of the world of course, but also opportunity, which can be converted into another word: evidence. Derived from Latin "evidere," "to see clearly," the word constantly belies its optimistic etymology. No evidence, no history; as a formulation this seems unexceptionable, yet much continues to be written about large-scale population movements and levels, the correlation of ancient and modern sites, the course of ancient empires, and much else on the basis of little or no credible evidence.

The more evidence that became available, and the more critically it was examined, the less certain historians have had to become. Not that the use of evidence itself, even 'good' evidence, guarantees that sound historical investigation will ensue. While we cannot write good history from bad evidence, it is all too easy to write bad history from good evidence. A goal of scholarship is to present interpretations that are least vulnerable to overthrow because they combine the use of evidence and argument to present a case vulnerable only to the onset of new data or techniques. This is achieved by aggregating all the available evidence, including whatever might seem peripheral, or generating arguments that explicitly take account of any resulting weaknesses and alternative hypotheses, whether or not already in the marketplace.

Provisionally, however, other tactics might be advisable. Laying out a purely speculative, but not overtly incorrect, argument can stimulate discussion that might bring to bear new evidence or new uses for existing evidence. It is important to make it unequivocally clear in this that the purpose is stimulus, not closure. Thus evidence and argument are inseparably intertwined—components in the production of history—and for this reason are coupled here. The arguments that follow here are austere. Their premise is that historical data do not often yield gracefully to the historian, no matter his imaginative powers or technical virtuosity.[3] In particular, the premise is that the quality of the evidence and the course of historical debate over the last century or two mandate caution, which should take the form of constant devil's advocacy—at all times each historian should be his evidence's, and his own, severest critic.

Successful study of the past requires that epistemological considerations always be on the front burner. We all suffer from the desire to treat belief and knowledge as much the same commodity, and wield words like "demonstrate" and "prove" indiscriminately. At the beginning of the twenty-first century we 'know' more about the past than ever before, if only because there are more scholars at work and using more, and more fruitful, diagnostic techniques. Even so, many areas of the past are no more favored epistemologically than they ever were, despite decades, even centuries, of analysis, debate, and repeated premature closure.

Whatever might be said for theory, it interacts with evidence like a teeter-totter; only one can predominate at any given moment. The thrust of the present work is that the study of history is better served when the teeter-totter favors evidence. Just the same, it is informed by an -ism of its own, although not one of the many -isms that have been closely associated with the study of history. Rather, it is pyrrhonism—the notion that judgments about reality should be tempered and cautious, closely tied to the available evidence, and provisional, if not so provisional that sensible progress cannot be made. In this view, progress is likely to be more substantial when constantly fueled by a spirit of vigilant skepticism that preempts closure in favor of sustained and open-minded inquiry.[4]

Such skepticism fosters a willingness to undertake the labor to get it right rather than accepting and aping conventional wisdom. The best historiography is the story of those who have been unwilling to believe what they have been told. When faced with discrepant information they seek out further evidence with the aim of keeping the question open, if only to corroborate the received version, which can be as likely an alternative as any other.

Another emphasis is at work here. Most works on historical method have concentrated on U.S. and European history, where the body of evidence is the greatest and most assured. It is just for this that I prefer generally to look to times and places for which the evidence is more exiguous and commensurately more interesting and methodologically provocative. Since, I would argue, at the level of thought rather than action, historians' modus operandi should be roughly congruent, I believe that this emphasis has representative value as well.

Ultimately, all evidence must be treated alike at *some* level, with no genres given special dispensation. The notion that the study of history should in some way be compensatory leads to a historiography that regards evidence with so little respect that it is constantly on the verge of implosion. There are no reasons to esteem testimony from the past for either its congeniality or its provenance. Medieval chroniclers gave special credence to clerical witnesses and we reprove them for their naiveté, even while we continue to give preferential treatment to testimony when it suits our own case.

IV

Historical method was once a centerpiece of the historiographical enterprise, but this day seems long gone. Samuel Eliot Morison, writing as President of the American Historical Association, voiced the new tone: "[i]t matters little what 'method' the young historian follows, if he acquires the necessary tools of research, a sense of balance, and an overriding urge to get at the truth. Courses on historical methodology are not worth the time that they take up. I shall never give one myself, and I have observed that many of my colleagues who do give such courses refrain from exemplifying their methods by writing anything. It is more fun to prick to pieces the works of their contemporaries who do write."[5]

Morison did not reveal the secret of acquiring critical skills without adequate training. Then again, he was not particularly critical himself, often lacked "a sense of balance," viewed his readers as landlubbers who should unquestioningly accept his self-proclaimed nautical expertise, and was emphatically not open to differences of opinion about his own work, for instance, his choice of Columbus's first landfall.[6]

Modern curricula tend to treat explicit and extended methods courses as housekeeping drudgery. Methodology is implanted into many topical courses, but only in idiosyncratic and fragmented ways. As a result, intending historians often absorb entropic and idiosyncratic views of method and are not allowed to reach common ground by arguing specific issues in a controlled yet competitive environment. Their epistemological and ideological premises are never overtly challenged, but formed by the Zeitgeist of their particular supervisor or departmental subdivision.

V

Contingency governs the writing of history, as well as its unfolding. For instance, although its general orientation would probably have been much the same in another time and place, the details underpinning my overall argument would have been culled from different bodies of data. When this was being written, I encountered materials that influenced my thought and arguments, and in their specificity these tended to displace materials I had collected earlier. A year earlier, a year later, a different library, and my arguments would have rested on different data, whether for better or worse.

I began with—I think—no preconceived notion of how to proceed, realizing that any number of approaches could be successful. In drawing on examples from a wide range of historical experience, however, I found that I was favoring nontraditional sectors of the past, and this emphasis on times and places for which evidence is slight became more deliberate. The more scanty the evidence, the more distant epistemologically, the more passionate the desire to discover new worlds, the greater the need for caution and discipline. I found too that I had grav itated almost imperceptibly to discussions about dating. I was only momentarily surprised. In my early days I managed to collect baseball cards, postage stamps, and Captain Midnight decoder rings. For reasons long forgotten, I also began to collect chronological lists of officeholders.

My guilelessness knew no bounds. Why should I have doubted that the rulers of Ethiopia descended in an unbroken line from the queen of Sheba, that scores of European dioceses originated in the first century CE, or that dozens of Indian dynasties dated to 3000 BCE? I remember no epiphanies, but my credulity began to be abraded when I encountered other lists for the same places, on which life threatening surgery had been performed. Whole sets of rulers and bishops evanesced, in their place commentary on why they never existed.[7] The more evi dence I encountered, the more confused and confusing it seemed, but at some point I came to recognize, as the Elizabethan epigramatist John Owen expressed it, that "[a]ll things I thought I knew; but now confess the more I know, I know the less."[8]

VI

The *Art de vérifier les dates* began by listing 108 estimates of the age of the earth, ranging from 6984 BCE to 3616 BCE, almost all relying on the bible and a few ancient sources such as Josephus, himself often derivative.[9] Today there are even more estimates, most less exact and featuring numbers with many zeroes. Each of these is thought to be demonstrably correct by at least one person, and proba bly more. Whatever is responsible for all this, historians have been sharpening their pens, and their wits, for a long time on matters of dating, creating a large body of literature, virtually all of it argumentative.

Diane Greenway captured the importance of dating: "[a]s ornithologists trap and measure migratory birds, marking them with rings, so historians capture and measure fleeting moments, marking them with dates."[10] Dating issues underlie most studies of the past, usually with some divergence of opinion. Efforts to define and refine chronology are among the earliest and most continuous in all historiography, and among the most confident. As William of Malmesbury put it in the 1140s, beginning his account with words of mixed caution: ". . . be warned that I guarantee the truth of nothing in past time except the sequence of events; . . ."[11]

Five centuries later, Edward Leigh was less sure: "[s]ome say the holy Ghost did obscure some things in Chronology to sharpen mens wits."[12] Earlier, John

Harvey had expressed a view that ignored the holy ghost: "[a]ll chronological computations are ambiguous, uncertaine, fallible, erronious and deceitfull."[13] More recently, T.P. Wiseman, a classicist, expressed this deference to chronological matters: "[t]he cardinal virtues of the historian are curiosity and suspicion. The passive and the credulous can only perpetuate unexamined orthodoxies, and there is no more unhistorical activity than that. But in practice, even the most original mind takes *some* things for granted—a chronology, for instance, or a basic narrative structure—which ultimately rest on earlier historians' hypotheses or combinations of evidence, but have been so universally accepted as to seem no longer worth critical examination." But, Wiseman was careful to add, "[t]hat can be dangerous."[14]

The quest for exact and reliable dating results in arguments that are coherent, similarly disposed, and remarkably focused. All parties to chronological arguments realize that only one answer can be correct, no matter how it is determined, and this fact alone has made chronological debates more conversational than most differences of opinion. The quest for exactitude has come to involve numerous disciplines—archeology, astronomy, dendrochronology, linguistics, paleography, volcanology—all of which must use many of the same sources as historians.

A further reason for laying special emphasis on dating issues is that the chronological table is the very epitome of the triumph of hope over experience, of canon over controversy. Should a list of the rulers of England include Lady Jane Grey or the "second" reign of Henry VI? What about all the Roman Emperors who never managed to secure senatorial approval? Or the "northern line" of Japanese emperors, banished from the official list of emperors by the eventual success of the "southern line." How and why do we legitimate some popes but demonize others as antipopes?[15]

VII

Bishop George Berkeley wondered famously whether "a tree in a solitary place where no one was present to see it" really existed.[16] Berkeley was tying reality with human sense perception and we can define the past anthropocentrically, as what we think we know about. Even though we can become aware of only an infinitesimal fraction of what happened in the past, the historian's duty is to add to that incrementally, even while falling further behind in absorbing new information. Taking history instead to be all that occurred in the past encompasses many times another possible definition—the detritus that the past has, so far, offered to the continuing present. Or we could include writing about the past in "history" acknowledging that historians have a heavy hand in creating the past rather than merely creating impressions about it.

In defending his first of many contributions to the hopelessly vexed issue of Indo-Greek chronology, A.K. Narain admitted that "certainties are not many, and I have been forced to make surmises, though they have been made with caution; I do not put forward my hypotheses dogmatically and I have nothing to advocate."[17] While Narain argued with diffidence, this could never reach the state of self-abnegation he proclaimed. It is hardly possible to write at any length without revealing some form of advocacy, whether or not conscious, and Narain went on to argue that some things in Indo-Greek studies were "certain." Forty more years of debate disallows this claim.

Narain's protestations reflect the endless debate over "objectivity," however defined. I take for granted that historians cannot ultimately be objective. Asking whether evidence has intrinsic meaning is useless and distracting. Most of the meaning evidence takes on is provided by those examining and interpreting it. An excavated site once housed a temple or a fortress or a residence only to the degree that scholars advance those arguments. If meaning inhered in a site, discerning it would be an act of observation rather than ratiocination.

Even though few historians any longer think of objectivity as a kind of accessible default goal, some deride even its pursuit as chimerical. I assume that the typical historian has a paradoxical view about objectivity. While he recognizes that it is permanently elusive, he sees the virtue in ignoring this as a way to address it—as a constraining and fettering measure, without which there can be no sensible treatment of the past. Thus in the formulation of the problem, in the search for evidence and in its use, and in interpreting the results, the historian assumes that there are better ways and worse ways, even right ways and wrong ones, and that adopting objectivity as a *working* belief helps to make the wiser choices each step of the way.

VIII

It was not quite by accident that I have organized many chapters around debates in the field. A well-conducted debate is a reciprocal interrogation—fertile ground for observing historical method, even in absentia. The debate setting precludes the opportunity merely to rush forward, assert, and then melt back into the crowd without further ado.

During the World Series of 1999, Pete Rose, who had been banned by Major League Baseball ten years earlier and had been campaigning for reinstatement, was interviewed. Jim Gray eschewed the mindless approach of such interviews (How did it feel out there today? Are you glad your team won?) in favor of an aggressive line of questioning. The interview had hardly concluded when the network and its affiliates received thousands of calls critical of Gray's stance. Several members of the New York Yankees and Atlanta Braves refused to talk to Gray on camera in solidarity with Rose. In the end Gray was obliged to make an apology to "the fans." Although no more than another tempest in another teapot, the Gray-Rose confrontation is a good microcosm of how historians treat both evidence and each other. Gray argued that he had given Rose "a window of opportunity" to explain himself and Rose had declined. Most historical evidence is more refractory than Pete Rose could ever be, and in questioning it we must be even more aggressive than most sports reporters would ever be.[18]

IX

While the ensemble of sources, conduct, and attitudes that characterize historiography are unique to it, historians are in danger of behaving like everyone else. Gleach expressed this when he wrote about John Smith that "[t]hese situations [where little or no detailed evidence is available] are common in the historical record, resulting in the oft-heard litany 'little is known of . . .' in all its variations. This may be accurate in some cases, but it is certainly not very satisfying . . . [and] we need some way to fill in these gaps." Gleach found his own way by positing a series of events that Smith did not write about only because he failed to realize that they were happening, and concluded that "[t]his certainly is an improvement over minimalist conclusions that nothing is known concerning Powhatan adoptions, or that these events might or might not have happened based on purely textual criteria such as when and how Smith published the accounts."[19] Gleach's lament and his defiant expediency warn us of the sometimes overpowering will-to-know in all inquiry. Keeping this in check is fundamental to the critical use of evidence. No historian's assumptions and point of view can be based on more than his own experience, and I have tried to make that experience as extensive as possible. In the process I have repeatedly found how disappointing it so often proves to be to accept testimony at face value, no matter how congenial, no matter how tempting it is.

Recently several works have appeared devoted to discussing the work of the historian, in most cases stimulated by the rise of theories that have the effect of treating the historian's task as so arduous and vexing. In their different ways each of these works makes the same general points. History is not a science and is not cumulative. Very little can be taken for granted and revisitation is an integral part of the historiographical enterprise. Narrative and analysis both have a place in improving our understanding of the past and can be used symbiotically.[20] I accept this line of reasoning, not because it justifies the historian's intellectual journey, but because more than two millennia of hard-won experience supports it. My objective is to discuss ways and means of raising probabilities, and sometimes of lowering them as well.

When traveling in certain atmospheric conditions, we often see what appear to be pools of water on the road ahead. As we near them, they invariably disappear. For the historian, congenial evidence often has the same evanescent quality. Haskell summarized this well: "The very possibility of historical scholarship as an enterprise . . . requires of its practitioners that vital minimum of ascetic self-discipline that enables a person to do such things as abandon wishful thinking, assimilate bad news, discard pleasing interpretations that cannot pass elementary tests of evidence and logic, and, most important of all, suspend or bracket one's own perceptions long enough to enter sympathetically into the alien and possibly repugnant perspectives of rival thinkers."[21]

Haskell refers to this attitude as "detachment" but I prefer to think of it as open-mindedness. It can be justified by numberless examples, such as the hoard of coins discovered in Afghanistan in 1992. This consisted of three to four tons of coins, perhaps 500,000 in all, but the find has not created euphoria among interested parties. Only a few specimens have been made available for scrutiny, many have been shipped off for sale, and it is feared that most of the rest will be melted down for their precious metal content.[22]

However dispiriting this case of lost, found, and possibly lost again might be to those for whom the evidence for the history of the period might have been increased many-fold, it also reminds us that most such evidence never surfaces at all. We can speculate as to what is missing and pretend that it isn't so in *our* work, but such examples should be both inspiring and chastening. The work of the historian requires a leaven of both, for the reasons expressed by the fictional C.I.D. Inspector George Hennessey: ". . . as I have grown older I have come to believe that if the sum of human knowledge was represented as a tennis ball, then on the same scale, the sum of what we don't know but is fact and awaiting discovery could be represented as a basketball."[23]

3

THE ANXIETIES OF AMBIGUITY

We all know that objective history is unobtainable . . . But
while we know this, we must still believe that . . . it is 99 per
cent obtainable; or if we can't believe this we must believe
that 43 per cent objective truth is better than 41 per cent. We
must do so, because if we don't we're lost, we fall into beguil-
ing relativity, we value one liar's version as much as another
liar's, we throw up our hands at the puzzle of it all, we admit
that the victor has the right not just to the spoils but also to the
truth.

For my part, as I went away, I reasoned with regard to myself:
"I am wiser than this human being. For probably neither of us
knows anything noble and good, but he supposes he knows
something when he does not know, while I, just as I do not
know, do not even suppose that I do. I am likely to be a little
bit wiser than he in this very thing: that whatever I do not
know, I do not even suppose I know."

I

Hans Goedicke conceded that his hypothesis about the relationship of the two
successors of Pepi I "cannot be confirmed by any written evidence (especially since the official tradition was changed later), but on the other hand no indi-

cation speaks against it, *wherefore* it possesses a high degree of likelihood."[1] Goedicke's comment is a bald formulation of the common attitude that no known evidence against a hypothesis is tantamount to evidence for it. Proceeding on such a principle is certain to ease the path of any historian as he presses forward. Yet contrary historical evidence is hard to come by for most periods and places. For Goedicke, it would require some unambiguous evidence about the relationship of two rulers of VI Dynasty of Egypt, for which there are many missing genealogical links and where the proliferation of similar royal titulature complicates positive identification even when filiations are mentioned.

In contrast, commenting on the work of another scholar, David Keightley was concerned:

> Professor Ho, I believe, is far more optimistic, far less austere than a historian should be . . . . I believe that the historiographical cautions required in other cultures are also required in dealing with early Chinese who were no purer, and no less human, in this regard, than other people. Professor Ho, by contrast, sees the Shang kings as honest rulers who kept true genealogical records, good and kind kings whose sayings have been faithfully preserved in [later] Chou and Han traditions that were equally pure in their historiographical intent; he views the early Chinese, in short, as different from, more pristine than, other peoples, and therefore deserving special historiographical trust. . . . I am not willing to concede his implied claims to an indigenous, uncorrupted, and credulous historiography.[2]

There is a potential hornet's nest here of course, but the relevant issue concerns the different views of probing the past that Ho and Keightley espouse. One wishes to take gratefully whatever evidence has come to light, realizing that there is unlikely to be much more. The other takes this very unlikelihood as reason to be cautious in his embrace.

II

John Thornton poses a question:

> Historians . . . do not possess infinite data; indeed, they are lucky to possess data at all. They are in no position to generate data of their own, but must take whatever people in the past, for their own purposes, deemed appropriate to

collect and record, winnowed by the inevitable losses of documentation wrought by the passage of time. As a result, historians have to start with the data they have and procede [sic] backwards (from the social scientists' point of view) to the questions. Rather than asking, "What are the relevant questions that I should ask about a particular process?", historians must say, "Here are my data, what questions can I answer with them?"[3]

This could be phrased in other ways. The historian might ask: "[i]s the evidence on my side"? Or he could ask: "[a]m I on the side of the evidence?" The second query encourages the accumulation of evidence, the exaltation of that evidence above the historian, and other salutary results.

As noted, some historians view history as whatever we happen to know about the past and nothing more. The more we know, the more history there is. While engagingly egocentric, this view of worlds past would not be worth considering were it not that it causes historians to adopt habits of thought that deprecate evidence in favor of interpretation, and interpretation in favor of the interpreter. A more sober view is that history is the sum total of the past, whether or not recorded. Historians make their living by learning more about this past, nibbling around it with the occasional inward foray. Our job is to blunder on, making the best use of evidence and argument that we can, always remaining aware that the next new discovery could show our path-finding to be deficient.

What determines which questions the historian asks when he encounters the infinite worlds of maybe? It is unlikely that a historian can come to his task unaffected by life's experiences. It is less likely yet that he could proceed with the task without being further affected by his discoveries, or the lack of them. Added together, these could be usefully, if loosely, labeled a personal philosophy—or ideology—of history. If the historian has frequently been disappointed, taken in by error, he might not resist taking a jaundiced view toward the reliability and authenticity of data he uncovers. Or he might take a more cheerful view of things. Since skepticism often results from a cumulatively observant view toward one's own experiences, this might be because he is young and still bereft of such experiences, or he might not have been as observant as he should, or has just been fortunate in his path through life. Whatever the case, we can assume some correlation between life as lived and the past as interpreted. Thus no two historians, even if they received the same training, will respond to their evidence in quite the same ways.

Is there real danger that the historian will project his life onto his work to the degree that they are inextricably bound together? Not if he learns and observes the rules of evidence, searches for evidence widely, learns the language/s of his sources, keeps a detached and open mind as to the results of his work, treats criticism as an opportunity, and thinks closure is a desirable but unrealistic goal. Historians with this attitude will produce careful work that draws rigorously on a wide range of sources, and will anticipate—even relish—criticism as a feature of their own interpretive journeys.

III

We can—some do—look at the past as an ineluctable process in which many things have happened because they had to. The twentieth-century's world wars were not only inevitable, but they would have occurred pretty much as they did in terms of causes, alliances, and results, no matter what. By this argument there is little point in studying the details of history because these embroidered but did not shape the overall picture.

Another, and better, way is to see the past as contingent. Many things could have happened even though only one ensemble actually did. One of Shakespeare's characters noted the precariousness of life's order.

> Take but degree away, untune that string,
> And, hark, what discord follows![4]

More recently, television featured a commercial in which a man and woman walked their separate ways down the street, in apparently intersecting paths. The accompanying music led viewers to believe that an epochal meeting was about to occur, but the couple missed each other by a few feet, and life went on as before. The message was that opportunities can be lost as well as gained

Treating one level of historical happening as contingent makes the historian's use of evidence more important, since evidence must replace predisposition as the basis of explanation. In truth, much of everyday life is contingent. In sports, victory or defeat is determined by who happens to be ahead after nine innings, ninety minutes, 5000 meters, or eight furlongs. Believing in contingency makes the historian's work more interesting, but also more insecure. He can uncover no wholes that are greater than the sums of their parts, will have more trouble extrapolating, and will not even bother to look for the historical elixir of life, which might help explain contingency's unpopularity in certain quarters.[5] He will be modest in his goals and methods, but would probably have trouble believing in himself otherwise. He will write in a mode that permits him to change his mind on the basis of new evidence or new insights. The door is not locked, it is not even fully closed.

It is unfortunate that the most prevalent expression of the past as contingent is counterfactual history. Few of us are so incurious as never to wonder about the what-ifs of life, or so lucky as to avoid the if-onlys. Such thoughts allow us to re-engineer our pasts in ways that better suit us. The elbow room in these exercises is enormous, constrained by plausibility (historian-defined), which has no necessary relationship with reality, but not by any historical record. The opportunities, indeed the need, for subjectivity arise from the very beginning and accelerate throughout the process. Perhaps this is why Richard Lebow notes that some (though not he) regard the exercise as consisting of "flights of fancy, fun over a beer or two in the faculty club, but not the stuff of serious research."[6]

Not all agree, of course; the cover of a book on biblical matters describes its contents. "[What if the exodus and conquest had really happened? What if we had no Assyrian account of Sennacherib's third campaign . . .? What if Paul had travelled east rather than west? . . . This is not fantasy or fiction [but] . . . serious scholarly inquiry into alternative scenarios and their potential consequences. The result is a trenchant demonstration of the ways historians set about working *with the evidence* in order to reconstruct the past."[7] *With* the evidence? *What* evidence?

Writ small, such reasoning figures in most historical analysis. If couched in more generally "what if" terms, it can cause readers to shudder with relief. Conversely, couched in "if only" terms, it creates regret. Writ large, it provides a pleasant diversion which allows readers to rate the cleverness and clairvoyance of the historian engaged in it. It has its disadvantages, however, at least when it goes so far as to limn alternative worlds. It assumes facts not in evidence; indeed, it assumes facts that can *never* be in evidence. Another of counterfactual history's fatal flaws is that, to remain plausible, it must have a large ceteris paribus element, which assumes that those variables the historian dallies with changed, whereas others, also at the historian's discretion, did not. No matter how sophisticated such exercises, no matter how plausible, they can only be tributes to historians' ingenuity and deserve no higher place.

Conveniently, the counterfactualizing historian—and only he—gets to decide just when to begin to deviate from the historical record. This alone effects dramatically any scenarios he might develop. Take the American Civil War. Historians have identified any number of occasions, ranging from the two-fifths amendment in the Constitution in the 1780s to the election of 1864, as crucial to the unfolding of events. Pick a later one of these to start with and certain possibilities are excluded; pick another, earlier, one and—hey presto!—they become fair game.

Its practitioners argue that playing the counterfactual game helps identify significant turning points in history—those situations where a different outcome would have had the greatest long-term effect. By this argument, the earlier the occasion, the greater the impact—if dinosaurs and homo sapiens had co-existed; if Eve had resisted the serpent; if the wheel and iron technology had been available to the Incas and Aztecs; etc. It also emboldens counterfactualists to transform minor events into major ones as part of their performance.

Consoling counterfactualizing is hardly a modern phenomenon. Livy took time out from his account of Rome's second Samnite war because "I have often silently pondered in my mind . . . how the Roman State would have fared in a war with Alexander." It is no surprise that he decided that it would have fared as well as it eventually did a century later against Hannibal. Alexander would have faced several military leaders, each superior to Darius III, and a republic not subject to the whims of a single leader. He would have been outnumbered and, like Pyrrhus, unable to replace losses.[8]

No doubt this reasoning pleased Livy. After all, uncontrolled counterfactual reasoning frees historians to create their own scenarios.[9] This also happened to Arnold Toynbee, who, in an essay entitled "If [Only] Alexander the Great Had Lived On," gave Alexander a second chance at life. By keeping him alive for another thirty-six years and having him beget a line of worthy successors, Toynbee was able to conjure a scenario in which a one-world government developed, ruled by Alexander's direct descendants, culminating in "the reigning (but not, of course, governing) World-ruler Alexander LXXXVI."[10]

Alternative histories are thriving at the moment. Several collections of counterfactual history have recently been published treating military matters, long a beehive of counterfactualist activity. The editor of one of these justifies his collection on the grounds that what-ifs of the past "can be a tool to enhance the understanding of history, to make it come alive. They can reveal, in startling detail, the essential stakes of a confrontation, as well as its potentially abiding consequences." He goes on that "[f]rivolous counterfactuals have given the question a bad name, and we avoided speculations such as what would have happened if Hannibal had possessed an H-bomb, or Napoleon stealth bombers . . ." He concluded that "[p]lausible then, is the key word."[11] Well, yes.

Unfortunately, many of the studies that follow his introduction challenge the usual meaning of that word. Is it plausible to treat as fact the biblical account of an "angel of death" that supposedly miraculously destroyed Sennacherib's invading army as depicting "plague"?[12] Is it plausible to assume that, if Cortés had been killed at Tenochtitlan, the most likely outcome would have been an Amerindian "constitutional monarchy" whose effect would have been to "have left the United States of today far smaller and bordering a nation of truly indigenous Americans?"[13]

It is necessary to distinguish carefully between garden-variety counterfactualizing, which all historians constantly do, and grand theorizing that assumes the fantasy and *begins* the argument there, in effect constituting a subset of utopian writing. It is perfectly valid to wonder what would have happened if Caesar had not been assassinated, had Hooker attacked Lee at Antietam when Lee's forces were split, had the atomic bomb not been dropped, or had Ted Williams not given five of his prime years to military service. Doing so simply helps us understand that contingencies underlie history.[14] It is pretending that these alternatives did happen and proceeding accordingly that renders so much counterfactual history entirely unaccountable and thus vacuous.[15]

In this respect, it is not a little offputting that the Library of Congress invariably awards counterfactualizing books call numbers within the history (D-DX) classification, rather than in the classifications (P-PZ) devoted to literary works. Thus, *The Napoleonic Options*, containing essays devoted to what might have happened but did not, has a call number (DC220.1N37) that places if squarely among works on French historical events that *did* happen.

Inevitably, playing these guessing games thrives in inverse proportion to the available constraining evidence. Hassig notes this when he defends counterfactual reasoning as "a sound approach for testing and proofing causal arguments that rest upon the inherently limited historical data typical of non-western and contact situations."[16] As noted above, his own case shows well enough how much damage removing these limits can inflict.

A close, and possibly more legitimate, relative of counterfactual reasoning is the application of historical method to works of acknowledged fiction, such as the Sherlock Holmes canon. This too might seem to be no more than *homo ludens* at work, but much can be learned about squeezing evidence from stones in the several thousand large and small studies that treat the issue. It shows that Arthur

Conan Doyle, like many other witnesses, was not interested in being consistent, a fact that probably accounts for most of the activity. Otherwise, the amount of ingenuity spent on arguing the tiniest detail provides a handy case study of the sheer variety of ways that historians can operate in ideal conditions.[17]

IV

Crucial differences among historians turn on the ranges they apply to words like "possible," "plausible," and "probable," and how they apply these to their own thinking. As historians we are forced to base our views on plausibility, and by extension on credibility, and on present-day mores, but we must also seek to understand the views of faraway generations on the matter. Is our plausibility theirs, or vice versa? How we answer this centrally affects how we proceed.[18]

In assessing Bernardino de Sahagún's heavily-used testimony about Nahuatl practices and beliefs, Browne makes the point that his "goal is to estrange the reader from Sahagún—or at least the Sahagún who looks a lot like a modern-day scholar."[19] This view exculpates the sources from wilful fabrication and also forces us to consider that historians in the past did not always view their evidence in quite the same ways as historians in the present.

Of course individual notions of plausibility are fashioned by the degree of faith we have learned to accept as necessary and tolerable. In 1999 the Vatican and several Protestant churches reached agreement in a five-century-long dispute over the relative merits of faith and good works in attaining eternal life. The Catholic Church changed its position that good works were necessary to one in which they were merely important. In this long dispute, faith has officially pre-vailed, at least for the moment.

A similar triumph of faith over evidence is palpably visible in the study of ancient Israel. In discussing the Abraham figure, A.H. Millard points out that many biblical scholars reject Abraham's historicity, even though they might accept that his story is a plausible expression of the times in which he is placed, Millard sums up his own views:

> [t]o place Abraham at the beginning of the 2d millennium B.C. is, therefore, sustainable. . . The advantage this brings is the possibility that Abraham was a real person whose life story, however handed down [for more than a mil-lennium], has been preserved reliably. This is important for all who take bib-lical teaching about faith seriously. Faith is informed, not blind . . . Without

> Abraham, a major block in the foundations of both Judaism and Christianity
> is lost; a fictional Abraham might incorporate and illustrate communal
> beliefs, but could supply no rational evidence for faith because any other
> community could invent a totally different figure . . .[20]

By this surreal argument, Abraham must have been real because faith demands
that he was. Reasonably contemporaneous external evidence would be welcome,
but it is not actually necessary. Millard is satisfied that there is no evidence
against his argument, without asking what that evidence could possibly be.

V

For many, the study of history is in the throes of one of its recurring crises.
Contrasting historical views at the turn of the twentieth century with some of
those prevalent today, W.H. McNeill saw significant differences: ". . . the personality and the biographical element in anybody's contribution to this temple of
learning were [sic] irrelevant. All that mattered was the careful criticism of
sources. This ideal prevailed for fifty or sixty years but has now, I think, been
very generally abandoned."[21] Choosing the scientific school of historiography
allowed McNeill's declaration to seem reasonable. Source criticism was an ideal
now recognized for what it was, and the appeal of the egalitarian source shows in
a good deal of recent history-writing.

A century earlier the question had been: how scientific can history be/come?
Later, historians struggled over the role of history-making in nation-building.
Then it was the matter of the role historians and their subject play in making the
world a better place. From this emerged the next crisis, which concerned the relationship between macro-theory and the historical record. Is it possible to find a
body of evidence, no matter how collected or how construed, that can single-
handedly contribute to grand theory? Or does theory serve as a multiplier, allowing the theorist to extrapolate from a few knowns, or givens, to a much larger
array of unknowns, which become knowable by dint of annexation? Most recently, historians have discovered themselves and they find their new objects of affec-
tion downright fascinating. This newest orthodoxy sees colloquy as immaterial—
historians can never be right, so they can never be wrong either. Why bother?

The paucity of historical sources rightly leads historians to seek out new ones.
Among the tenets of much contemporary historiography is that conventional historical evidence is inadequate for present requirements, requiring us to locate

sources that do not partake of their defects. Often these already exist but have been disregarded in favor of sources that were intended, or at least had the effect, of reinforcing past status quos. In other cases, historians take part in creating new sources, oral history being the most obvious example, designed to help redress the balance.

So far, so good, but historians sometimes make further assumptions that endanger the rigor of the historiographical enterprise. The one that probably matters most is that, since all testimonies are affected by the experience, persona, and bias of witnesses—whether author or informant, translator or editor, or the reader himself—this evidence has little extrinsic value, so no piece of evidence need be arrogated over any other piece. This leads to a form of counter-nihilism in which every source and every interpretation is of roughly equivalent value. Since each is as "true" as any of the others, not only is reaching objective truth, and of realizing this, impossible, but objectified truth itself becomes a siren whose call historians are well advised to resist. If the historian's purpose is to seek out the truth about past events, processes, causes, and effects—not necessarily by determining what happened but by establishing degrees of probability and determining what did *not* happen—then the notion of multipliable truth is subversive to the very core of the enterprise. If there is no objective, there can be no quest.

It has never been a secret that different investigators will value—and even discern—evidence differently, but it has not normally been assumed that all the resulting disparate conclusions will be of comparable value, so that new interpretations can flourish simply by being advanced. Like hypercredulity, this debilitates the desire to seek out all sources of data—because these have now become potentially infinite, yet indistinguishable—and evaluate them in different contexts, working alternately with and against the evidence, sifting and winnowing in order to establish probabilities.

One of the characteristics of postmodern argument is its seductiveness. If objectivity is an illusion, if truth is idiosyncratic, and if science is artfully camouflaged opinion, then what is to keep from choosing what to believe, what not to, entirely on personal grounds? In this scheme of things there is no need to develop arguments that can resist reasonable criticism or be responsive to the weight of available evidence. An inevitable result is that rigor, persistence, a critical eye, and an open, questing mind are all abandoned in favor of overweening introspection, in which the evidence of the individual historian's senses is regarded as paramount. There is no real danger that the historian can be more than technically and trivially at fault. Acceding to the inevitable, historians who practice this strain of historiography grant themselves immunity from error. Against this is pitted the traditional approach to evidence, which holds that, while no single available source might contain the truth, all of them cannot do so, since there is not enough truth to go around.

In *Telling the Truth About History*, Appleby, Hunt, and Jacobs write that "postmodernism raises arresting questions about truth, objectivity, and history that cannot simply be dismissed."[22] Of course they cannot, or at least should not be without confronting them, but crediting postmodernism with parsing these age-old questions is badly off-base. Exactly how badly is suggested by a discussion about a prominent historian, in whose work there are over 1100 examples of "extensive authorial interruption," i.e., first-person references. More than forty times this historian "interrupts the ongoing tale to make comments . . . which expressly call into question the truth of the version of events he records." The modern author goes on: "[w]hat kind of historian expressly rejects his own data, without going on to put something better in its place? What kind of historian warns us that much of what we read in his history is simply untrue?"[23]

What species of historian indeed? Not, as we might expect, a self-contemplative contemporary postmodernist at all, but Herodotus, often accused of excessive credulity and not, to my knowledge, a historian ever admitted into the postmodernist pantheon. Countless historians since have done the same, and it is pretentious or ignorant to imply or argue otherwise.

Writing with a very specific theoretical agenda in mind, E.H. Carr devoted the first chapter of his *What is History?* to warning readers that "facts" are seldom what they seem to be. In writing that "[t]he facts speak only when the historian calls on them," he did not go nearly as far as those who take the notion of fact to be fictional, but Carr underscored the subjectivity of historical inquiry in much the same way as they do.[24] If he did not write with their passion and rhetorical overkill, it was probably because he realized he was merely reiterating a widely-accepted epistemological position rather than pretending to stake out brave new ground.

As individuals and as scholars, each of us has the right, often the obligation, to disbelieve something we experience—otherwise, magic would be miraculous and professional wrestlers the world's greatest athletes. This does not allow us to evade our responsibilities to test evidence—and ourselves—before we draw conclusions. Nor does it warrant putting ourselves constantly at the center of our enterprise, forcing critics to sight in on an ever-moving target. Least of all does it allow us to pontificate on the fragility of knowledge in order to excuse indolence in addressing loose ends, elusive sources, or irksome discrepancies.

VI

Prefaces and prolegomena were invented centuries ago so an author could present himself before proceeding with his argument. Before the nineteenth century, few historians claimed anything like objectivity; even Thucydides admitted only to trying. Even more rare was the historian who insistently belabored his own presence.

It would be foolish to suggest that either the historian or the evidence should be given top billing as a matter of course. Deficiencies in training, predisposition, and indolence always have, and always will, influence historians' results and conclusions. While it would be panglossian to think that we can always overcome these, the best defense is a open and critical mind engaging as much of the evidence as possible as energetically as possible, reckoning both the possibilities, the probabilities, and the impossibilities, and in the process visibly ceding center stage to the evidence.

It does not require a particularly observant eye to notice the many contradictions that mar postmodernists' arguments. One of their more bemusing positions is that the only certainty concerns postmodernism's own inevitability. Thus Keith Jenkins turns pre-ordinist when he roundly declares that what he preaches is not "a position we can choose to subscribe to or not . . ." No longer a skeptic, he assures us that this is nothing less than "our fate."[25]

If consulting and evaluating evidence is all but pointless, consulting the works of each other and paying homage to a group of semi-deities whose works always seem above reproach is de rigueur. In the process the work of congenial thinkers is used uncritically to elevate and legitimate all sorts of garden-variety assertions. This seems not only paradoxical, but downright disingenuous. Perhaps it would be entirely ungracious to think of postmodernism as bearing a certain resemblance to the recovered memory movement in psychology, which effloresced, was paramount for a short time, and then quickly faded, leaving much damage and a group of unrepentant practitioners in its wake.

VII

I adopt another approach here—the comparative, even the eclectic. This apparent lack of focus is intentional, designed to suggest—space limitations disallow any more—that the extant historical record can and does support arguments for caution and testing based on a variety of times and places. In effect I advance arguments by exemplification, less designed to convince than to give pause and incite further investigation.

I present one or more examples that support the particular argument and argue that these have general as well as specific significance. The advantage to this approach is that any dubious reader can test my case by checking the examples I have chosen before proceeding. I accept that it also forces readers to accept my assertions that enough other similar cases exist to render the examples competitively plausible. In short, it requires suspending disbelief about arguments advocating a suspension of belief.[26]

The range of examples included here is both purposeful and accidental. Some I know well from previous investigation, whereas others might escape my firm grasp. The intent is to suggest that the historian can gain perspective—and with it a sense of in/congruity—from a wide acquaintance with the historical record. While this approach can become too eclectic, this is not the case here since the universe in this respect is truly vast. If anything, I feel a lack of exemplification imposed by practicalities. Bare boned, the question is this: which is the more important, the historian or the evidence?

Nancy Nolte expressed the dilemma of writing critical history: "[Michael Jones] spends far too many pages and too much of the reader's time discussing the evidentiary difficulties of all his topics. His emphasis on the negative aspects of evidence undermines the credibility of his conclusions."[27] Readers prefer affirmative arguments, so an author who faces up squarely to problems of evidence is in danger of sacrificing his own case in the court of scholarly opinion. Jones might have compressed his discussion of evidence to a preface or relegated it entirely to footnotes, or he might have dispensed with it altogether. Readers might then have been more persuaded by his conclusions than he was himself. Does any historian have that right?

VII

The historian who regards posterity and his own scholarly conscience as his main target audiences often sacrifices immediate impact, but manumits himself from the attendant constraints. This is just as well since, as the Nobel laureate George Stigler, points out—and which has been confirmed empirically in other fields—"[p]eople demand much higher standards of evidence for unpopular or unexpected findings than for comfortably familiar findings."[28] Experience shows us that plumbing the past has its own irregular and unpredictable cycles of taste and treatment. Today's historian who writes for tomorrow might never find himself in much favor, either as observer or database entry. Just the same, all historians have an obligation to write as though their work will be timeless as well as timely.[29] In particular, they need to consider how important it might be to put in place an interpretation that is precisely heterodox and above the moment. Among posterity's perquisites should be that its past—our present—bequeath a range of choices for them to consider.

4

UNRAVELING GORDIAN KNOTS

I doubt everyone until the last page. That's how I made
Lieutenant.

I have the gravest doubts upon the subject. But I intend to
crush them. This is no time for scepticism. There is too much
scepticism in the age as it is.

I

An episode of a radio show began with the keeper of a "differential integrator" regaling his audience with its wondrous powers. It could perform in sixteen minutes work that would take a team of twenty mathematicians ten years to accomplish. One of his audience innocently asked: "How do you know the answer's right" unless "twenty mathematicians work ten years to do it over again?" Another added that he thought "it's absurd for a bunch of great big high-powered scientists to build a gadget like this and then take its word for everything without question." The custodian stammered and blustered that these doubts lacked a "proper scientific approach," but later he tested the computer by asking it what 2 + 2 equaled. To his chagrin, he received a different answer each time and the plot drifted along other lines.[1] "How do I know?" "How did my sources know?" are questions that every historian must ask himself frequently, so their own plots can thicken.

Any examination of historical thinking requires a chapter devoted to doubt simply because the vast majority of what was once generally believed is no longer generally believed. Sources continue to come under scrutiny, sometimes to be compromised, sometimes to be rejected outright. It is easy to imagine that we happen to be the lucky generation at the culmination of knowledge about the past. Whether this is so or not, only future generations can answer. In the meantime, the least we can do is to maintain a contextual modesty dictated by the cumulative experience of our predecessors.

II

Young Washington Irving needed a role model, and he found him in Christopher Columbus. The journal of Columbus's first voyage had just been published for the first time, inspiring Irving to write a life of the navigator. He was determined not to denigrate his new hero—there was already too much of this: "[t]here is a certain meddlesome spirit, which, in the garb of learned research, goes prying about the traces of history, casting down its monuments, and marring and mutilating its fairest trophies. Care should be taken to vindicate great names from such pernicious erudition."[2]

A few years later, William Gilmore Simms echoed Irving. Writing on the work of Barthold Georg Niebuhr, Simms lamented:

> It is not our purpose to disparage the learned ingenuity, the keen and vigilant judgment, the great industry, the vast erudition and sleepless research of this coldly inquisitive man;—yet, what a wreck he has made of the imposing structure of ancient history, as it comes to us from the hands of ancient art. Whether the simple fact, that what he gives us is more certainly true than what we had such perfect faith in before, is, or should be, sufficient to compensate us for that of which he despoils us, cannot well be a question with those who have a better faith in art, as the greatest of all historians, and as better deserving of our confidence than that worker who limits his faith entirely to his own discoveries. We prefer one Livy to a cloud of such witnesses as M. Niebuhr.[3]

By the standards of today's even more skeptical school of early Roman history, Niebuhr was no demolitionist. For Simms, however, he personified the first post-Enlightenment generations of historians who insisted on checking and comparing an increasing variety of sources with one another and with newer critical ways of regarding human behavior. For them, Romulus did not disappear in a thunderstorm, nor did C. Mucius Scaevola sacrifice his right hand for Rome's survival.

Bringing us up to date, some thirty years ago Sherburne Cook and Woodrow Borah argued that "[c]redence requires less faith than inflexible disbelief."[4] Although Cook and Borah treated doubt and disbelief as one and the same, their remarks distil well the unnatural sentiment that believing is more intellectually challenging than questioning. Given Borah and Cook's own lack of skepticism, their arguments are not unexpected; certainly others have acted as they did, even if not boasting about it.

III

These examples remind us that, historically, doubt has been deplored more often than deployed. Yet with astronomers, climatologists, dendrochronologists, geneticists, historical linguists, and a score of other arcane specialists crowding in on the study of the past, today's historian is increasingly forced to make ill-informed decisions. Does he accept or reject an argument he cannot understand, or does he suspend judgment? Accepting is the easiest, but possibly the most dangerous, alternative. Rejecting is almost as easy, and often less immediately dangerous. Suspending judgment will probably eventuate in some degree of both acceptance and rejection, but only after much drudgery. As Richard Hamilton puts it: "[o]n first hearing a claim, one should, as a didactic exercise, negate it and then ask, Can I defend, justify, or support the negation? The result might not be a full-scale confrontation, but a small-detail emendation, a specification, is itself an addition to our knowledge and understanding."[5] Only calculated doubt affords the historian the chance to act judiciously, and should be the most heavily-used weapon in the historian's ordnance. Sometimes, after all, the true meaning of a well-plowed written source is more impenetrable than many scientific formulations.

Skepticism is not inborn, but an ineluctable product of watchful experience.[6] The form it takes varies according to walks of life and can range from the token to the nihilistic. We routinely live beyond the evidence in our daily lives. When we telephone someone and no one answers, we tell ourselves "nobody home," even when we make it a practice of not answering our own phone, and we especially tell ourselves this if we know that the person has caller ID. This spectrum of belief plays out every day of our lives. Instant replay in sporting events illustrates this. Remote observers are exposed to this on virtually every play, even though, except for professional football, it has no effect on the game as played. Those inclined to knee-jerk belief in constituted authority will regard the instant replay as unnecessary, even dangerous. For them the officials' calls are authoritative *because* they are officials and to challenge them is unseemly. Nihilist skeptics will argue that it does not matter whether the call proves to be right or wrong, since these distinctions are arbitrary, even interchangeable. The cautious skeptic agrees that officials are usually right, but were they right in this *particular* case? Since more evidence (slow motion, various camera angles) is available, why not avail ourselves of it before making our own judgments?

There are similarly divergent critical attitudes toward historical testimony. Some take the sources as read, as a kind of decontextualized reportage waiting to be mined. Their gold is real. Those unwilling to trust the sources so blindly spend more time analyzing and assaying them and less time drawing conclusions that are categorical. Perhaps they once saw gold, but were embarrassed to discover that it was really pyrite. As a result they tend more quickly to spot incongruities and are less eager to wish them away. Whatever the case, interpretations that are squeezed from the sources rather than poured from them stand a better chance of withstanding the assaults of time and the hostility of posterity.

IV

Skepticism takes many forms—I am concerned with pyrrhonist skepticism. In theory, and often in practice as well, the pyrrhonist doubts but seldom denies. Instead, he prefers to suspend judgment about truth-claims on the grounds that further evidence or insights might alter the state of play. Pyrrhonists demand that, to be successful, all inquiry must be characterized by rhythms of searching, examining, and doubting, with each sequence generating and influencing the next in a continuously dialectical fashion.[7] As a result, issues are visited and revisited as often as needed. The result can be to strengthen probability or to weaken it— odds that might seem too risky for those who believe that progress must be inexorable. The considered suspension of belief does not ordinarily pertain in matters that are self-evident or trivial, but expressly applies to cases where more than one explanation is possible.[8]

Given this caveat, the practical advantages of pyrrhonism are patent. The most important is that declining to accept or believe keeps questions open as long as necessary. Practitioners learn to flinch when they meet terms like "certainly," "without doubt," "of course," or "prove/proof" in their reading, seeing them as discursive strikes designed to persuade where the evidence, or its use, prove insufficient. They have learned that, since new evidence and new techniques are constantly coming forth, they are sensible to withhold final judgment.

V

In scolding his most persistent critic, Marshall Sahlins asks: "[w]hy, then, this stonewalling in the face of the textual evidence? Probably because [Gananath] Obeyesekere's main debating game is a negative one, . . . the object being to cast doubt."[9] Sahlins could not be more wrong, if understandably miffed, in regarding the raising of doubt as a "negative" thing. It is its polar opposite—accepting as true statements based on little more than authority—that has had the most deleterious impact on the advancement of knowledge. Those who have followed the Sahlins-Obeyesekere quarrel—discussed further below—might choose to support one or the other or adopt a position between the two. Whatever the case, they are more likely to be edified and educated than if Obeyesekere had not entered the lists. They will see that "the textual evidence" that, Sahlins implies, is unproblematical, is nothing of the kind. The most interesting skirmishes in this war have occurred precisely over the likely meaning of the eyewitness accounts of Captain James Cook's death.

Sahlins's anathematizing of doubt and doubters scarcely stands alone. In an extended logomachy with the monster doubt, W.W. Hallo expresses concern about what he considers defeatist attitudes toward the ability of certain evidence to answer important questions. In particular he is concerned about the influential views of A. Leo Oppenheim, who was "forever cautioning against the dangers of synthesizing from partial (or partisan) evidence, forever repeating the warning 'we do not know'."[10] But, Hallo argued, this was too harsh, too gloomy. "Perhaps we do not know *yet*, but future discovery will reveal; or perhaps *we* do not know, but the ancient sources *did*, and will let us in on their knowledge if we choose to read between the lines; or again, we may not *know* but possibly we can frame a working hypothesis that *approximates* accurate knowledge."[11]

Apart from the enigmatic comment about reading interlineally, Hallo almost sounds like a pyrrhonist in good standing, but as he continues, Hallo abruptly parts company: "[w]e should not expect to know more than the ancient sources *knew*, but we can hope to know more than they chose to *tell*."[12] At this point a certified optimist might suggest that we *can* know more than the ancient sources by applying extraneous evidence (e.g., ice cores) to the data. Soon though Hallo is worrying again about Oppenheim, who wrote that "[t]he literary history of Mesopotamia" cannot yet be written for want of sufficient material.[13] These views Hallo thinks "counsels of despair."[14]

Moving on to F.R. Kraus, another scholar of ancient Mesopotamia, Hallo sees him as "preach[ing] a kind of scholarly abstinence or at least reticence," obviously not a good thing. Hallo goes on to speak of "the sacred line between the self-evident and the inferential," treating it as a line that is as unmovable as it is sacred.[15] After having shifted from pyrrhonism to a kind of measured optimism, Hallo proceeds apace: "[i]f my estimate is correct that cuneiform texts provide the most abundant archival documentation before the European Middle Ages, when or where on earth are we to go to reconstruct the society, the law, or the economy of a given culture if we cannot do it for the ancient Asiatic Near East?"[16]

Where indeed, when "abundant" and "sufficient" become functional synonyms? Later Hallo asks a pair of rhetorical questions that are also red herrings: "Must we wait until *all* the evidence is in before we construct hypotheses? Or can we not rather base such hypotheses on the data already in hand and analyzed and then modify the hypotheses in light of subsequent discoveries? I would argue that we not only can, we must!"[17]

Hallo closes with a statement that carries a weighty ideological load: we are "to treat the evidence, precisely because it is limited, as a precious resource—none of it to be ignored or squandered, but every fragmentary bit of it critically sifted, *so that it fits into our reconstruction* of the history of antiquity . . ."[18] Hallo's pilgrimage from pyrrhonism to predisposition is hurried but thoroughgoing. His ringing declaration that historians have an obligation to cram their evidence onto procrustean beds of interpretation is entirely untenable. Not only is it the antithesis of zetetic skepticism, but of all forms of historical practice that presume that evidence must speak as more than a ventriloquist's dummy. Hallo's apodictic coda shows that he has completed his odyssey. "However limited th[e] documentation may be, the only limits it imposes on us are to set reasonable limits to our own skepticism."[19]

Hallo's argument forces us to recognize that the knottiest aspect of knowing is knowing that one knows or could know. At what point can Hallo not only assert that a particular theory best suits the evidence, but also demonstrate this beyond cavil? At what point could he be sure that he—and others on whom he relies—have made no transcriptional or translation errors? What evidence can he possibly regard as "self-evident?" In particular, at what point can we be certain that "all the evidence is in?" As recent discoveries (e.g., the Khorsabad tablets, Mari, Ebla) in his own field show, significant new data continue to turn up for the ancient Near East, only to have a harrowing—but ultimately salutary—effect on existing views.[20]

In stark contrast, one of the so-called minimalists sees the stock of evidence for the ancient Near East rather less optimistically. "If we want to say something about the ancient Near East, we have to make do with what we have, not what we would like to have. This should not cause us to take over any potentially useful bit of data uncritically; on the contrary, the state of the sources should make us recognize the limits of our knowledge and the need to scrutinize all sources carefully. On the other hand, the paucity of information means that no potential sources should be dismissed without critical analysis."[21] Comparing the total evidence now available for two millennia of ancient Near Eastern history with, say, that for five years of medieval English history only demonstrates the fatuity of Hallo's roseate outlook, no matter the increase in that stock over the past century.

VI

The premise of evidential sufficiency surfaces everywhere. In criticizing a review of a book on the dating of the crucifixion, Norman Walker chastised the reviewer: his "rejection" of a particular chronology "simply because this point cannot be 'scientifically' proved strikes one as high-handed, unhelpful, and unscientific[!]." After all, he went on, "[t]he said chronology does indeed harmonise the Passion accounts in a wonderful manner, and until [the reviewer] or anyone else has a better one to displace it, must rightly hold the field. The onus lies on [the reviewer] or others to produce a satisfactory counter-hypothesis. *It is more important to build than to destroy.*"[22]

H.S. Smith had earlier argued that ". . . it is bad historical method to assume that a document of this type is radically inaccurate until there is strong external evidence to that effect." Smith was disputing arguments that the date of I Dynasty of Egypt should actually be about 750 years rather than 955 years before XI Dynasty began. Smith argued that "the average for generations of kings over the whole period of I-VI Dynasty seems acceptable," yet that number is still not known today.[23] This sort of *laisser-passer* is most frequently awarded sources that contain unique information desirable for developing arguments. The Turin Canon's data are irresistible starting points for modern chronological schemes, and they might well be generally correct. But there is no incontrovertible independent evidence that they are, nor any strong internal likelihood that such long durations would be calculated, remembered, and recorded—time and time again—in Old Kingdom Egypt.

Referring to the provenance of the Qumran documents, about which there is high controversy, Hartmut Steggemann speaks with similar pre-emptive and proprietary confidence: "[t]his [i.e., his] theory fits the evidence best and should no longer be doubted."[24] In discussing Josephus' testimony about Masada, Cohen is less imperious, candidly writing that "[r]ather than simply admit ignorance, I offer the following conjectures."[25] Cohen then offers a scenario that, while more plausible than that of Josephus, is necessarily based on testimony in Josephus, and moreover is untestable, even though it does not conflict with the available archeological evidence. Innumerable others have perforce taken a similar line. Regarding England's most famous—and most elusive—monarch, Snyder puts the issue squarely: "[there] is no contemporary proof for an historical Arthur, but neither is there proof of his fabrication, and it is fair to ask whether it is the job of an academic historian to build a negative case."[26]

These rationalizations—and the litany could easily be immensely longer—sound as if the more that historians believe something (or the more of them who do), the truer it is. Such sentiments betray a fundamental estrangement from honest doubt. To answer Snyder's peculiar, but useful, question: it is very much the object of scholarship precisely to determine the likelihood that a notion is true by first testing to see whether it is false.[27] Whether or not a theory "best" fits the evidence, vowing not to question it creates one of those self-fulfilling prophecies we all are warned about. The history of scholarship is littered with theories once thought to fit the evidence best, and sometimes actually did for a while, but were abandoned when new evidence, new techniques, and new angles of vision—including doubt—entered the picture.

VII

Is it really always more important to build than to destroy? This, after all, is the fundamental question that describes the disdain with which much skepticism is regarded. Should the skeptic feel bound to replace discredited ideas with better ones? Walker and the others are far from alone in thinking so. Zvi Yavetz, for instance, argued that "scholarly reassessments are legitimate only if new evidence that invalidates the old is discovered, if a new method of research is applied, and/or if a new outlook emerges."[28] H.W. Montefiore agrees: "[i]f the story of the Magi is unhistorical (in the sense that it is not based on what actually happened), then some satisfactory account must be given of the origin and development of the tale."

This ridiculous stipulation cannot be carried out; nothing like the necessary information is available. In fact, Montefiore went on to offer a few half-hearted suggestions, only to disown them: "[n]one of these explanations seem to be adequate to explain Matthew's tale, and the possibility must be investigated that Matthew based his story on historical events."[29] Such indulgent policies are disastrous for progress, since restricting the grounds for such reassessment all but grants immunity to much of the work already done. It actually favors those who have produced no evidence for their interpretations.

Gary Rendsburg is also worried about the effects of doubt in his field: "[b]iblical studies has [sic] gone from consensus to crisis," and he is not pleased by developments. Those who have challenged the consensus—and thereby created the crisis—are involved in "an unhealthy and deconstructive project," perhaps as a result of being "left over from the 60s and 70s, and whose personality includes the questioning of authority in all aspects of their lives." With such a "political agenda," it is no wonder that their work is "baseless twaddle."[30] William G. Dever followed with yet another denunciation of the biblical revisionists: "[t]hey strip away history, but they don't replace it with anything else." He went on portentously that "[t]hey are nihilists, and nihilism leads to a vacuum, and as we have seen before in Europe, a historical vacuum leads to fascism. And we all know where fascism leads. Jews, of all people, know what can happen. We need to speak up before it goes too far."[31]

It is not necessary for skeptics to provide a satisfactory counter-hypothesis, which merely begs the question of sufficient evidence. In fact, the zetetic process has several steps, one of which is testing. Just as a mathematical theorem or a prefabricated I-beam is tested to ensure its explanatory power or tensile strength, so a historical argument should be tested in all its parts. Referring to eight references in Josephus to a capture of Masada, James McLaren observed that "[i]t is a matter of principle that is raised here. Where there is more than one account it is important to be sure that they refer to the same event before they are used together . . . The alternative—accepting a link but then finding there is not one—requires an element of destruction. The approach used is partly based on the premise that it is easier to put something together when all the possible pieces have been properly studied than it is to undo and repair something that has been hastily constructed without all the individual pieces being assessed."[32] In short, hypotheses that fail scrutiny should provisionally be rejected and possibly—but only possibly—replaced by another argument that resists testing more effectively. If failing the test creates a vacuum, so be it, since the first step to improving hypothesizing is recognizing the need to do so.

Viewed pragmatically, expressing skepticism can be a useful form of self-protection. As he lays out his argument and his evidence, each historian should imagine himself his own worst critic, and he might feel free to entertain well-considered doubt. When he does so, he should not feel nearly as apologetic as William Murnane, who began an article with the self-deprecatory comment that it had "no higher purpose than to raise doubt."[33]

Hallo, of course, is right: skepticism can be limiting, but it also can be liberating. It does not tie but tether. No one looking at the historiography of any subject can fail to notice how much opinion has changed over time. Whether it is the age of the earth or the universe, the contact population of the Americas, the rise of Christianity, the Aryanization of India, or a thousand other topics, scholarly opinion has ebbed and flowed then and now. Each ebb, each flow occurred only because someone began to question, to unearth new evidence, and ended up modifying or overthrowing the existing wisdom. Looking at this pattern conspectively assures us not only that we can doubt, but that we must.

VIII

What limits should we set on skepticism? James Barr, a member of neither extreme group in biblical studies, nevertheless argues that "[t]here may well be no extra-biblical information to confirm this or that event referred to in the narrative. This in itself, however, does not seem to me to be in itself [sic] adequate ground for doubting the reality of the event."[34] Barr's approach is casual rather than systematic, and perhaps he fails to make any distinction between doubt and disbelief when, in fact, the differences are enormous. Whatever the case, barring incontrovertible confirmation, doubt is obligatory, even (i.e., especially) for scripture.

Oracle bones provide precious independent corroboration for the last nine of twenty-nine Shang rulers mentioned in traditional histories of early China.[35] The question is whether—and to what degree—this allows us to draw conclusions about the first twenty rulers. Some regard partial confirmation as warrant for treating the remainder of the traditional account of the Shang, and even that of the allegedly preceding Xia dynasty, as correct, at least in outline.

Until the 1920s the Xia and Shang dynasties were archeologically unattested, and no unambiguous evidence yet exists for the Xia. Ho referred to Chinese historians early in the last century as "hypercritical" and "iconoclastic" because they doubted that which later became known, and went on to argue that the "lists of seventeen [Xia] rulers may not be summarily dismissed either."[36] In using "summarily" Ho is right, and "iconoclastic" is fair enough, but is he correct to refer to those who doubted in the absence of corroborative evidence, as "*hyper*critical?" One can argue that their only obligation was to be willing to abate their skepticism if the required evidence came forth, the discovery of which was partly spurred by the iconoclasts' reservations. In retrospect, and in light of this new evidence, it is easy, but unfair, to condemn such licit doubts. Those who continue to distrust the traditional accounts of the Xia dynasty are equally duty-bound to do the same.

IX

A recent example of the salutary effects of systematic doubt is the study of the *Walam Olum*, a series of 183 glyphs on wooden tablets purporting to be a list of over ninety chiefs of the Delaware Indians from before the time they crossed "over the water, the frozen sea . . . the stone-hard water." To some, this was welcome, if unexpected, corroboration of the Bering Strait land bridge hypothesis, but to others it smacked of forgery or feedback. No one ever saw the original tablets except, if we are to believe him, Constantine Rafinesque, a scholar and charlatan of mixed repute, who self-published the contents of the alleged tablets, with renderings.[37] Given Rafinesque's reputation, and the intrinsic implausibility of the record, arguments have raged over whether the *Walam Olum* is both authentic and reliable, one or the other, or neither. The available evidence was inadequate to answer with the double negative, with the effect of keeping the question open for over 150 years. At least one elaborate cooperative effort favored both reliability and authenticity, complete with detailed itineraries and various datings—from 366 BCE for crossing the Bering Strait to "about 1327 [CE]" for "crossing the Alleghenies."[38]

There the matter might have been left—a battlefield draw—but David Oestreicher decided to test the indecision by looking more closely at Rafinesque's personal papers and other sources from the period. This canvass produced the preponderant evidence that had been lacking, and it fell on the side of inauthenticity and unreliability. Oestreicher was able to show how Rafinesque had plundered Indian language dictionaries and grammars to forge the *Walam Olum*. By applying systematic doubt to an issue that more random doubt had already long kept open, he was able at last to approach certainty. If his solution does not surprise most observers, it is no less of value for that, for it reminds us that even the most refractory historical questions can yield to sustained inquiry.[39]

Is the glass half full, or is it half empty—and why does it matter? This age-old question is commonplace in literature. In fiction it turns up in such expressions as: "I answered defensively. 'But there's no proof that Joseph [of Arimathea] *didn't* come to Britain after the Crucifixion, any more than there's proof that he *did*."[40] If this helps to sustain a story line, so be it, but in historiography it is not the story line that counts most. Just the same, the feeling that half-full is better than half-empty finds expression everywhere. Tim Cornell, who believes that much of early Rome existed pretty much as Livy described it, upbraids skeptics: "[t]here is no reason in principle why [a] tradition should not be a romanticised version of events that really happened. It is arbitrary to dismiss the rape of Lucretia (for instance) as fiction, when we have no way of knowing whether it is fiction or not."[41] As T.P. Wiseman glossed this: "[t]hat is, it purports to be true; it could be true; why should it not be true?"[42]

X

Of the three roads described at the beginning of this chapter, that occasioned by systematic doubt is the costliest in time and possibly least potent in short-term effects. Its advantage is that it is also the least vulnerable to overthrow because it provides its own embedded devil's advocacy. For some, short-term success will be sufficient; for others the goal is to present a case that dissidents will find difficult to falsify. No claim about the past is beyond the responsibility of justifying it. Despite all the arguments favoring a skeptical attitude, however, it is unlikely ever to prove popular. When Neville Morley advises his readers that "[w]hatever you do, don't just believe everything you're told; every statement should be taken apart and scrutinised before, reluctantly, you accept that it might conceivably be true," he probably realizes that the sheer amount of work he suggests will put off most of them, yet his advice is unerringly on the mark.[43]

In addition to the labor involved in opposing certainty with doubt, there is another variable that might count for more. It seems unnatural to distrust our expertise, our power of guessing the truth. Have we not been trained precisely for those purposes? In truth, the skeptic would prefer to believe, despite seeing that doing so often implies a failure to learn from experience, and he subjects his evidence to every possible test *in hopes of failing*. But when he does not, when the evidence proves vulnerable, then he acts accordingly. Effective devil's advocacy must meet—or, better, beat—the opposition on its own terms. It is not enough to disagree at the generalized level—the case is not presented logically; Marx (et al.) has been forgotten; arguments are undocumented; etc. These might all matter, but can be shrugged off as subjective. But criticisms that detail disingenuous citation practice, faulty mathematics, or syllogistic deficiencies can be ignored only at eventual serious risk.

XI

At this point readers will see why I praise pyrrhonism yet disparage postmodernism. Where is the line to be drawn between them? Or are they partly overlapping? If so, how great is the overlap? Or is it total—is there no difference at all between them? These questions arise because of the widespread misuse of notions like skepticism. For instance, one of the more prominent biblical minimalists does his cause no good when he equates "continually practic[ing] the hermeneutics of suspicion" in one sentence with "the tidal wave of postmodernism" in the next.[44]

Whereas postmodernism rejects the possibility of truth, pyrrhonism does not. It does not pretend that this search is easy, nor promise that it will eventually be successful. Those who practice it should ignore the threadbare criticism that their work reduces rather than increases the fund of historical information.[45] They should find it no hardship to side with Darwin when he wrote to a correspondent who advised him that he had found an error in work dealing with Russian wheat: "Permit me again to thank you for the thorough manner in which you have worked out this case, to kill an error is as good a service as, and sometimes even better than, the establishing a new truth or fact."[46] Or, as Thomas Jefferson aptly put it: "[i]gnorance is preferable to error; and he is less remote from the truth who believes nothing, than he who believes what is wrong."[47]

5

WHEN TOO MUCH IS NOT ENOUGH

To have lost such men and events may seem impossible in our
age of massive documentation, multimedia, and information
overload. Yet, the problem afflicts much of ancient history
(representing *over half* of "recorded" history).

There is no such thing as enough evidence.

I

Imagine a historian a millennium or two in the future attempting to write a history of some part of the world at the end of the twentieth century. Suppose that he was forced to work with less than one percent of the evidence that now exists. Suppose further that this evidence consists of a few general histories that often disagree with one another, fragmentary economic data, a few literary works that occasionally relate to the real world, and nothing else. All newspapers and similar documents have disappeared, so any reflection of continuity rests only with the general historical works, which, unfortunately, have large gaps in them. Some physical evidence remains, but it is scattered and incidental. How is he to proceed?

Is it fair to describe our own situation this way? Do we really lack 99 of every 100 pieces of evidence from certain very large nooks of the past? No one can know, but it is easy to believe that, if anything, this is conservative. We lack written records from the New World before the end of the fifteenth century, for

Oceania and most of Africa from even later. There were scores of statelets in pre-Zhou China; we know the names of a handful. We might think of Roman history as well documented, but we cannot construct a list of the governors of even one province completely and certainly.

II

The recent movement away from evidence requires explicit attention to the nature of sources. In a way, the best sources are those never intended to have a future, or even much of a present—for example, the economic documents that so dominate the record from places like Ebla, Mari, and other sites in early Mesopotamia, or the Geniza records from Cairo. Such records are always fragmentary and, while we can usually take them at face value, the next step—putting them together—is more difficult. The result is often a pastiche featuring various kinds of possibly representative transactions, but without enough interconnected data to form a discernible and defensible whole.

All evidence is vestigial. The sources in which it is embedded cannot possibly replicate the events that, wittingly or unwittingly, they testify to. They can never be treated as *representing* a larger reality, but only as hinting at it. Just the same, there is a lot already known and much more to be discovered. The first question that historians are likely to ask of their sources is: why and how were they created? Knowing this is to take the first long step toward understanding them better. It is the historian's business to ferret out the old and hope to find some new.

Conventionally, sources are arranged ordinally—primary, secondary, tertiary, etc. There hardly seems much reason to consider the "etc.," except as historians are interested in how historical knowledge seeps from their own rarefied climes into the larger public domain. How it trickles to succeeding generations is a more important issue. Concepts, even lowly definitions, are important here. We can treat "primary" as absolute or relative. The latter approach allows considerably more latitude, perhaps too much, in that whichever sources we have that are—apparently—closest to the events we are interested in are duly termed "primary," even though they might be separated by centuries from these events. By this way of thinking, historians would always have access to something called "primary" because each historian can define the term idiosyncratically.

Obviously this can lead to confusion, as historians use the same term to describe different circumstances. Leopold von Ranke, and before him John

Lingard, held a more stringent view; only a source that was at least "contempo-rary" can justly be considered primary.[1] This sounds reasonable and would help provide consistency, but "contemporary" can be a complex notion itself. The *New York Times* and the *Podunk Gazette* might both carry a story on the same day, but with vastly different emphases and depth of detail. Were both reporters (or nei-ther?) eyewitnesses to the events? Were they equally well placed to observe? Were they equally perspicacious? Did they have equally retentive memories? The answers, of course, can all be no, and it is conceivable that in any given case the honors will be to the *Podunk Gazette*.

There are ordinarily three levels of primary evidence: participant, eyewitness, and hearsay.[2] Although the first might seem the most reliable and the last the least, it might not be so. Columbus's journal of his first voyage to the Americas exemplifies a common problem with sources. This exists in holograph, but the handwriting is that of Bartolomé de las Casas, writing as much as two generations later. Barring the miraculous recovery of any original in Columbus's own hand, interested parties must make due with this recension and call it a primary source. Until recently they could only consult the original or the published facsimile of it. A good place to start, surely, but it meant that every party would need high lev-els of paleographic and historiographical skills to make the most of the opportu-nity, and few did. Instead they relied on transcriptions calling themselves edi-tions. That this was false advertising became clear with the appearance of two text editions in the 1980s. The first concentrated on paleography and lexicogra-phy and was a valuable addition to the Columbianists' arsenal.[3]

From the historian's point of view, the second edition was better yet. Taking advantage of new word-processing capabilities, the editors produced an edition that in spacing, sizing, and general appearance, closely replicates the handwritten manuscript. Moreover, it was accompanied by extensive historical and calli-graphic commentary, even a concordance. No one working on Columbus's activ-ities should now be content simply to peruse the sixteenth-century manuscript; even less should they be willing to progress without doing so. Ideally they will engage in a bit of scholarly tennis-viewing, looking first at one source, then the others, back and forth a thousand times or more. Somewhere in the process, they are likely to lose track of which is the primary, which the secondary source, for the manuscript and the editions will have fused together into a whole that is truly greater than the sum of its parts.

Despite its tardy appearance and uncertain provenance, Columbus's journal has been used endlessly to retell that adventure and argue specific points about the trip. Trusting that Las Casas got Columbus right, and that Columbus got himself right, most historians have taken comfort, but the journal is riddled with inconsistencies and incongruities, suggesting a massive early rewrite by Columbus for his own purposes.[4] It can also be shown that, as a transcriber, Las Casas wielded an attitude as well as a pen.[5]

One danger in relying on secondary sources is illustrated by what often happens when these are traced back to their origins. When Philip Curtin tracked estimates of the Atlantic slave trade back through the published record, he found that commonly-cited numbers in the range of fifty million ultimately derived from a journalist's account from the mid-nineteenth century. This encouraged him to approach the subject anew, and his resulting estimate was little more than one-fifth of some figures that had become canonized by repetition.[6] Belief in a smallpox epidemic in Hispaniola in 1507 also gathered speed and credibility by a chain of reciprocal, if often unannounced, dependence.[7] Estimates of bison population blindly followed an early estimate of 75 million or more, whereas the most recent estimate considers 30 million to be the maximum possible figure.[8] Only three examples, but a clear pattern that shows the need to test the apparent independence of our sources, and reminds us that, while we might begin with the source nearest to the events described, we should certainly never end with it.

III

One of the historian's most formidable tasks is distinguishing among sources. It is tempting to treat a source as primary if it says what we want it to. It might well be primary or it might be a dependent source masquerading as primary. The excavated site of Pompeii itself is the primary source and any eyewitness accounts, which once were primary, become relegated to lesser status. On the other hand the site itself becomes progressively less primary, as more and more excavations take place, material is removed, reconstructions occur, and so forth. It is conceivable, though incongruous, that the site itself will become less primary than accounts of it before renovations began. Pompeii is an example of a dynamic situation, where the status of sources can change. Even when they do not, there is no compelling reason to treat all primary sources as intrinsically more valuable than any other sources.

All this underscores that sources as we have them are often the end-products of a long, complicated, unpredictable, and indeterminable gestation.[9] Jakob Benediktsson aptly compares such sources to medieval churches that "one generation after another goes on building and altering, until it becomes very different from what the first builders had planned."[10] Paul Zumthor said much the same when he spoke of *mouvance*, or the continuous alteration of a text—oral or written—over time, as it serves the changing collective memory and self-identity of a community.[11]

The protean task of distinguishing primary, secondary, tertiary, even quaternary sources is made especially clear when realizing how the same text can be any of these. As long as an inscription is extant, the stone on which it appears is the primary source. When this are not readily accessible, latex squeezes are often taken to serve as simulacra. Since there is usually only one of these as well, photographs are used to propagate research opportunities, but might suffer from inadequate lighting, underexposure, and other travails of field conditions. Finally, if the inscription is published, it is often redrawn for clarity. Here, in a nutshell, are four hierarchical layers of evidence; most will have access only the last and least.

IV

David Potter asks a rhetorical question that underlies every attempt to understand a source: "[h]ow can anyone give a fully objective account of an incident at which he or she was not present?"[12] We might frame the same question omitting the "not" or even putting the question mark after the word "incident." Potter was discussing the caution necessary when consulting ancient historical sources, mostly compiled long after the events they relate, and transcribed several times since. Historians instinctively warm to evidence that purports to be eyewitness. How much more primary can a source be? Historians from Herodotus to the present have taken care to assure their readers that at least some part of their testimony was ocular. Some scholars regard Herodotus's visit to Egypt as fictional, but this is hardly Herodotus's fault. More than thirty times he assured his readers that he saw or heard what he wrote.

In the fraudulent account of the Trojan war once attributed to one Dictys of Crete, the author wrote: "[e]verything I have written about the war between the Greeks and the barbarians, in which I took a very active part, is based on firsthand [eyewitness] knowledge."[13] The claim is a standard one, inviting belief—and often receiving it. It is debatable what actually constitutes eyewitness status. A participant in a battle is unlikely to have many chances for an overview and, while able to provide gripping details at the personal level, will not be able to account for the ebb and flow on the larger battlefield. A remotely but advantageously sited observer is likely to do a better job at this, but it is possible that hearsay will provide the best and most complete evidence of all. If the reporter for the *Podunk Gazette* was able to interview a wide range of combatants and commanders, ask the right questions of them, and synthesize the answers well and quickly, then the *Podunk Gazette*'s report might well be the finest available to the historian of the occasion.

A stern test of the historian's integrity comes when he is faced with evidence that is particularly full and seems to offer aid and comfort to his argument. Four chronicles of Hernando de Soto's expedition through the southeastern United States are known to exist. Three of them appeared within a few years of the return of the survivors, the fourth sixty years later. The first three are first-person participant accounts, not without literary flourishes, but largely matter-of-fact in their approach. The fourth claims to be based on reminiscences of an unnamed participant, and is a paradigm of Humanist rhetorical froth. Despite its remoteness in time and testimony, this account, written or edited by Inca Garcilaso de la Vega, is longer than the three earlier accounts combined, providing a cornucopia of details about what both Spaniards and Indians did, said, even thought.

For modern students of de Soto's activities the choice is clear. If they want to learn a great deal about the expedition, they must rely on Garcilaso more than on the other three. Most do just this, whether they are interested in pinpointing de Soto's route, estimating the Indian population of the Southeast, or trying to build a local ethnography. Even in its practical details, however, Garcilaso's account taxes credulity on every page. Sizes of rooms and fields, distances that arrows bounced off helmets, the giveaway florid speechifying by all hands presumably remembered by his remarkable informant—these and scores of other clues warn us that Garcilaso is not to be trusted very far.

Coming to him with doubts compels us to pursue the matter, to suspect, for instance, that his account was based on the earlier accounts and embellished to taste.[14] That Garcilaso is a fragile historical source is hardly the most interesting aspect of this case. More to the point, his divestiture has done little to limit reliance on his account. True, there are now some feeble and formulaic cautions expressed by those haring after de Soto's route. But once expressed, these are cast aside, and the hunters continue to use Garcilaso unflinchingly, just as if he had passed every test rather than failed them.[15]

Caesar's *Gallic War* purports to be largely eyewitness written in the third-person "I", but the earliest surviving manuscripts date from the ninth to twelfth centuries, and the two major manuscript traditions differ in numerous ways. The same circumstances apply to most works from antiquity that survived long enough for monastic amanuenses to transcribe them yet again. Using these sources uncritically forces historians to assume that nothing happened to alter them in the millennium or so between their first writing and our first glimpse of the text. As a working assumption this is unavoidable, but it can seldom bear the onus of serious scrutiny.

Several narratives stipulating participant status have recently come under fire as possible fabrications. A work professing to be a pre-Marco Polo account of southern China recently appeared, but the 'editor' of the work has steadfastly refused to reveal the whereabouts of the manuscript on which it purports to be based, daring critics to disbelieve him, and they have obliged.[16] In another case, the editor/author has also declined to produce one of the manuscripts on which he claims the work is based. This work has been used heavily and been granted the weight of its claims. It was published by a university press and assertions about its accuracy and authenticity accompanied it, so why not just believe?[17]

V

Having discussed authenticity, we need to address reliability. Is the evidence irrefutable that eyewitness accounts are ipso facto more reliable? The question can be answered only by comparing such accounts of a particular event, winnowing out the discrepancies, and testing these against the accumulated weight of evidence. A recent work assembled more than 100 eyewitness accounts of Lincoln's assassination and its immediate aftermath.[18] Reading these reminds us of the omnipresent Rashomon effect, and also that a secondary account that collects and evaluates a number of primary sources might actually be preferred to these, even when it paraphrases them, as long as it does this well, and as long as it allows access to all the evidence.

This procedure will often be impossible, but we have many studies, usually by psychologists and usually in forensic contexts, about eyewitness testimony. These have arisen because of juries' tendency to grant eyewitness testimony greater credence than circumstantial evidence. The studies in question have generally demonstrated that eyewitnesses are discouragingly fallible, even when tested shortly after the occasion.[19] Even the most reliable eyewitness accounts, when aggregated, fail to reproduce the larger picture. Often, eyewitnesses have limited purview of the events. Those watching a football or soccer game seldom concentrate on the off-the-ball action, even though it might directly influence the outcome. For this reason, announcers often divide their watching brief in order to provide a conspective analysis.

Eyewitnesses in history are unlikely to have been as systematic. Had they been, would it have been good enough? We can hardly re-enact the life experiences of eyewitnesses from the past to judge their capacity with respect to memory. The alternative is to conduct large-scale and repeated experiments that test various kinds of memory. As noted, hundreds of these have been carried out and in general the results have not been encouraging for any historians who might wish to believe eyewitnesses implicitly.[20]

VI

Testis unus, testis nullus, runs the Roman legal dictum: "one witness [is] no witness." Or as a less exalted source put it: "Unsubstantiated? It means that no other person than yourself has claimed to have witnessed these things or been able to show that they existed."[21] Most of what we think we know about the past, we know from, or by way of, a single source. There is a natural tendency to treat unique evidence with kid gloves.[22] Since such sources cannot be tested by comparison, this might seem appropriate or just serviceable. On the other hand, that fact by itself should persuade the historian to apply every form of internal criticism possible.

Another approach would be to treat historical sources as commodities in a competitive capitalist economy—perhaps not entirely an unfair characterization of the guild of historians. Here supply and demand compete in the marketplace in a kind of zero sum enterprise. When one dominates, the other can only be adversely affected. The less available a commodity, the more it is valued, and when there is a monopoly, the supplier has a stranglehold on determining value. Just as we place greater value on a monopolized commodity by paying more for it, we treat monopolizing sources in the same way. Since Josephus is virtually our only source for domestic events in first-century Palestine, historians place a higher value—greater credibility—on his testimony because there are no competing commodities to measure his against.

Two scholarly books on the so-called Star of Bethlehem recently appeared almost simultaneously.[23] Each author accepts that there was some kind of astronomical phenomenon, but each identifies it differently.[24] The two works are the latest of scores of studies of this occasion. Of interest is not just the variety of arguments, but that the account is a salient case of the single source. Although universally a part of the modern retellings of the story, the star is mentioned only in one of the four gospels, that attributed to Matthew. Luke's gospel, although it narrates details of the occasion, fails to mention such a star. Today's accounts that incorporate it are essentially Matthew grafted onto Luke.[25] Substantially more attention has been paid to trying to determine what Matthew might have meant than to wondering why the other evangelists failed to mention it at all.[26]

Since they must have traveled in some of the same circles, one reasonable scenario is that both Matthew and Luke heard the story and that Matthew chose to believe it whereas Luke chose not to. Written at about the same time and from within a similar milieu, Luke's silence weighs heavily against accepting Matthew's version, and suggests that this unexpectedly comprehensive disagreement is the real mystery, and that all studies devoted to defining and dating the Star of Bethlehem are largely futile.

Even more than the bible, the Book of Mormon is our sole source of information on a reputed emigration of several groups of Israelites to the New World and their adventures there between ca. 600 BCE and the fifth century CE. We are told that the angel Moroni delivered the text of the Book of Mormon to Joseph Smith in the form of a number of brass and golden plates of diverse origins, and that Smith caused them to be translated and printed in 1830. In all, eleven of Smith's followers claimed to have seen the plates, but no one since has been so fortunate.[27] A substantial apologetics industry has been at work for several generations, using historical arguments to invest the work's provenance with credibility inside and outside the community. Attempts to provide modern equivalents of ancient toponyms, find Semitic roots in certain words, or calculate population levels and dates and sites for Mormon forerunners, are all designed to bestow historicity on the Book of Mormon's unsubstantiated account.[28]

VII

Historians ordinarily depend on sources that relied on other sources themselves, so the question becomes: how reliable were these earlier sources and how well were they used? As if anticipating these questions, Josephus wrote this about his accounting of Tyrian history: "[f]or very many years past the people of Tyre have kept public records, compiled and very carefully preserved by the state. . . It is there recorded that the Temple at Jerusalem was built by King Solomon 143 years and eight months before the foundation of Carthage by the Tyrians." To bolster his case he quoted a certain Dius, an otherwise unknown historian, as well as Menander of Ephesus, about whom little is known.[29]

Josephus's testimony is surprisingly, even suspiciously, rich. He provided not only the lengths of reign of several rulers, but their ages at death as well. For the succession from Ithobaal to Pygmalion, this is the gist of Josephus's account (birth/accession-death, using the dates provided by one modern interpretation):

Ithobaal (904/888-856); his son Balezor (895/856-850); his son Metten (853/850-821); his son (?) Pygmalion (842/821-774).[30]

According to Josephus, Ithobaal succeeded to the throne by assassinating his predecessor.[31] By this testimony Ithobaal was a wonderfully precocious young man: assassin at sixteen, but father at nine! And if Pygmalion was Metten's son (implied though not stated), then Metten was a father at eleven.

Naturally this genealogical chronology has occasioned many pratfalls among those who attempt to date this Tyrian royal line to accommodate the results to biblical synchronisms. A variant reading shows Ithobaal succeeding at age thirty-six rather than sixteen, and Katzenstein grasped this providential straw, not so much to explain Ithobaal's prodigious paternity but to squeeze his reign onto the procrustean Biblical chronology.[32] Katzenstein was forced into this gambit because he asserted that "[t]he reliability of the document is uncontested by scholars, and the fact that the numbers which pertain to the life-spans of the kings or their regnal years are not rounded, underscores the veracity of the list and its contents."[33]

Katzenstein spoke for many others in his optimism, but this sanguine view had already been severely tested when an Assyrian inscription came to light that mentioned a Tyrian king who did not seem to square with Josephus, a certain Ba'limanzer, who paid tribute to Assyria in 841 BCE.[34] Those who believed in Josephus's regnal list were forced either to accept this name as a form of Balezor or consider it to be the name of an unknown ruler accidently omitted by Josephus or his sources. Those who chose the former were obliged to ensure that their chronological scheme had Balezor safely ruling in all or part of 841 BCE, whatever else they chose to argue. Katzenstein did this by quadrupling Balezor's reign in order to include the new date.[35] Reconstituting Tyrian chronology, Lipinski managed to have Balezor (to whom he gave six years, 847-841) live just long enough.[36] Peñuela had already come to the same conclusion (although for him Balezor reigned from 855 to 841), using a different set of arguments.[37]

This legerdemain allowed Josephus and the Assyrian scribes to appear to agree with one another, but others found the name forms similar but incompatible. W.F. Albright fell into this camp, but found a ready solution: "Ba'al-manzer may, therefore, represent a Tyrian king whose name has fallen out of the list because it so closely resembled that of his precursor (or successor) Balezoros." So Albright merely inserted this name into Josephus's list without otherwise threatening its integrity.[38] No one who grappled with the problem regarded the Assyrian evidence as a grave threat to Josephus's information, but simply accommodated it in one way or another.

The inscription of 841 BCE is only one problem. Modern reconstructions of the Tyrian kinglist are tripartite. First comes a sequence of eleven kings as propounded by Josephus and ending with Pygmalion's death, usually ascribed to ca. 774 BCE. Two of these names are also known from the Bible, no others from any source. After a gap of 25 or 30 years comes a sequence of about five names known only from Assyrian records.[39] This is followed, after another lacuna of about a century, by another Josephus-based sequence of nine rulers covering, it appears, less than sixty years and ending ca. 532 BCE. In short, Josephus stands virtually alone, forcing those who wish to fill in Tyrian history to believe that both he and his sources were unimpeachable.

Garbini thinks that Josephus fabricated much of his evidence to provide the bible with outside corroboration, "relying, evidently rightly, on the gullibility of readers who would have found it quite natural that what happened in Jerusalem was recorded in Tyre, not to mention calculating the year with reference to future events."[40] Such gullibility has had a long half-life. Josephus's chronology has continued to be the point of departure for calculating Tyrian chronology and is one of the principal grounds for arguing dates for Solomon and other Israelite rulers.[41] Handy, for instance, is unwilling to suggest any more than that the numerous internal discrepancies in dating "might also caution against too quickly accepting the list of [Tyrian royal] names as *totally* correct."[42]

Historians have been impressed by Josephus's appeal to the Tyrian "archives." Barnes argued that: "[f]ew would dispute the basic authenticity of Josephus' tradition, especially," he continued, "in light of his own appeal to the 'public records' to corroborate his polemic against the enemies of the Jews and his attempts to glorify the Jewish people."[43] Barnes's very language seems to make a case against him—a case strengthened by thousands of examples of false referencing throughout history. Garbini's question as to why Tyrian archives would record the building of Solomon's temple is a fair one, but a better one might be:

how did these records survive as late as the third century BCE (Menander's floruit) anyway?[44] After all, Tyre was besieged several times by the Assyrians, Egyptians, and Chaldeans. In 332 BCE Alexander the Great captured and destroyed it, and according to Arrian several thousand lives were lost and even more Tyrians deported.[45] It is unreasonable to expect the Tyrian "archives" to have survived, and even less justifiable to profess it without discussion.

The modern historian's dilemma is to wonder whether to attribute the peculiarities in Josephus's account of Tyrian royal chronology to Josephus himself, to the sources he named, or to some anonymous post-Josephan scribe/s. Any choice—whether or not to believe, how to integrate the Assyrian data, how to correlate Tyrian chronology with that of the bible—can be based only on the flimsiest evidence, and attempts to rehabilitate Josephus by bouncing Balezor around like a pin-ball (866-849? 859-853? 856-850? 856-830? 855-841? 848-830? 847-841? 846-841?) do nothing for the credibility of either Josephus or modern historiography.[46]

Attempts to reconstruct Tyrian chronology—which presume that Josephus was right and that it is our task to prove this, no matter what changes we make to his received testimony—remind us once again how indomitable the will to answer all historical questions can be. Whether any or all of Josephus's Tyrian kings actually ruled must await further evidence—Josephus and the bible are merely reciprocal refractions in this. In the meantime we can provisionally assume that the king list as Josephus passed it down, and as modern historians have grasped it, is as much parody as history.

VIII

A cardinal attribute of sources is their independence. It has long been the policy among law enforcement officials to question witnesses or suspects separately, providing the opportunity to elicit damaging discrepancies, or bolster cases by apparently unprompted consistencies. Say a robbery was committed by a person well disguised in a black body suit and hood. Suppose that a person confesses to the crime, but provides no details that only the perpetrator could know. Suppose further that four witnesses identify the confessor, one by his teeth, one by his shoes, one by his gait, another by his general build, and that none of the four witnesses was in communication with the others. Finally, let's say that the robber bit one of his victims and both the dental imprints and DNA evidence from the saliva confirm the confession and the eyewitness identifications.

This sounds like an airtight case; most prosecutions depend on much less. Nowadays DNA evidence is probably the most damning independent strand of evidence, even though this too can be compromised. The least certain is the confession, since it is well known that individuals confess to crimes they did not commit, and when a confession does not reveal otherwise unknowable facts, it must always be suspect. Perhaps, even today, the four independent identifications would impress a jury most, as long as it could be demonstrated conclusively that they *were* independent.

It is not hard to see why this is so. Members of juries might be inclined to distrust the scientific evidence because they don't understand it. If the defense produces 'expert' witnesses to challenge the conclusions of the prosecution, the jury might regard the whole matter as a write-off. Confessions can be retracted or ruled inadmissible. But if the four witnesses maintain their positions, most juries would be convinced. The confession is akin to unelaborated statements in sources that such-and-such happened in such-and-such a way. We are at liberty to accept or dispute such statements based on what we know about the occasion, about the sources, or about our own sense of what is contextually credible. The DNA evidence is not much different than radiocarbon dating, thermoluminescence, or dendrochronology, all of which have been proved to be wrong on occasion due to contamination at the source or during testing or interpretation. Independent testimonies that converge on a single point of view are likely to impress historians in the same way they impress a jury—indeed, historians *are* the jury.

Thus it is that historians strive heroically to demonstrate—or just assert—the independent status of sources on which they depend. Pondering the historicity of the Acts of the Apostles, Joseph Fitzmyer writes that "[t]here are a number of incidents that Luke has recounted that find confirmation elsewhere."[47] It turns out that "elsewhere" is seldom farther away than the epistles of Paul. For many, this will seem too few degrees of separation. Nonetheless, welcome confirmation sometimes does occur. Egyptologists constructed a list of eight rulers of I Dynasty from fragmentary sources. The composite nature of the list compromised its credibility until an inscription of the last ruler was unearthed that listed all the rulers of I Dynasty and confirmed the names and sequence that scholars had patiently built up.[48] While this obliging datum bodes well for other reconstructions, it cannot be taken as a warrant to rest satisfied with results in other reconstructions, but only to continue to assimilate new evidence into existing theories with care.

The load-bearing capacity of an argument based on a string of unconfirmed sources is dangerously modest. The probability that such an argument is correct founders on the axiom that probabilities multiplied are probabilities diminished. Since no single testimony can have a probability of 1.0, each time these are associated with (i.e., multiplied by) another one, the overall argument is increasingly in danger. Even three sources that the historian deems 75 percent correct amount, when used in concatenation, to a probability of $.75^3$ or about 4 in 10. Reduce the individual probabilities to 60 percent and the result is barely 20 percent. And so on.

IX

Numismatic data are of interest only to a small specialized group of scholars, but they distill well some of the problems that using evidence entails. For certain areas of the past, numismatic evidence assumes great importance, including early and medieval India and environs, where coins are used to ascribe dynastic affiliation, dating, and extent and character of rule. Often, numismatists make connections based on coins being found in the same hoard, which might be fortuitous, or on "style"—that is, coins (like pottery) that look alike are assumed, lacking other evidence, to come from roughly the same time and place. Historians also look to the metrology of the coins to draw similar inferences. The trouble with coins is that, while the information they contain can be important, it is also strikingly disembodied, only connecting certainly with other coins when they are coins of one ruler overstruck by another. There is no room on coins to tell much of a story. Although they often contain dating, it might be in regnal years rather than in the years of a datable era.

No set of rulers has created more controversy than the congeries of Indo-Bactrian, Indo-Greek, and Kushan dynasts of western India, Afghanistan, and contiguous areas from the third century BCE to the third or fourth century CE. Many of these are known only from their coins, leaving it to modern historians to fit a multitude of pieces together.[49] No two scholars of the period agree. As Cribb points out, the imputed range for the accession of Kanishka, an important ruler, is about two centuries. He adds that "[a]n answer cannot be reached by averaging out the answers or by holding a vote among scholars as to which view they most favour. . . Just as in the natural sciences, where there can only be one correct description of a given phenomenon, so there must also be one accurate answer to the dates of the Kushan kings which renders all other solutions incorrect."[50]

Cribb prefers a date of 107/120 CE for Kanishka's accession. He realizes that many other dates (78 CE, 128 CE, 132 CE, 144 CE, 232 CE, and 278 CE) compete with his preference. In fact another contributor to the same volume argues for 232 CE and a third for a date between these two.[51] Will we ever know the genealogy and chronology of the fifty or so rulers who have left records proving their existence and their claims, but little more? Frankly, it is hard to see what could effect this. Certainly not more coins—there is already an embarrassment of riches, which often adds new names but no place to put them.[52]

<h1 style="text-align:center">X</h1>

An unrecognized problem in treating sources is knowing what their authors took for granted and so underreported. The chroniclers of the past seldom wrote for us, but for those around them—an audience not likely to require, indeed to resent, having every detail elucidated. Our hypothetical historian from the fourth millennium will not find in his scattered sources much information on the "American way," the multiplicity of automobile models, or the detailed workings of government and how to distinguish between theory and practice in them. His sources will not be accompanied by glossaries. All manner of discourse is certain to elude him. If he encounters the phrases "get to first base" or "make hay while the sun shines," what will he make of them? Or "if pigs could fly" (maybe they *will* fly by that time!).

No event in the past has been survived by all the sources for it—most have been survived by none at all, leaving historians to determine how the extant evidence can be used to throw light on the events in question. One choice has been to adopt the notion of "providential preservation." Popular with religious fundamentalists and defenders of the King James version of the bible, this concedes that all sources have not survived, but insists that all the *right* ones have—the evidence, their very survival. This enables work to progress, but suffocates the critical process at birth.[53]

In the end, the historian's attitude about the relationship between his work and his sources comes down to whether he grants the latter civil liberties or not. Is evidence to be treated as true until proved false? Or the reverse? And what will constitute proof? And, short of proof, what degree of probability is sufficient to build on? Should greater efforts be made to prove or disprove evidence and hypothesis? Should the weight of the readily available evidence suffice, or should the search for new evidence continue regardless? What are the consequences of being wrong? But if historians are the jury, they are also the prosecution and the defense, or at least have an obligation to take on these roles as part of their investigation of the past, unless certain issues become so debated that the courtroom scenario is replicated.

XI

The president of the James Cook Society was downcast. He had learned that an arrow reputedly made from one of Cook's bones was actually made from an animal bone. Undaunted by the palling effects of technology, he expressed confidence: "[o]n this occasion technology has 'won.' But I am sure that one of these days . . . one of the Cook legends will [prove] to be true—and it will happen, one day."[54]

Thornton's lament underscores two points. The first is that hope continues to spring eternal. The second is that modern technology is a two-edged sword for the hopeful believer and has made a habit of throwing cold water on historical myths. Zachary Taylor did not die of poisoning. Thomas Jefferson was not celibate after his wife's death. George Washington did not wear wooden teeth. Arthur and Guinevere are not buried at Glastonbury Abbey.

This fact should encourage rather than discourage the increased use of appropriate modern scientific techniques to throw light—or water—on physical evidence from the past. Failing to do so is voluntarily to pluck important weapons from the historian's arsenal out of fear for the results of their use—a cardinal sin by any measure. Ignoring this type of evidence can have serious repercussions since it can also validate data that might otherwise seem wildly improbable. A startling example is the apparent substantiation of the claim by Afghan Hazaris to be descended from Genghis Khan, until now taken—and rightly so—to be just another origin myth.[55]

6

THE MANY BIRTHS OF FRANK LLOYD WRIGHT

"I thought Oz was a great Head," said Dorothy. "And I
thought Oz was a lovely Lady," said the Scarecrow. "And I
thought Oz was a terrible Beast," said the Tin Woodman.
"And I thought Oz was a Ball of fire," said the Lion. "No, you
are all wrong," said the little man, meekly. "I have been
making believe."

There's plenty of room for differences. In fact, they're essential. If two bobbies see somethin'—*anythin' at all*—in exactly
the same way, then it's a waste of time them workin' together.
It's the differences which make a team good or bad—an' I
want us to be a good team.

I

In 1911 Raymond Pearl conducted an experiment based on Mendelian genetics.
532 kernels from the same ear of corn were counted and categorized by fifteen
different people. Pearl had divided them himself on a genetically expected 9:3:3:1
breakdown for color and texture, but found that "[n]*o two of the fifteen highly
trained and competent observers agreed* as to the distribution of these 532 kernels." He attributed this to the fact that "every individual has bias, or 'personal

equation' in his observing and measuring. There is no way completely to eliminate its effects."[1] Thousands of more casual observations continue to demonstrate
the truth of Pearl's comment.[2]

II

Historians who accept the tenet that one witness is no witness at all are in a
quandary, since seeking out more sources almost always confuses matters. We
can hardly replicate the past experimentally, but the results of surrogate experiments are nonetheless significant. Like it or not, the "personal equation" has been
part of every recorded—and transmitted—observation from the past. While this
does not forbid us from reaching an approximation of truth, it does enjoin us to
query every datum we meet in our work. The range of disagreement can be large:
minor differences of emphasis and content; silence vs. non-silence; major differences in content, sequence, and dramatis personae; all of the above, with one or
all accounts denouncing the others.

The Copper Scroll was discovered in the Judean desert in 1952, and became
the object of uncontrolled hypothesizing even before it was unrolled three years
later. This continued until rival scholars published editions of it in the early
1960s. The apparatus to these "contained evidence of a major shift in their
authors' interpretation[s]" of the scroll, as each moved away from some of his
earlier theories about its dating and content.[3] Once the scroll had been studied,
and fully published, interest seemed to lag—perhaps a case of too much evidence
impeding untrammeled speculation. Eventually the dust settled and, as Al Wolters
later put it, "of the six paradigms which emerged in the first dozen years of
Copper Scroll study, only two remain as viable contenders in contemporary
scholarship."[4] The Copper Scroll is only a single piece of evidence, but the case
is a relevant microcosm of the way in which scholarly debate often works itself
out—the less the evidence, the greater the scope for free-based guessing, the
greater the allure. Once the Copper Scroll came firmly into the public domain,
interested parties simply shifted to other manuscripts among the Qumran documents, to undertake the voyage of discovery and controversy once again.

Our knowledge of Julius Caesar's eight years of campaigning in Gaul, on
which his military reputation largely rests, depends entirely on his own eyewitness testimony. Reading *The Gallic War* tells us whatever Caesar wanted the
Roman people to know and little else. We learn that Caesar made a few tactical

and strategic errors, but that he overcame them all resoundingly. We learn that, while he had several able subordinates, whenever he was absent, the conquest faltered. We learn that millions of Gauls died on the battlefield or in their encampments, with nominal Roman losses. We learn that the craven Senate tried to recall Caesar, risking depriving Rome of a splendid new conquest. We learn how Caesar courageously evaded recall until his work was done. Historians who doubt these propositions have little more than Caesar, and a little bit of Cicero, to guide them. Caesar adopted a shrewdly understated style, and seems to be telling his readers of his endless exploits only reluctantly. Modest in discourse, he seems to be asking them: can you believe all this? We cannot know whether alternative, possibly discrepant, accounts might once have existed because victors get to produce the canonical version of how they triumph.

Yet when we read of protracted complex processes like the Spanish conquest of the Aztec and Inca states, the British conquest of India, or the Crusades; single events like Little Big Horn, Isandhlwana, or Panipat, or even momentary events such as the assassinations of Abraham Lincoln, Franz Ferdinand, or John F. Kennedy, we must wonder about events on similar scales that are less well documented. What would we learn about any of these nine, or 9000 others, if we were forced to rely on a single account?

III

The discrepant nature of the sources is matched by the range of responses to them. Those who find themselves wondering about the efficacy of combining source and interpretation in explaining the past will find strong impetus in the number of studies which, though based on the same sources, come to wildly differing conclusions about the subject at hand. Frank Lloyd Wright became a public figure in his twenties and remained one for over sixty years, but this was not enough to ensure that we know such simple facts about him as where he was born. It is generally conceded that he was born in Richland Center, Wisconsin or its vicinity, but there are seven opinions as to the exact site. The dispute has become heated, as the town seeks to capitalize on its good fortune, but finds that the differing opinions make it difficult to offer tourists a definitive answer to what seems like a simple question.[5] If a particular site is officially designated, it will probably be a matter of politics rather than the weight of evidence.

Two thousand years earlier, Livy, like Herodotus, constantly agonized over differences in his sources, and often refrained from choosing among them or chose the source that reflected best on early Rome and/or worst on the Rome of his own time.[6] Thus, when musing on the early history of the city, he could write: "[t]he authors are not in agreement. I would prefer that it has been falsely reported that poisoning killed those whose deaths by plague made the year [331 BCE] infamous. Nevertheless, in order that I not deprive any writer of credit, the matter must be set forth just as it is reported."[7]

Those who would regard Livy's words as unduly ingenuous or revealing would not be much interested in what Janet Abu-Lughod has to say, in comparing her work with that of another historian: "[u]nbeknown to each other, [Alan] Smith and I had evidently been researching our books at roughly the same time . . . Not unexpectedly, we were consulting many of the same books and articles for the time period covered in *Before European Hegemony*. Indeed, a glance at his bibliography revealed that we had read at least fifty sources in common for that period. Despite our overlapping sources and our similar questions, however, we came out with entirely different interpretations and narratives."[8]

Most scholarly disputes pale when compared to the learning squandered on identifying Columbus's landfall. He reported that the inhabitants called it Guanahaní and, once he left for other parts after only three days there, hardly mentioned it again. This has proved no obstacle to those in hot pursuit of Guanahaní, who have advanced arguments in favor of practically every island in the Bahamas, as well as other locales.[9] The most significant similarity between Columbus's track and a host of other examples is that proponents of different landfalls all rely on the same set of texts, only to part company when interpreting that evidence. They do this by seeing different words than others; by interpreting certain words in a variety of ways; and by questioning the reliability of the transcriber. In the last they are abetted by the fact that the journal is confessedly only about one-fifth Columbus's *ipsissima verba*, the rest being some kind of paraphrase by Bartolomé de las Casas.

IV

A couple of recent differences of opinion illustrate how easily scholars become their own Rashomons. The acrimonious debate over the reasons for, and significance of, James Cook's murder in Hawaii in 1779 opened when Marshall Sahlins argued that Cook's death was a matter of unfortunate timing. The first time Cook landed, the Hawaiians were at a point in their ritual cycle, the Makahiki festival, that caused them to see Cook as the embodiment of their god Lono, and so he was worshipped. When he returned, only ten days later, the cycle had moved on. Cook's bad luck was now to be treated as the embodiment of Ku, another, and this time warlike, god. So the Hawaiians killed him because they had to.[10]

Gananath Obeyesekere criticized Sahlins's interpretation as contrary to the evidence and demeaning to the Hawaiians, arguing that Cook-as-Lono or Cook-as-Ku was not a Hawaiian myth but a European one. Obeyesekere points out that none of the several eyewitness accounts mentioned the Makahiki festival by name, and that Sahlins's attribution, and with it his entire thesis, is incorrect.[11] Sahlins retaliated by accusing Obeyesekere of distorting the same sources, albeit in different ways.[12] Nothing loath, Obeyesekere in his turn criticized Sahlins's critique in an afterword to the second edition of his own work.[13]

For historians, the appeal lies in the fact that Sahlins and Obeyesekere, and their partisans and critics, exploit almost entirely the same corpus of primary sources, the accounts published by various members of the crew on their return to England. We cannot know what the Hawaiians actually thought then, and so must reserve judgment, but in the matter of the battle of the texts, historians would probably accord honors to Obeyesekere, but also appreciate that Sahlins opened an issue that provided so instructive an example of clashing over the same body of evidence.

The second example concerns two studies of Alexander the Great published one year apart. The authors are widely recognized as the leading authorities on the subject. Each used precisely the same primary sources and largely the same secondary sources. Each drew conclusions diametrically opposed to the other. N.G.L. Hammond's title tells the story. In the tradition of W.W. Tarn and Arnold Toynbee, he sees Alexander as directed by "a visionary, spiritual dimension which stemmed from his religious beliefs."[14] The undoubted excesses of his reign were beyond his control, as Hammond enters on Alexander's behalf the familiar plea of ignorance.

If the names were missing we could only think that A.B. Bosworth was writing about a different historical figure entirely. Bosworth's Alexander is determined, even ruthless, in his behavior toward both the enemy and his own inner circle. As Bosworth puts it: "[t]he price of Alexander's sovereignty was killing on a gigantic scale, and killing is unfortunately the perpetual backcloth of his regime."[15] Bosworth's Alexander resembles Julius Caesar in Gaul more than Jesus Christ in Galilee.

What to do? The critical reader is likely to find that Hammond's arguments are more strained, his credulity more on display, his avoidance of problematic issues more studious. On the other hand, Bosworth himself might occasionally seem Javertian in his pursuit of Alexander's darker side. Although there is evidence aplenty for the events themselves, there is much less about guilty knowledge, programatics, and culpability. Hammond and Bosworth have reached this polarity by a lifetime of study of the same ensemble of evidence. If neither is right, those interested in Alexander as phenomenon can only form their own opinions.[16] In time other Alexanders will no doubt emerge from the sources.[17]

V

History is seldom allowed to repeat itself, although we have made this happen with the use of instant replay at sporting events. We can now be almost completely sure whether the ball beat the runner, the receiver caught the pass inbounds, the shot clock did or did not expire, or the pass was made while the recipient was onsides. Since in many cases the replay is available from six or even more angles, the Rashomon effect comes into full play. Some views are obscured by players or officials or equipment, while others offer an unobstructed view. By slowing history down and capturing it from a variety of perspectives, the instant replay mimics the historian's ideal.

Commenting on the results of the corn-counting experiment discussed above, Pearl concluded that:

> It may fairly be said that Ear No. 8 carried 532 kernels. The testimony of fifteen independent witnesses agrees with this. Perhaps with as great warrant as is ever attainable we may say that we *know* that Ear No. 8 had 532 kernels. But how many white starchy kernels did it have? I mean how many did it *really* have? There must have been some determinate number because it is certainly *known* that *some* of the 532 kernels were white starchy. But *how many*? It seems a simple problem. One only has to count them. They do not run away or change. But still I should like to *know* how many of them there were on this ear. And still more I should like to know some method by which *definite and certain knowledge* on the point *could possibly be obtained*, by the use only of visual observation of the kernels themselves and the process of counting. Examine the fourth column of Table 13 and think it over.[18]

Pearl drew no conclusions about interpreting historical evidence, but we can say that the degree of disagreement there is likely, in principle (e.g., not everything can be observed, there is no fixed number of data), to be rather greater. To many, Pearl's ruminations will seem defeatist. These will argue that he gave up too soon, did not work hard enough at conflict resolution, chose to accentuate the negative, and the like. But, as Pearl put it, it only *seems* a simple problem.[19]

7

DESTROYING IN ORDER TO SAVE

What the right story is can be contested ground: contested by
archaeologists with differing theoretical and methodological
positions; increasingly contested by different political factions
at the local and national level; and sometimes contested
between archaeologists and indigenous people. Presenting the
past we think we see must be done with an awareness that the
ground is contested and who the combatants are.

If a C^{14} date supports our theories, we put it in the main text.
If it does not entirely contradict them, we put it in a foot-note.
And if is completely 'out of date', we just drop it.

I

In 1998 *Biblical Archaeologist* changed its name; it was now to be called *Near
Eastern Archaeology*. As the editor put it, the "decision . . . emerged from a
lengthy and agonizing process." Earlier, the title change had been described as
"emotionally difficult," and it ran against the grain of subscriber sentiment.[1] The
purpose was to "reach a wider audience," but the change was also emblematic of
a longstanding debate having little to do with audience.[2] One group of archeologists championed the change because they objected to the notion that the purpose
of their work was to validate the biblical version of history in Palestine for the
last two millennia BCE. Those who voted to retain the old name charged their

opponents with failing to give due credit to the only written historical source, at least for Palestine, for most of this period, certainly the only source that purported to deliver a continuous history.

The name change was a pre-emptive strike as well. Those advocating it sought middle ground to defend against the arguments of a newly-coalesced group of scholars. Called "revisionists" and "minimalists," or in certain contexts "nihilists," they attribute a late date for the Hebrew Bible's composition and question the historicity of almost everything mentioned in the Old Testament. Drawing away from the appearance of being bible-ridden offered those opposed to the new school to widen options, as was demonstrated in an article in the maiden issue of *Near Eastern Archaeology*.[3]

II

Ronald Mason characterizes archeology as "a primitive science with high aspirations."[4] The lengths to which we will go to learn about the past is illustrated most unequivocally in archeology, where the cost-benefit ratio would be unacceptable to any bottom-line enterprise. As Deetz put it, ". . . historical archaeology is the most expensive way in the world to learn something we already know."[5] The benefits, on the other hand, at times seem miniscule, indeed non-existent, which goes a long way toward explaining why archeological explanation differs so much from that in history.

History and archeology have long enjoyed a symbiotic relationship, but on an epistemological level there are striking differences. Historians can only marvel at the enormous gap between the means with which archeologists work and what they make of their results. Historians have much more evidence, both in content and contextually, from which they tend to draw conclusions that seem modest in comparison. Conversely, even the most fortunate and most cautious archeologist must make one leap of faith after another.

This is compellingly demonstrated in an article co-written by an anthropologist and two archeologists, who make the following claim about retrieving the past through archeological means: "[w]hile it is true that not all archeological sites survive in the strict sense, the truth is that usually it is only the small campsites of nomadic foragers that are likely to disappear from the archeological record."[6]

A view as polyannic as this will only encourage those who rely heavily on archeological evidence. But how true is this claim? For that matter, how true *can* it be? It implies that eventually archeologists' patience will be rewarded as long as they are not working among "nomadic foragers," and that the heavy costs of archeological work will usually bear fruit sufficient to warrant them. Historians, and for that matter many archeologists, are likely to find this claim risible, not from inclination but from bitter experience and reasoned thinking. For instance, it is estimated that from 1000 to 2000 actual and potential archeological sites have been or will be inundated by Three Gorges dam project on the Yangtze river. This is just the latest in a series of similar planned inundations: most famously, the Aswan dam in Egypt, but also the Volta dam in Ghana, the Kariba dam in Zambia, the Birecik dam in Turkey, and various dams in India.

Pompeii has been intensively excavated for over a century, and had survived nearly intact until digging began, yet there is hardly a question about Pompeii that has been definitively resolved. Estimates of its population vary three- to four-fold; the purposes of certain structures remain in dispute, as do the number of stories in many structures; the amount of area given over to residences is still moot; the exact dimensions of the city (defined by our standards, of course) are also questionable. Pompeii exemplifies the truism that the more the data, the more difficult it is to reach definitive conclusions as to their meaning.[7] There are few sites like Pompeii—and more like ꞔUbar, Cahokia, or Nan Madol—where the lack of evidence, and the propensity of archeologists to claim more than they can defend, come prominently into play. ꞔUbar was scarcely discovered before it was trumpeted as the source of the very frankincense mentioned in the gospels. Cahokia's sheer size has led some to claim a large population and imperial status for it. Nan Madol, a huge complex of artificial islets, is a site without compare and questions as to its date, purpose, and construction proliferate.

The inordinate costs of archeological work no doubt play a role in the frequency with which archeologists make flamboyant declarations of victory, only to be followed by glorious debunkings. The need to propound overarching interpretations (archeologists occasionally profess to see their discipline as a science) based on exiguous data inexorably leads to an epistemological climate that sees little need for consistently tying evidence firmly to interpretation. Instead, a sprawling edifice of conventions has been adopted in which apparently like conditions are attributed to like causes and, in turn, like effects are hypothesized.

III

Alan Swedlund and Duane Anderson point out that "[i]t is now commonplace to report [archeological] findings in the public media well in advance of scientific presentation."[8] They contrast this with earlier practice, when members of the public were among the last to hear. Perhaps the public should be among the first to hear about new archeological interpretations. Often enough, after all, it is their money that is being spent. Still, the temptation when treating the public as prime consumers is to sensationalize the evidence, cull out the doubts, smooth the rough edges, and make a quick, if ephemeral, splash. In the very recent past, many such phantom discoveries have been challenged, abandoned, or (seldom) openly retracted, leaving behind a legacy of misinformation and false hopes.

Special care is needed when one of the partners is scripture, particularly the scripture of the interpreters. At a symposium honoring W.F. Albright, one of his students conceded that "Albright's great plan and expectation to set the Bible firmly on the foundation of archaeology buttressed by verifiable data of many kinds seems to have foundered, or at least floundered. After all the digging done and being done, how much has been accomplished? . . . Archaeology has not proved decisive or even greatly helpful in answering the questions most often asked by biblical scholars and has failed to prove the historicity of persons and events especially at the early end of the scale."[9] That such a statement could be made after a century of the most intensive archeological work ever carried out speaks eloquently about the limitations of both evidence (too little) and interpretation (too much) in the field.[10]

An inscription found in 1993 appears (although some think not) to contain a reference to "the house of David." If so, it would be a rare extra-biblical reference to affairs in Judah for a period before other external sources become available. More to the point, it could be taken as proof that the biblical account of the rise of the Israelite states accorded with perceptions elsewhere. The discovery brought in its train an enormous outpouring of academic and popular studies, far in excess of almost anything that appears in the field of history, no matter how controversial.[11] Hällvard Hagelia found that 170 articles and books devoted to it appeared within ten years, as well as 33 editions of the fragments, and presumably his search was not complete. With only as few exceptions this literature treated the inscription as testimony supporting the biblical account of the reigns of David and Solomon and of the Divided Monarchy that followed.[12]

IV

A recent article cites the view of a prominent Japanese archeologist: "[a]ccording to Terasawa, this allows dating Furu 4 to the beginning of the fifth century; if we calculate backward, the number of intervening styles multiplied by an estimated average duration per style (20-25 years) places Furu 0 at the end of the third century."[13] The politically- and culturally-charged milieu in which hypotheses on Japanese origins operate might have obliged Terasawa to jam his evidence onto the unprotected and unsuspecting pottery users, but M.H. Wiener expresses the same attitude, writing that "[i]t is difficult to believe that the marine motifs of the Volcanic Destruction Level at Thera can be separated by fifty years from very similar motifs of the Marine Style pottery of MN 1B Crete."[14]

Well aware of the dynamics and contingencies of the historical record, historians can only be baffled and alienated by such comments. Is it really too much to accept that stylistic practices in parts of the world could not have endured for fifty years or more? The odd notion that past societies routinely and obligingly changed pottery styles in order to help posterity date them comes fresh from the traditional larder of archeological conventions. Pottery shape and design, and especially changes—or imputed changes—have been used to explain migrations, political change, ethnicity, gender relations, size of populations, absence/presence of raw materials, and a dozen other matters. Could this simply be because pottery remains are by far the most common relics from the past, awarding the excavator of just about any site a ticket to the debate?

The royal cemetery of El Kurru in Sudan illustrates another facet of the parlousness of archeological interpretation. The site contains sixteen tombs, the last two of which are those of the first two known rulers of Kush. Three views are currently held regarding the chronology of the cemetery. The tombs, each one of a male ruler, cover fourteen generations, representing continuity with the last known period of Egyptian overrule, which ended about two and a half centuries before the Kushite conquest of Egypt. Or the tombs represent as few as six generations and include the rulers' chief consorts as well, resulting in a much shorter chronology. Or finally, they represent only about six generations, but continuity is preserved by accepting a foreshortened chronology.[15]

The last loses credibility because of its resoundingly circular shape. The first must be rejected on the grounds that it assumes fourteen generations, each with a single ruler, and covering about 250 years. Biologically, fourteen generations in 250 years cannot be made to work, while fourteen rulers in as many generations has occurred only once in recorded history.[16] Thus, while Timothy Kendall points out that "in almost every aspect of our field we can never hope to reach secure understanding of, or agreement about, any particular historical situation," his six-generation, non-continuous, chronology is prima facie more credible than a longer one.[17]

Historians rely on paleodemographers to provide estimates of skeletal age and gender, which historians use to draw conclusions about the larger population purportedly represented by the remains. Claims of physical anthropologists that the procedure known as the Complex Method results in an 80-85 percent accuracy rate in aging skeletal remains to within two to five years of real age can only have cemented this alliance.[18] Put to the test, however, these claims have been exposed as unduly optimistic. Of nearly 1000 skeletons exhumed from the crypt of a London parish church, it was possible to link nearly 400 to coffins with plates that indicated the names and life spans of the dead.[19] Blind estimates of age were then made from skeletal remains and compared with the biographical information and "less than 30 percent of the sample were correctly aged—ie to within five years of the real age."[20] Fifty percent fell within ten years either way and about 75 percent within fifteen years (that is, a thirty-year range). This is barely one-third the success rate claimed by proponents of the Complex Method—more than enough to shift the chances for success in any given instance from likely to unlikely.

V

The problematical aspects of archeological evidence can be traced to one ineluctable aspect of the practice of archeology. Whereas the purpose of historiography is to discover and preserve texts, that of archeology can only be to discover and destroy contexts.[21] This begins to happen the moment the first shovel—or bulldozer—scratches the surface, and continues unabated for the life of the excavation and beyond. Only pale imitations of such sites can be preserved, and then only by the most careful—and expensive—procedures in excavation, interpretation, and conservation. Archeological sites cannot be photocopied, they cannot be purchased at the nearest bookstore, and they cannot be borrowed on interlibrary loan. They are never available in more than abridged translations.

A chasteningly precise example of the magnitude of this reality comes from Israel, where 335,400 sherds were excavated at Gezer Field VII. Of these, 87,240 were initially saved, but eventually only 37,345 pieces were deemed "suitable for the final selection process."[22] Historians often use no more than ten percent of the evidence they collect and sift, but ordinarily the remainder is left intact for others. It would be unfair to call this disposition of sherds wanton, but it suggests the real difficulties that archeological interpretation must surmount, as well as the equally real epistemological handicaps that must ensue. Moreover, it is not only the evidence itself that comes to be destroyed, but the context in which it was discovered. No matter how carefully a site is mapped—and this is a fairly recent development—that map is at best a secondary source, and often less than that.

Any archeological evidence that seeps into the public domain, therefore, is not primary but secondary data. No offsite party can share in the discovery of the evidence, only in its disposition. In this sense it shares the weaknesses of oral data, and of much written data as well. Yet written sources are able to retain a certain integrity and are constrained in their journey by recognized canons of intelligibility. In contrast, archeological evidence can undergo any number of transformations that will be undetectable even if suspected. This applies to today's carefully, even meticulously, implemented archeological digs and a fortiori to those that have proceeded on less rigorous standards.[23]

VI

Forms of evidence that we can treat as archeological are inscriptions on stone, copper, or other materials left behind by societies where paper was not a practical option or not regarded as sufficiently durable. In this sense it differs from the normal run of archeological evidence that often consists of unintended remains not designed for the eyes of remote posterity. Inscriptions are practically the only form of evidence from much of the ancient world and especially from early and medieval India, where they are so common and central a source for the study of political, social, and economic history that a considerable bureaucracy exists to discover, interpret, and protect them.[24] Generally, inscriptions should be treated in much the same way as other types of evidence, but there are a few twists peculiar to the genre. More than most forms of written evidence, inscriptions exist in isolation, are more difficult to discover and study, and are less forthcoming, since the difficulties in producing them often led to elliptical forms of presentation.[25]

In India the great majority of inscriptions are land grants. Often found in hoards, they often lack the random distribution to be entirely trustworthy guides for inferring larger socio-economic practices and patterns. Such inscriptions have long been used to construct the complicated and fragmented dynastic structure that characterizes modern views of these early periods. Many inscriptions provide the name of a ruler and sometimes his ancestry and a date, either in years of his personal rule or in the years of one of the many historical eras that arose in the sub-continent. At first glance they appear to provide firm evidence of filiations and spheres of political control, but this evidence is seldom unambiguous.[26]

The fault for this often lies in modern interpretations. It has long been de rigueur to treat the genealogies in these inscriptions as king lists as well, despite evidence to the contrary. Or to assume that the latest ruler known from inscriptions was also the last ruler of the dynasty, and the first known, the first. Or that the latest year mentioned for a ruler was in fact his last year or close to it. Or that the modern site of an inscription was also its original site. Or that identical names in different inscriptions are those of the same person, allowing stray inscriptions to find a sanctuary that might not really belong to them.[27] This pretense at completeness persists despite repeated counter-indications. It is only somewhat surprising that the inclination to splice errant genealogies has scarcely abated in the face of the complications that arise from it. The need to find new room on filled dynastic dance cards, though not peculiar to Indian history, is most intensively practiced there.

A stele of the pharaoh Merenptah again illustrates the penchant to make much of little. Dating to the end of the thirteenth century BCE, the stele mentions a polity called "Israel" (as reconstructed from hieroglyphics anyway). Many biblical scholars take this as evidence—all there is, really—of a biblical Israel two centuries before and two centuries after the date of the stele itself. In short, they treat it as testimony to four hundred years of continuous history. They do not notice, or do not heed, that the relevant passage reads something like "Israel is laid waste [and] his seed is not," apparently stating Merenptah's claim to have extirpated the inhabitants of whatever polity this was.[28] If the stele is evidence of anything, it is that Merenptah claimed to have wiped out a group of people with a name similar to that which the bible later gave to people who purportedly left Egypt and who several centuries later established a state in the same area.

The paucity of archeological evidence exacts a methodological and epistemological toll, well illustrated by William Dever's rodomontade: "[a]rchaeology is now in a position to write a *fully fleshed out* social history, or account of everyday life in Israel and Judah in the later monarchy, *even without the texts of the Hebrew Bible*."[29] Such claims show in sharp relief the difference between the goals, the terminology, and the epistemological sensitivity of historians and archeologists. Moreover, given the weight biblical testimony is inevitably granted in interpreting the archeological data, to claim that it is incidental to historical reconstruction amounts to disingenuousness.

Just the same, this making much of little has characterized the study of the frozen and well-preserved body of a man discovered in the Ötzaler Alps in 1991. Dating techniques eventually put his life span at about 5300 BP. The case made headlines everywhere and archeologists and physical anthropologists quickly gathered to study the remains as thoroughly as possible.[30] Ian Hodder recently recapitulated their work, and offered arguments and inferences as to the significance of the find. Many are plausible, some less so; none is demonstrably correct.

Nonetheless, Hodder lost no time in making transcending claims: "[t]he fleeting moment of the Ice Man's life and cold and lonely death provide us with a window through which to peer at the playing out of larger structural and systemic transformations. The find of his body allows a different perspective on these abstract and objective forces. It helps us to see how the structures were mediated and transformed, how they were played out in the practices of personal lives—how individuals performed and transformed the large-scale historical movements."[31] Really? This places quite a burden on the poor Neolithic fellow. If only one set of armor had survived from the Middle Ages or one mummy from ancient Egypt, would we dare use them to infer "larger structural and systemic transformations" in these societies?

VII

Unfortunately for historians—and no doubt for archeologists too—archeology and nationalism have been inextricably intertwined since the beginning.[32] Americans are unlikely to realize the extent of this. Since much of their national and pre-national history is amply documented by the written record, archeological findings play a refining role and usually at the level of small or under-represented groups. Elsewhere archeology is much more important in describing and defining ethnic and national self-identity, and so has been at the beck and call of special interests, including the dominant political powers. At best, this means that historians interested in tapping the archeological record must come to terms with the historical unfolding of that record.

The exiguity and ambiguity of archeological evidence, together with the proven appeal of material remains, have long combined to saddle archeology with unwanted parasites—nationalism, tourism, lunatic fringeism—wherever the place and whatever the circumstances. No discussion of archeological evidence can ignore the relationship between that subject and history in the modern Near East, in particular in Israel, where "digging" has been called "a veritable form of prayer," and where discoveries and interpretations always serve public purposes.[33] No one travels abroad to visit the archives unless they are actually using them. But tens of thousands of tourists are drawn to the "Holy Land" (or Pompeii/Paestum, Xian, Machu Picchu, and other sites), because monumental remains are more exciting than words.

If excavated Israel is a cynosure for various religious groups to spend money, it is also the most notorious case of archeology in the service of ideology. For centuries all such work was contextualized and informed by biblical testimony. Lately, some scholars have attempted to interpret findings on their own terms, with the predictable result that their interpretations diverge from biblical testimony. Equally predictably, this approach has raised cries of blasphemy from traditionalists.

The extraordinary costs of site preparation, excavation proper, laboratory tests, and dissemination of results force archeologists everywhere to seek funds incessantly. To be successful, they need to be attuned to, and sometimes in thrall to, official imperatives. It is simply not possible to conduct such work without buying into official ideologies about the past. Since most funding comes from official or quasi-official sources, there is a built-in temptation to satisfy benefactors. Archeology requires the long-term goodwill of the host government, and with this comes a sense of obligation that might manifest itself in various regrettable ways. For instance, archeologists might well find themselves contractually obligated with regard to the disposition of finds. Moreover, archeology is a collaborative and recurrent activity, which means a need to satisfy the local archeologists over long periods of time. Even after leaving a country after completing excavation, ties remain stronger than for the departing archival researcher—for instance, the greater the likely need to ask later for favors in terms of artifacts, photographs, etc.

Nationalists are well aware that properly promoted archeological sites have more propaganda value than a hundred scholarly books. It is no exaggeration that hardly a month goes by but an article appears in the popular press describing some exciting new find. In turn these generate tourism and prestige. Machu Picchu played no known role in Inca history but is the most famous Inca survival. Angkor Wat played a central role in Khmer history, but few people who know Angkor Wat as a monument through site visits know or care anything of this history.[34]

VIII

When archeological evidence confronts written evidence, to which should the honors go? Given the number of possible variables from one case to another, this question is unanswerable, but suppose that it is positive archeological evidence vs. negative written evidence? Several separate digs in and around Bergen, Norway turned up indications of a major conflagration there ca. 1225-30, but the relevant annals record no fires between 1198 and 1248. Archeologists have considered, and rejected, the hypothesis that a number of coeval small fires—each too small to make the annals—account for the available archeological evidence, leaving it a straight contest between the two forms of evidence.

An archeologist and a historian collaborated to treat the Bergen fire as a test case, and decided that in this instance archeology proves more reliable than written history.[35] Surveying the sagas and annals, almost all emanating from Iceland rather than Norway, they concluded that these recorded fires selectively—for plot advancement, to curry royal favor, or because there were illustrious victims. The Bergen fire evidently failed to meet any of these criteria. If true, this episode should encourage those using the medieval written records to be more careful about arguments from silence than they might have been in the past. While no one thought of these sources as comprehensive, it had seemed reasonable to assume that, if they recorded as many fires as they did, then they probably attempted to record all major fires. That they apparently did not do this after all throws unwelcome light on both their completeness and their objectivity.

IX

While archeologists debate among themselves endlessly, there is remarkably little direct colloquy between archeologists and historians, despite the symbiotic relationship that exists in their respective work and conclusions. As Umberto Albarella put it: ". . . a quick browse through the literature can easily show that archaeologists and historians often ignore each other's evidence."[36] In particular, such discussions should feature canons of proof, where, it seems to me, historians occupy higher ground, but need to know how much higher. Merrilee Salmon, a philosopher of archeology, offers a clue to the size of the abyss: "[g]iven scientific fallibilism, expressions such as 'verification' and 'validation' of hypotheses, 'proof,' and 'incontrovertible evidence' are not intended to suggest that absolute certainty is attainable. In the context of scientific inquiry, the limits of these terms are well understood."[37] This double-speak is alarming for anyone who exercises the right to apply everyday meanings to everyday words, and suggests that historians need to worry whenever they encounter any archeological argument. Is it being made "in the context of scientific inquiry?" Do words like "proof" mean what the rest of us think they mean?

Undeterred, archeologists press forward. Discussing the vexed case of the location of a polity mentioned in the Chinese annals, Okazaki Takashi is optimistic: "[o]n the other hand, archaeological findings cannot *yet* furnish a definite answer either."[38] With even more optimism, an Israeli archeologist has been quoted as saying: "[w]e found almost certain proof that the story of the entry into Israel is very believable. The relevant materials are in the field. *We only have to find them.*"[39] With such visionary hopes and ambitions, there is clear danger that archeologists will not find the time to view their enterprise overtly from an epistemological perspective, will never really ask *how* they know, and will forget that their epistemologies are not supposed to differ so much from those of the rest of us.

8

SPEAKING OF HISTORY

Tradition does not reach far, where there is neither pen nor
pencil to perpetuate the memory of events. . . . Oral history is
very uncertain at best. Every repetition varies the language at
least . . . [a]nd fiction would often be called on, to supply
lapses.

What was that sequence? He was certain that he had left
something out, and it made him reflect on the unreliability of
evidence. Something very important and very enjoyable had
just happened to him, yet he could not even hold the details in
his mind.

I

In 1971 Leonard Berkowitz published the results of his investigation into how
a famous psychological experiment had been assimilated into textbooks since
1951. Berkowitz found disappointing results: "[t]he findings are correctly reported in very few of these works" and "[t]here are serious omissions and representations regarding the results in some of the best known texts." He compared this
to the well-known phenomenon that "details tend to be omitted [in transmitted
messages] and often only those items consistent with the communication's central theme are reported." Moreover, "[t]he transmitted information may be dis-
torted so that there is a better fit with the theme than actually existed at the begin-

ning." He was especially disappointed that the fact that this phenomenon is well known "has not prevented social psychologists from exhibiting the same types of errors when they relay messages."[1]

II

In stark contrast, English Catholic theologians living in exile in the seventeenth century wrote tracts attacking the credentials of the protestant churches, in part by arguing that oral tradition was vastly superior to the written word.[2] According to Serenus Cressy, "Orall Tradition" was "more secure from errour and mistakes then writing" because it was "*not written with inke* and on paper, *but by the spirit in mens heartes* by which means the sense sunke into their Soules, farre more effectually than if wordes onely has swomme into their braines "[3] Kenelm Digby agreed that "though the wordes be uncertane . . . the sense is constant."[4] Others thought orality was more demotic, yet others that the very virtue of "tradition" was that it could change to accommodate new circumstances. Most saw the advantage in being able to claim apostolic succession, but this required using "tradition" as the principal means of transmission and authentication.

Anglican theologians were prompt to wonder how oral traditions could satisfy the requirements that these theologians imposed on them. John Dryden momentarily turned critic when he turned these arguments against their proponents:

> If written words from time are not secured,
> How can we think have oral sounds endured?
> Which thus transmitted, if one mouth has failed,
> Immortal lies on ages are entailed;
> And that some such have been is proved too plain;
> If we consider interest, church, and gain.[5]

Not only did Dryden's sentiments rhyme, they have the makings of good historical critical thinking as well.

The shortcomings of the oral medium, of course, were noticed long before Dryden. For example, a Hittite treaty from the thirteenth century BCE contained the following clause: ". . . if the words of the messenger are in agreement with the words of the tablet, trust the messenger. . . . But if the words of the speech of the messenger are not in agreement with the words of the tablet, you . . . shall certainly not trust the messenger and shall certainly not take to heart the evil content of that report of his."[6]

III

This did not—nor should it have—impede recent developments that have led to the flowering of oral historiography as a means of extracting information. The effects, and probably the intent, of the oral history boom have been democratizing—more voices and more perspectives. The rise of oral history in the academy began in earnest with the decolonization of the historical enterprise after World War II. Part of this process involved learning more about the soon-to-be-liberated societies that largely constituted the moribund imperial systems. Heretofore such information had been gathered by anthropologists and missionaries either in the employ of an imperial power or sharing its goals. The new atmosphere required upgrading this paternalistic process, and academics began to treat non-European pasts by actually traveling to the field, seeking out informants to relate their societies' history, recording it, and finally publishing their own versions of it.

At first there was a feeling that this was not quite real history and not historiography either.[7] For Africa this began to change early in the 1960s when Jan Vansina, trained as a medievalist but the veteran of years of fieldwork in central Africa, published *De la tradition orale*.[8] Vansina applied many of the rules for medieval history to early African history and helped bring credibility to modern oral historiography. By comparing, rather than contrasting, the various types of sources for medieval history and Kuba history, Vansina transcended arguments that oral historical sources could be nothing more than idle chatter masked as accounts of the past. He pointed out that historians from the Middle Ages, whom modern scholars treat as precursors, did in fact gather data directly from informants by word of mouth or co-opted accounts that had been transmitted from earlier times. The ways they worked were not so different from the new breed of historians who went out to the field. Time hallowed the work of these earlier historians, time and the fact that after being written down, the material they had gathered contrived to appear more like the work of their intellectual descendants of later centuries—us.

IV

Vansina wrote little about collecting and sampling oral historical data, but others soon filled the gap. Strong advocates for the new initiative, their attention to method was for the moment designed to justify and authenticate their own work. They tended to be introspective only insofar as it helped to convince them of prospects for their own success. In time, however, more serious attention was given to the cons, as well as the pros, of oral historiography.[9] This was necessary because there are remarkably important differences between consulting paper and consulting people. While all the principles discussed elsewhere apply to interpreting oral tradition, an entirely new set of procedures was needed for collecting it, since historians not only collect oral data, but help create and shape it in the process.

Of course this can apply to using written sources as well. A historian can start off by choosing an inferior edition or a faulty translation or by working in a language with which he insufficiently familiar, and never recover. But while this is possible, it is not endemic, and when it happens it could be found out because the same sources will usually be available to other interested parties. The oral historian can make the same mistakes by choosing poor informants or interpreters, asking the wrong questions, establishing inappropriate interview environments, and the like. If he does, no one else need ever know, since he can easily win more credit in print than in the field; hence the importance of establishing and promulgating detailed and explicit guidelines, including full disclosure.

The process begins with the selection of a topic and a group among which to work. The oral historian operates under constraints in this. Besides being interesting to him, the topic must be appealing to those he plans to exploit, not least those who control access in areas of the world that oral historians find most attractive. Thus the historian must anticipate judiciously, but often without any grounds for informed choices. Once the preliminaries are carried out, he must acquire at least a grounding—and one would hope more—in the local language/s. This represents considerable effort and expense, but can seldom be avoided lest the result be akin to studying the history of ancient Athens without knowing classical Greek. Most oral historians will require an interpreter during early stages of fieldwork, yielding yet more chances for error, for an interpreter must not only be skilled in the language, but should sympathize with the historian's goals, while yet being considerate of the concerns of the society in which they are working.

Finally, the historian is ready to engage his first living primary source. The first crux is developing a preliminary set of questions that will acquaint informants with the historian's interests, while not giving away too much. The questions must not be couched in ways that lead informants to answers they feel are desired; the researcher is there to be informed, not edified. He has ensconced himself amid the people whose past interests him, and over a period of time has gained, without displaying too much overt interest in doing so, some sense of local mores and worldviews, helping him discriminate among possible inform-ants and protocols.

Wishing to be productive, fieldworkers often collect information from groups of people whom they can interview en masse before they move on to interview more groups of people, and the result can be group-act and group-speak. The dynamics of a group interview can provide his interpretations for the historian, but not in ways he should find acceptable. Oral historiography seldom benefits from haste; trial group interviews provide impressions about the present, but sel-dom useful information about the past, although they might be useful in establish-ing likely informants and developing a more effective modus operandi. There is something to be said for noticing particularly those who appear to dissent from the consensus and making sure to pursue inquiries with them.[10] The view that emerges at first will likely be consensual and based on such incidental issues as strength of personality, deference to authority, and desires to keep information private. In the circumstances, any historian satisfied with group interviews is con-tent to be a bystander to his own research.

The core of oral history involves a scenario with the researcher, the intervie-wee, and (sometimes) an interpreter. These are private, yet social occasions. They are also occasions of unequal benefit. Books don't mind being used, but people often do, and the oral historian is treating his informants just as he would treat a book—as a means of furthering his own interests. This is a delicate matter, and is not to be resolved on a crass pay-as-you-go basis, which will tempt informants to treat data as commodities, with disastrous results.[11] Instead, the historian must find ways of conveying his own excitement and standards of truth about the value of the research.

The oral historian can never be sure that he has succeeded, or indeed whether he has succeeded too well, because his informants did their best to keep him happy. Engaged in the labor-intensive task of eliciting individual or societal memories from one informant after another, the historian could find his critical instincts blunted by a series of answers that he wants to hear. Nothing should start red lights flashing faster than answers that correspond closely to the historian's needs. Is this accidental, or has he telegraphed his punches? If the latter, is it pos-sible to recoup the losses? If not, what should his new strategy be? The historian must interview as many informants as practicable, or design a defensible sample, asking roughly the same questions and seeking, subtly but deliberately, to elicit different answers. If he fails in the latter, he bids to succeed in the overall enterprise.

He must also provide for interviewing selected informants more than once at widely-separated intervals. This is akin to the various built-in controls that characterize experimental science and is a sine qua non. It is a dangerous maneuver, just the same, for it exposes the historian to one of the dread realities of oral research—that informants change their testimony for a variety of reasons that include faulty memories, differing micro-environments, a new take on the research/er, changes in health or social status, and/or a penchant for mischief-making. Such a result is distressing, but rarely fatal—no different than the typical Rashomon effect that governs so many written accounts. The historian can apply the usual canons to help him determine what it all means, but above all he must provide himself with that opportunity through multiple interviewing, just as the historian who uses written sources seeks out all those that could be relevant, even if versions of the same text, and studies them again and again.

Other worlds are seldom simpler worlds; the historian entering the field might find a society divided along any number of fault lines not easily discernible to the neophyte observer.[12] If he becomes aware of matters, he will, presumably, wish to avoid being seen to take sides, but that choice might not be entirely his. At best—and assuming partial success—the information he gathers will be affected by the division, leaving him to sort things out. At worst, he will find that dealing with one side will be regarded as consorting by the other, leading to a boycott or similar avoidance behavior. Since there is probably no way to preclude some unfortunate result falling somewhere along this continuum, the fieldworker's most effective mechanism might simply be to do his homework before entering the field—a truism that is not always true. Foreknowledge will prevent him from bumbling into an awkward situation unawares or, worse yet, never quite coming to realize that it exists at all.

V

The historian of the written word has several options for converting his sources to his own use. He can take notes; hand-copy the texts verbatim; or photocopy, photograph, or microform them. The last are the most advantageous, for they preserve intact the form and format, allowing the historian to consult it at any later time for any reason. For the oral historian the range is similar, but the options different. He too can take notes trying to catch the flavor of the testimony. To do this verbatim he would probably have to resort to shorthand, not a reasonable alternative. Or, when allowed, he can tape-record testimony and transcribe it later. This, the photocopy-equivalent, is standard operating procedure among field historians, since it preserves the chance to consult and probe the testimony at leisure. It is superior to photocopying because not only are words revealed, but often the mood behind them—the hesitations, the snickers, the confusions all emerge, each one a possible clue to the normative value of the testimony, each an opportunity for the researcher to make more informed judgments.[13]

Research based on fieldwork is often begun in the field, where it helps to frame further research activity, and completed somewhere else. This is not much different from normal practice with archival work. Fieldwork is typically less systematically carried out, however, leaving the historian with a heavier load in turning the raw materials into a finished product. At this point the question becomes how to establish a set of priorities that seem best to ensure an effective use of time.

In a study of Newfoundland folktales collected in the field, Halpert and Widdowson make explicit their concern with getting the transcription 'right.' "The texts presented here," they claim, "are not literary reworkings but are transcribed verbatim from oral tradition." But, they admit, this task is no easy one, and they claim only limited success. They point out that "[o]ne of the greatest present-day illusions in fieldwork is that the tape recorder effectively secures the exact words of a speaker, which can then be easily transcribed and presented in written form." They add that "[i]n transcribing the Newfoundland audiotapes, it proved impossible to do more than hint at the many nuances of vocal expressiveness used by tellers." They recognize that "it is impossible to transfer more than a fraction of this multifaceted oral performance to the unidimensional medium of print," and admit that the "principal aim in this collection is to explore some of the possibilities of such transference."[14]

This caution and care are commendable, and Halpert and Widdowson's discussion is one of the best available on the issue of transcription as translation. It is an unpleasant surprise then to learn that, despite their conclusions as to the inferiority of transcriptions, the tapes themselves *may in due course* be made available for scholarly reference."[15] Because such field tapes are so important, it is the responsibility of every researcher to preserve them and eventually donate them—sooner rather than later—to a depository that will permit consultation by qualified persons. Although no different than citing an archival source accurately to permit someone else to investigate it, this duty has been fulfilled with embarrassing laxness in the forty to fifty years of active oral historiography.[16] As a result, many works based on oral field research remain hopelessly detached from their evidence and from the opportunity to test their conclusions, and run the risk of being treated as curiosities.

Taking the time required to transcribe tapes accurately forces most historians to make choices that might more often be expedient than responsible. From the researcher's point of view these are hard-won 'personal' property, as well as means to professional success. On this view the right time is never, but this attitude is unprofessional, if not unethical. Sharing should occur about the same time as the first fruits of fieldwork are published; any earlier would be a burden for the researcher, much later would be an evasion.[17]

VI

An important benefit of conducting oral research is the historian's first-hand exposure to the Hawthorne Effect, which occurs when "the introduction of experimental conditions . . . has the consequence of changing the behavior it is designed to identify. When people realize that their behavior is being examined, they change how they act."[18] The term derives from an experiment carried out in the 1920s at the Western Electric Co. in the Hawthorne neighborhood of Chicago. This involved introducing a set of variables (e.g., lighting, incentives, variations in shift times and pay schedules) one at a time in order to determine their impact on productivity. Well into the exercise, however, it was discovered that workers had learned that they were participants in an experiment, which fatally compromised the possibility of determining which variables mattered most, which least. Instead, a new variable was introduced, and one of incomparable significance— the psychological effects of knowing that others were interested in the workers' daily tasks, sometimes called "operant conditioning" or "experimenter effect."[19]

Whatever we might call it, this imponderable explains why survey research lacks the essential criterion of objectivity. Working with an outsider, as is normally the case, with an individual agenda, also normally the case, cannot help but have indeterminate effects on informants' behavior. From the very moment a researcher arrives in his target area—whether it be a village, a family, a congregation—previous attitudes and settings change. Exchanges of pleasantries, not to mention information, now have unanticipated consequences—reward, fame, obloquy—that never existed before. It is ludicrous to expect that respondents will not reorient their views about the subject in light of new and reconfigured sets of opportunities and consequences.[20]

VII

Nearly two thousand years ago the rhetor Quintilian put it succinctly: "[w]ritten evidence and oral evidence often conflict" and went on to argue that the two had different means of support. [21] Like many historians, John Vincent also treats oral and written evidence as mutually exclusive: "Historical study requires verbal evidence, with marginal exceptions. And this verbal evidence, with all respect to the fascination of oral history, is nearly all written evidence."[22] Admittedly, the two are distinct at certain stages in their development, but an important benefit of the recent flourishing of the study of oral data is the sharp relief it brings to issues of transmission by reminding us that the printed word is often only the latest of several stages in the processing of information.[23]

Historians who use oral data ostensibly several generations old are coming to consider the implications of scores of transmissions on content. In particular they need to be concerned that in many societies conveying tradition has performative aspects to it. Certainly it has been true that modern fieldworkers find that informants treat the transaction as an opportunity to excel as entertainers, and there is no reason to presume that this has not been the case in any transmissions that preceded the most recent occasion.

By definition, performance is an attempt to triumph over the text. Not content merely to interpret, musicians add cadenzas to works they perform that impress their own individuality on the work, and conductors shape instruments and voices as much to their own liking as to that of the composer. Shakespeare might not be treated quite so rudely as Handel or Mozart, but each actor strives to bring a personal perspective to his plays. One of the principal ways a performer gains esteem is by improvising his text to delight and impress his audience. Is it wise to assume that performers in oral societies are any less egocentrically driven about historical texts?[24]

Some do think so. About the only way historians anxious to put traditions to historical use can develop an argument is to claim that such traditions were learned and transmitted word-perfectly time and again. Many remain stolidly undaunted by all the interpretative hazards and prefer to credit members of oral societies with extraordinary capacities—and wills—to remember. Stuart McHardy argues that the "conservatism" of oral tradition in Scotland is reason enough to accept that "accurate information" on the Picts (that is, before the mid-ninth century) was preserved in folktales nearly to the present. McHardy even goes so far as to wonder aloud whether a folktale collected in the 1980s "might be truer to the original [1000-year-old] form than the early medieval manuscript version."[25]

In seeking to impose a chronology on pre-European Maori history, J.B.W. Roberton asserted that "[t]he mental retention of genealogies acquired during this process (a spare time hobby) makes it easy to believe that the transmission of genealogies by word perfect repetition was no very great feat . . ." Roberton continued that "[t]he assumption that records [sic] cannot be [accurately] transmitted orally over some centuries is untenable." He concluded, somewhat dubiously, that "[e]xperimental support for such a negative assumption would be very difficult and I have not heard any quoted."[26] Any experiment to test this would indeed be "very difficult," but many of us have participated in, or heard of, party games like Chinese whispers in which the object, often unachieved, is to transmit only a short sentence accurately and only along a chain of ten to fifteen people, all in on the game.[27]

Those who champion generations of word-perfect transmission espouse one theoretical possibility that can model such an unverifiable process. Another is that of the fallible transmitter. Failure to transmit accurately can have a host of causes. Mere forgetfulness or carelessness need no explanation. A subversive persona is another. The trickster is an element of many personalities—if only from a desire to crosscut the consensus. In the case of prior transmissions of oral tradition, no evidence would remain, leaving us with nothing but the duty to suspect. More common is the impact of social, political, or religious exigencies on tradition. Societies change constantly, requiring compensating changes to the portrayal of the past that underlies all societies' views of themselves. Such myth-making in written records occurs constantly and with no regard for the fact that it is detectable. For oral data the process is immeasurably easier and possibly more tempting. The lack of written records about the past renders each occasion for transmission a clear opportunity to influence both present and future.

All things considered, the closer we look at issues of transmission—the opportunities and the temptations—the more difficult it is to treat any oral data as unadulterated, even though we can seldom offer a binding argument to that effect. In the absence of this, the historian must decide how credulous he is willing to be, and his own interpersonal experiences will probably weigh suitably heavily. Anyone who accepts the notion that something is lost or altered in transmission cannot treat oral tradition as largely accurate, even though in principle, it could and might be.

VIII

The role of the oral in written historiography is drawing unaccustomed attention at last. Several works on ancient Greece, medieval and early modern western Europe, and the biblical world have appeared in the last decade or so. Susan Niditch's study of the interaction of the oral and the written in ancient Israel is one example.[28] Niditch analyzes the biblical text to discern passages that spring from an oral source and those that appear to have undergone the kind of elision and tidying up that are more characteristic of writing. Niditch does not conscript the full range of material that could throw light on the most important question concerning the relationship of the oral and the written: what are the effects of constant transmission and transition on the process? Oral data might have existed for centuries before being committed to writing, and involved perhaps hundreds of individual or collective transmissions.[29] Each of these had a potentially corrosive effect on the integrity of the subject matter, but we can know nothing about these effects because we know nothing about the transmission process. Faute de mieux, we must infer from results that are available about other transmissions and assume a congruent pattern between the observed and the unobserved.

IX

The oral history movement has provided us with experience and insights into how best to deal with historical sources that are now written, but once were oral. Sometimes this orality is victualed by ingesting written information into the oral food chain. Or the data in the oral universe can be less osmotic and remain there until they eventually are lost or extracted by an outsider, to be turned into the written word. Herodotus metamorphosed the oral into the written without pretending to do otherwise. His successor Thucydides, though vastly different in philosophy and execution, aped Herodotus closely in this regard. And they are but the first two names in an immense Rolodex of historians through the ages. Many of these explicitly acknowledged their modus operandi; others did not, but clearly must have operated in this way.

Hundreds of cases suggest that, when an oral society needs to change its perception of the past, it is willing and able to reorder available knowledge. One of the great benefits of orality to its practitioners—its ability to forget the past in aid of reconstituting evolving sociopolitical relationships—is at the same time one of its bleakest characteristics for those who would use it to reconstruct that past.[30]

Almost everywhere in Africa, oral traditions have been shamelessly (from the historian's perspective) used to realign local interest groups and take advantage of the vagaries of colonial rule. The coming of the written word allowed oral tradition to become fixed at a certain point in its evolution, but this seldom happened immediately and sometimes not at all.

One of the first effects of the onset of new sources has been an alacrity in oral societies to co-opt them into their own traditions as a new form of competitive one-upmanship before any petrification sets in and severely reduces the scope of the exercise. This operation is well documented throughout the world and can be found for the looking.[31] Typically, traditions collected after the publication of certain histories of an area or the dissemination of biblical information would include some of these new data, whereas traditions collected earlier did not. Scrutinizing the records available often discloses unrepentant admissions that such feedback was in spate. Just the same, later traditions continue to include this spurious information and to treat it as if handed down for generations.

Some recent claims for Aboriginal traditions in Australia go much farther; some of them are truly extraordinary. Barry Blake found "clinching evidence that Aborigines had an oral tradition that embodied memories of the cataclysmic events of 10,000 years ago."[32] Not to be outdone, R.M.W. Dixon made the point both stronger and longer: "[t]his [part of one story he was told] suggests that the story of the volcanic eruptions may have been handed down from generation to generation for something like 13,000 years." Dixon had no qualms about arguing that as many as 500 or more oral transmissions had little corrosive effect on content; in a revealing non sequitur, he finds it "not implausible, since Aborigines are known to have been in Australia for at least 40,000 years."[33]

Not implausible? A series of lucky guesses would be a more likely hypothesis than thousands of years of accurate transmission. Far the most likely explanation, though, is simply that during two hundred years of missionizing and other forms of acculturation, notions such as these seeped into the corpus of Aboriginal tradition, only eventually to be disgorged and accepted as primeval. Claims like this, and those that use tales of megafauna to argue for deep-time reliability of oral tradition, or for the survival of such animals until fairly recent times, overlook the numerous pathways available for such information to reach and affect traditional accounts in modern settings.[34]

Despite all these impediments to belief, there has been an upsurge recently in claims for the efficacy of American Indian oral tradition over the very long term. Roger Echo-Hawk exemplifies this when he writes under a cloak of false mod-

esty that ". . . I speculate that the majority of oral traditions that contain historical information generated by firsthand observers can go back no further in time
than about 40,000 years."[35] Echo-Hawk seems unconcerned that he is positing
not fewer than 1600 transmissions without significant loss or gain of content to
use to postulate detailed and kaleidoscopic patterns of population movements
over most of western North America in deepest prehistory.

Echo-Hawk's optimism is shared by others. In attempting to correlate volcanic eruptions with Dene tradition, D.W. Moodie and A.J.W. Catchpole claim
that "[t]here can be little doubt that ancestors of the Dene witnessed the second
of these events and that memories of this terrifying experience . . . were transmitted orally from generation to generation for a period of over twelve hundred
years."[36] In supporting the American Indian position on Kennewick Man, David
Hurst Thomas argues that ". . . most tribes maintain rich oral traditions, which
describe *in detail* their remote past . . ."[37] Echo-Hawk and Thomas defend the historical accuracy of oral tradition as part of larger arguments defending the rights
of certain Indian groups to block the study of various artifacts. Many tribes assert
that their traditions claim autochthony and thus the right to claim *any* early
remains as "ancestral." The only way to render this plausible is to maintain that
there has been a millennia-long accuracy of these traditions, even in their details.

Such reliance might not be one of the future's options. Ironically, just as the
study of oral evidence has come into its own, conditions detrimental to the well-
being of orality have also become more pervasive in once largely oral societies.
Richard Roberts notes four reasons why oral tradition is in danger: the passing of
the generation reared in the early colonial period, the disruption of generational
forms of transmission of historical knowledge, the proliferation of the radio and
cassette player, and the rise of national broadcasting.[38] Roberts is talking about
West Africa, but the process of change and degeneration has existed in all times
and all places, even if the motives and mechanisms have varied.

X

Those who worry about how much hidden change oral tradition masks are often
told that it is virtually impossible to efface the past so effectively that tell-tale
traces of the effort do not lurk in later tradition. That the content of oral traditions
does not survive well the passing of time must remain a belief—or an intuition—
for those periods for which there are no other data. To support this notion, the historian must seek evidence that new views of the past can supersede older ones,
preferably in as brief a period as possible.

In 1908 the largest meteorite known to have struck the earth in historical times fell in Siberia. Contemporary sources tell us that the impact was accompanied by unprecedented pyrotechnics and acoustics, as well as unusual seismic activity. E.L. Krinov writes that "newspapers not only reported the fall of a very large meteorite accompanied by threatening phenomena [but also] the extraordinary luminous effects observed in the atmosphere during the following days." Nonetheless, "in a comparatively short time the fall of the meteorite was almost forgotten and memories had to be revived fifteen years later."[39] We can only imagine what exciting events blotted out these memories or just what "reviving" consisted of.

Another case, from the Trobriand island of Kitawa, is better documented and much to the point, since it affects the ethnographer who recorded it. Giancarlo Scoditti relates that when he, an Italian, first visited Kitawa in the 1970s, he was regarded as a Kitawan, and his friends on the island used to "kid" him about the circumstances of his parentage as they imagined it. Twenty-five years later, "[w]hat started as a joke has now become in many younger people's minds a historical fact."[40] Those who know better will die off and the younger generation's "historical fact" will establish a new truth, at least until it too is replaced by yet another generation's interpretation. That cases like Scoditti's can occur under the scrutiny of the modern world is disquieting, even if it is precisely the confrontation of this world with oral worlds that spawn these kaleidoscopic changes.

9

SENSING INCONGRUITY

The vice of this method of handling the inscriptions lies here:
that it involves a playing fast-and-loose with well-attested historical documents; hailing them eagerly when they say at once
what you want them to say, but discrediting them with all your
might when their utterances are troublesome to you; it means
that you are unwilling to wait, unable to hold questions of harmony in abeyance, . . .

I am president of an explorers' club which meets once a quarter and tells each other stories, greatly embellished by imagination and wishful thinking.

I

The Library of Congress classification system is almost universally used in the
world of academic libraries. It is not without faults—one of these is that the
scheme originally separated "works of literature" from "works of history," and
that division ostensibly remains today. Thus the history of Classical Antiquity is
covered by classes DE, DF, and DG, but sources for that history fall into the PA
class. The Library of Congress's attempt to distinguish between literary and historical works is not an isolated case. Cicero might be praised for his high latini-
ty, but his writings are often as important to historians as the more clearly historical approach of his contemporary Sallust, and it becomes impossible to justify

drawing lines. This segregation of history and literature has other harmful side-effects in the way in which texts are approached and assessed.

II

Johan Huizinga saw the writing of history and literature as all but mutually exclusive. In history writing "[t]here is an absolute craving to penetrate to the genuine knowledge of that which truly happened . . . The sharp distinction between history and literature lies in the fact that the former is almost entirely lacking in that element of play which underlies literature from beginning to end."[1] This hermetic boundary is being eroded, however. Modern literary criticism is increasingly an exercise in determining authorial intent, usually by comparing one version of a text with another. The opportunities to do this for sources from faraway times and places are much fewer, but knowing the results when it can be done alerts us to the dangers of assuming that our only source is also the rendition its author preferred above all others, as well as one that intermediate scribes have not manhandled too rudely.

Frederic Holmes wrote about the evolution of Antoine Lavoisier's ideas from one version of his writings to the next: "[w]e cannot always tell whether a thought that led [Lavoisier] to modify a passage, recast an argument, or develop an alternative interpretation occurred while he was still engaged in writing what he subsequently altered, or immediately afterward, or after some interval during which he occupied himself with something else; but the timing is, I believe, less significant than the fact that the new developments were consequences of the effort to express ideas and marshall supporting information on paper."[2]

Holmes captures the notion that the process of writing and thinking, thinking and writing, should be studied as a dialectical whole. He can do this because drafts of Lavoisier's works exist, from laboratory notes to final publications. Is this a luxury or a nuisance? Some historians would answer one way, some the other, depending on how much of a hurry they are in. Sometimes the temptation is to accept the final—usually the published—version of a text as authoritative, by assuming that the author rejected all previous versions ipso facto, but this deprives historians of an invaluable opportunity to assess sources dynamically, a chance that should never be missed.

For literary and textual critics, changes are important because they often allow them to trace textual lineages and influences. Historians have less reason to be grateful, but dare not let ingratitude blind them to the issue. Texts that are deemed literary rather than historical tend to be categorized and treated differently, and by scholars with different kinds of training and temperament. It is hard to see the logic of this; all texts are inherently literary and many literary texts ultimately, and sometimes immediately, have historical significance. Uninterested in the techniques and theories of textual criticism, historians risk forgoing important insights into the production and influence of their sources. It is one thing to let textual critics set an example, but should historians let them do their work as well?

III

One of the great lessons to be learned from literary scholars is how unstable texts are. The practice of treating texts diachronically exposes their uncertainty and confusion, and makes it more difficult to determine whether a particular text is a destination or merely a convenient way-station. Transcriptional errors are important in interpreting texts. Most historical sources are written, and we readily accept the notion of error since we've all committed them ourselves. Some errors are inadvertent and trivial in their execution, but significant in their implications ("now" for "not" or vice versa, moving a decimal point in either direction or adding or omitting integers, haplography or the skipping of words, misunderstanding abbreviations, various errors due to mishearing, etc.).[3]

Other changes are purposeful. Conjectural emendation, especially when unsignaled, is the bane of all historians, yet alarmingly common practice among scribes and editors of both yesterday and today.[4] Transcribers and editors also suppress material for various reasons. Then there are those changes that are inadvertent at one level but advertent at another: the so-called Freudian slip. Determining these requires special knowledge about the context of the transcription and the transcriber, unless the changes can be identified by comparison with other versions of the same text. There are often good reasons to consider transcriptional error as a possible resolution to textual cruxes, but graduating from possible to certain requires independent evidence.

No texts have proved more elusive than travel accounts, which have attracted both literary scholars and historians widely. Since early travel accounts are a principal source of information for those not studying western Europe, this courtship deserves particular attention. Travel accounts profess to be eyewitness versions of the observations of those who recorded them, sometimes on the spot, sometimes after the occasion. These accounts are often the only information on particular places and peoples at particular times, and inevitably are highly valued.

All these factors operated at high levels during the heady days of exploration and imperialism. Many important sources for the expansion of Europe are neither more nor less than travel accounts. This was especially the case for the chroniclers of the Indies, east and west, all of whom wrote within this genre, whether or not palpably. Later, scarcely a traveler to Africa, Oceania, or Southeast Asia did not fail to regale some audience on his return—or even before his return, and later regaled other audiences with a version that was at least slightly different.

The travel account as historical source began at least as early as the Egyptian Sinuhe, who reported on a trip ca. 1950 BCE. Differences of opinion about the value of travel accounts also begin with Sinuhe. Did he travel to the Levant or merely to the Sinai peninsula? Or nowhere at all? Is his narrative fact, fiction, fictionalized autobiography, political propaganda, a didactic book of conduct?[5] If authentic, is it also reliable?[6] Can his testimony be used to illuminate archeological data? Scholars answer these questions variously and, as Greig put it, "[i]t is impossible to prove conclusively that Sinuhe is either a work of non-fiction or fiction."[7]

Reasons for this ambivalence are neither hard to find nor to accept. Travel accounts quintessentially represent an observer with a particular cultural makeup trying to make sense of cultures with quite different, if not alien, sets of mores— Gullivers among the Houyhnmhms. Travel accounts are also unparalleled opportunities for self-aggrandizing hyperbole. Readers were not in a position to contradict the travelers, who alone had made the voyage, they alone the observations. Raising the stakes only served to enhance their own albedo.

Almost by definition, travel accounts are likely to undergo more changes than most texts. They are usually formulated in a sequential but fragmented fashion, often while the author is in a state of wonderment and disorientation. The physical evidence is often placed at risk owing to time, weather, enemy action, or lack of proper materials and preservatives. Whatever survives is often rushed into print to satisfy a clamoring public, and changed in the process for any number of obvious reasons, including coherence, continuity, addition of information gathered later, the sense of the public and official mood, and bowdlerism. In the end, there might be three or four recensions in the public domain or otherwise available to the industrious researcher.[8]

IV

We can divide travel accounts into the imaginary travel account disguised as fact; the partly fictional travel account, also disguised as fact; the travel account written to be factual but suffering from traveler's awe; and the travel account that is largely accurate. The fantastic posing as the factual is a dismayingly commonplace form of writing.[9] During certain periods—the Hellenistic age and Roman times, as well as in early modern times—it was much the vogue to write of fantastic and unknown places in an understated style precisely to convince readers that these places really existed. Some early editions of *Gulliver's Travels* included a picture of Lemuel Gulliver, complete with fictional address, should any interested parties care to drop by and chat about Brobdingnag. Readers were thus offered the choice to believe or disbelieve, but they were provided with few tools for the second alternative. As a result, many of these works had a longer shelf life of credibility than their contents warranted.[10]

The second category puts less emphasis on selling the fantastic. Sometimes an entire trip is fabricated, other times it is a matter of embroidering a real trip with additional itineraries. If its critics are correct, it began with Sinuhe's account; it has certainly flourished ever since.[11] A work by Jean-Baptiste Douville purporting to chronicle two extensive journeys in west-central Africa appeared in 1832. In addition to the text, there were many accoutrements designed to convince, e.g., dated astronomical events, meteorological tables, and a word list.[12] Almost immediately critics roundly condemned Douville's account of all or part of his travels.[13] A century and a half later, Anne Stamm demurred, writing that "having followed Jean-Baptiste Douville in all stages of his journey, having verified, analyzed, weighed all the information contained in the some thousand pages [of his *Voyage*], it appears impossible to dispute the greater part of his exploration."[14] Joseph Miller challenged this attempt at rehabilitation by pointing out that Stamm failed to use sources that undermined part of her argument, and that archival data showed that Douville was at one place when he claimed to be elsewhere.[15]

Douville and numberless others were tripped up because they wrote of extended journeys, but were not clever enough to tie them to feasible timetables. Thus it is easy to discredit them on logistical grounds. As Marion Johnson points out (after citing several examples where later authors accepted John Duncan's version of his travels), "if this part of [Duncan's] narrative is demonstrably false it becomes more difficult to rely on other parts of his account."[16]

V

Fortunately, not all scrutiny condemns. *Madagascar, or Robert Drury's Journal of Fifteen Years' Captivity on that Island* was published in 1729. Like other such works published at the time, it has a Robinsonesque aspect to it, and the anonymous editor felt obliged to assure readers that it was "nothing else but a plain, honest narrative of matter of fact."[17] For many, this assertion smacked of the standard-issue testimonial designed specifically to sell fiction as fact. Worse yet, some thought they could see the hand and mind of Daniel Defoe, no mean incubus for seekers after reality. As a result, historians and ethnographers of Madagascar treated Drury's *Journal* as a piece of fiction that they dare not be caught citing.

In the 1990s an archeologist working in southern Madagascar compared words and things in the *Journal* with local conditions, and concluded that it "is not a work of fictional realism nor is it a fancifully embroidered account based on a few authentic pegs. It contains a large number of exaggerations, errors, misconceptions, and probably a few deliberate lies, but where we can match it against a thorough knowledge of the Antandroy past and present it comes through remarkably well."[18] It is not often that a work attributed to Daniel Defoe is rehabilitated as likely fact. Robert Drury's *Journal* has many of the hallmarks of the fictional travel accounts of the period and those who were cautious about using its testimony were justified. Now they are no less justified in changing their minds and using it to supplement the few sources otherwise available. Parker Pearson's work shows the efficacy of approaching travel accounts with an open mind and using the specific kinds of evidence that can test them on their own terms

It took less time to vindicate James Bruce. His tales of a five-year sojourn in Abyssinia met with acclaim at first, but soon critics were denouncing them, and the ensuing five-volume printed narrative, as a hoax.[19] They regarded his account, which included claims that he had been governor of a province and had led cavalry into battle, as the work of a vainglorious mountebank. Since such influential *littérateurs* as Samuel Johnson and Horace Walpole were among their number, the work rapidly fell into disrepute.[20] This opprobrium lasted only until other visitors to the area confirmed much of Bruce's account. In 1809/10 Henry Salt interviewed Ethiopians who had met Bruce, removing forever the stigma that Bruce's account was nothing but an elaborate charade. Salt did not go so far as to say that Bruce was always reliable, and he spoke of Bruce's exaggerations, contradictions, and troubles with dates.[21] Henceforth, though, all travelers of the time and all historians of ours could ill afford to dismiss Bruce's testimony.

VI

Translation has a long history of being subversive. Translating the bible, when the various vernaculars became important as the Renaissance drew to a close, proved contentious business. Some translators, like Erasmus, used the occasion not only to demystify scripture but to challenge the prevailing orthodoxies. Earlier John Wyclif had organized a translation into English. Wyclif was a prominent churchman, but his translation work immediately made him unpopular with ecclesiastical authorities, who feared for their lucrative monopoly on purveying god's otherwise incomprehensible word.[22]

Amid the diplomatic flurry preceding the dropping of the first atomic bomb came the Potsdam Declaration, calling for Japan's immediate unconditional surrender. The Japanese cabinet addressed the demand and issued a statement on 28 July 1945, in which the word *mokusatsu* was used to indicate the cabinet's attitude. The official Japanese translation bureau rendered this as "ignore" in the official response, but they had other choices, for the term can also mean, among other things, the less defiant "withhold comment," and some argue that this was its intent. At any rate, the communiqué went forth with the word "ignore."[23] Two weeks—and two atomic bombs—later, the Japanese finally surrendered, without complicating matters by using the word *mokusatsu*.

Few translations exact so high a price. But historians who prefer to use translations continue to pay a price for their lack of enterprise. It is the rare historian who does not occasionally require dealing with a translation of a primary or secondary source. The temptation might be to rely on the translation rather than seeking out and deciphering the original text. If that text is in a language unfamiliar to the historian, it is sometimes possible, and always desirable, to seek out a colleague who can provide some help. However, it does not require outside help to track down all other translations of the same text for comparison. If these are consistent, the historian should probably feel safe in proceeding, while remembering that full consistency in translation occurs only as a result of imitation, and not because a text offers no alternatives.

The word "cielo" appears 33 times in the journal of Christopher Columbus's first voyage to the Americas. In Spanish the word can mean "roof," "ceiling," "sky," or "heaven." Ruling out the first two meanings still leaves translators to choose between the last two. Context, of course, helps. When Columbus used the word to report on atmospheric conditions, we can assume that he was referring to the sky, but he also used the term to refer to where he thought the Indians believed the Spanish came from. In these cases Samuel Eliot Morison translated the term as "sky," while Dunn and Kelley always preferred "heavens" and B.W. Ife always chose "heaven."[24] Twenty years earlier, Morison had preferred "Heaven."[25] This variety tells us much about the translators, something about Columbus, and nothing at all about the Indians. Dunn and Kelley stake out an ingenious middle ground. They seem to have the same idea as Morison, but express it more colloquially and ambiguously. Ife takes a stand that is ambiguous in quite a different way, translating "cielo" as "heaven" in all relevant references, only to observe in a footnote that "[i]t should not be forgotten that 'cielo' also means 'sky'," making no attempt to resolve the implications of his interposition.

These translations of the journal's "cielo" encapsulate the irresoluble differences that translators face in confronting even single words. It is unlikely that any of the translators deliberated long on their choices, yet the question is not without its appeal. Choosing "sky" is the simplest solution. Whether or not the Indians shared our notion of heaven, the sky was as real to them as it was to Columbus. In choosing "heavens" to represent "cielo" Dunn and Kelley dealt with two horns of the dilemma by finding a third horn to grab onto. Ife's "heaven," and especially Morison's "Heaven," are the least appropriate choices, for they suggest that Columbus attributed to the Indians some notion of a place from which wondrous beings emerged, even though he also observed that the Indians had "no religion."

The differences between "heaven" and "sky" are so great because "cielo" is an anachronism reflecting a time when, for most people, the sky was merely the visible face of an eternal dwelling place. Translators who choose "heaven" or "Heaven" open a Pandora's box wide—that the Indians believed in an afterlife; that they believed in a system of earthly reward and punishment; that their paradise was also beyond the skies; that they believed in supernatural beings who visited the earth from time to time; that Columbus imagined things in moments of evangelical ardor; that the Amerindians were relicts of the lost tribes of Israel.

This leaves us in a quandary, because we cannot know what Columbus (or Bartolomé de las Casas, the transcriber/editor of the journal) intended by the word, or even to what degree the choice was based on what the Indians did rather than what he thought they were doing. As a result, every user of the journal must decide for himself whether he is reading Columbus, Las Casas, or the translator. This is no easy task, and one reason why the journal has served so many disparate purposes so usefully.

Another example from Columbus's journal extends the point. The word "angla" appears eight times in the journal, and these are the first known appearances in Spanish of the word—borrowed from the Portuguese, where it means a large bay. Dunn and Kelley translate it as a concavity in the shoreline four times, and four more times to mean the opposite, a promontory or cape.[26] In none of these cases does context provide certain justification; rather it is a matter of Dunn and Kelley being certain that Columbus was where there is either a promontory or a bay.

VII

Other translations of the chronicles of the Indies are more calculated. Those imputing very high numbers to the contact population of the Americas invariably translate the word "enfermedad" (normally, "sickness" or "illness") as "disease."[27] In this way they provide themselves with a much-needed lexical weapon in their campaign against the evidence, and one that allows them to account for almost any purported decline. Readers not aware that they are firing blanks might well permit themselves to be disarmed.

In his account of wandering across the southwestern United States and northern Mexico, Alvar Núñez Cabeza de Vaca wrote that he and his companions had been "espantados" on visiting an Indian village to find that many residents were blind because of clouded eyes. Henry Dobyns took this to be the aftereffects of a smallpox epidemic that had struck the area with high mortality. Dobyns did not translate "espantados" directly but it is useful to wonder why Cabeza de Vaca used this particular term and what he meant by it.[28] "Espantado/a" can mean "startled" or "alarmed" or "surprised" or "astonished" or "astounded." Although treated as synonyms to "espantados," these words are hardly synonyms with each other. "Startled" hardly seems appropriate in the circumstances, but what about "alarmed?" If Cabeza de Vaca recognized smallpox symptoms and had escaped the disease's ravages while growing up in Spain, then he might well have been alarmed. But if he saw only the effects of smallpox and not the active disease, why be frightened? For that matter, why not speak of the universal hallmark of smallpox, pock marks, instead of this rare side-effect?

The remaining choices—"surprised," "astonished," and "astounded"—are three points along a continuum that can be treated *en ensemble*. To me (but to others?) "astounded" implies an extreme reaction, as though a confidently expected event had been turned upside down in practice. Cabeza de Vaca could not have expected *not* to see any blind Indians, so that he would be "astounded" when he did. This leaves "surprised" and "astonished." Although more severe as a reaction, "astonished" seems to me the best of the five alternatives. Complicating matters, Cabeza de Vaca wrote many years after these events and his account exists in four very different versions, including one in which he claimed to have cured most of the blindness. This allows us to suspect that the episode was a fable or parable, and that any modern translations and interpretations of "espantados" might not matter very much after all, except as a technical exercise.

Robert Denhardt looked at Bernal Díaz del Castillo's account of the conquest of Mexico, where Bernal managed to note the color of the horses of sixteen of the conquistadores. Denhardt then looked at four modern translations of Díaz's chronicle and added a fifth translation, his own. For thirteen of the horses, the translations vary, and in four cases Denhardt's translation differed from any of the others.[29] Knowing the color of these horses adds little to our knowledge of the Spanish conquest, but recognizing the vagaries of translation does remind us of something of value.

Intrinsic to translating, whatever the text, is the battle between the stylists and the purists or, if you will, those who regard a text as a work of literature and those who treat it as a historical source. Burton Watson, who translated part of Sima Qian's monumental *Shiji* took the former view: " . . . it is not enough merely to bring across the meaning of the Chinese; one must do so in a manner that reads like natural, idiomatic English."[30] Translators have treated Columbus's journal much the same way. Morison tried to make Columbus speak like a New England-bred graduate of Harvard.[31] However fluid his edition read, it could not provide completely reliable information on what Columbus wrote or meant. It was necessary to wait another twenty-five years for this, with the appearance of Dunn and Kelley's edition of the same text.[32] Their edition is a difficult text to understand, festooned with question marks and alternatives, but an honest text. No parties interested in Columbus's activities during the six months in question should ever turn to Morison for insights into Columbus's mind, for all they will get are insights into Morison's mind better left to the preface and notes.

IX

Few historians have the stomach to prepare and publish extensive critiques of translations already in the public domain. Some would argue that the gain to scholarship is too slight, the work itself too pedestrian, or the audience too limited. Some or all of these might be true; nonetheless, the appearance of such studies can only be welcome, not only when they throw better light on a particular text, but because they put translators on notice that their work is important enough to do as well as possible.

Good translations, like good text editions, require space and time. In 1703 Willem Bosman, a Dutch merchant on the Gold Coast in the 1690s, published an account of his experiences. Two years later an English translation appeared and this was reprinted in 1967 to accompany the modern rise of African studies, and historians use the more accessible reprint to come to grips with Bosman's testimony. Unfortunately, the English translation was as defective as it was prompt—so defective that it took over half as many words to correct the mistranslations as there are in the original text.[33] Published serially and separately from Bosman's text, the impact of this massive correction process is likely to be less than optimal. Historians who do not read Dutch—the last edition in which was published in 1737—will continue to rely on the 1967 reprint, with its myriad mistranslations, misimpressions, and outright frauds.

Any historian using translations extensively owes it to himself to consult a thin quarterly called *The Bible Translator,* dedicated largely to short articles on translation issues. These are concerned not only with issues of word-for-word translation, but with larger matters such as introduction of notions (sin, the afterlife, the soul, etc.) into societies where they did not exist and therefore for which there are no words to adopt.[34] These case studies usually end up on a somber note, with confessions of failure or at least of doubt.[35] Or we might adopt the breezy attitude of a Mormon student of the bible: "[w]e believe in the Bible on a conditional basis—only insofar as it is translated 'correctly,' or is in accordance with modern revelation."[36] As always the choice is ours.[37]

10

POISONED CHALICES

. . . and yet I often think that it is odd that [history] should be
so dull, for a great deal of it must be invention . . . I am fond
of history—and am very well contented to take the false with
the true.

In talking about the past we lie with every breath we draw.

I

In baseball record books Ted Williams is credited with hitting .406 in 1941, and
with six American League batting titles during his career. Behind these statistics are some intriguing variables. One involves the fitful evolution of the sacrifice fly rule. Except from 1931 to 1938 and 1940 to 1953, a fly ball out that drove
in a run was not counted an official time at-bat. In 1941 Williams hit six sacrifice
flies, but in that year a sacrifice fly was just another out. Deduct these six at-bats
and he would have hit .411, as he would have had he exactly replicated his 1941
season just two years earlier or thirteen years later. Deducting just those six at-
bats would also have raised Williams' lifetime batting average enough to round it
off at .345 instead of .344.[1]

In 1954 Williams had a batting average of .345 and Roberto Avila an average
of .341. But from 1951 to 1956, in order to be eligible for the batting title, a player needed at least 3.1 *official* at-bats for every game his team played, and bases
on balls did not count. Over his career Williams drew the third highest total of

bases on balls in history, and in 1954 he led the league, as usual, with 136 walks, whereas Avila had only 59. As a result, Williams had only 386 official at-bats and was deemed ineligible.[2] The rule was changed two years later, but this did Williams no good in the record books, because Major League Baseball does not attempt to rationalize its checkered rules history.

II

As Alfred Hiatt aptly puts it: "[f]orgery never goes out of fashion. It is not unique to any period or any people; it can occur across a variety of media (including printed, handwritten and, now, electronic texts, artworks, and currency of both paper and plastic varieties); its eradication seems, at the beginning of the twentieth-first century, impossible."[3] This is hardly an exaggeration, and in the circumstances any historian must keep the possibility—sometimes even the probability—that some of his sources were intentionally falsified, either from the beginning or at some point along the way to the present.

An important way to test sources is to search ruthlessly for anachronisms. The notion of anachronism is fundamental to the study of history. It is well known, for instance, that the surest way to unmask a pseudepigraphical document is to detect some mention of an event or person that postdates the time supplied or implied by the document. More importantly, historians learn to be wary of assuming that the past thought and acted like the present. Finally, historians must take no less care in avoiding assuming that what was taken as true in a historical record was also true outside the time/space referents of that record. Nowadays we have learned enough to recognize some of the overdeveloped credulity of our professional forebears. Still, it would be fatuous to feel either that no such sources remain or that we can detect them on sight. Methods must be in place to assist in the defrocking. No forgery can survive a proved anachronism unless it can also be proved that it was a rogue later interpolation.

Wriggling out of a patent anachronism is one of historians' more grueling challenges. It is most difficult with a document purportedly written by a single author within a restricted period of time—worse yet if the document claims to be holograph. An entry in Samuel Pepys's diary mentioning something that occurred after Pepys died—or even for that matter after the date of the entry, given Pepys's professed modus operandi ("and so off to bed")—would immediately raise danger signals and put Pepys's diary in dire trouble as an unalloyed primary source. Works in which an original author and later editor-scribe collaborate, offer more scope—and more perplexity. Thus the journal of Columbus's first voyage can accommodate up to sixty years of apparent anachronisms, although in cases where more evidence is available, the judgment can be more peremptory.

In the 1980s a copybook turned up in Spain containing nine letters attributed to Columbus. Unchallenged Columbian writings are much scarcer than historians would prefer. Those who want the detailed letters in this *libro copiador* to be authentic must necessarily look to catch it out; how better than by discovering anachronisms? I treated the word "Jamaica" as anachronistic, but explained it away as later scribal intervention.[4] I could make this argument because all agree that the *libro copiador* appears to have been copied in the second third of the sixteenth century, or many years after Columbus could have written it. Perhaps the form "Jamaica" had come into use in some quarters in the intervening period, but until it could be demonstrated, this, any other anachronisms, and the obscure provenance of the *libro copiador* combine to make well-wishers very cautious.

Unfortunately, I had not done my homework well enough. As early as 1516 Peter Martyr had used that very spelling in his *De Orbe Novo*.[5] Thus a scribe writing twenty years or more later could easily have substituted the new term in an authentic Columbian text. Still, two issues remain. The first is that there is no evidence that Columbus himself ever used the term "Jamaica" elsewhere, although, given how little of Columbus's presumed written oeuvre survives, this is a tenuous argument. The second issue is more serious. Assuming that Columbus did not use different spellings in two sets of texts presumably written about the same time, then scribal intervention, not exactly a blessing itself, is the only alternative to forgery.

For the moment most scholars provisionally accept the *libro copiador* as authentic. They are especially impressed by the quintessentially Columbian "style" of the documents. But style is elusive and the desire for more sources unquenchable. If Columbus can be found to have used the term "Jamaica" outside the *libro copiador*, it would be a relief, but until the document is ransacked for other possible anachronisms, the matter must remain sub judice. If none are found, it increases the probability that the letters in the *libro copiador* are authentic, but hardly assures it.

The argument that a usage came into existence earlier than supposed as "proved" by the document itself has restricted application—it might work for lexical problems, but not for unique events. In asserting Abraham's historicity, A.R. Millard adopted rather an nonchalant argument: "[n]aming a place after a people whose presence is only attested there six or seven centuries later than the setting of the story need not falsify it." He followed with a defense against the argument that the mention of camels in Genesis is a sure sign that the account was written many centuries later. As he put it, "[i]t is as logical to treat the passages in Gen 12:16, 24 as valuable evidence for the presence of camels at that time as to view them as anachronistic."[6] This time the escape clause is an argument against silence. None of the inscriptions emanating from the area before ca. 1200 BCE mention camels. Yet this silence is to be overthrown by a much later literary text on the grounds that that text either was divinely inspired or was not later after all.

Some anachronisms kill, while others only paralyze. William Groneman suspects that a diary alleging to be from the 1830s is a forgery, in part because it contains the phrase "crimes against humanity" three times. He points out that this diarist could have devised this phrase a century before its otherwise first attested occurrence, but thinks it unlikely. It might well be unlikely, but it is not as though this short phrase is so distinctive as to have had only one birth; had it been "crimes against Mensheviks," the case would be unanswerable. As it is, any critic would need to build a stronger case before rejecting the source outright.[7]

The common meanings of words and measures change often enough to make it dangerous to presume the same meanings over centuries. In the sixteenth century the word "montes" in Spanish meant not only "mountains," but also "woods" or "forests," an issue that has vexed various efforts to hunt early explorers down. It is not enough to whip out a modern dictionary and look up a word; nothing short of recourse to a good etymological dictionary is enough—but not quite enough to tell the historian just how his sources *meant* words, only that they had certain choices, forcing the consequences of those choices back onto us.

III

Anachronistic arguments by historians are usually hard to spot, especially if they speak to readers likely to think the same. No one today can find a favorable word to say about slavery and the slave trade, the promiscuous butchering of bison in the western United States, or the treatment of the Aborigines in Australia. Summarily indicting those who practiced these is often unavoidable, but it is an issue that the historian must address, preferably explicitly. A less volatile example is the way historians brandish the word "usurper." The concept is applied to explain current political legitimacy—losers become usurpers by losing. History has no problem in applying the principle, and William Shakespeare is a principal culprit. Macbeth, king of Scotland and archetypal 'usurper,' actually had a better right to the throne than Duncan did under the succession practices then in vogue. Not one of the fifteen rulers of Scotland between the union of the Scots and Picts ca. 850 had succeeded a direct ancestor, whereas Duncan had succeeded his grandfather, Malcolm II. Macbeth, a collateral relative Malcolm II, claimed the throne on grounds of legitimacy rather than force majeure—or excessive uxoriousness. The later success of Duncan's son Malcolm III combined with Shakespeare's literary license to cast the latter as one of the great villains of all time, quite out of tune with views in Macbeth's own time and place.

Richard III's story bears some differences, but Shakespeare mythified history here as well. Richard might have been a usurper, but then so was his older brother Edward IV, Henry IV, Stephen or Matilda, Henry II, Henry I, and William I, and Shakespeare's own protagonist, Henry VII. The real difference is that they succeeded in maintaining themselves, so that their history could be written by sycophants and successors. Richard III was not so lucky, and could safely be depicted as a hunchbacked personification of evil.

Another of history's quintessential villains, Aaron Burr, also became demonized by the success of his rival and a change in succession rules. Under the provisions in force in 1800, voters cast ballots for two men, without specifying which was their choice for President and which for Vice-President. As a result, Thomas Jefferson and Burr found themselves with the same number of electoral votes, leaving it to the House of Representatives to choose Jefferson after a great deal of logrolling. Few might care to argue that the choice should have gone the other way, but the basis of their argument has more to do with character and less with the notion that Burr played loose with the Constitution—or that he did this more than the Jeffersonians, who promptly saw to it that the Constitution was amended to preclude any further contretemps.

IV

An anachronistic attitude with serious consequences is assuming that observers in the past held accuracy with the same high regard that we profess to.[8] Today the methods and motives that we impute to some of our sources—plucking numbers from the ether, cribbing other texts shamelessly, inventing eyewitness status—strike us as utterly unprofessional. And so they are—today. But we cannot allow ourselves to forget that the notions of factual truth and authorial objectivity do not date from prehistory, but are fairly recent ideas—two or three centuries old at best if treated as common property. To think otherwise is to think anachronistically, with all its fatal results.[9]

A natural desire to bring consistency to—that is, to impose it on—the past is distinctly a form of anachronism. The effects show up clearly, again, in the statistical history of baseball. Over the years rules have come and gone, some lasting only a year, most much longer. As a result, the numbers that baseball aficionados see are not always directly comparable. In 1887, and only in 1887, bases on balls counted as hits, and batting averages for this year were naturally much higher than for any year before or since. Ignoring this ephemeral rule change would drop the highest batting average in 1887 from .492 to .435, still higher than any since, but not by very much. It is hard not to be ambivalent about this. Walks are like hits in that the batter becomes a base runner. On the other hand walks do not advance any men already on base unless it is first base or the bases are loaded, so it is less effective than many singles would be. Then too the fact that this rule was in effect only one year makes it totally aberrant when looking at the 135-year-long course of baseball. On the other hand, to make 1887 conform arbitrarily is to dehistoricize it; like it now or not, the rule *was* in effect then.[10]

Smoothing out baseball's historical statistics to be "consistent" opens a fairly capacious pandora's box. Like life, baseball is dynamic, and more has changed than the rules. Players have become better nourished, better conditioned, and more athletic.[11] The balls and bats have become better as well, and teams do not try to make the ball become mush by using it for an entire game. But then fielders' gloves have also improved. Night baseball and quicker (if longer) trips might cancel each other out. The height of the mound, the width of home plate, and the official strike zone have changed back and forth. Pitching would seem to have become comparatively stronger with the advent of various kinds of relief pitchers, but expanding from sixteen teams to thirty-two might have diluted talent in turn. The sizes of fields have shrunk to favor hitters, compensating for the old rule that balls that bounced out of the playing field in fair territory counted as home runs. African-Americans and Hispanics have added talent pools that were not exploited before the 1940s. In one league a designated hitter bats for the pitcher but not in the other, and not before 1973. Who can judge what the overall effects of all these—and more—changes have been?

There is one further imponderable—the role of the official scorer. He or she, and not the umpires, determine hits and errors. Making such decisions day after day affords them a cumulative, and quite immeasurable, effect on batting and fielding averages, no-hit games, and the like. The role of official scorers has been consistent for well over a century, but their behavior has varied from one day, even one play, to the next, resulting in many thousands of micro-variables that taint the notion that statistics are overridingly objective.

V

In recent years several highly publicized forgeries have found a brief moment in the sun before being cast into the shade. Many others like them have had much longer, and far more subversive careers, before being unmasked—if unmasked at all. In introducing his history of Alexander the Great, Arrian shared some of his criteria for choosing among sources. He noted that he relied most heavily on an account attributed to Ptolemy I Soter because "as he himself was a king, mendacity would have been more dishonorable for him than for anyone else."[12] Historical inquiry is handicapped by the fact that too few kings wrote about the past, and the present by the fact that public figures are now regarded as those *most* likely to lie. Historians must contend with authors who might not always have told the truth—or even tried to. The study of the past is littered with unfortunate cases where historians have relied on sources that were nothing less than inventions designed to amuse or deceive.[13] As already noted, the accounts of Dares and Dictys, long taken to be first-hand reportage of the Trojan war, were both fabricated in the first centuries CE.[14]

VI

The Catholic liturgical calendar was once glutted with phantoms and, despite some effort to purge them, still is. Many resulted from forgeries concocted in late Antiquity and the early Middle Ages. One interesting case was not a forgery, but a modern blunder that made it one. In 1802 three tiles were found in an ancient tomb in Rome. In situ, they read LUMENA/PAX TE/CUM FI. This did not make enough sense for the excavators, and the tile with LUMENA was resituated at the end, creating the phrase "Peace to you, Filumena." Not much of a start, but enough to have one biography produced almost immediately, and several more thereafter.[15] Several miracles were attributed to the epigraphic "virgin and martyr," and the French saint-to-be Jean-Baptiste Vianney popularized her cause by announcing that she was his personal intercessor. Eventually, her cult became among the busiest in the Catholic church.

Archeologists raised doubts early, but no one listened. The authors of a standard work on Catholic saints remained unmoved: "[t]he miracles and benefactions wrought by God when we ask for the intercession of a certain saint, whom we call on by the name of Philomena, are indubitably known to us: nothing can shake them, or our gratitude to her."[16] Eventually, church authorities disagreed and finally expunged Philomena from the official roster of saints in 1961, after a successful innings of more than 150 years.

Once in the public domain, a forgery can always be revivified. Early in the nineteenth century Irish nationalism was beginning to ferment and needed some historical support. Rushing to fill the gap, a work called *The Chronicles of Eri* appeared, allegedly written much earlier, with a pseudonymous author and quite a story to tell, purporting to give a history of the island from 5357 BCE, providing along the way a host of details. It was "balderdash from beginning to end," but scholars "for a long time could not provide a definitive falsification of this fictitious trumpery."[17] Disproof came in due course, but the *Chronicles* still managed to enjoy a brief moment of resuscitation in the 1930s before finally expiring, perhaps forever.

Fortunately, not all forgeries have long shelf lives. The Canek manuscript, discovered in 1988, claimed to be an account of a missionary's trip in 1695 to parts of the Maya country still outside the Spanish orbit and provided details of Maya life not otherwise known. The discovery was initially lauded as "an auspicious event" that "shed important new light on Itza Maya culture," and it was quickly accorded a text edition.[18] Only a few years later, another scholar denounced this and three other texts as forgeries compiled after 1950 by detecting anachronisms, borrowing, and suspiciously similar calligraphy.[19] The testing and, even more the accompanying acknowledgment, helped make the career of this particular pseudo-source one of less than a decade.[20]

VII

Literary texts are sometimes treated as historical sources on the grounds that they contain information known from other sources. As already noted, Barrett points out that several characters and places mentioned in the Acts of the Apostles are known from other sources, and that those asserting the historicity of Acts can use this to support their case.[21] Indeed they can, yet we expect even a forgery or a late compilation to contain a modicum of reliable data, if only to warrant reliability by the appearance of reality. In fact, undisguised historical fiction often contains historical characters on the fringes of the plot. Lindsey Davis's detective M. Didius Falco moves in a society that features real emperors, real politicians, and real literary figures, but these are the only things that are real, and the plot is never allowed to affect them and thereby become palpably unhistorical. Real names feature in such works precisely to reassure readers that, while the stories are not true, they are at least true to life.[22]

All forgeries are inauthentic, but there is a murky middle ground in which the word "forgery" cannot be used, even if the word "inauthentic" can. Biographers of Abraham Lincoln reckon that he produced three examples of outstanding literary quality. One of these is a letter of condolence to a woman named Bixby, who claimed—a claim since refuted—to be the mother of five sons killed on the Union side. Lincoln signed the letter, but did he also compose it? Opinion has been divided, with those favoring undiluted Lincoln in the majority. Lincoln's secretary John Hay later claimed to have written the letter, and many other such letters, as a routine part of his duties. It was Hay against the Lincoln partisans and the question remained unresolved until a scrapbook of Hay's was discovered that seems to demonstrate beyond cavil that he composed the letter, presumably at Lincoln's request, and above Lincoln's signature. While the letter was not a forgery in the usual sense of the word, attributing it to Lincoln by confusing composing with signing has led to a protracted and ongoing debate—and an enhanced profile for the letter itself.[23]

The case of the Bixby letter would be of little consequence except that it reminds us that signing a document, or even rendering the entire text in one's own hand does not make one the author. This is especially the case with public figures, who routinely assign such writing chores to others with more time and talent. Does signing a text imply acceptance and co-optation? Can it make it authentic? Should the speeches of U.S. presidents be collected together under their authorship, even if the words are those of someone else? How far can the content and tone of these speeches be used to assess a president's character, temperament, and achievement?

VIII

Basil Thomson thought he detected history after comparing two legends from Polynesia: "[a]fter I had left Tonga I asked an old native of Futuna whether he knew any legends of a Tongan invasion. He wrote down for me an old Saga describing an invasion by the King of Tonga. . . . The only difference in the two stories was that the Futuna account describes the utter rout of the Tongans with so great a slaughter that stacks were made of the dead bodies. Traditions so corroborated rise at once to the dignity of history."[24] Thomson did not consider that Tongans and Futunans had been in communication for centuries, especially during the half century before he wrote. If he had, he might have been less sanguine in his claims.

In 1975 Robert Temple published a book that turned out to be a popular, if not critical, success, arguing that extraterrestrial beings visited the Dogon people in West Africa in the distant past.[25] Why? Because the Dogon appeared to know about Sirius B, the dwarf companion of Sirius and a star invisible to the naked eye. Temple's premise was that the Dogon had existed from time immemorial unaffected by outside, but terrestrial, influences, and thus any "lore" was to be accounted for internally. Temple's arguments were based on the few ethnographic accounts of Sirius knowledge among the Dogon, but he chose unwisely and, as a result, believed unhesitatingly.[26]

Kenneth Brecher suggested an alternative etiology. Suppose that a French missionary or administrator (the French presence was over fifty years old when the Dogon purportedly divulged their knowledge of Sirius B) happened to mention it to some Dogon, knowing of their interest in the visible Sirius? And then, on receipt of this new information, suppose the Dogon had co-opted it into their ceremonies? Brecher reported that "I am told by anthropologists that culture transfer of the sort I am supposing could not possibly have happened; there is no chance, they say, that missionaries, ethnographers, and the like could have smuggled modern notions into the core of a sacred tradition." Even so, Brecher remained confident that his hypothesis was "no doubt the most likely explanation for the knowledge possessed by the tribe."[27]

Years later Walter van Beek went to Dogon country and asked specific questions about the fieldwork that constituted the evidence for this strange set of beliefs. He soon learned that the story of Sirius B, as recorded only by Marcel Griaule, éminence grise of Dogon studies, in the 1940s and 1950s, had fallen out of the Dogon's ceremonial repertoire—if it had ever been there. Moreover, one of Griaule's principal informants told van Beek that Griaule, who had studied astronomy in his youth, had taken the informant's comments on other, visible, stars in Canis Major to refer to Sirius B.[28]

There is good reason then to suspect that in this case Griaule had been informant, not collector. Temple's extraterrestrial scenario allowed critics to write him off without much ado. But his case is interesting because he did what Griaule had apparently done before him—treat the Sirius case as undiluted indigenous knowledge, without considering other possibilities. Brecher was right to resist the misplaced certitude of his anthropological colleagues and insist that outside information is at the heart of this element of Dogon cosmology.

IX

The story of Sirius and the Dogon exemplifies an important class of data that, while neither plagiarism nor forgery *strictu senso*, are derivative. Generally speaking, they are unlikely to be easily noticed—anachronisms are few and the thrust of the testimony is congenially corroborative. They are sources that lay blame where the historians think it belongs, whose sense of which historical actors and factors reflect well those of the historian, and whose chronological depth is appealing. Yet there are many dangers embedded in congeniality. It reduces the chance of discovering that sources are often created precisely to satisfy the needs of historians or other groups and they adopt means of expression, and incorporate content purely with this in mind. This process might be called feedback, since it emulates the muted echoes that occur in sound reproduction.

The greatest incidence of feedback occurred with the imposition of colonial rule throughout the world.[29] With hegemony came efforts to determine existing local circumstances by consulting with local leaders and intellectuals about the past in order to devise a present that, while it entirely overthrew this past at one level, tried to exploit it at another. A common practice was to impose a new administrative layer at the top while retaining the semblance of the old political structure at various subordinate levels. In British colonial parlance this was termed Indirect Rule, but the practice had existed at least from the time of the New Kingdom in Egypt, which established or retained client rulers in neighboring Palestine in the fourteenth century BCE.[30] The Romans adopted the policy, and even at the end of empire, Roman authorities often convinced themselves that the rulers of pesky "barbarian" groups were actually operating under their aegis.

With the expansion of Europe, the mechanisms of indirect rule were revivified and expanded. When the Spanish conquered the Aztecs and Incas, they took to themselves all real authority, but left subordinate indigenous rulers in place pending good behavior or replaced them with other local-level authorities. The system reached its zenith when maps of the world began to be colored with British pink. First in India, then in Africa and southeast Asia, existing rulers, or their doppelgängers, were a prominent feature on the new colonial terrain. But this did not usually happen without formal inquiries into the legitimacy, British-style, of those individuals or lineages who happened to be in control when the British arrived to set up shop.

The inquiries inevitably were conducted along British legalistic lines: informants were identified, testimony collected, and in the interests of British fair play all sides were represented. At first, local rulers scarcely knew how to respond to this new and unwelcome dispensation, but they quickly learned how to outfox the colonial masters. Records from the incessant stool disputes in southern Ghana show numerous examples of the content and presentation of arguments, moving from failure in early times to success as time passed, in large part because indigenous authorities learned what the British wanted to hear and were pleased to let them hear it.[31] At first these informants recounted vague and discrepant traditions about political authority, but by the end of the interwar period they were quoting from books published in the colonial metropolis and even from the documents of earlier inquiries. They had become lawyerly, and with it more successful in pressing their claims.

X

When the Spanish arrived in Peru in 1532, two brothers were contesting the Inca throne. To read early accounts, this case of fraternal rivalry was as unique as it was untimely, perhaps occurring one other time in a history that the Spanish thought must have lasted for three hundred years or more. This opinion was firmly based in the various accounts largely written in the first half century of Spanish rule. Several Spanish chroniclers wrote about the pre-conquest Inca state on the basis of Andean informants, sometimes members of families into which they had married or otherwise established relationships. These accounts generally agree as to the course of Incan history, sharing with one another the trait of imputing a list of as many as a dozen Incas who succeeded each other from father to son. At the level of detail, however, there are numerous discrepancies and contradictions, and modern historians of the Incas have tended to pick and choose among these data to construct their own coherent accounts. In this they have been aided heroically by the work of Inca Garcilaso de la Vega, the mestizo son of an Incan royal female and a high-ranking Spanish invader.

Inca Garcilaso's consuming passion was that the Spanish recognize the antiquity, proto-Christianity, and cultural and political superiority of his maternal civilization. As the repository of indigenous testimony on the one hand, and the beneficiary of a well-placed Spanish education on the other, he was in a position to tell his story precisely in ways to induce belief. His work, the *Royal Commentaries of the Incas*, presented a very linear and elegantly told history of the rise, apogee, and sudden fall of the Inca dynasty, and it was to prove persuasive in fashioning modern opinion about the extent, administrative character, and remorseless expansion of Inca rule. No extensive modern account of the Incas fails to rely, either implicitly or explicitly, more heavily on Inca Garcilaso than on any of the other chroniclers, with the possible exception of Pedro Cieza de León.

By the mid-1960s a fairly homogenized modern vision of Inca history was in place, in which the expansion of the state could be chronicled cartographically, the dynastic politics rendered lineally, and the administrative aspects admired uncritically. If there were no coherent contemporary records to support the picture, it was nonetheless regarded as history, subject to a certain degree of modification, but hardly enough to do more than re-arrange the details, depending on which sources might be privileged. R.T. Zuidema upset this propitious equilibrium when he published an interpretation that based itself on a close assessment of Andean dualist cosmology. The subject had been addressed before of course, but Zuidema suggested that due attention to these elements of Andean life could produce an entirely new version of Inca history.[32]

Some years later Pierre Duviols pursued the argument by claiming that the Inca rulers did not reign successively, but in two parallel dynasties centered on different parts of the Inca capital of Cusco and responsible for different areas of the Inca realm. Duviols cut Inca history in half, not by arguing ethnographic generalities but by looking at the standard sources with an entirely different eye, arguing that they could be interpreted in ways that supported Zuidema's notion as further expounded by himself.[33]

Historians have been wary of accepting this paradigmatic sea change, but some have taken an approach that has the same effect, although without some of the alarming implications, by treating much of early Inca history as myth or legend. Thus María Rostworowski begins her account of Inca history at the time of the putative seventh or eighth Inca, Kusi Yupanki (Pachakutec), and treats his war against the Chancas as "the point of departure for the formation and subsequent expansion of the Inca state" rather than as an episode well into its imperial career.[34] Rostworowski hardly mentions earlier rulers, treats the traditional founder Manko Qhapac as "legendary," and others as possibly historical but also probably in some way concurrent with each other and with other polities.[35] She disposes of traditional Inca chronology with an unnerving observation: "[a]n analysis of the information *provided by the chroniclers themselves* indicates that their often-cited affirmations concerning succession from father to son reflected their own European cultural assumptions rather than accounts or observations of actual Andean traditions."[36]

Rostworowski's claim is supported by a large body of evidence from other areas.[37] But most discomfiting is her argument that the evidence for her radical reinterpretation has been there in the traditional sources for all to see. This is a direct challenge to Andean historians: while they might reject the work of Zuidema as that of structural anthropologist, and doubt Duviols because he relied too heavily on Zuidema, it will be harder to dismiss Rostworowski since she has replicated their findings through a substantially different approach.[38]

The nature of Inca historiography in 2005 is dramatically different than it was just forty years earlier, although the issue is scarcely resolved, and probably never will be. J.H. Rowe's once-canonical list of Inca rulers, complete with dates, still has many adherents among those who dislike uncertainty, but it no longer serves as the default measure of the Inca dynastic period.[39] In a very tiny measure this is due to being able to use a few new sources—fuller and better texts of some important chronicles—but it results largely from an increasing appreciation of the need to understand better the worldview of the unnamed sources that lay behind those we do know.

But it is fair to suspect that this began much earlier—when informants were trying to parse and please their new masters—and themselves—by saying what they thought they were expected to quote. Evidence about interviewing tactics is seldom available for sixteenth-century Peru, although Rostworowski and others base their conclusions partly on testimony presented at various investigative *visitas* conducted in the fifty years or so after the conquest. A thoroughgoing analysis of the sources for the early chroniclers might uncover further evidence of intertextuality, as well as networks of affiliated and like-minded informants, especially since the roster of such informants is fairly well confined to the higher echelons of Inca society, who managed to acculturate early and often, much to their own benefit.[40]

We can suspect that when latter-day imperial agents saw indigenous rulers whip out a recently-published book and quote from it on behalf of their claims, they recognized the birth of a new tradition and were suitably amused. When it suited them, this tradition was allowed to blossom. They had no reason to think that later generations would want to regard the testimony as bona fide historical data, but these local histories have prospered in post-colonial historiography. For

Ghana the means to squelch credulity exists only in the archives there and might already have disappeared. Springing from the occasions themselves, these records leave no doubt about the process by which written data were transformed and incorporated into oral tradition. Other cases are less subject to demonstration, but this should not prevent a thorough canvass of the chronicles, as well as testimony in the Andean *visitas,* which were very much like the stool inquests in the Gold Coast.[41]

XI

The potential for forgeries and feedback to do harm directly correlates with the degree of belief they manage to instill. Reflexive belief leads historians down paths that can be at best dead ends and at worse embarrassing, even mortifying. Questioning them, on the other hand, not only separates some wheat from some chaff, but has distinct heuristic value for probing other sources, since historians gain in the process a heightened appreciation that the boundaries between the 'true' and the 'false,' the 'original' and the 'borrowed,' the 'welcome' and the 'unwelcome,' are protean and indistinct. Some black, some white remain, but the predominant color ends up being a polychromatic, and challenging, gray.

11

SCOTCHING THE MYTH-MAKING MACHINE

A myth is like a mercenary,
it can be made to fight for anyone.

To forget, and I will even go so far as to say to get one's history wrong, are essential factors in the creation of a nation;
and thus the progress of historical studies is often a danger to
nationality.

I

Abner Doubleday is a widely-recognized name in American sports history. Most who know his name also "know" he invented baseball. In fact, Doubleday had no more to do with the development of the game than his biblical namesake. After baseball became the national pastime, the game's authorities felt impelled to document an indigenous origin. The game did not develop from English rounders, but had a founding moment, a founding locus, and in Abner Doubleday, a founding father. The Doubleday fable is based on the testimony of a single octogenarian, who was force-fed his recollections by those in charge of the commission of inquiry sixty-eight years after the alleged genesis.[1] Real enough as a person and as a general officer in the Civil War, Abner Doubleday gained his greatest fame for something he never did because baseball and feelings of national pride had become inextricably intertwined.

II

In 1869 Japanese Emperor Mutsuhito gave his chief minister an imperial rescript in his own hand. The Emperor wasted no time in coming to the point. The first sentence ran: "[h]istoriography is a for ever immortal state ritual and a wonderful act of our ancestors," and continued with prescriptions that were to govern historiography thenceforth.[2] After centuries during which the Japanese Emperors were *rois fainéants*, Mutsuhito had restored the imperial line to active power. A lot of history needed rewriting, and historians in Japan spent the next seventy years at work on this project. Not all governments have been so obligingly explicit in expressing their palling concern for the ways in which the past is represented, and not all historians' communities have been as obliging in their turn. Just the same, the symbiotic relationship between historiography and national interest is of long standing and well understood.

Corporate self-identity, animated by corporate pride, is one of historians' great nemeses. To it can be attributed more historical nonsense than to all other causes combined. Here I discuss instances of such myth-making, enough perhaps to make the point, but a tiny fraction of the available universe. Although we see historical myths constantly being shattered, we cannot fail also to see how assiduously and successfully new ones are created and old ones refurbished. The reasons for this inexorable decline into myth deficit are several. The content of myth is specifically designed to appeal to human nature by telling stories—some completely false, others loosely based on reality—that answer questions and boost individual and collective egos in appealing ways.

For our purposes myth can be defined as explanations for past and present, usually accompanied by stories, that, although usually not true, are contextually plausible. By this definition, much of what was once believed is now held to be untrue to one degree or another, often to be entirely false. Although we can hope that the future's falsification of the present's beliefs will be less cataclysmic, some of what is firmly believed today will certainly be shown to be as false as Chicken Little's falling sky. Myths travel along too many avenues to be easily suppressed. Humankind has been making myths far longer than it has been making history, and the process continues unabated. Some myths are true, others false. Some exist for one reason, others for another. Some are born as myth, others gain the status later in life. Whatever the case, all myth is purposeful. Historians and others have long felt a need to come to terms with particular myths, but often at the cost of creating new ones.

III

Common sense tells us that a story about the past can operate as myth and still be a true recollection of true events. Experience tells us that this seldom happens. The rise and decline of one contemporary myth shows why this is so. In his *Jewish War* Josephus recounted the unedifying history of the Sicarii, a group of brigands and assassins who operated in Judaea during the Roman suppression of Jewish autonomy between 66 and 70 A.D.[3] After the fall of Jerusalem, the Sicarii retreated to several mountain fastnesses, including Masada, from which they pillaged the surrounding countryside. Eventually, the Romans invested Masada. After a siege of several months, all but seven of the 967 defenders allowed themselves to be killed by a chosen few, who then committed suicide. In describing these events Josephus generally took a contemptuous attitude.

Schwartz et al describe Masada as "one of the least significant and least successful events in ancient Jewish history," and it long escaped the attention of Jewish historians.[4] Then, beginning in the 1920s the story of Masada began to be transformed into the myth of Masada. After independence in 1948, Masada helped meet the pressing demand for powerful symbols of defiance, endurance, and hope for the future common to all newly-born nations.[5] With one President of Israel quoted as saying: "[f]or us Masada means the will to live," the myth could hardly fail to flourish.[6] A few wrinkles needed ironing out. Since the Sicarii, by Josephus' account, could hardly be deemed appropriate models for the new country, the defenders of Masada had to become Zealots, a related, but milder-mannered group. In this version, the Zealots helped defend Jerusalem against the Romans and only then retreated to Masada to continue the freedom struggle. History was being turned sideways.

Archeology contributed notably to this metamorphosis when Yigael Yadin, a prominent military and scholarly figure in Israel, undertook excavations on the site in the 1960s.[7] Yadin made his contribution to myth formation in the simplest possible way; wherever Josephus had referred to Sicarii, Yadin substituted "Zealots." Whereas Josephus had never used the word "Zealots" in referring to Masada, Yadin used it every time but one in his own work. Other than this airbrushing, he merely took Josephus at his word. Yadin made no pretense to objectivity, proclaiming that "[i]t would be one of the tasks of our archaeological expedition to see what evidence we would find to support the Josephus record."[8]

Yadin thought he had found what he was looking for, and he wasted no time publicizing and popularizing his discoveries, or rather his interpretations of them.

Although Josephus mentioned no face-to-face hostilities between the defenders of Masada and the Romans, and although Yadin professed to believe in the mass suicide, he still described the occasion as "a heroic stand" that "elevated Masada to an undying symbol of desperate courage."[9] With the publication of Yadin's account of the excavations, the Masada myth appeared to be firmly entrenched and Masada itself quickly became a lucrative tourist attraction.[10]

Still, not all subscribed to the new orthodoxy.[11] Critics argued that Yadin had produced an interpretation that was a "thinly disguised romanticism of Israel's past."[12] It hardly mattered since, soon after Yadin's paean to the Zealots appeared, the Masada myth began to wane, or even to turn on itself. Israel's spectacular and unexpected success in the Six Days' War in 1967 allowed a refurbished national self-image to emerge unassisted by the remote past. Masada could now be seen as a shameful example of a defeatist complex, and the Masada myth began to give way to the Masada complex.[13] This volte-face allowed minimal tactical doubt of Josephus's account to creep into the discussion, if on expedient rather than scholarly grounds.

It is worth looking at Josephus's account as if it were history rather than the basis for myth. Writing as a self-described social scientist, Ben-Yehuda argues that Josephus's accuracy is "irrelevant" to understanding the myth, although he refers to Josephus as "the only true [sic] account we have" and supports this assessment by generally accepting his version.[14] Shargel, on the other hand, thought that "the first problem is the credibility" of Josephus.[15] Here I must side against Ben-Yehuda, while agreeing that what we believe is distinct from, and often more important than, what is actually true. Historians, however, while they might find myth-making instructive in certain diagnostic ways, have the additional obligation of determining as far as possible to what degree the myth is accurate.

We could believe Josephus regarding both numbers and style of death. We might choose to believe in the numbers but not in the suicide explanation, or the reverse. Finally, we could reject the entire story as a fabrication. Predictably, modern myth-makers have oscillated among the first three, while eschewing the last. There is something to be said for this. Josephus was writing only a few years after the occasion and nothing in his account is palpably impossible, as distinct from implausible. Best of all, his version has no ancient competition. Some have questioned Josephus's account of the manner of death. Mass suicide contradicts rabbinic teaching and has the aspect of the unthinking and cowardly about it.[16] Some who have addressed this issue have found ingenious arguments that accept the suicides (and thus the symbolism) without transgressing Judaic law.[17] Others point out that mass suicide was a topos in ancient Greco-Roman writings dealing with warfare, works with which Josephus was familiar.[18]

Generally, though, opinion is divided in the absence of evidence beyond Josephus. Cohen finds Josephus's story to be "very dramatic but utterly incredible;" Ladouceur thinks it "induce[s] skepticism;" for Newall "the familiacide and suicide of 960 Sicarii on Masada did occur historically."[19] Without any concern for whether the defenders of Masada were Sicarii, Zealots, or Martians, at least four elements militate against digesting Josephus's testimony whole: the speeches he put into the mouth of the leader of the defenders; the logistics of the site; the silence of the Talmud; and what archeologists did not find.

Two speeches of Eleazar ben Ya'ir, the leader of the defenders, are central to Josephus's narrative, and he reproduced them as verbatim.[20] In his account, Eleazar's first speech fell on barren ground, so he immediately tried again and this time changed the mind of every one of his listeners—how, we are never told, nor how Josephus came into possession of the text of these speeches. He does offer an explanation: one of the survivors who had hidden in "caverns" below the site emerged and reported on "both the speech and how the deed was done."[21] But the two speeches combined run to over 2000 words (in English). Can we believe that this survivor, cowering at some remove from the site of the speech, could have heard it, remembered it, and passed it along to the Romans, who would then in turn have remembered it well enough to pass along to Josephus in good enough shape for him to treat it as direct speech—all this while crossing language barriers?[22] What is surprising is how often the contents of these speeches have been used in probing the mindset of the defenders rather than that of Josephus.[23] Sometimes those who reject the provenance of the speech, which constitutes about half of Josephus's relevant narrative, insist that doing this does not adversely affect the rest of the story.[24]

Josephus's number of 967 defenders, which he also does not provenance, has led some to question whether the site could have provided so many with adequate food and water.[25] We know too little to judge the merits of either case here, but logistical constraints are a legitimate tool for raising doubt. Although Feldman regards the absence of any mention of Masada in the Talmud as "baffling," others have offered a variety of possible explanations.[26] Some of these are reasonable enough to breach the argument from silence, but of course none can be conclusive.

Possibly the most serious impediment to belief is that, while the archeological excavations have not contradicted Josephus's account—how could they?—only about 25 skeletons were unearthed. Since it would be reasonable to assume that when nearly 1000 people die at the same time and same place, more than 3 percent of the bodies would survive, this number is both too high and too low.[27] Defenders of Josephus's veracity have mounted several hypotheses, the most popular of which is that the bodies were burned outside the walls, even though their own source says otherwise.[28] Only a few have challenged Josephus's figure as exaggerated, even though earlier in the *Jewish War* he had unblushingly written that 1,100,000 Jews died during the siege of Jerusalem a few years earlier.[29]

To complicate matters, these skeletons are a matter of controversy; some think they represent the defenders, while others identify them as Roman. Intent on verifying Josephus, Yadin took no measures to preserve the context of the skeletons, and valuable in situ information was irretrievably lost. Yadin's insistence that the bodies he found (and which he had reinterred before they could be examined scientifically) were those of defenders weakens his case for relying on Josephus, since we would expect that either a large proportion of the bodies would be found or none at all. Cohen is one of the few to doubt Josephus so far as to call his account a "farrago of fiction, conjecture, and error," although he concedes that "[a]t least some of the Sicarii killed themselves rather than face the Romans," though probably not nearly 1,000 of them.[30] Cohen's interpretation trumps alternatives that the siege never occurred or that, however implausibly, Josephus found himself in a position to report all the happenings conscientiously and accurately.

The rapid evolution of the Masada myth shows—yet again—how extraordinarily different views of the occasion rest on a single description of a few thousand words. Everyone who presses one of these discrepant views claims to do so as a result of trusting the accuracy of Josephus. Yadin was the most outrageously impudent, yet also the most influential—it is he and not his detractors who caught the eye and ear of and interested public.[31] It is unlikely that one in a hundred of those who trek to Masada have the least notion that so much about Josephus has been questioned. There they hear about Eleazar ben Ya'ir or Yigael Yadin, but not about Trude Weiss-Rosmarin or Shaye Cohen.[32]

IV

Several treatments of Masada have noted how closely it resembles one of our own myths, the siege of the Alamo. The much larger body of evidence for the

Alamo has not impeded the growth of the myth, which features a belated appearance of a series of heroic gestures and another impossibly-recorded speech.[33] This all helps to demolish the myth at a scholarly level, but there is little evidence that the uncongenial realities have filtered very far into public consciousness.[34]

The moving frontier has probably created more myths than any other aspect of the U.S. past. No American can live very long without seeing the myths of the "Old West" reinvented and disseminated almost daily in the movies, on television, in popular works of history and/or fiction.[35] In form and function some of these resemble the Masada myth, if inverting the details. For most, this period and place of our history is painted in black and white, chiaroscuro at best. It is populated with bluff and simple figures, who seem to be either good or evil incarnate although, as in the cases of Billy the Kid, Wyatt Earp, Joaquín Murieta, and others, the two often mix indiscriminately. In other cases, the good is allowed to mask the bad with remarkable perdurance.[36]

Textbooks are major entrants in the myth-making sweepstakes. The salient attraction of any textbook is its marketability. In an era where the evidence suggests that children and young adults know little history or geography, it is more important than ever that textbooks avoid offending or challenging cherished beliefs. The past must be simplified—historical figures are not portrayed as complex individuals, most events have one or a few proximate causes, the discourse is direct, and competent revision of the past is anathema.

In this world historical characters are either preternaturally good (George Washington, Abraham Lincoln, Horatio Nelson) or preternaturally bad (Richard III, Benedict Arnold, Aaron Burr), and events stand as synecdoche for processes. Textbook authors have little choice in the matter; there is no interest in finesse and perhaps no room for it. Those whose knowledge of the past derives largely from textbooks will come away with a satchelful of myths, not the least of which is that both the past itself and its study are uncomplicated.

A salient recent example is Christopher Ehret's casual observation that "two of the early [pre-3500 BCE] African religions . . . were distinctly monotheistic thousands of years before the idea of monotheism ever occurred to Middle Easterners or Europeans." Ehret supports this really extraordinary claim, well within the relaxed textbook tradition even if outsized, only by reference to a single word that occurs in several African languages, leaving it to students to accept or reject the claim willy-nilly.[37]

The standards that allow such claims to reside unadorned and unchallenged in textbooks have long been recognized and lamented, but there is little evidence of appreciable gains, but only some movement toward prevailing political correctitude. Nor is it easy, given the circumstances, to imagine that meaningful progress could be in the offing, leaving impressions of the past that are entirely divorced from reality to sink inexorably into the minds of those who are not likely ever to have the chance to be disabused of them.[38]

V

Today's myths appeal to today's belief systems, so they lack gods, dragons, and physically impossible deeds, but they are no less pervasive for that. The historian attempting to combat them often faces overwhelming opposition.[39] Commenting on the reception to his debunking of rampant centenarianism in England, William Thoms lamented: "Let no one who has the slightest desire to live in peace and quietness be tempted, under any circumstances, to enter upon the chivalrous task of trying to correct a popular error."[40] Several Norwegian and Swedish historians were all but ostracized from the guild for their unappreciated efforts to undercut the historical value of the sagas. As a result, demythologizing has become an intramural affair, one in which historical scholarship is estranged from its natural public. It is hard to imagine what could change this; for 4000 years or more, nothing much has worked.

12

IRRECONCILABLE DIFFERENCES

We are therefore confronted with two well-supported, but conflicting theories, about the age of landnam in Iceland. . .
Experience tells us that we should not try to disprove one theory with the arguments of another, but rather that we should
scrutinize the supporting evidence of both theories and examine
potential sources of error until all reasonable doubt has been
expelled.

Unfortunately there is hardly any sound evidence with which
this generalisation can be validated; yet it seems more attractive
than any alternative I can think of. There are several pieces of
evidence, each insufficient or untrustworthy in itself, which
seem collectively to confirm it. I call this the wigwam argument: each pole would fall down by itself, but together the
poles stand up, by leaning on each other; they point roughly in
the same direction and circumscribe 'truth.' I realise that it is
dangerous to accept the general tenor of the evidence while
doubting the truth of individual pieces. But this is what we are
forced to do in reconstructing even the crude outlines of
Rome's early social structure.

I

One of the best-known stories of all time is that of the "first Christmas." This popular tale is actually a composite of elements from the gospels of Matthew and Luke—the other gospels start Christ off later in life. The elements in Matthew's gospel (the "star," the magi, Herod's slaughter of the innocents, and the flight to Egypt) and those that appear in Luke's gospel (Elizabeth the cousin of Mary, the census, the shepherds and the manger scene, and the singing heavenly hosts) are mutually exclusive.[1] We would expect the two accounts to diverge—if they did not it would be suspicious in itself—but hardly to such an extent. Luke confirms nothing that Matthew wrote, nor Matthew that which Luke wrote. Since the two were not only contemporaries but associates, this is peculiar. Did each milk entirely different traditions? If so, how did they diverge so quickly? Caution requires that we treat neither account as authentic or reliable enough to earn widespread belief. The modern version contains nine elements, but we have no right to treat the separate threads as elements to be added to, rather than pitted against, one another. In this case the gospel texts survive to warn us, but they can hardly tell us how often such things happen unevidenced.

II

A ceaseless, and sometimes aggravating, task for historians is reconciling the variant testimonies they collect during their work. Ideology intrudes when deciding how best to treat disparate evidence bearing on the same topic. The tendency is to be additive, treating the body of material as auspiciously accumulative rather than dangerously discordant. Consider the numerous attempts to rewrite the chronology of the ancient Near East to preserve biblical testimony intact. Immanuel Velikovsky did this by conjuring otherwise unknown, and impossible, celestial phenomena. In his turn, Hans Goedicke relied on geology, calling on the massive eruption on Thera to explain the biblical story of the parting of the Red Sea. In this way he was able both to date the exodus and explain its marvelous aspects.[2] In these exercises, and any number of others, Biblical chronology plays the role as a silent bed of Procrustes on which all competing chronologies must be accommodated. The problem arises because, whether we treat the bible as history or literature, it seems virtually impossible to regard it with the same jaundiced eye that we might routinely turn on similar sources such as the Avestas or the Rigveda.

As noted above, four written accounts of the expedition of Hernando de Soto survive, all apparently independent and all dealing with the same events, although in different ways. Using them is inescapable: "[t]o ignore [de Soto chronicles], . . . would be to close up shop since they are virtually all that scholars have to study the Soto *entrada*."[3] The two shortest are by named officials in the expedition, men in a position to know, and with the obligation to record, what transpired. These two accounts surfaced within a few years after the return of the survivors. A third narrative was published pseudonymously some fifteen years later. It was longer and more literary, clearly designed as much to tell a story as to record useful logistical details. The fourth version appeared only sixty years after the end of the expedition. It had a named 'editor,' Inca Garcilaso de la Vega, who ostensibly aspired merely to tidying up and transmitting the reminiscences of an unnamed veteran. Longer than the others combined, this is written with all the literary flourish that a committed Humanist could summon.

All agree that Garcilaso was trying to sell a story; the question is, how much of it is true? To judge from the uses to which *La Florida* has been put trying to establish de Soto's exact itinerary, just about all of it. Laborers in this vineyard use all four sources, but rely most heavily on Garcilaso since he is so forthcoming with the details they relish. When the other accounts mention a distance, a direction, or a topographical feature, Garcilaso often spreads gild on the lily by adding a picturesque detail that encourages seekers to narrow their choice. When one source for the expedition mentions *A* but not *B* in a particular description, whereas a second source mentions *B* but not *A*, the characteristic response has been to assume that both *A* and *B* occurred, not that one or another of the sources is confused. And when Garcilaso adds *C* and *D*, modern students of the route believe that they have access to four pieces of solid evidence that complement each other, rather than one, or maybe none. Testimony is rejected only when it is demonstrably impossible or disagrees with modern hypotheses.

Looking at the sources for de Soto's expedition synoptically shows that Garcilaso is so seldom likely to be right that bringing his account into the discussion poisons it irreparably. It also shows that the three other accounts often disagree with one another to the point where it is not always possible to choose among them. There is no evidence that the recorders on the expedition were particularly concerned with such details as exact distances and directions, nor that they were in a position to record these correctly day after day, year after year, even if they had wanted to. The official accounts were designed to present evidence at court, not to guide modern trail hounds. It was sufficient to generalize—and important to dissimulate.

The authors of the three early sources were traveling companions for nearly 1500 days and nights, and we should not assume that they did not confer with each other about their work, both then and later. If so, we lack certainty even when two or all of these sources seem to corroborate each other. This might seem defeatist, but it is a more realistic assumption than any that posits that each of these accounts arose independently, remained uninfluenced by the others, and was reasonably accurate even ex post facto. Thus, while we can assume that information in these sources often supplements that in the other sources, we can be very less sure when and how this happens.

III

Unfortunately, evidence from one genre seldom meshes well with existing data from another. Whatever the cruxes in early Egyptian chronology, it is often affirmed that beginning with the XVIII or XIX Dynasty, there is virtually no room for disagreement in dating individual rulers. The vacuity of this claim is illustrated by a recently-edited Assyrian inscription that throws new light on the date of Shebitku of the XXV Dynasty.[4] Donald Redford points out that at least four postulated dates—702/701/699/695—are already on the books for the accession of this Pharaoh, but that this inscription seems to point to a date no later than 705. Since other evidence clashes with this dating, Redford calls on the deus ex machina for so many dating dilemmas in the ancient Egypt—the co-regency. Whether further evidence will uphold his suggestion—and he admits to being "diffiden[t]" himself—remains to be seen.[5]

The Se(v)una (or Yadava) dynasty is one of few medieval Indian dynasties for which two kinds of evidence co-exist. There are inscriptions that provide some names and dates, but little narrative. There is extant as well the *Vratakhanda,* a work of the courtier Hemadri that purports to offer a continuous history of the dynasty from its mythological origins. Each source contains information not found in the other, forcing modern historians to make a number of choices. Naturally, these depend on their views of the reliability of the competing evidence. Hemadri was not a historian, and we know neither his angle of vision or his sources and how he used them. If we assume that he used the same epigraphic sources available to us, but more of them, we are likely to lend his work more credence than if we assume that he worked with less credible sources or was fueled by an unknown ideology.

Such differences of opinion play out in attempts to establish a regnal chronology. The inscriptions provide few dates, while Hemadri provides none at all. There are names in Hemadri for which there is no epigraphic evidence, and genealogical relationships occasionally differ between the inscriptions and the *Vratakhanda*. Worried about a "gap" in the inscriptions between 1058, the last known date of Bhillama III, and 1069, the first known date of Seunachandra II, A.V.N. Murthy is content to fall back on Hemadri: "[i]t is known from Hemadri that three princes . . . succeeded one another" between these two rulers, and they find a firm place in his reconstruction of Seuna dynastic chronology.[6] In contrast, J.N.S. Yadav distrusts Hemadri and prefers to rely on the epigraphic evidence. He notes that "the epigraphic records . . . are silent" on Hemadri's three rulers and concludes that this "raises a doubt whether they were successive rulers at all," and they find only a provisional place in his reconstruction.[7]

Murthy's "gap" is a mere eleven years, and does not need to be accounted for. On the other hand Hemadri does include three names at this point and the question is whether they ruled consecutively or simultaneously, independently or as contenders, or not at all. Given the exiguousness of the epigraphic evidence, Yadav's implied argument from silence is worthless. At any rate, in number, genealogical filiation, and dating, no two modern reconstructions of the early Seuna dynasty are very alike.[8]

Luke's and Matthew's Christmases, de Soto's wanderings, and the Seuna genealogies are just three examples of how easily, and how subliminally, narratives from the past become modern reformulations of haphazard data. In the case of the Seunas, combining differing forms of evidence gives historians several choices not ruled out by the existing evidence. They can prefer the literary over the epigraphic, and thus the continuous over the sporadic, or they can devise a chronology that retains a particular succession of officeholders, but reduces the period it covers. Or they could construct dual chronologies, each based on one form of evidence and let the reader decide—or decline to.

IV

Consider the case of the tombs of the rulers of Jin, a Chinese principality during the time of the Zhou dynasty. From early written records we have a list of these rulers, which has been presumed to be substantially correct. Since 1992 the tombs of several rulers have been unearthed and studied. None of the names attached to these tombs matches the names in the list that has come down to us, leading the excavators and others to engage in fruitless match-the-names exercises, no two of which agree with each other and none of which has competitive plausibility. As one scholar puts it: "[g]iven a cemetery of Jin lords and a classic text purporting to list those lords, [the excavators] seem to have been determined at all costs to bring the two into correspondence, no matter how insufficient or contradictory the evidence. But this rush to judgment cannot be countenanced . . . [It] give[s] a false and misleading air of certainty to an archaeological sequence that cannot be regarded as firmly established."[9]

As usual, there are several possibilities. The names on the tombs might be otherwise unknown personal names that might one day be matched up on stylistic or placement grounds. Or perhaps they just happen to be six rulers who were omitted from the king list for whatever reason. Or conceivably the list itself is, at least in part, fictitious. Or the tombs commemorate someone other than rulers of Jin. This is not a particularly attractive potpourri of choices, and was probably not anticipated by historians and archeologists as the work commenced.

The new problems thrown up along with the soil are sure to test the wit of those attempting to resolve them; at the moment the evidence is insufficient to rule out any solution. The conundrum of the cemetery of Jin illustrates well what makes historical inquiry so exciting. The evidence there was entirely unanticipated and has already engendered attempts to make the new evidence match the old. Xu points out that this must, at least provisionally, be accounted a failure.[10] In time, perhaps attention will be drawn to more radical—and certainly, to some, undesirable—alternatives.

V

Historians have availed themselves of the results of radiocarbon dating for more than half a century. The greatest appeal lies in its ability to provide ever narrower ranges of probability for the relicts of events that might otherwise be undatable. Radiocarbon dating is popular in efforts to confirm, or make more precise, dates already reasonably well documented in the historical record. More often that we would like, history and carbon disagree. This happened often enough that eventually it was concluded that there were localized variations in the half-life of carbon, as well as variations over time. While this has helped reduce some contradictions, it remains to be seen where the next soft spot turns up.

Various attempts have been made to date the explosion on the island of Thera, a major event in the ancient Mediterranean world. Until recently, archeological evidence (mostly pottery 'styles') was thought to suggest a date late in the sixteenth century BCE. More recently, radiocarbon dating, dendrochronology, and ice-core dating suggest a date about a century earlier.[11] This seems to be a strong case for converging evidence, except that none of these can demonstrate that the eruption at Thera—and only the eruption at Thera—accounts for the atmospheric conditions in ca. 1628 BCE. So, while the evidence converges nicely, the final step is still missing, and those who accept the new dating are forced to change many other datings for the second millennium BCE, while lacking the gravitas to justify these.[12]

The agitation that can result when physical and written evidence clash is particularly evident in the case of early Iceland. According to such reputedly unimpeachable sources as the *Islendingabók* and the *Landnámabók*, the first permanent settlers arrived in Iceland from Norway in 870/74, a date which, for Icelanders is as important as 1066 to the English, 1492 to (some) Americans, or 753 BCE to the Romans. In 1966 Kristján Eldjárn, the state antiquarian (and later President) of Iceland, decried efforts to ascribe certain archeological remains to Celts as "weird," arguing that archeological evidence validated the story of a relatively sudden and quick settlement of the island by the Norse beginning ca. 870. Archeology and literature were in harmony.[13] Eldjárn's views summed up well the prevailing feeling about the relationship of the two forms of evidence in this case; the first was expected to support the second.

There was some consternation then when a series of radiocarbon dates was derived in the 1970s that suggested that parts of Iceland had been settled as early as ca. 700. It is no surprise that this dating was strongly resented and resisted. One line of defense was to postulate a "local depression . . . in atmospheric carbon dioxide over Iceland," which would imply that "all samples from Iceland would give an apparently too high age."[14] Ingrid Olsson, its proponent, had done work on early dynastic Egypt, where this actually was the case and so the theory, if a bit circular, was not entirely implausible. Unlike Egypt though, it was not required by a mass of interconnected historical evidence.

Other evidence soon undercut Olsson's expedient, but this had no effect on national sentiment, which rates the written sources too highly to be overthrown by a set of geochronological data. The reaction in Icelandic scientific circles was to forgo using C^{14} dating at all, while the excavator of the site in question even declined to include the disputed results in the final report.[15] Margrét Hermanns-

Audardóttir, however, accepted the apparent evidence of the C[14] dating. Her published argument was accompanied by a number of critical comments, most of which faulted her for arrogating science above literature, but also criticized her use of non-Icelandic written sources.[16]

V.O. Vilhjálmsson was critical of early efforts to correlate archeology with written documentation, and was dubious of Olsson's expedient, but preferred to reject the 700 CE date on various grounds, including the possibility of contaminated samples.[17] Adolf Fridriksson agreed that Hermanns-Audardóttir's conclusions "must be dismissed entirely" on the grounds that she had not met the standards required for overthrowing an existing orthodoxy—which apparently are loftier than those required to establish it in the first place.[18]

This controversy prompted Páll Theodórsson to undertake a thorough investigation of the issues. He looked at three possible reasons for rejecting the dates—laboratory bias, initial age of samples, and locally concentrated depressions—and concluded that there are insufficient grounds for rejecting the testimony of the dated samples, and no grounds at all for rejecting them out of hand.[19] In summing up, Theodórsson cast doubt on the evidence of the *Islendingabók*, pointing out that it was written only in the twelfth century and was based entirely on "folklore"[20] He laments that Icelandic archeology is "in deadlock," but he does not foresee a quick or painless resolution.[21]

Why this strong preference for a problematical written source against a growing body of scientific evidence? One reason is that geochronological dating is less secure for Iceland than for most other places: the lack of old forest growth rules out dendrochronology; Iceland's low-maintenance society left fewer artifacts behind; and constant volcanic activity introduces troublesome variables. A second reason relates to national ethos. Iceland expressly defines itself by its compact history and the world-famous literature that describes and defines that history.[22] The new dating strikes at the very core of this almost reverential attitude, with the result that, almost uniquely, Icelandic society firmly rejects the opportunity to be of greater antiquity than it had believed it was.

VI

The *Landnámabók* and *Islendingabók* are members of the not very exclusive club of single sources whose provenance is dubious and whose testimony is compromised, if not contradicted, by other evidence. The fact that Icelanders have made these works their social and political charters in no way enhances their credibility. Although about one-quarter of the C[14] dates from Iceland can support a pre-870 settlement, the issue is far from resolved.[23] There are as yet too many imponderables to accept the earlier dating, but the anguished outcry is wildly incommensurate to the strength of the alternative evidence. The compilation of the *Landnámambók* and *Islendingabók* culminated centuries of dynamic oral tradition. They were compiled in part to legitimate and codify the then-existing land distribution and social hierarchies on the island.[24] In short, these were documents of their time. The discrepant radiocarbon dates serve to remind us of this as much as they force us to consider an earlier dating for settlement. For now though, most Icelanders adamantly prefer to retain the "first settler" Ingólfr Arnason as their symbolic national ancestor.[25]

These examples, though few, serve well to underscore Arthur Marwick's slightly over-precise comment on the need for caution: ". . . at least 80 per cent of what a scholarly historian writes is likely to be soundly based—but the reader should always be ready to reject up to 20 per cent, which can be due to bees in the bonnet, sycophancy towards a patron, the desire to be in fashion, humble error, or various other reasons . . ."[26]

In fact, there is no point in evading an unpopular truth that plays a crucial role in helping us to decide whether or not to take information at face value. In discussing several recent scandals in American historiography, Peter Hoffer put it succinctly but damningly: "We lie because the truth is harsh or hurtful; because we see an advantage in the lie; because lying is easier than explanation. We lie to save ourselves from extra work or the consequences of the truth. We lie to make ourselves look smarter, bolder, richer, or more worthy of another's admiration or friendship. We lie to save souls teetering on the edge of the abyss of damnation. We lie to bring those whose guilt is clear to us but may not be as clear to others. We lie because we are paid to lie. Some of us have a compulsion to lie."[27] Historians might not like the sweeping nature of this comment, but, as they proceed, they must act as though they believe it anyway.

13

"WE'RE CHANGING EVERYTHING . . . AGAIN"

> At the end of the day one will have to admit that one is wasting
> one's wit on an endless study, and that one will not wish to add
> to the numerous folios of existing chronologies. The best rule
> will be to withdraw into the area of historical certainty, and to
> content oneself with approximations measured in generations or
> centuries where prehistoric times are concerned. The earliest
> limit will not reach far back beyond the first Olympiads, as the
> destruction of Troy, though the fact itself can not be doubted,
> already belongs entirely to a mythical age.
>
> Of course there are many other possibilities, fourteen in all, but
> since we are unable to choose between them, I suggest the above.

I

John Locke saw chronology and geography as saving history from being "only a jumble of Matters of Fact, confusedly heaped together without Order or Instruction." But scholars need only be concerned with "the general part of it." He elaborated: "[w]hen I speak of *Chronology* as a Science . . . I do not mean the little Controversies, that are in it. These are endless, and most of them of so little Importance to a Gentleman, as not to deserve to be inquir'd into, were they capable of an easy Decision."[1] Nowhere have "the little Controversies" been so much a centerpiece of the discourse than the centuries-long efforts to apply a defensible dating framework to the ancient Near East.[2]

Sturt Manning records the reign of Amenemhat II of the XII Dynasty of Egypt as "(c. 1935/29/22/21/17/11/01/1877/76/751903/1895/82/76/66/43/42/40 BC[)]."[3] This might seem like a typographer run amok, but those familiar with Egyptian chronology know better, for it reflects the range of modern opinion on the dating of this reign. The competing views of the chronology of the ancient Near East epitomize ways in which knowledge about the past is gained—and lost—incrementally. Although composed of thousands of cellular components, the process is a symbiotic one, where modifications to one piece of information ramify widely, so that it seldom is possible to proceed without a more global awareness. At no time has there been consensus, and seldom even an undisputed majority opinion.[4]

II

Before the critical study of ancient Near East chronology was launched, the available sources consisted of a few chronicles that had survived from ancient times and, most importantly, the bible. Gradually sources became available that undermined the bible's determinate authority. This was accompanied by the beginnings of serious archeology, which now included excavation as well as observation.

Writing under the Ptolemies, the Egyptian priest Manetho presented Egyptian history as comprising thirty discrete dynasties before Alexander the Great. To all appearances, these succeeded one another in relentless fashion, each unifying the entire Nile valley under its rule, although the capital tended to move around. Beginning with the excavations in Egypt during Napoleon's ephemeral control there, an enormous literature developed trying to decide whether Manetho was right and, if not, how and how much he was wrong.[5] R.S. Poole published an early reading of the evidence that was both precocious and ingenuous. Poole was willing to consider dynastic overlaps and co-regencies, and he dated Menes, the first ruler, later than almost anyone since, as late as ca. 2640 BCE, but he acted for wrong reasons and achieved wrong results. His objective was to validate biblical and Herodotean chronology, and he made dynasties contemporary that we know not to be the case, even subsumed some dynasties into others, yet accorded the alien Hyksos rule a period three times as great as current theories allow.[6]

Like Poole, early modern chronologists of the ancient Near East had only their credulity to guide them and this proved treacherous. Poole's efforts were a dead end, but it became clear that the easiest way to differentiate chronologies lay in deciding whether or not to accept Manetho's implication that dynasties succeeded one another in linear fashion.[7] If they did, modern scholarship could

establish the chronology of ancient Egypt by adding up the figures Manetho provided, subtract them from the date of Alexander's visit and determine the date of
the accession of Menes.

As a result Menes was initially backdated well into the sixth millennium
BCE.[8] For instance, in the 1890s the influential W.M. Flinders Petrie proposed a
date for Menes of 5546 BCE and had reduced this only to 4320 BCE. in his last
work, published in 1939.[9] He persisted in this dating even though virtually all
other Egyptologists had lowered their own dates for Menes to ca. 3400 BCE or
even later. His basis of belief was peculiar and circular, but revealing: "the
[ancient Egyptian] historian would not include a duplicate line, however great it
was" and "[t]he principle therefore seems clear that, where there were contemporaries, only one line was selected and others ignored, in order not to upset the continuous reckoning"[10]

The discovery of such texts as the Palermo Stone naturally led to another flurry of confident reckoning. De Ricci captured this in 1917, when he wrote that
"[t]he day when it will be possible to combine the six known fragments of this
text, the chronology of the earliest rulers of Egypt will rest on bases as certain as
those of the twelve Caesars."[11] Writing after more than eighty years of further
work, however, the author of the most extensive analysis of this source could only
write that "[i]t seems unlikely that a definitive, or even plausible reconstruction
of the annals will ever be possible, infuriating as that may be."[12]

Roughly speaking, there are now three datings proposed for the founding of I
Dynasty. Some posit a date of ca. 3400 BCE, while another group prefers a date
of ca. 2950 BCE. The largest group advocates a date of ca. 3100 BCE, largely
based on the figure in the Turin Canon of 955 years before the beginning of the
VIII Dynasty, a statement that can be confirmed or disconfirmed with equal facility. All three groups call C^{14} dating to their aid, and each can make a case,
depending on which (5730 or 5568 years) half-life they choose and how many
standard deviations they can abide. The statement by a committed participant in
the debate sums matters up, perhaps slightly optimistically: after a century and a
half of intense debate "[i]n Ancient Egypt, the earliest agreed fixed date is 664
BC."[13]

The state of affairs in Egyptian chronology is reflected in the fact that between
1987 and 1997 several full or partial chronological schemes were advanced, each
differing from the others, even when the author was the same.[14] They disagree on
the absolute dating of dynasties, their length, and the lengths of individual reigns.
The reasons for this chaos are obvious: there are too many choices and too little

independent evidence. For early periods there are few synchronisms with other parts of the ancient world, and authors must treat co-regencies, concurrent dynasties, and lengths of reigns in virtual isolation.[15]

The imputed chronology of the better-documented XVIII and XIX Dynasties (ca. 1550-1190 BCE) underscores the fragility of these exercises. Speaking of the former, Patrick O'Mara concludes, rather wistfully: "Must we not be content with some sort of multiple solution conveying a grid of probabilities?" He offers four dates—1365/1354/1351/ 1340 BCE—with some evidence in favor of each, for Akhenaten's first year.[16] Modern scholars credit Seti I of XIX Dynasty with a reign from 10 to 19 years and Merenptah from 9 to 19 years, and put forward five different years (1304, 1301, 1290, 1279, 1276 BCE) for the accession year of Ramesses II, who intervened between them.[17]

III

The history of Mesopotamian chronology is even more turbulent yet expressed even more confidently. In 1862 H.C. Rawlinson announced that he was "glad to be able to announce to those who are interested in the comparative chronology of the Jewish and Assyrian kingdoms, the discovery of a Cuneiform document which promises to be of the greatest possible value in determining the dates of all great events which occurred in Western Asia between the beginning of the ninth and the later [sic] half of the seventh century B.C."[18] Only a few of the dates and names that Rawlinson went on to propose are now accepted. In fact, like W.F. Albright, discussed below, Rawlinson went on to change his own mind several times before he finally ceased to conjecture.

More serious efforts began in 1884 with the discovery of tablets that provided the names of the rulers of several dynasties. As usual, the assumption was that these represented consecutive rather than partly concurrent periods of rule so that, once again, dates could be provided merely by working back from the earliest date that could be regarded as fixed. Even so, a raft of varying dates resulted during the first twenty years of the exercise. Almost all rejected concurrency.[19] Any illusion of sufficiency was gradually eroded as more inscriptions became available, some of which established synchronisms ("well-known names in new and startling combination") that were impossible by hundreds of years under the reigning orthodoxy.[20] This stage culminated with the appearance of L.W. King's study of the then extant chronicles of early Mesopotamia, which included a list of 15 dates proposed between 1888 to 1903 for Hammurabi, the sixth and most famous ruler of the First Dynasty of Babylon.[21]

The chronicles King studied showed three early dynasties—then called Dynasties I, II, and III, and now known as the First Dynasty of Babylon, the Sealand dynasty, and the Kassite dynasty—as (apparently) ruling in succession for 304, 368, and 576 years. Totaling these and projecting them back from the mid-twelfth century, when Kassite rule ended, resulted in figures of ca. 2400 BCE for the beginning of the First Dynasty of Babylon. The Sealand dynasty was gradually elbowed out of the chronological sequence entirely, reducing that date to the twenty-first century. The freefall continued and had backward effects as well—when the dust temporarily settled, Sargon of Agade had lost over a thousand years of antiquity.[22]

In 1921 Stephen Langdon and A.T. Olmstead expressed wildly divergent opinions about our grasp of early Mesopotamian chronology. Langdon was confident: "[w]e now possess, in almost complete form, trustworthy material for reconstructing the chronology of the early history of Mesopotamian civilization."[23] Olmstead was feeling quite the opposite: ". . . [new discoveries] force a complete re-writing of almost every page in the earlier Assyrian history."[24] The differing opinions are not surprising; that they were expressed within a few months of each other is not very surprising either.

Three years later the new *Cambridge Ancient History* summed up matters: "[a]lthough the discovery that the first three dynasties are not be reckoned consecutively has narrowed the extent of the divergence in modern computations, the chronological schemes that have been proposed vary according to their reliance upon the trustworthiness" of the later inscriptional durations "and of the figures in the Royal Lists and other summaries."[25] The number of schemes approximately matched the number of scholars proposing them. Ernst Weidner's bibliography covered less than nine years but included over 1800 items.[26] In 1946 Böhl reported that in the preceding seven years "as many as eighteen treatises" on the date of Hammurabi had appeared.[27] There was also a constant thread that sought to base the chronology of the ancient Near East on the chronographic data in the bible, Herodotus, Berosus, Eusebius, and others. The presumption was that there must have been good reasons why these ancient chroniclers offered the numbers they did.

IV

The discovery of the so-called Venus Tablets in 1912 resulted in a host of new arguments. The tablets dated to the reign of Ammisaduqa, the fourth successor of

Hammurabi.[28] The astronomical data in these were deemed of central value in establishing Ammisaduqa's dates and, by extension, those of the entire First Dynasty of Babylon and dynasties, like that of Larsa, for which synchronisms existed. By making certain assumptions about the locus and accuracy of the observations, and bearing in mind the cyclical nature of the phenomena observed, the tablets could countenance several specific dates. At first they were used to date Hammurabi to the twenty-first century. As time passed, the accumulation of evidence slowly forced Hammurabi's dates downwards.[29] Eventually the tablets were used to support arguments that three different dates could apply to Hammurabi: 1848-1806 BCE, 1792-1750 BCE, and 1728-1686 BCE, which became consecrated as the "high," "middle," and "low" options.[30]

The Venus Tablets have little independent significance—their usefulness is in their flexibility. Still, they have undergone several challenges as to observational and transcriptional accuracy.[31] Cryer recently expressed this unpalatable argument: "there is no reason to place any great faith in the Venus Tablets for the purposes of reconstructing the chronology of the second millennium."[32] If so, Hammurabi is untied from any specific date, although still tethered by a growing body of contextual evidence seemingly restricting him to an ever narrower ambit. Recently an international colloquium was held, which brought astronomical, archeological, and literary arguments to bear solely on this issue. The inconclusive results suggest that a great many more data will be required before the issue can be narrowed much further.[33] The relentless chipping away at the Venus Tablets evidence means that some day their fault line will be reached and they will crumble under the onslaught. When this happens, it will be time to wonder why the mystique lasted so long.[34]

V

Much evidence suggests that Assyria was ruled by a long line of rulers who succeeded one another without serious breaks. A complete list of these rulers was slow to unfold. Until 1921, when Weidner published an inscription that added numerous further names, only a few rulers before Aššur-bil-nišešu (now no. 69 on the list!) were known.[35] Finally, in 1942/43 the Khorsabad King List was published, which contained 117 names from before 2000 BC to the seventh century BCE. This list, and a few others since published, have become the backbone of Mesopotamian chronology. They measure up well to the fragmentary lists of eponyms that have survived, and from the time of Šamši-Adad I, a known contemporary of Hammurabi, they present few peculiarities of any consequence. If the intensity of the study of Mesopotamian chronology remained high, its limits are permanently constrained by the Assyrian evidence, which has become the default arbiter of most chronological arguments.[36] Those that did not, or could not be made to, fit with the list were inevitably weakened or rejected ipso facto.

Do the Assyrian kinglists have the load-bearing capacity for this onus? In general, the answer is yes. Except for its earliest parts, which have no broad chronological implications in any case, the Assyrian King List is one of the most plausible such lists in the public domain, and the few problems are not sufficient to undermine its general credibility. There are no rulers with unacceptably long reigns, no genealogical filiations that defy biology, no names that are wildly incongruent with the general nomenclature. In short there are no substantial prima facie grounds for rejecting the Assyrian kinglists. At the same time their very value dictates that they be scrutinized regularly for signs of weakness.[37]

Nonetheless, a few knotty issues arise. From ruler no. 67 all the reign lengths are included, but two rulers (nos. 84 and 85) are given no years of rule, and we also meet a pair of rulers (nos. 65 and 66) whose regnal lengths have been broken off all copies of the list. Taking the evidence to indicate that rulers 84 and 85 ruled only a very short time, dead-reckoning back to ruler 67 will be as accurate as the kinglists' evidence. At this point, this technique loses its applicability, unless reign lengths can be assigned to rulers 65 and 66. Arno Poebel, the editor of the Khorsabad King List set an unfortunate precedent when he assigned these two rulers zero time on the grounds that the missing portions "must have" indicated as much—as the result of his own "calculations."[38]

Rulers 42 to 47 create the greatest challenge, being recorded in the kinglists as ruling *tuppišu*, a term usually taken to represent zero elapsed time, so all six rulers are held to have occupied a handful of years at most, thus effectively denying any chronological significance to almost one-tenth of the Assyrian rulers (nos. 42-47, 65, 66, 84, 85). The appeal of this expedient is obvious, even though no independent evidence requires it. It helped Poebel fit the kinglist evidence into the low chronology he espoused and it effectively eliminates our ignorance of ten reign lengths as a complicating issue in the debate, and banished the specter of leaving Assyrian chronology high and dry before the sixty-seventh ruler.

There is no escaping the unpalatable fact that rational explanations are compromised when the kinglists record six consecutive *tuppišu* periods. This leaves several hypotheses temporarily viable:

[1] that these rulers were all rivals for the throne, but that this was the only time in Assyrian history that this occurred and also the only time that the kinglists mentioned contending rulers by name.

[2] that five of the six names (ruler 47 excepted) existed at various other times but were collocated to show a time of troubles just before the establishment of a new ruling dynasty

[3] that *tuppišu* actually was meant to convey a sense of indeterminacy because the tenures of these six rulers (and two later ones) became lost during the many centuries that the Assyrian King Lists were expanded and recopied.

Two of these suggest that the kinglists are encrypted in ways that have so far escaped us, and all imply that a determinable chronology before ruler no. 48 is presently impossible, leaving entirely nugatory the value of the Assyrian King Lists in dating Šamši-Adad I and his contemporary, the linchpin Hammurabi. If Assyrian chronology underpins that of Mesopotamia after the late fifteenth century BCE, the reverse is true before that time.

The zero-year expedient is recognizably utilitarian then. Less congenially, nowhere in recorded history has there been another instance where six, or even four or five, rulers successively occupied a throne for less than a year in total. These alone are grounds for treating the zero option as divorced from reality. But regarding the six named rulers as contenders for the throne who were quickly eliminated opens a pandora's box—that the kinglists are not always a record of consecutive reigns. Of course, it is possible to evade the issue by declining to offer dates for a period earlier than the latest *tuppišu* rulers, recognizing the dilemma, but not the need to resolve it in the present state of the evidence.

VI

One of the most intriguing features of this vast literature is the gusto with which so much of it is permeated. Poole, whose attempt to create an epigraphic chronology of Egypt was radical, had no compunction that he was right. Subsuming several dynasties into XII Dynasty, he assured his readers that "this is now so well proved that it cannot admit of the least doubt."[39] It has been doubted ever since. In a paper in which each dynasty paraded after its predecessor with no overlap, Langdon wrote with similar panache: the accuracy of the date of 2474 BCE for the founding of Ur III "seems indisputable . . . [t]he names of nearly all the kings from 4200 onward are ascertained, and the lengths of the dynasties established, except for small margins of uncertainty in two cases." From 3188 BCE "there is no longer much uncertainty in fixing the chronology of Sumer and Accad; . . ."[40]

Hot on the heels of the first analyses of the Venus Tablets, Thureau-Dangin revisited early Mesopotamian chronology. After offering five alternatives, he wrote that "there are only two possible solutions, B [Hammurabi, 2003-1961 BCE] and B' [Hammurabi, 2011-1969 BCE], and B is clearly more probable than B'." Thus Thureau-Dangin felt competent to choose between alternatives only eight years apart.[41] In 1931 J.H. Breasted was no less confident about Egyptian chronology; suitable restoration of the Turin kinglist should result in "recover[ing] the chronology and history of early dynastic Egypt with some approach to finality."[42] In 1946 Böhl argued that "all chronologcal difficulties would be removed" by accepting dates of 1748-1716 BCE for Hammurabi's contemporary Šamši-Adad of Assyria.[43] Two years later Goossens was slightly more circumspect about Mesopotamian chronology: "[t]he date of 1531 [BCE] for the end of the First Dynasty of Babylon is not *absolutely* certain," he admitted, but patently held no doubts himself.[44]

Ten years later S.A. Pallis surveyed in excruciating detail the scholarship between 1884 and 1929 regarding Mesopotamian chronology. He looked at nine attempts to date the founding of the First Dynasty of Babylon from 2232 BCE to 2040 BCE, but rejected them all. He concluded that "[a]ll that is left to me, then, is to try to strike out a path for myself."[45] Accepting no overlap between this dynasty and the Sealand dynasty, he felt "fully justified" in adding a tenth date, 2185 BC, to the nine he had surveyed, and he placed Hammurabi at 2083-2041 BC.[46] Pallis' timing proved to be exquisitely unfortunate. Although he regarded his datings as "definitive," his calculations disappeared root and stem almost at once.[47] With the Mari discoveries and the publication of the Khorsabad King List beginning in the very same year in which his own work appeared, everything changed. Since then Hammurabi has never been seriously dated earlier than ca. 1900 BCE, and sometimes as late as the seventeenth century.

VII

William Foxwell Albright picked up where Pallis left off, and his resoluteness marks him as a handy exemplum. Albright nominated himself as a sort of rapporteur on chronological matters. In quick order he published a trio of updates on chronology as it was affected by ongoing excavations and reinterpretations. In the first, he dated Hammurabi to "about 1870 B.C. . . . some eighty years later," he noted, "than the latest hitherto proposed date." Although he considered this reduction to be "drastic," he was confident that it provided "a solid framework into which to fit our new data as they come from the excavator's *chantier* and from the scholar's study."[48]

Just two years later Albright was obliged to rethink things. He remained sure that now "[t]he Assyrian chronological data are . . . sufficiently precise and detailed to allow a very satisfactory system to be set up." But Hammurabi had to relocate again, this time to "about 1800 B.C," even though Albright feared that this date "may seem sensationally low to historians and Orientalists."[49] In the end Albright was satisfied: "[i]t is clear that the new chronological scheme which we have set up, is the only possible one, allowing for a scope of error which may amount to as much as a half century but which is probably not over twenty or thirty years."[50]

Less than three years later Albright changed his views and took Hammurabi along for yet another ride. The publication of the Khorsabad King List prompted the next round of evanescent certitude. Relying on Poebel, Albright calculated that these data dated Šamši-Adad I to the middle of the eighteenth century BCE. For more precision Albright turned to the Venus Tablets, and declared that "we . . . must place Hammurabi 1728-1686 B.C."[51] Once again, Albright closed on a triumphant note. "There can be no doubt that the Mari documents and the Khorsabad List make a really organic picture of the historical evolution of the ancient Near East possible for the first time. Henceforth ancient Near-Eastern history becomes *history*, not merely a congeries of more or less refractory data."[52]

By the 1940s Albright was a seasoned veteran of the chronology wars. As early as 1921 he had published a list of Assyrian rulers in which he inferred rulers to suit his hypothesis, muddled the sequence, and dated Šamši-Adad over 300 years earlier than he was later to do. He criticized Weidner for dating the Kassite dynasty remarkably closely to today's opinion, and ended his argument with the claim that the dating he espoused was "practically certain."[53] Only three years later he was at it again. This time he was writing because "the situation is radically changed again, with the suddenness we have learned to expect in such matters." This was a good thing, because "the various statements of the [ancient] Assyrian historiographers [now] become quite harmonious, and it is no longer necessary to resort to the somersaults of which we have all been guilty."[54]

For Albright the solution was deceptively simple. If all synchronisms before the fifteenth century were discarded, "all difficulties seem to vanish automatically!"[55] He began by accepting most of the durations between rulers mentioned in later inscriptions—and asserted that "round numbers [in sources] are almost never too low." He reconstructed the Assyrian royal line after Šamši-Adad I in a way that was quickly refuted by new evidence; had Nineveh as "a religious center of the Mitannian state;" dated Šamši-Adad I "about a century after the close" of the First Dynasty of Babylon; argued that the Sealand dynasty ruled all Babylonia and that its founder reigned "certainly after the fall of the First Dynasty and the retirement of the Hittites;" regarded any overlap between the Babylon and Kassite dynasties as "an incredible supposition," and invented a second Kassite dynasty to account for some stray royal names.[56]

Albright was exemplary in providing updated overviews of a kaleidoscopically changing situation, but in matters chronological he was wrong far more often in his long career than he was right.[57] He must have realized this, and it would not seem too much to expect that, as he kept revising himself, he would learn to curb his discourse and temper his enthusiasm for the latest hypothesis, which, his own experience should have reminded him, was likely soon to need revising. Instead of looking back on his own record, which comprised at least four different dates for the accession of Hammurabi (2123/1870/1800/1728 BCE), he repeatedly professed to being certain that each revision was to be his last one. And eventually it was; when he finally settled on lowest of his choices, he maintained it vigorously and frequently against the claims of the middle and long chronologies until the end of his career.

VIII

The authors of the latest assault on Mesopotamian chronological orthodoxy waste no time in challenging interpretations of the Assyrian King List evidence. They begin by arguing that "none of the regnal lengths cited for the period before the middle of the eleventh century can be verified by other evidence."[58] Their aim is to test the middle chronology dating (ca. 1813-1781 BCE) for Šamši-Adad I, Hammurabi's contemporary. In the absence of evidence either way, they approach this by a series of lowest-choice arguments. They posit a lunar year calendar in Assyria before 1114 BCE, and with it a reduction of 21 years. They continue by arguing that the term *tuppišu* assigned to several Assyrian rulers signifies zero years. Since this is the common opinion, this saves nothing in their scheme. When the various kinglists have discrepant reign lengths, they choose the lowest, reducing, for instance, the reign assigned Išme-Dagan I, son of Šamši-Adad I from 40 years to 11.

When the dust clears, Šamši-Adad is redated to ca. 1719-1688 BCE and Hammurabi to ca. 1696-1654 BCE, 96 years later than the middle chronology and 32 years later than even the low chronology.[59] Gasche et al find useful elbow room in, and add to, recent reinterpretations of the Venus Tablet data. These release modern scholarship from choosing from a very limited—if still too broadly distributed—list of dates, with acceptable dates now available at eight-year intervals, so Gasche et al's task, and the task of any others, is simply to be sure that they choose that eighth year that serves their purposes best.[60]

This effort constitutes the most extended challenge to the high/middle/low triad in nearly sixty years, just when the matter seemed to have settled down to arguing differences of a few years or decades. Gasche et al point out several weak spots in traditional chronological arguments. For instance, they uncouple Muršiliš's capture of Babylon from the end of First Dynasty, events which, they note, are "nowhere directly connected in ancient sources" but result from a modern need for benchmarks. On the other hand—and the authors do not deny it—their interpretation is tied to a series of choices designed to push the envelope.

More troublesome, the authors rely heavily on an imputed continuity of pottery styles to jump-start their case. The relationship between pottery remains and human dynamics is notoriously controversial and is considerably more subjective even than most other forms of archeological interpretation. Such statements as "that [ceramic] material nevertheless suggests that the Middle Chronology is too long by something on the order of 100 years" are problematic and reflect the authors' idiosyncratic sense of pottery use as much as it does any independent evidence.[61]

The temper of their case is somewhat compromised, and certainly constrained, by their final paragraph:

> . . . every piece of evidence with historical significance from the Near East belonging to the earlier part of the second millennium and dated by reference to Babylonian chronology will have to be adapted. This includes, but is by no means limited to, evidence for the relevant Elamite dynasties, the Old Hittite Kingdom, and the Levant in the Middle Bronze Age. The repercussions are therefore far-reaching. An analysis of them, however, is beyond the scope of the present investigation, as is any analysis of the chronological relationship between the activities of Tuthmoses I and Muršili I in Syria and the number and lengths of the generations that separated Muršili I and Tudhaliya I.[62]

Here, as if preordained, is the familiar heady language of the field, implying that others will be as convinced as they are—odd given their self-proclaimed role as devil's advocates.[63]

IX

The study of ancient Near East chronology is an epistemological purgatory. It is not possible even to capture the latest orthodoxy in toto, nor to claim finality in even a single case before ca. 700 BCE, if not later. Despite two centuries of ebb and flow, assertion and retraction, hope and despair, despite the tremendous accretion of evidence, the editor of an inventory of early Mesopotamian inscriptions, could still make the chastening observation that "[o]f the nearly sixty rulers represented by inscriptions in this volume, we are certain of the length of the reign of only one . . ."[64] Since the accumulation of evidence is responsible, it allows progress toward a final solution, even if that will remain a chimera barring the most miraculous of eventualities. One consequence is that authors routinely use one chronological system or another with no hint that there are differences of opinion, and carry out non-chronological arguments wielding different dates.

Discussions of ancient Near East chronology resemble panels in a geodesic dome. Sometimes, changing opinions have little ripple effect, but most are interconnected and proposed changes need to meet global as well as local specifications. Perhaps the first footnote of any article in which dates appear should carry an appropriate warning, however tiresome this might seem to the combatants. The phase of the study ending in 1940 now seems like prestidigitation. We encounter hundreds of textual and astronomical calculations, culminating in Pallis's efforts to fix datings in the third millennium.[65] This posturing took place in contexts where authors were either suggesting or reporting rectifications of previous chronological systems, sometimes their own. Yet not a single conclusion regarding absolute chronology from that period is deemed correct today.

Yet these were largely good faith efforts grounded in some part of the available evidence, often showing ingenuity, if also relying on problematic data and retrocalculation. The discovery of certain synchronisms in the Mari evidence and the publication of the Khorsabad King List created one of those paradigm shifts that we have become familiar with. Everything *did* change around 1940, but the debates continue to this day, more circumscribed to be sure, but no less fierce—and no more conclusive.

In sum, it is easy to agree in principle with Manning when he writes that "[a] fixed correlation is all that is necessary. However, when available, it is quite likely we will find neither the High, Middle nor Low chronologies to be right; instead a new chronology will begin to emerge independent of the unsatisfactory Venus Tablets, and the contradictory king-lists."[66] It is harder to imagine what piece of evidence could be uncovered that would tell us—once and for all—just when Hammurabi succeeded his father Sinmuballit as ruler of Babylon. Experience has shown that Manning's "when" is optimistic, simply the latest in a long, and ultimately fruitless, litany of similar expectations.

This continuing vulnerability is illustrated by asking a series of hypothetical (but not impossible) questions. What if a tablet from Mari should mention an identifiable Egyptian ruler? What if evidence for longer reigns for, say, three XII Dynasty rulers than otherwise attested should come to hand? What if an inscription of a person not named Hammurabi, but who is described as the son of Sinmuballit should be discovered? Or what if a record showing Sargon of Agade and Gudea of Lagash (now placed about two centuries apart) to be contemporaries came to light? None of these is likely, but discoveries just like them have necessitated many a pratfall in the past and, as we are well aware, both the past and its study have the habit of repeating aspects of themselves.[67] Despite this, will we continue to assert confidently time and again that certain dates are incontrovertible?[68] The number of dogmatic assertions that pepper the literature of the past century or so—of which the examples cited here are but a tiny fraction—serves only to remind us that assurance is not a trait lacking in those interested in this subject. Still, and despite the aura of déjà vu all over again, evidence for ancient Near East chronology continues, if often fitfully, to converge, but not quite on a single focal point.[69] The astigmatism remains uncorrected, but the prescription is getting better.[70]

14

RULE LIFE VS. REAL LIFE

... if we assume that one of the four Venus chronologies is
correct, the odds favoring the Long chronology over the other
three are about 10000 to 1. If we drop the assumption that one
of them must be true, we still can assert that the Long
[chronology] is correct, with a probability of error below 1%.

Chronology and astronomy are forced to tinker up and reconcile, as well as they can, those uncertainties. This satisfies the
learned—but what should we think of the reign of George the
second to be calculated two thousand years hence by eclipses,
lest the conquest of Canada should be ascribed to James the first?

I

In 1994 A.T. Fomenko published a two-volume work with the imposing title
*Empirico-Statistical Analysis of Narrative Material and Its Application to
Historical Dating*, in which he called for a revision of "some important ancient
historical events."[1] This was modestly put indeed. Fomenko had Nero as a con-
temporary of the Holy Roman Emperor Henry IV, the later Roman Emperor
Arcadius, the legendary Roman king Tullius Hostilius, and the Merovingian
Pepin II, and placed events described in the New Testament in eleventh-century
Italy.[2] Fomenko conceded that the narratives to which he applied his techniques
are "really very complicated, multifaceted and sometimes subjectively embel-

lished material," but claimed that mathematics "is capable of giving a new vantage point from which to view the problem of chronology."[3]

The advent of new technologies forces historians to make uninformed decisions far too often. When an author whose business affiliation is the Institut für Mittelenergiephysik disagrees with an author whose address is the Nuclear Structure Research Laboratory, what is the historian to do but follow his own predilections? Yet historians now depend increasingly on a wide assortment of scientists for information about the past. Now we must consult, and try to understand and trust, astronomers and geophysicists for details of eclipse paths; physicists for particulars about wiggles in radiocarbon dating; epidemiologists for details about how diseases spread; geneticists for DNA results from preserved body parts; metallurgists for the properties and provenances of ancient coins; etc., etc.

II

William Whiston knew full well that eclipses were natural phenomena, but he was unable to rid himself of the thrall to his beliefs, and thought of an earlier solar eclipse in these terms: "[t]h[is] Eclipse of the Sun, . . . appears now to have been a divine Signal for the End of over-bearing Persecution in the ten idolatrous and persecuting Kingdoms, which arose in the fifth century in the *Roman* Empire, the *Britains* and the *Saxons*."[4] Today eclipses have become a kind of god from the machine rather than, as for Whiston, from the heavens.

Even so, historians often turn to astronomical dating in hopes of gaining precision. The aim is to combine the objective celestial evidence from astronomy with otherwise undated terrestrial events. Each time this is done successfully, the event is dated, which is often confused with proof of its actuality. Hundreds of entries in the historical record mention what could be an eclipse of the sun, but seldom present the phenomena in these terms. Instead they refer in some diagnostic way to a darkening of the sky during daylight hours. The presumption is that some kind of solar eclipse must account for the description. The parade of examples showing the record to be frequently false has not discouraged historians and astronomers from continuing to search for eclipses and using them to date actual and imagined events almost to the minute.

III

Much scientific attention has been paid to dating the crucifixion of Christ. Josef Blinzler listed over one hundred scholars who had chosen dates between 21 CE and 36 CE for the Crucifixion.[5] Each of these held no doubt about his choice. As one of them put it: "Friday, April 7, 30 A.D. is established as firmly as any date in ancient history."[6] One of the most elaborate attempts to date the crucifixion using eclipse data is that of C.J. Humphreys and W.G. Waddington, published in a widely-read scientific journal. "We have sought to reconcile the documentary evidence that exists with our reconstruction of the Jewish calendar and we have used calculations of the occurrence of a lunar eclipse which, if accepted, allow the day, month, and year of the Crucifixion to be determined precisely."[7] That day, they conclude, was Friday, 3 April 33 CE.

The first step in judging these exercises is to determine whether the Gospel references to "darkness" are astronomical, atmospheric, allegorical, or alleged. Problems also arise with the word "lunar." Matthew and Mark speak only of a darkening, whereas Luke attributes this to a darkening of the *sun*. Humphreys and Waddington refer to this disagreement only in a codicil to their paper, and then only to rely on the undefended—and indefensible—argument that a scribe "wrongly amended the text [about a lunar eclipse] to refer to a solar eclipse."[8] Humphreys and Waddington eliminate eleven of the twelve lunar eclipses they claim were visible in Jerusalem during the time in question. They ignore the biblical data that Christ was born before Herod died (in 4 BCE) and lived 33 years, but their real failure is to evade mentioning that opinions diverge widely as to just what the evangelists' word actually mean.[9]

Why do no gospels refer to a lunar eclipse, they wonder. Besides scribal incompetence, it is because "[t]he gospel writers were not primarily interested in providing clues for chronologists[!]"[10] Humphreys and Waddington do not consider that such references are neither to eclipses nor to real events, but are allegories designed to strengthen the case for the faithful. As Raymond Brown put it: "[d]iscussion of this issue makes sense only if we assume that the evangelists are reliable for the minimal chronological references that they all . . . supply, namely, that Jesus died in Jerusalem on a day before the Sabbath at Passover time during the prefecture of Pontius Pilate."[11]

Precise astronomical dating requires demonstrating that the relevant sources are equally precise and correct. Although Brown believes in the historicity of much Gospel testimony, he is reasonable enough to ask "whether any of the evangelists had personal knowledge of the precise day on which Jesus died." He continues that "[o]ne can doubt that without descending into the nihilism of assuming that no writer knew or cared about anything that happened in Jesus' passion."[12] If granted, this argument renders it wasteful even to pretend to arrive at a precise date for the crucifixion.

IV

A 68-page essay on the chronology of ancient China appeared in 1999.[13] Replete as it is with tables and arcane astronomical arguments, it seems churlish to resist accepting it as definitive. In fact, it is only the latest salvo in a barrage of publications about this very question, about which opinion is riotously divided. This interest is almost entirely a modern phenomenon, and has been inspired by the possibilities of astronomical dating. When Sima Qian compiled his monumental history of China to his own time, ca. 100 BCE, he addressed the issue of providing dates for the earliest times because "[w]hen I examine their calendrical records, . . . the ancient writings are all different; completely contradictory!"[14] He decided to provide no dates before 841 BCE.

More recently. Joseph Needham expressed similar reservations about the value and use of astronomical data: "[t]he success of this has depended on the source from which the observations were taken; when the historical records were reliable, as from the Former Han period [second-first centuries BCE] onwards, the results were valuable; but when weight was placed on texts of the semi-legendary period, . . . the results were not, and only served to discredit Chinese materials. No small amount of paper and ink has been wasted by writers and computers whose sinological basis was highly insecure."[15]

The quest that Needham found chimerical was already proceeding apace, however. The early written sources offer various datings for the Xia, Shang, and Zhou dynasties. I will concentrate here on the debate over the end of Shang and the beginning of Zhou, for which three dates have been retrocalculated—the equivalents of 1122, 1051/50, and 1028/27 BCE. The first emanates from the second century BCE, while the second derives from a later recension of a document discovered, we are told, in 281 CE in the tomb of a ruler who had died almost 600 years earlier, and has come to be known as the *Bamboo Annals*. The third derives from fragments of an earlier version of the *Bamboo Annals,* as cited in other extant sources. No outsider can pass sensible judgment on the arguments over the authenticity and reliability of the *Bamboo Annals*, but anyone familiar with the topos of the "found" document must be uncomfortable with the story of their discovery.

Given the volume of published arguments, any discussion must be selective. Between 1924 and 1932 Léopold de Saussure provided a thoroughgoing treatment of the subject and concluded that 1044 BCE was most likely the date of the advent of Zhou.[16] In turn, C.W. Bishop rejected astronomical data on the grounds that many of them were "interpolations dating from a time when Chinese astronomers had learned how to calculate them backward," but he did conclude that "it would seem reasonable—in fact almost definitely determined—that the founding of the Chou dynasty took place during the middle of the eleventh century B.C."[17] These cautious views did not go unchallenged. W.P. Yetts proposed a date of 991 BCE for the end of Shang, perhaps the latest date ever seriously suggested.[18] Bernhard Karlgren criticized this dating, and Yetts later argued for a date of ca. 1050 BCE.[19] The following year, Karlgren himself argued for 1027 BCE, calling it "a comparatively very well documented date."[20]

Nor were Chinese and Japanese scholars idle, advancing dates of 1111, 1066, 1062, 1055, and 1018 BCE. Ong judged that "none of these reconstructed chronologies is satisfactory or acceptable" and that "the question of both chronologies remains unresolved," But he still preferred that some choice be made: "[f]or the sake of simplicity, scholars would be wise to follow either the orthodox chronology [1122 BCE] or the calculation [1027 BCE] based on the genuine" *Bamboo Annals*.[21] Ping-ti Ho was less ambivalent; basing himself on information in the *Bamboo Annals* and apparently independent data that could be construed to support this dating, he concluded that the excerpted *Bamboo Annals* date of "1027 B.C. should certainly be accepted as the absolute date for the year of the Chou conquest."[22]

V

Before more than a few years had passed, all these postulated dates were challenged by a spate of astronomical datings that rejected both 1122 BCE and 1027 BCE in favor of a range of dates clustered between the two. David Keightley's discussion of the *Bamboo Annals* was the first act in this new play, although hardly of a piece with what followed. Keightley was frank and direct: "I should like to propose . . . that such emphasis on the *Chi-nien* [*Bamboo Annals*] as a source for Shang-Chou chronology is probably misplaced."[23] Keightley feared that there were errors of transmission from the now-lost original *Bamboo Annals* to later citations of its contents, and that "there was probably nothing reliable to transmit in the first place."[24] Keightley cataloged anomalies, anachronisms, confusions, and outright errors in the extant versions of the *Bamboo Annals*, and raised pertinent questions about why and how the chronological data could have been accurately preserved for so long. He closed with a piece of advice: "[t]o rely upon the *Chi-nien* chronology simply 'because it is there' is unjustifiable."[25]

Keightley's admonitions were repudiated on all sides. Three years later Edward Shaughnessy investigated the conquest date on the basis of another early source, the *Yizhoushu*, which he believed "Confucian obscurantism" had unfairly caused to be maligned and underused. Relying on its astronomical information, Shaughnessy arrived at an entirely new date, 1045 BCE, for the conquest. More than that; the culminating battle was fought on 15 January of that year.[26] A year later David Pankenier begged to differ, once again on astronomical grounds. Pankenier's interest was piqued by a reference in the *Guoyu,* a third-century BCE source, to "a particular alignment of Mercury, Jupiter, the sun, and the moon" near the time of the Zhou conquest. For Pankenier these were "what appear to be actual astronomical observations made at the time the conquest campaign was mounted."[27] Pankenier was familiar with Keightley's warning, and asserted that he would "rely heavily on the *Bamboo Annals*," in ways that would palliate Keighley's concerns.[28]

Sounding not at all like Keightley in the event, Pankenier proclaimed that he would "vindicate" not only the original fragmentary version of the *Bamboo Annals*, but the "less well authenticated" later version, which dated the conquest to 1051 BCE, and would "provide the first true astronomical dates for events in this early period."[29] Pankenier did this by finding a planetary conjunction that seemed to conform to the description in the *Guoyu*, and which he dated to 28 May 1059 BCE. After discussing possible accession year and regnal length usages and much labored exegesis, Pankenier concluded that it is "quite evident" that the final conquest took place on 20 January 1046 BCE.[30]

Pankenier then sought to establish the date of the foundation of the Shang dynasty on similar grounds. He found an "astonishing" result—the *Bamboo Annals* record a similar planetary conjunction "in exactly the right year," which served as a portent for the imminent overthrow of the Xia dynasty. Using this almost astrologically, Pankenier calculated a date for the end of the Xia dynasty, 1554 BCE.[31] Pankenier hinted that more calculations could be in store, perhaps extending back to the mythical period of Chinese history, based on his "establishment of strategic footholds based on astronomical fact."[32]

Sharp on Pankenier's heels came David Nivison. Nivison too regarded the *Bamboo Annals* as a reliable guide, if only certain modifications were introduced.[33] These would be based partly on astronomical evidence and partly on yet another reinterpretation of the early sources. When he had finished, Nivison concluded along with Shaughnessy that the final battle of the conquest was fought on 15 January 1045. BCE Nivison asked himself: "[h]ow firm is this result? What, if anything, could cause me to change my opinion?" His answer was that: "I must continue to think that I am right, unless I am persuaded that the "Wu ch'eng" dates are faked, *and* some incompatible dates are correct; *or* that my analysis of lunar phase terms is wrong, *and* some incompatible analysis is correct. . . . I would need to be shown an analysis that accounted satisfactorily for all known dated inscriptions. I do not think that such a counterproof could be mounted that would be convincing enough to carry against all my other arguments, unless we have some new and quite surprising archaeological discoveries."[34]

All things considered, Nivison must have been seriously nonplussed when he found it necessary almost immediately to publish a research note in which he declared that "the date [of the conquest] must have been 1040."[35] Among other things. he concluded that some dates for Wen Wang, the Duke of Zhou, were not after all "beyond reasonable doubt," found that lunar eclipse data now corresponded better with this later date, and concluded, decidedly lamely, that "[o]ne of the more conjectural revisions of the chronology, probably accepted for many centuries during the Chou dynasty, must have had the date 1045."[36]

At about the same time, Pankenier published a note following up his earlier analysis of planetary clusters. If these presaged the fall of both Xia and Shang, then why not earlier, especially as he had located such a conjunction on 26 February 1953 BCE? As he noted, this date "is only thiry-six years from 1989 B.C., the date which the *Bamboo Annals* assigns to the founding of Xia!"[37] But 1953 is not just 36 years *from* 1989, it is 36 years *after*. This would remove it from portent status into that of coincidence, except that Pankenier decided that "we may conclude that Shun's fourteenth year was simultaneously the first *de jure* year of Yu the Great's reign as the founder of the Xia dynasty, or, in our terms, the year 1953 B.C.!"[38] Quod erat demonstrandum.

VI

Nivison, joined by Kevin Pang, took his own turn at pushing astronomical dating back beyond the Xia dynasty. Using the *Bamboo Annals,* but "correcting" them by 72 years to fit their hypothesis, Nivison and Pang constructed a new astronomically-based chronology in which Shun, the last of the mythical emperors, reigned from 1967 to 1917 BCE. and Yü founded the Xia dynasty three years later. They concluded that "[p]erhaps not only the Xia 'Dynasty,' but also Yü 'the Great,' and even the legendary 'Sage Emperor' Shun, are not myths (or not just myths) but in fact belong to precisely datable history."[39] They assisted their case by randomly interpolating two-year interrregna between several Xia rulers.

Several critiques followed Nivison's and Pang's contribution. A basic support for Pankenier's dating of Xia was that the planetary conjunction allegedly mentioned in the ancient records was so rare that the one must refer to the other. Huang Yi-long disagreed, calculating that such conjunctions visible to the naked eye occurred six times between 1973 BCE and 1497 BCE.[40] Huang's parameter (a maximum of 30° separation) was wider than those of Pankenier and others, which raises the issue of subjectivity and perception that shows that more than one answer is possible. In any case, Huang concluded on a pessimistic note: "[t]he five-planet conjunctions said in literary sources to have occurred in ancient times are mostly not records of actual observations, but were very possibly portents concocted by later writers to prove the theory of the mandate of heaven [and] one ought to be extremely careful in using them as important evidence for ancient chronology."[41]

Next came David Pankenier, who predictably found Nivison's and Pang's use of sources undependable.[42] He now regarded the *Bamboo Annals* with far less favor than they, arguing that it was riddled with interpolated astronomical calculations. He proposed a series of "safeguards" and claimed that Nivison's and Pang's results "clearly fail the test" he put to them. In particular, Pankenier thought it risible that the Chinese understood "celestial mechanics and eclipse prediction" in 1900 BCE.[43]

Zhang Peiyu, the next respondent, assumed that the oracle bones' corroboration of late Shang dynastic history could be extrapolated. As a result, "the scholarly world now generally [sic] assumes that the Xia genealogy . . . must also have a historical basis." He went on that, by "[u]sing scientific methods, . . . it is possible to reconstruct and pinpoint the date of some historical events." Zhang was not sure though that Nivison and Pang had done this right; perhaps they had been too arbitrary in their "corrections." The chronology in the reconstructed *Bamboo Annals* is "the result of willful manipulation on the part of its re-editors."[44]

Zhang felt that the eclipse record of 1876 BCE noted below, so crucial for astronomical dating schemes, had "evol[ved]" for a purpose. He went on to calculate that there had been 128 solar eclipses visible in the relevant area between 2166 and 1860 BCE, too many to extract one to match the historical record. Worse yet, the one Nivison and Pang chose had a magnitude of 0.38, invisible even with foreknowledge. On the basis of regnal lengths in various sources, he dated Xia's beginning to ca. 2120 BCE, earlier than any of the astronomical datings, and nearly as early as the largely discarded traditional date of 2205 BCE. He favored three eclipses and three planetary conjunctions as most likely to fit, reversing the procedures of the other contributors to the debate.[45]

Nivison and Pang, who responded separately, were unmoved. Culling through the sources, Nivison found "a textual record" of exactly what he is looking for— a reference to an occasion where "the sun and moon did not meet harmoniously," and decided that it refers to an annular eclipse. He lighted on "October 16, 1876 B.C" as "the only correct date" for this.[46] He noted that the data in the *Bamboo Annals* differ slightly from the result of his own calculations, but brushed this aside. Pang closed the multilateral discussion by claiming that "[t]he traditional dates for the beginning of Xia [2205 BCE] and the extraordinary floods that occurred at the time of Yao and Shun require drastic revision."[47] Pang, an astronomer, overlooked that many scholars of early China have revised Yao and Shun and the entire Xia dynasty out of existence, and with it any need to date any events associated with it.

VII

In his study of the sources for Western Zhou, Shaughnessy remained sanguine: "[s]ober-minded historians would almost surely advise me to follow Sima's lead [no dates before 841 BCE] and be content with a relative chronology that does not insist on precision. Nevertheless, I am firmly convinced . . . that an absolute chronology is desirable and, eventually, if not yet, possible."[48] Regarding anything as "essential" is remarkably often prelude to finding it. Shaughnessy devoted seventy pages to the quest. He indicated the dimensions of the problem by listing twenty-two different datings between 1127 and 1018 BCE advanced or supported by nearly forty scholars. Having discussed fifteen criteria for evaluation, Shaughnessy regarded the planetary conjunction of 1059 BCE as "[t]he foundation to any solution."[49] Ultimately, he decided that 1045 BCE, the year he had advanced earlier, and which Nivison had first espoused and then divorced, "best satisfies all of the evidence with a claim to historical validity." Still, he was slightly cautious: "the chronology proposed here, though likely not the final word on the topic, can be used with some confidence . . ."[50]

In her review of Shaughnessy's *Sources of Western Zhou History* Sarah Allan contended that his "absolute chronology" is "demonstrably incorrect." She based her assessment on an inscription which she dated to the reign of Mu Wang, the most celebrated ruler of Western Zhou. If Allan is right, the information on the inscription would date it to 999 BCE, much too early for any of the astronomically-based end-of-Shang dates.[51] In fact, the only dating system this fits comfortably is, of all things, the traditional dating of the fall of Shang to 1122 BCE and the reign of Mu Wang to 1001 to 947 BCE.

In the midst of this industrial-strength improvisation, Noel Barnard offered a challenge. "Sinological researchers into the astronomical data and the problems of pre-Han chronology as recorded in ancient literary sources have expended great effort in mastering the science and mathematics of astronomy. Unfortunately there is apt to be a lack of comparable attention to crucial aspects of the data as they appear in the transmitted Chinese literary records."[52] Barnard went on to discuss the authenticity of the *Bamboo Annals*, and their "easy acceptance" by those who argue for the their accuracy without succeeding in demonstrating it.[53] Barnard reminded readers that the *Bamboo Annals* have no visible provenance before the end of the third century CE.

Barnard concluded with a point that apparently is not obvious: "[w]hen it comes to using 'portent data,' of which eclipses are just one type, the researcher should attempt to establish beyond question the historicity of the event. If this preliminary step is not taken, the time and effort spent on the astronomical side of the research and writing is not only wasted but may also create misapprehensions in the field of astronomy studies itself."[54]

VIII

A uniting thread in these efforts is the way in which evidence is handled. Throughout, there is an unexamined, and largely undefended, belief in the sources. Despite this, there has been a grudging, but nevertheless effective, acceptance by non-scientists on grounds of an inability to criticize the techniques themselves. As one Sinologist put it: "We are awed by the scholarship of all their arguments."[55]

What is the historian to do, beyond being awed? It is easy to be persuaded by the first argument met, but what happens when the historian meets the next appeal to astronomy? And the next? And these are all different? What, for instance, is the non-astronomer to make of the discrepancies in Huang's and Zhang's separate determinations of possibly relevant planetary conjunctions? Each found a large number of five-planet conjunctions that could match the historical record, but the two sets of calculations—and therefore the two sets of results—diverge widely even though the criterion (30° of separation or less) was the same. Between 1973 BCE and 1497 BCE, Huang showed conjunctions in 1973, 1953, 1813, 1734, and 1535. For the same period Zhang showed over twice as many: 1973, 1953, 1951, 1913, 1875, 1813, 1772, 1734, 1716, 1674, 1576, and 1535. Moreover, the exact degree of measured separation differed in four of the five common examples.[56]

The historian who runs across one or the other of these studies is likely to be impressed—and perhaps persuaded—by the surfeit of exact calculations that characterize them. The historian who stumbles across both of these (and perhaps there are others?) will be disabused of the comforting but unsupportable notion that both science and scientists are necessarily both objective and specific.

The outpouring of ingenuity, enthusiasm, and determination in support of three dates that are only six years apart might seem unprofitable, but it is by no means uninteresting. The fact that three superficially plausible cases have been developed, no more than one of which can possibly be correct, is consequential for the viewpoint of the present overall argument. Most consequential of all is that, with the exception of Nivison's seceding from himself, none of the combatants has shown the slightest inclination to be moved by the best arguments of any of the others. Once Nivison, Pankenier, and Shaughnessy formalized their arguments, they have stalwartly adhered to them.[57] Pankenier summed up this aspect of the case forthrightly: "[n]othing has occurred [since 1981] to prompt me to revise [my] view;" indeed, further research "has strongly reinforced t[he] conclusion" that the Shang dynasty ended in 1046 BCE, rather than one year or six years later, or at any other time.[58]

IX

As with astronomy, so with dendrochronology, the study of tree rings. M.G.L. Baillie tries to establish its importance as a dating technique, arguing that it is "difficult . . . to date anything pre-*c.* 800 B.C. with any reliability other than by dendrochronology."[59] Using tree-ring calibrations, Baillie produces new datings for Egypt, China, even Ireland.[60] By his reckoning, for instance, the end of the New Kingdom in Egypt would be dated nearly a century earlier than all other evidence requires.[61]

As aberrant a conclusion concerns Baillie's dating of the Shang dynasty. Relying on only one source, Baillie speaks of "the so-called 'traditional' dates for the Shang" from 1617 to 1122 BCE, even though the traditional date for the establishment of the dynasty is 1766 BCE.[62] Baillie needs a duration of 496 years because of one dendrochronological date; "frost rings in a new foxtail pine chronology, from the Sierra Nevada, at 1132 B.C." This, he enthuses, "was a marvellous revelation," and he hurries on to conclude that "the Shang dynasty can now be dated 1627-1132 B.C. *until proven otherwise.*"[63] Baillie appears completely unaware that his date for the end of the Shang dynasty conflicts with every single recently suggested astronomical and traditional date, just as he is unaware of the tribulation with his Egyptian chronology.

Turning from the forest to the skies in another work, Baillie further rearranges ancient chronology, this time to suit his theory of frequent cometary bombardments as reflected in the tree-ring record. Eventually, he addresses the absence of any of this in the historical record: "[w]e have seen that tree-rings and mythology and odd little footnotes allow the building of a fairly conclusive picture wherein the earth appears to have been affected by atmospheric loading associated with bombardment . . . So if this is correct and we were bombarded, why were we not told? Why would anyone want to suppress such information? Why, indeed? Let us see what we can come up with."

What Baillie comes up with is a conspiracy theory; he concludes that the events he hypothesizes were "mysteriously overlooked."[64] Baillie's god from the machine—that all he thinks happened really did happen, but all were neglected by all the sources—underscores, perhaps slightly extremely, the propensity to crush evidence under the weight of hypothesis. While scientists might be masters of their particular -ology, they have a penchant for eschewing science's rigorous standards rather than applying them to a discipline that merely fancies itself a science.

X

In his environmental interpretation of human history, Jared Diamond sets a lofty goal: "[t]he challenge now is to develop human history as a science, on a par with acknowledged historical sciences such as astronomy, geology, and evolutionary biology."[65] The goal is not only lofty but unattainable. Too often, scientists seem inclined to treat the documentary record in much the same way as they would treat physical phenomena, a mistake with implications. They write as if describing the results of a successful experiment—with assurance, expressing no doubts that, properly applied, their sophisticated techniques can resolve one chronological conundrum after another. In the process they pay scant regard to the range of sources, and none whatever to their complexities and contradictions. As a result, their expositions tend to be argumentative juggernauts that aim to bludgeon readers into either accepting them or feeling inadequate.

The hostilities between science and history encapsulate well the dilemmas that confront historians in the face of more, and more complicated, avenues to the past. We are not trained to understand either scientific argument or scientific proof, nor does it seem that scientists are well trained to appreciate the problematical aspects of historical evidence, where, unlike experimental science, they have no firm control of the variables. Nonetheless, scientists seem more willing to discredit historical argument than historians are to call into question scientific conclusions about historical matters. Baillie's revised chronology of several major events in recorded history encapsulates the notion that the accepted versions of history are grist for the mills of scientific endeavor. And even though Baillie's views have received a wider public hearing than those whose work he attempts to overturn, there is no appreciable evidence that historians care very much, as if ignoring other opinions is sufficient to render them harmless.

When scientists play the dating game, treating the historical record as no more problematic than their own laboratories, they act naively and ahistorically. By and large, they seem unaware that the likelihood that traces from the physical record actually reflect particular events that occasionally turn up in the historical record is infinitesimal. They do not ask how to distinguish between astronomical or meteorological phenomena observed, remembered, calculated, or borrowed because they fail even to see this as an issue. Given this estrangement in both thinking and in evidence, it behooves historians to treat scientific claims about chronology—and perhaps much else—very gingerly indeed. For us there can be no parsimony.

15

WHEN MIGHT MAKES WRONG

Strange, thought O'Neill, how a categorical statement can
immediately place a doubt.

[N]o word has a meaning *inseparably* attached to it; a word
means what the speaker intends by it, and what the hearer
understands by it, and that is all.

I

In 1999 millions of people laughed when the President of the United State publicly quibbled over the meaning of the word "is." Their amusement sprang
from the circumstances of the occasion, but also from an intuition that "is" cannot have too many variant meanings, and that the President was being uncharac-
teristically pedantic. No doubt he was, but this should be no argument that the
meanings that words convey, whether individually or *en ensemble*, do not matter
a great deal.

The great physicist Robert Boyle was careful to make this point to his readers:

> Perhaps you will wonder, . . . that in almost every one of the following
> essays I should speak so doubtingly, and use so often, *perhaps, it seems,*
> *it is not improbable*, and such other expressions, as argue a diffidence of
> the truth of the opinions I incline to, and that I should be so shy of laying

down principles, and sometimes of so much as venturing at explications. But I must freely confess to you, . . . that having met with many things, of which I could give myself no one probable cause, and some things, of which several causes may be assigned so differing, as not to agree in any thing, unless in their being all of them probable enough; I have often found such difficulties in searching into the cause and manner of things . . . that I dare speak confidently and positively of very few things, except of matters of fact.[1]

II

Historians do not create their evidence—we hope—but they have a lot of control over how it reaches the public domain. It is not how assiduous the historian is in amassing evidence, or how careful in assessing it, that matters, but the way he tells his story. Through his exposition, the historian's evidence becomes his readers' evidence. For the moment, "discourse" is the preferred word for this aspect of historiography. I use it here to mean the stylistic ways in which argument is communicated, and which will vary from person to person, one evidentiary situation to another, one language to another, and one audience to another.

Writers are urged to embrace the active voice, the indicative mood, the easily diagramable sentence. If their writing is crisp, the message will be lucid and convincing. This view treats discourse as a grammatical sharp knife cutting through warm historical butter and anathematizes most sentences in the present work. It is best applied to genres like fiction, where the author is in full command of his story. The crisp thought crisply expressed is more enemy than friend to the careful and cautious historian. In history-writing the impersonal construction, the passive voice, and the subjunctive mood each has its place, as do qualifying clauses or phrases and relevant asides. These parts of speech accommodate doubt, uncertainty, and nuance; without them history, at least in its writing, becomes reductive.

Authors envisage an audience before they write, but often change their targets as they proceed.[2] The idealized audience consists of four groups: those who already agree; those with slightly open minds, but who are likely to agree with the slightest nudge; those with more open minds who are ready to be convinced, but only by a strong argument; and those who are certain to disagree with everything. Which should be the target audience? The third group, of course, the swing voters; why waste time on any of the others? Assuming that this group will be slightly antagonistic, because they are agnostic, will ensure that the case is presented as forcefully as possible. The historian should always imagine that his worst critics will line up eagerly to take their best shots at his work.

We might think we are well equipped to differentiate among truth, error, invention, and possibility, and also at conveying this circumstance to readers. There are any number of ways to convince our readers that we are right. One is to proceed cautiously in what we say and how we justify it. This requires a number of discursive detours—phrases like "if [e.g., I am right], then;" "in the present state of the evidence;" "on the other hand;" and the like. There would need to be explanatory asides and footnotes as well, even in some cases excursuses and appendices. Historians suspect that readers generally do not like this approach, preferring a style that permits them to read at speed and believe with equal speed. This more palatable style of discourse also has its catch phrases—"as is well known," "all agree that," "this proves," "surely," and so forth. It avoids plodding and helps readers realize more clearly just how they are expected to think.

III

A wonderful example—quite too wonderful to overlook in any discussion of discursive legerdemain—encapsulates this genre of the pre-emptive discursive first-strike. This appears in a book whose author, John Prevas, is attempting to follow Hannibal's footsteps through the Alps—the latest of many such efforts over more than two thousand years. Prevas is not daunted by these previous efforts, which of course he deems largely failures. On the contrary:

> We know from the ancient sources that Hannibal covered the distances of the march in stages and within given time periods. First, we know that he marched for days from the place where he crossed the Rhone to the "island," . . . Second, we know that from the "island" he marched ten days and nearly a hundred miles along an unnamed river, and into the foothills of the Alps. Third, we know that the first ambush happened on the tenth or eleventh day after he left the Rhône. . . After five more days of marching, Hannibal came to another gorge where he was ambushed a second time. Finally, we know that the second ambush occurred in a place that was less than a day's march from

the final pass where Hannibal crossed over the Alps and came down
into Italy.[3]

Where to begin with this delightfully ingenuous piece of argument? Perhaps
with the Rhône, which is only one possible alternative for the major river mentioned in the sources, and not one adopted by all students of the itinerary. Or
should we begin with the notion that Hannibal marched "nearly a hundred miles"
in a ten-day stretch? This calculation is strictly Prevas's, and is reached in circular fashion. Or we could begin where Prevas begins—with the ancient sources.
These are Livy and Polybius, who often disagree with one another and neither of
whom tells us quite how they gathered some of the unlikely details that they
decided to include in their accounts. In short—and despite Prevas's insistently
battering discourse—we "know" nothing. And neither does he. The virtue of this
passage is in providing a clear example of the well-known notion that the strength
of arguments are often inversely proportional to the strength of the evidence
underlying them.

IV

The longest standing, most widespread, and most influential form of discourse is
the absence of discourse. Ignoring inconvenient evidence or differing opinions
has always been a prominent weapon in the rhetorician's arsenal. Readers hardly
need to be told that the historian's work is one of selective interpretation. Much
has been omitted, not least in the historian's own sources, but readers need to
know something about what has been left out and why. In answering these questions, the historian not only fulfils a professional obligation, but helps to understand his own ways of proceeding better.

For this undertaking, scholarship has the preface among its weaponry. The
preface has a long and distinguished history, and at one time was treated as a persuasive art form of its own.[4] Lately, however, it is being relegated to a brief presentation of thanks and almost never finds a home in anything but a book. Yet the
preface can be the most illuminating part of any scholarly argument. It is a vehicle by which an author can explain himself and seek the goodwill of readers. In
a good preface the historian explains *why* he has written that which follows. He
explains *how* he has gone about gathering the evidence and framing it. If relevant,
he explains *whom* and *what* he is challenging. He might even explain *when* and
how his ideas developed, precluding the need to trespass throughout.

The historian can use the preface to explain the limitations he has set himself, which can disarm readers—and reviewers—who might wish for a different book. The process of writing it forces him to come to terms with the personal and the pragmatic, as well as the intellectual and organizational, aspects of his work. A preface can serve to discuss the ambiguities of the subject under discussion, allowing the historian to be candid with the reader without incessantly interrupting the discursive flow that follows. Even in a short article, the historian can allocate a footnote to fulfilling such obligations to readers. The importance of the preface suggests that it deserves nearly as much attention as the body of the work. Writing the preface first, as a point of departure, and then rewriting it last, as a measure of the distance that point has shifted, should always be a salutary experience. As readers, we should go straight for the preface in a work, and as authors we should be intent on shaping our own prefaces to fulfill the promise of a work's title.

V

A piece by William G. Dever serves to illustrate the ways in which discourse can stand surrogate for reasoned argument.[5] Dever opposes the "minimalists," who claim that the so-called historical books of the Old Testament are not very historical after all, and he labels them "postmodern," a surefire way of condemning their modus operandi as "malarkey." Worse yet, from Dever's point of view, they often brush off claims that archeology can fill the vacuum. Unlike standard-issue postmodernists, who believe that no source can tell us enough, and so there is no point in trying, the minimalists do not argue that all history must be a literary construct, only that these biblical texts are literary at heart and date from so late as to jeopardize their value as primary sources. This is no different than the tack taken by critical historians everywhere.

Dever continues that "[m]ost Biblical scholars and virtually all archaeologists have tended to dismiss revisionism as a passing fad, not worthy of being addressed seriously."[6] He is prepared to be more generous: "[w]e cannot, however, avoid the basic historiographical issues that the revisionists have raised."[7] Dever does not so much address the issues, however, as those who have raised them. To keep readers in line, he passes judgment early in his discussion: "What weighs in finally is not 'truth,' for there is none, but rhetoric, the more extreme the better." To prove his point, Dever quotes or paraphrases several "typical statements," but fails to cite a source for any of them. Just two paragraphs later, he castigates the latest work of one of the more prominent minimalists as "hardly ... scholarship, since it does not contain a single reference to support any of the countless cavalier assertions that are made."[8] One can only marvel at the lack of self-awareness. This assault on extremism is odd for someone who has gone so far as to claim that "we [archeologists] will write a history of ancient Israel, and we will also write the *only* competent histories of ancient Palestine."[9]

Linda Newson introduced a discussion of the impact of European diseases in the Philippines by providing a little background: "[i]t has been estimated that the native population of the Americas may have declined by about 90 percent from about 50 to 60 million in 1492 to 6.5 million in 1650." She cites a source that makes this argument, and another that advances even greater depopulation. Newson then goes on: "[t]he scale of the disaster remains a matter of debate, partly because it depends on estimates of the pre-contact populations that are hotly disputed."[10] For this statement she provides no citation. Readers are given only one set of numbers to remember; they are not told whether those who disagree with these numbers think them too high or too low; and they are provided with no leads to pursue.

If Newson had declared her own interest and role in the controversy, readers would learn two useful things: if there is an answer to the numbers of American Indians at contact, no one knows it; and that Newson has actively participated in the debate as a partisan of one school of thought on the matter. Knowing these things would provide them with the chance for a more informed reading of what follows. Newson adds that ". . . the role played by [the] introduction of Old World diseases in this demographic collapse is *now* generally recognized," as though this was an insight springing from recent findings and arguments.[11] As Newson must be aware, observers from the sixteenth century on frequently made this connection, although usually without resorting to the kind of overblown number-crunching that she and others practice.

The bloated claim probably—one hopes!—reaches apogee with Gavin Menzies's grandiloquent claim that "[t]here's not a chance in a hundred million that I'm wrong." Menzies was defending his theory of Chinese global exploration, which is uniformly rejected by scholars in the relevant fields, apparently taking umbrage at the charge that his work is "inexorably circular, its evidence spurious, its research derisory, its borrowings unacknowledged, its citations slipshod, and its assertions preposterous."[12] Bemusing as Menzies's lack of diffidence is, it differs only in degree from hundreds or thousands of similar, if less apocalyptic, protestations designed to inhibit doubt by their very assuredness.

VI

When considering the characteristics of published discourse, we cannot allow ourselves to forget that this is often only the culmination—or at least the first visible incarnation—of oral or unpublished written exchanges of possibly long standing. Only rarely is any hint of such preceding discussion available, since it is usually regarded merely as prologue, but its potential importance is exemplified in a study by Colin Flight of the minutes of a seminar at the University of London regarding the processes by which the Bantu-speaking peoples of eastern and southern Africa came to be where they now are. At the time, the 1960s, the evidence was especially exiguous—largely linguistic with a smattering of archeological data—in sum too little on which to build overarching explanations that were credible. Nonetheless, these were built and pressed with some force on the unyielding record. As Flight pointed out, this development arose largely from the effects of small group dynamics. The process was more attuned to power, prestige, and partnerships than to unimpeachable evidence, but the result was the birth of one of African historiography's most enduring orthodoxies.[13]

VII

A character decides to believe a witness's story: ". . . on the whole, I thought so many details made it unlikely he was making it all up."[14] The reader never learns whether this is an accurate assessment since the witness is soon murdered. Along the same lines, Robert Wright writes that "the basic criterion of scientific judgment" is that "the most plausible story wins."[15] It is not clear whether Wright defines plausibility as evidence-based or discourse-based, or a bit of both, but historians of all periods—indeed, all writers—have realized that plausibility resides in the details.

Greek and Roman historians knew a thing or two about the role of the corroborating detail in fostering plausibility. In wondering why little attention had been paid to Thucydides' careless use of the stade as a linear measurement, Simon Hornblower suggests that "his confident, detailed figures for stades, . . . make us *feel* he is doing something reassuringly accurate."[16] As Oakley puts it, more generally, "for the ancient historian plausibility was part of the evidence." Unfortunately, Oakley continues, "[t]he ancients were ill equipped to distinguish between what was plausible and what was true, and what was fictitious and what was true."[17] Perhaps if Arrian had written that Alexander had a small mole on his left cheek, six toes on his right foot, or a ring that he couldn't get off, his readership would have taken this as a sign that Arrian's source/s had been eyewitness and would have accepted more of his account more uncritically.[18]

Plausibility buys credit very cheaply, witness the penchant to sequester the plausible from the implausible to inoculate against disbelief. As noted above, the four accounts of Hernando de Soto's expedition vary in length, detail, and plausibility. The latest of these is also much the most detailed, but behind the veneer it is also wildly implausible. This has not been enough for those tracking down de Soto, who badly need Inca Garcilaso's surfeit. Their modus operandi is to accept any of his statements that could conceivably be true—that is, are plausible—and reject those that fail this test, even if the two appear in the same sentence. For instance (not a real example), if Garcilaso described an Indian town on the left bank of a river near an island and containing 5,000 people who lived in glass houses, de Soto hunters would use the geographical description to site the town and the population estimate to project regional populations, but would studiously ignore the glass houses, at best treating them as copying errors.

This demeanor toward the plausible is a serious impediment to critical historiography, especially if we consider that forgeries try particularly hard to be just that. After all, most historical sources do not entirely lack plausibility, even those produced when the notion had a wider definition and lower standards, and merely airbrushing out the impossible—to us—and accepting the possible—also to us—is no way effectively to come much nearer historical reality.[19]

VIII

The use of footnotes deserves more attention than it generally receives.[20] Treating discourse as a simulacrum for evidence amounts to abandoning the normative aim of scholarship, which is to make a case. Justice systems depend on providing juries at least the semblance of full and equal access to relevant data. In many cases the defense or prosecution will present the better case, with or without the help of the evidence. But when only one side is able to present arguments at all, and then chooses to present only that evidence that might support its case, we read about it in the papers or see it on newsmagazines. Historians are not obliged to present an equal case, although a full one is preferable, and footnoting allows them to take sides without cheating the jury. Dissenting opinions can be afforded at least token representation there as an alternative to using the central text, and footnotes can be used for developing a context that would be a burden on the main text.

Most historical manuals treat the use of footnotes, if briefly. Readers are advised not to footnote common knowledge, nor to bring to bear an entire arsenal of supporting evidence. This is sound advice, but the second admonition needs to be refined and contextualized. When the discussion is part of an ongoing debate or, especially, a challenge to received wisdom, the historian is obligated to trace the course of the differences of opinion fairly and fully; distinguish between persons and their work; and provide not just the argument but the reasoning and the evidence behind it. Footnotes can be seen as authors' challenges to those whom they anticipate will disagree. It speaks to their assurance and puts the obligation squarely on those who would dispute their findings.[21]

Publishers of books and journals have contributed to the lower-class status of footnotes. The footnote apparatus was once an undesirable added expense, requiring special typesetting and larded with italics, numbers, and other features that require scrupulous attention. Even today, some publishers expect authors to consolidate footnotes at the ends of paragraphs, creating much mischief and adversely affecting the beneficial uses to which authors and readers can put footnotes.

It was the supposed cost-ineffectiveness of traditional footnotes that led to the social-science system of referencing. Here citations are interpolated directly into the text with untoward effect. If, in the older system, readers' eyes could be drawn to the foot of the page—or to pages somewhere else in the book—in this system the foot of the page leaps up and seizes possession of parts of the central text. Worse, the social-science system has somehow led to the steady erosion of page numbers from these parenthetical citations. Even quotes are no longer invariably referenced. One author—unusual in degree only—published an article that contains 169 citations, which might seem impressive until the reader is faced with using them—not a single one of them contains specific page numbers.[22]

IX

Iteration is a popular form of authenticating discourse. Defending the traditional chronology for the settlement of Iceland against a number of contradictory radiocarbon dates, Orri Vésteinsson begins by dismissing this evidence entirely, asserting that archeological approaches had "not proved fruitful avenues of research in as much as nothing has turned up contradicting the long held view that Iceland was settled by Norsemen around and shortly after AD 870," and continues that "archaeological investigations continue to support" a date of 871—in fact this date "now seems . . . so accurate that it is almost uncanny." Finally, Vésteinsson mentions that some radiocarbon dates suggest an earlier settlement, but dismisses that evidence in favor of tephrochronological evidence that "produces the date 871, with a margin of error of less than two years." Other hypotheses, he continues, have been "refuted," and "the settlement of Iceland commence[d] shortly after 871."[23] Throughout, Vésteinsson refers to those who arrived ca. 870 as "the very first settlers." If nothing else, the wearied reader is persuaded that Vésteinsson rejects any hint of an earlier settlement.

There is also the discourse of imminence. Here readers are encouraged to believe that resolution of problems, like the Rapture, is largely a matter of patience. Speaking of the population of pre-monarchical Israel, William Dever writes that precise population levels are not known because "[u]nfortunately, demography is not yet a science in archaeology."[24] Dever does not reflect on what miraculous breakthrough will legitimize his use of the word "yet." Many readers will not take him seriously because they too cannot imagine what this would be, but others will find comfort in the hope he provides.

There is no aphorism to the effect that certainty sells, doubt repels, but unqualified statements confidently expressed have no trouble finding receptive audiences who want their thinking done for them. In reprising the history of the tangled debate over the homeland of the Indo-European speakers, Mallory quoted A.H. Sayce on the matter:

> 1880 "This Aryan family of speech was of Asiatic origin."
> 1890 "This Aryan family of speech was of European origin."
> 1927 "So far as my examination of the facts has gone it has led me to the conviction that it was in Asia Minor that the Indo-European languages developed."[25]

Apparently Sayce, like W.F. Albright, was never more sure that he was right than when he was changing his mind. Also like Albright, his bombastic confidence led others to follow his interpretations during his lifetime, although neither Europe nor Asia Minor is now generally thought to be the elusive homeland.[26]

Even apparently minor words must be chosen carefully. Most words have epistemological value, but some more than others. To some, "much" and "most" might seem interchangeable, or at least reciprocal, but when an author chooses "most" he is implying that he believes that the portion he is describing has a lower limit—one more than one-half of the universe in question. If he is not sure of this, he uses "much," which tells readers that he is not sure, and if it is important, he might even explain why he chose one four-letter word over the other. Readers have the right to make such inferences themselves and to hold authors accountable for their failure to be as precise in proclaiming their knowledge, or their ignorance, as they can.[27]

Particularly to be shunned is discourse that mixes the historian's and the sources' opinion. This requires constant attention on the part of both author and reader. K.C. Chang wrote that "[i]n the *Bamboo Books*, historical accounts on bamboo found ca. A.D. 280, a passage describes how the duke of Zhou, after his conquest of the Shang ca. 1100 B.C., . . ."[28] There are no dates in the *Bamboo Annals*; Chang is supplying his own date, but in such a way that unwary readers could be misled. Anson Rainey blithely wrote that "[i]t is hardly coincidental that 925 [BCE] is the fifth year of Rehoboam (and Jeroboam I) according to the chronology in Kings."[29] The bible also provides no dates and few useful synchronisms; this date is Rainey's reconstruction, and, as discussed elsewhere, several other dates have been advanced for both rulers.[30]

Charles Aling refers to "a major treaty" between Ramesses II and "the great Hittite king Hattushilish III."[31] Aling of course is doing only what many others do as well, but the royal name "Hattushilish III" is really a schizoid application; Egyptian texts refer to a ruler named "Hattušiliš" all right, but the ordinal is a modern construction based on reconstructions of a Hittite regnal genealogy that is murky and beset by many very similar royal names, which makes it difficult to defend applying ordinals to most rulers of the kingdom.[32] Although venial sins by any standard, such assumptions remind us how reflexively the present can impose itself on the past.

Historians also need to be especially punctilious when describing relationships among sources. Writing about the battle of Hastings, S.A. Brown notes that "William of Jumièges and William of Poitiers followed by Orderic Vitalis all state that Harold's intention was to take William by surprise, the last two adding even the possibility of a night attack."[33] Brown's language leaves the reader in doubt as to the relationship of the three authors. "Followed by" might, but hardly need, suggest a dependent relationship between Orderic and one or both Williams, but the last clause suggests something slightly different—either a relationship between Orderic and only one William or, since Brown uses the word "even," that the two accounts are independently derived. The common opinion is that Orderic is derivative and his information probably ought not to be included in Brown's formulation at all, since citing him has only the apparent effect of strengthening an argument.

X

Attempting to write global history constrains the historian's discourse by forcing him to squeeze the nuances out of the evidence in order to suggest much in very brief ambit. Most recent efforts reflect this, but a discussion of population dynamics from the rise of hominids to the present makes the point particularly well. Fekri Hassan deals with population growth and decline, but in order to offer gross numbers he accepts sources as he encounters them, with sometimes dire results. Hassan writes that "the population of the Roman empire is estimated at 54 million." True enough, this represents *one* set of opinions, but other estimates flourish as well. He writes that "[i]n Mesoamerica, about 35 million people occupied an area of 1 million square kilometres." This not only accepts the highest estimates ever offered, but inflates them by several million.

A few paragraphs earlier Hassan writes that "Persia controlled an empire of 5.5 square megametres around 600 BC." Whatever the extent of the Achaemenid empire, it did not come into existence until ca. 550. Hassan also speaks of "[t]he Inca empire, which covered five times the area of Europe between AD 1100 and 1400."[34] The Inca state rose only ca. 1450 and at its apogee exercised vague suzerainty over an area of about 1.6 million square kilometers.[35] Europe, including Russian Europe, contains about 10.5 million square kilometers, or almost seven times the area of the Inca empire. Hassan either overstates the relative size of the latter by as much as thirty-fold or quietly redefines "Europe."

This is an intolerable incidence of error in two paragraphs. This is not inevitable, but results from relying on secondary and tertiary sources, without checking their value in order to contribute, as one world historian put it, toward devising "'a simple, all-encompassing, elegant idea' with the power to order all human experience."[36] In a shootout between elegance and evidence, one can triumph only at the expense of the other, and all-encompassing theories need the first rather more than the second. And this burden is most effectively—and most easily—sustained by discourse.

16

SIX HUNDRED BARRELS OF PLASTER OF PARIS

"I see nobody on the road," said Alice. "I only wish *I* had
such eyes," the King remarked in a fretful tone. "To be able to
see nobody! And at that distance too!"

"But you will admit, gentleman," I said, a little desperately,
"that my theory holds water, that is, in default of actual information?"

I

From time to time we see hypothetical reconstructions of gigantic dinosaurs, with an indication of the osteological basis of the reconstruction. Nearly a century ago Mark Twain addressed the problem when referring to what we knew for certain about a famous literary figure: "[William Shakespeare] is a Brontosaur: nine bones and six hundred barrels of plaster of paris."[1] The problem persists; more recently a diagram of a "Seismosaurus," estimated to be about 130 feet long and weighing about 45 tons, was published with the caption "[t]he black vertebrae are those found so far"—just two of these plus another two or three leg bones.[2] In time more bones were excavated. and it became possible to work from knowledge of a complete skeleton of a relative, Diplodocus, and, within the limits of skeletal anatomy, to extrapolate this and argue that it was now to be estimated to have weighed 100 tons or more and to have been as long as 170 feet.[3]

173

David Gillette estimates that about one percent, perhaps less, of dinosaur physical remains have survived. As he put it, calculating even less generously, ". . . using [a] 10 percent figure, from a population of, say, a million individual dinosaurs that died in a given century during the late Jurassic, perhaps only 100,000 skeletons were buried successfully; 10,000 survived decomposition during early stages of burial; 1,000 survived deep burial; 100 survived shallow burial; and only 10 became exposed. Of those 10, only one survived on the surface long enough to be discovered by a paleontologist. . ."[4] Historians must identify with this ruthless winnowing process. A past event has to be witnessed, then the observations recorded, the record preserved for varying periods of time, then found, and finally understood. Of course we cannot know the numbers, any more than Gillette could know his numbers, but the degree of disappearance has been phenomenally high. In this chapter I discuss the implications of this silent majority.

II

The period before the onset of dynastic rule in China is known as *wan-guo*, "the ten thousand states."[5] We know something about one to three of these states. If we believe the figure of 10,000, then we know some small part about from .01 to .03 percent of them. If we reduce that by 99 percent, then we are in the slightly less unenviable position of knowing something about as much as 3 percent of the states. Assuming that further archeological work will increase the evidence, perhaps tripling it in time, when all is said and done, and making certain favorable assumptions, we will be informed about a greater part of that 3 percent and just possibly about polities beyond these three states.[6] It is not entirely a pleasing prospect for the ambitious.[7]

A Chinese annal, the *Wei zhi* from the mid-third century, mentioned 100 countries of the "Wa," thought to refer to Japan, of which 30 were in contact with the Wei dynasty. We know nothing more about the polities of the Wa than this single report and a few summary notices of tribute-paying Wa rulers. The *Wei zhi* also mentioned several "countr[ies]," including 21 such polities "beyond" the principal state of Yamatai.[8] About these we know nothing either so, however valuable the information in the *Wei zhi*, it serves as well to remind us how much we do not know.

Discovery of the Qumran documents or Dead Sea scrolls was more than a reminder that odd sources can be oddly salvaged from the ravages of time, but they prove cause for pessimism as well. About 1000 such scrolls have been found, but one scholar estimates that as many as 200,000 scrolls were created.[9] Thus, however precious the documents have proved to be, before treating them as representative we must remember that they might constitute no more than .5 percent of a putative total and that even this modicum represents a totally unanticipated leap in the body of available evidence.[10]

<h1 style="text-align:center">III</h1>

Expressing a prodigiously nonsensical—and technically indefensible—view, Clemens Reichel asserts that "[i]t is probably safe to say that every historical event leaves some traces in the material record. Minuscule as these traces may be, they can often be recognized by careful observation and a good amount of detective work."[11] In fact, of course, much of the record of the past is suffused with impenetrable silence, and the bulk of historians' interest is inevitably directed toward the sounds. David Hackett Fischer wrote that "evidence must always be affirmative" and went on that "[n]egative evidence is a contradiction in terms—it is no evidence at all."[12] In the sense that it is invisible, and if decontextualized, this is certainly true, but the historian must respect contextually suggestive silence. It must be plumbed, found to be true—or not—and brought into arguments where it is relevant.

Although historians sometimes pretend otherwise, and despite comments like that of Reichel, the past has not been benevolent in preserving itself for the present. Nor is there reason to assume that what little has survived is somehow representative of all that has not. Historical argument is strongest when it relies on evidence that is already available, less strong when it requires evidence that might become available, and fatally weak when it requires evidence that cannot realistically ever become available.

It is necessary to recognize silence as either a friend or an enemy in hiding, and expressly address it in historical arguments. The first step is realization; after this, the historian has a choice of tactics. One is to take measures to assure that silences are real and not a product of failing to pursue all possible lines of inquiry. This sounds simple, but pragmatics and the desire to be efficient combine to inhibit the investigation. Casting the net more widely might require further linguistic competence or travel expenses. When the result might be detrimental to a working hypothesis, the inclination might be to forgo the effort.

Once provisionally identified, silences should be treated as diagnostically significant.[13] The classic argument from silence sees it as reflecting reality and bases specific arguments on that. This works best when the silence is so comprehensive, yet so counterintuitive, that any general argument needs to account for it. Silence in the historical record, however, often results simply from failing to engage all possible sources. If further research finds no breach in the silence, then the argument can move forward. If breached, arguments in favor of the reality of some corner of the past are measurably strengthened. Another approach is using silence to devise further hypotheses and stimulate further research. A third avenue is to treat silence as expected and accepted, without further ado. This strangles further research at birth merely to ease the historian's lot. Worse yet is to treat silence as evidence *for* some occurrence, by arguing, for instance, that it proves that such and such event occurred after the period of silence or that somehow silence demonstrates by itself that some event occurred. Here I discuss each of these responses, and some variants.

IV

The danger of wasted work is especially great when historians make explicit arguments from silence, attempting to show, for instance, that the absence of any reference to an event until long after it allegedly occurred is evidence that it never occurred. Although risky, this is vital whenever an event and its recording appear to be separated by a suspiciously long time. First in order is the historian's visceral trait, curiosity—in this case, wondering whether a historical reference in hand is really the earliest known. It is wise never to accept that it is, even if follow-up research uncovers no earlier ones.

Frances Wood created a sensation when she published a work provocatively entitled *Did Marco Polo Go to China?* and answered in the negative. Prominent among her reasons was that Polo's account failed to mention mainstays of the Chinese cultural and visual landscape such as tea, foot-binding, and the Great Wall. Her argument was that no outsider could spend more than fifteen years in China without noticing these things, but we can ask whether such an outsider could have noticed these things but failed to record them, especially while he was languishing in prison back in Italy and dictating his experiences to a second party. Few have agreed with Wood's conclusions, but in disagreeing they have put the discussion of Polo's testimony on a firmer footing by explicitly seeking ways to defend it.[14]

Stafford Poole's challenge to the historicity of an alleged apparition to an Indian peasant in 1531 of Our Lady of Guadalupe draws heavily on silence. The apparition has long been an important unifying symbol for a much-divided society. Exhaustively canvassing all the available sources from the period, Poole was able to state that the first written account of the event did not appear until 1648, although some allusive oral tradition might have existed earlier.

A successful argument from silence must be powerful, but Poole has mounted a strong case. He chronicles, for instance, numerous occasions before 1648 when any apparition should have been discussed had it been common knowledge. The most damning evidence is a letter written to the author of the 1648 work, in which the vicar at Guadalupe confessed that he and his predecessors had been "sleeping Adams." This suggests that the apparition was news to him, although he promptly boarded the bandwagon with his own book designed to stimulate profitable pilgrimages.[15] As a full-fledged argument from silence, Poole's analysis cannot be definitive; perhaps one day a document from the 1530s will turn up referring to the apparition. Until then, however, Poole has rendered the story more tenuous than ever, and his work has shifted the onus to those who would believe.[16]

<h1 style="text-align:center">V</h1>

While these examples—and hundreds like them—are of interest to small groups of specialists and to the wider guild as examples of a particular issue, others take on a wider significance. The most portentous silence facing early Christians was the vexing absence of secular sources about Jesus Christ. Ever since opponents of Christianity began to think historically, they have invoked the dearth of materials on someone named Jesus in the right time and place. The first known mention outside the bible that arrogates him to preternatural status is a passage in Josephus's *The Jewish Antiquities*, written about sixty years after the events it purports to describe.[17] The passage, known as the *Testimonium Flavianum*, speaks of a person named Jesus, calls him "a wise man, if indeed one ought to call him a man," goes on to say that "[h]e was the Messiah," and speaks of a resurrection after three days.[18]

As the earliest apparent corroboration of the New Testament, this passage has "generated a debate over its authenticity that encompasses every position imaginable, from total acceptance to total rejection."[19] The theory that the passage is fraudulent gains support from the fact that between Josephus at the end of the first century and Eusebius at the beginning of the fourth century, there is no extant reference to this passage, even though several Christian writers quoted or cited other parts of Josephus.[20] Attempts to overcome this disconcerting muteness have been vigorous and ingenious, but unconvincing.[21]

Further silences throw doubt on the New Testament version of things. Perhaps what the early Christians thought epochal was for the Romans merely a tempest in one of their many teapots, but the pall of silence remains. The pervasive uncertainty surrounding this brief passage encourages arguments to be made from every possible angle. G.A. Wells has capitalized on it to argue against the existence of a Christ figure, whereas Murray Harris has used vague allusions in early Latin authors as strong evidence for just the opposite.[22] The ambiguities allow all parties to believe as they choose, with no fear of direct refutation, but also disallows any of them from fully answering the case of the others.

Doubtful authenticity is only one problem with treating Josephus's testimony as corroborative. Its late date means that he could have been repeating matter he had heard from Christians or read in their writings, many of which were already current, rather than citing independent strands of evidence. There is nothing in Josephus that is not in the gospels, which is not what we would expect had Josephus relied on non-Christian sources. However, no interpretation makes better sense than that certain phrases in the *Testimonium Flavianum* were added by Christian scribes and that the remainder of the text derives from information Josephus acquired from Christians of his acquaintance. Josephus's statement might be an independent source regarding Christ's existence, but neither Josephus nor any modern interpreter has provided the evidence to prefer this notion over choices that relegate Josephus's statement to being information about beliefs and not about Messiahs. The principal reason why this question must remain unanswered is the sixty-year span of silence followed by two more centuries of the same until Eusebius breathed life into it.[23]

VI

The Bugandan kinglist was exiguous when it made its first appearance in the 1860s. The first published list contained only eight names, but during the next twenty years this number more than quadrupled.[24] Perhaps J.H. Speke, who collected the first list, was either incompetent in gathering data or indifferent to publishing all of them. Conversely, the historian might argue that Bugandan informants withheld material about their past until they could be more certain of the motives of their uninvited interlocutors, a sensible policy decision not unknown today. More skeptical historians would depart from another point along the spectrum. The Bugandan authorities came to recognize the importance of antiquity to the new arrivals and responded by manufacturing rulers and passing them along to those who clearly welcomed them. This too would be sensible public policy and one with ample imitation.

There is little difference between empty spaces and empty faces. Anonyms in the sources nag—vacuums of no great size, but temptations still. Lot's wife had no name worth reporting, and the same is true for Noah and his three named sons, all four with wives without names. Ancient and medieval authors wrestled with this problem and often came out winners. Francis Utley collected citations to 103 names (including variants) posthumously conferred on Noah's wife, and he was sure that many had escaped his canvass. In the process he also found thirty names for Shem's wife, thirty-five for Japheth's wife, and twenty-nine for Ham's wife.[25]

As for the Old Testament, so for the New, where many figures, whose names we think we know, acquired them retrospectively. The Wise Men, the names of the 72 (maybe) disciples, the companions of Christ on Calvary, and numerous others, all had names bestowed much too late for these names to be regarded as reliable. Metzger sums up his discussion of this phenomenon: the names " . . . are a testimony to the fertility of pious imagination down through the centuries and the reluctance to respect the silence of the New Testament narratives. How many of the traditions rest upon historical data will be differently estimated by different persons, but in any case the number will be very small."[26]

VII

Many historians choose another way to cope with silence; treating it as a vacuum, they fill it with must-have-beens, could-have-beens, should-have-beens, and their concomitants. As one author put it, "[t]his article represents one of the first attempts to approach the issue of the epidemics that *must have* swept through the Indian population before the arrival of the conquistadors in the region of what is nowadays Costa Rica."[27] Such assertions remind us that arguments *against* silence are common, as historians impose their views on an unaccommodating record. Ibarra Rojas mimics a body of must-have arguments that presuppose that European diseases struck throughout the Americas before Europeans had done more than establish a few beachheads. She argues further that such diseases struck other parts of Mesoamerica after 1520, and lists expeditions that sailed or marched near the area, beginning with Columbus's fourth voyage in 1502.

Ibarra Rojas has the frisson of a case based on propinquity; others have presumed that these newly-introduced diseases spread hundreds of miles in every
direction within a very few years, killing off millions of Indians (whose own existence is presumed on the basis of the diseases themselves!). Ibarra Rojas admits
that "at the moment no documentary evidence" exists that any epidemics struck
Costa Rica, and there is none for the other areas either.[28] Purveyors of such reasoning are adept at turning silence to advantage. Henry Dobyns, foremost among
many, argues that the modest numbers of Indians observed by the early explorers
are proof that disease had preceded them and killed off millions Indians who
therefore were not there to be counted.[29] In the same vein Paul Martin has argued
that a lack of evidence actually supports his notion of the "spontaneous extinction
[of North American megafauna] by prehistoric overkill" occurred within a few
generations.[30] He does not explain why animals dying in a short time would leave
less evidence than if they had died over a longer period of time or why it is
unlikely that such evidence will be forthcoming.

VIII

Although those who wield arguments from silence wish them to outlast all com-
ers, they cannot be designed to be eternal. Several examples can show why caution is appropriate. None is more minatory than the demolition of Alex Haley's
identification of his ancestor Toby with a certain Kunta Kinte, which took his
ancestry back to Africa, and made his own fortune. Haley's claim was that Kunta
Kinte arrived in Virginia on board a particular ship—the *Lord Ligonier*—on a
specific date, 29 September 1767. This information was not provided by any contemporary written source, but on data Haley had gathered in the Gambia, to
which, he deduced, Kunta Kinte had been native.[31] Haley then went to the
archives and found "a lengthy deed" dated 5 September 1768 which mentioned
"one Negro slave man named Toby"[32] Voilà!

Unfortunately, not "voilà" after all. Haley had made the fatal error of working
only forward from September 1767 in the archives. Other researchers, not encum-
bered by a vision, worked backwards and soon discovered that Toby "appeared in
six separate documents of record over a period of four years *preceding* the arrival
of the Lord Ligonier." Haley's documentary silence had been exposed as a sham,
and the only possible conclusion was that "Toby Waller was not Kunta Kinte."[33]
At this point Haley had three choices: retract his identification; ignore the new
evidence (which had appeared in much less public a forum than his own work);

or try to re-establish the identification by finding another ship which had arrived earlier than the first reference to Toby Waller. The last would have been difficult, probably impossible, and scrutiny would have been intense. The first would have been honorable but humiliating. Haley chose the second alternative and lived not to regret it.

It has long been almost universally held that the ancestors of the American Indians arrived in the New World via the Bering Strait about 12,000 years ago, based on the fact that no certainly human-associated remains had been found that could be dated earlier. As a result, Clovis Man (from the find-site in New Mexico) became the embodiment of the earliest immigrants. As time marched on and this absence of evidence appeared to pass test after test, it became difficult to resist the orthodoxy, although many archeologists believed that eventually such evidence would be forthcoming.

Their patience seems to have been rewarded at last. In the past several years, sites in Chile, Brazil, and the eastern United States have been explored and, especially at the Monte Verde site in Chile, have withstood unprecedented critical scrutiny.[34] It is to be dated about 2000 years before Clovis. With this, new horizons beckon; for instance, if the Bering Strait hypothesis is still accepted, why should the breakthrough come from a site as far away geographically as possible? Either the Bering hypothesis must be abandoned in favor of some unlikely trans-Pacific alternative (or, possibly, coastal route), or numerous other sites much closer to the Bering Strait remain to be discovered.[35]

It is now being conceded—here and there anyway—that "[t]he possibility of previous abortive colonization attempts as early as 40,000 years ago cannot be unequivocally rejected."[36] The word "abortive" might be seen as acknowledging irresistible new evidence without endangering the reigning paradigm. The question of the antiquity of humans in the New World is more likely to be settled by evidence such as DNA than by all the excavations ever done on the matter. The issue, however, is not when humans first reached the Americas, but how even relatively feeble arguments from silence can gain a stranglehold on scholarly inquiry, for the lack of pre-Clovis sites should never have been taken seriously enough to build a hegemonic orthodoxy on it.

For many of its entries the *Oxford English Dictionary* provides "first" citations. The first editor of the *OED* was suitably dubious, if blasé, about this: "earlier instances will, I doubt not, yet be found of three-fourths of all the words recorded."[37] Despite this authoritative warning, the *OED* has frequently been cited for its information on the first written appearances of particular words.

Many of the 1,904 words originally credited to William Shakespeare's facile genius, however, are now ascribed to earlier authors. Discussing this, Schäfer points out the paradox involved in the very notion: ". . . a search for absolute first citations is, method[olog]ically speaking, impossible, since every newly discovered antedating is potentially antedatable in turn. We shall never be able to say positively that an early citation for *any* given word is the very first, . . . nor could this be an object of serious scholarly investigation."[38]

IX

Arguments from silence are often attacked by those who find them unpersuasive or unpalatable. Hershel Shanks refers to a work on the Torah in which the author writes: "[t]he reader should be aware that we have no direct evidence of the existence of characters best known to readers of the Bible, including—but not limited to—Abraham, Sarah, Isaac, Jacob, Esau, Moses, Joshua, Deborah, Gideon, David, Goliath, and Solomon."[39] Shanks does not deny the truth of this; instead he argues that "[t]he absence of specific reference to these figures in contemporaneous extra-Biblical sources is next to irrelevant. For a simple reason: We would not expect them to be mentioned in the sparse written records that we have."[40]

Shanks does not insist that all these individuals existed, but he knows, better than most, that very many—and very ephemeral—Egyptian, Assyrian, and Babylonian rulers and non-rulers left remains, as did rulers and citizens of places like Ebla and Ugarit that antedated the rise of Israel and existed on no larger a scale. It is fair to ask: where *are* the discoveries for Israel and Judah that would rival those of Ebla, Ugarit, Alalakh, and others? We have contemporary records of many pharaohs who ruled only a few years; why then have we nothing for David and Solomon, who supposedly ruled eighty years between them?[41]

Attempts to rehabilitate John Smith's credibility remind us that an argument from silence can be opposed by another form of itself. Smith's account of Pocahontas and his near-death experience first appeared in his writings in 1624, after both Pocahontas and her father Powhatan had died, and also after Smith had already written on his experiences in Virginia. This has led his modern detractors to suggest that Smith had to wait because his story was a fabrication. Frances Mossiker and J.A.L. Lemay, on the other hand, point out that several of the original Jamestown settlers were alive in 1624, and in a position to contradict Smith's story, but apparently none did, although none appears to have publicly supported the story either.[42] Other authors have since tried, with some success, to rehabilitate Smith's veracity in other cases, but the matter must remain open, precisely because it is inescapably a case of choosing between equally suggestive silences that happen to fall in opposite directions.[43]

X

Unexplained silences in the historical record serve as catalysts for new ways of thinking. Applying the argument from silence to epidemiology is a high-risk venture, but a recent work has done just that. Modern epidemiological theory links classic bubonic plague (*Yersinia pestis*) with rats—no rats, no plague. In the Middle Ages and early modern times, the "plague" swept through western Europe several times and this has routinely been diagnosed as bubonic plague, but contemporary descriptions fail to mention the requisite dead rats. In analyzing nearly fifteen hundred letters among Jesuits in the sixteenth century, A.L. Martin notes that the correspondents "made observations on the climatic conditions of wind, humidity, and temperature and reported on ominous astronomical phenomena but still failed to notice a single dead rat." Martin's final sentence sums matters up: "[a]s a result of all these factors the retrospective diagnosis cannot be an irrefutable, probable, or even likely plague but must be 'plague?'."[44]

Martin's question mark illustrates that he makes no categorical claims, but historians of epidemics must seek alternative explanations to the notion that these Jesuits were simply an unobservant lot. One would be that there were no dead rats to notice, and this in turn would lead to other hypotheses—either the disease in question was not classic bubonic plague after all, or its symptoms and method of transmission have changed over the centuries. In the first instance the observational powers of previous generations are put at serious risk, with consequences for historians of disease—or anything else—who rely faithfully on such sources. In the second instance, medical historians are put at risk, since they assume that disease manifestation and transmission have remained much the same from time immemorial.[45]

Earlier, David Davis had noted that "no mention of mortality of rats occurs in accounts of the Black Death in the fourteenth century, and he concluded that "[t]he accumulated evidence . . . does not support the traditional view that black rats were responsible for the Black Death."[46] Davis' sample, though large (about 300 sources) was too circumscribed to support his conclusion categorically, and Martin's contribution has raised the stakes. In part the latter's work is designed specifically to test the assumption, which he calls "regressive history," that modern solutions can always be applied to historical problems.[47]

The missing rats answer no questions; their value is in justifying raising them. It is a temptation that appears not to be very tempting. Davis commented that "[s]ome 300 references were examined but not reported here because the data did not mention rodents or were inconsequential."[48] When consulting 300 sources results only in a single dismissive footnote, it is easy to see why the process is not very often repeated, and also why there are many silences in the record that are not recognized to be as potent as they might be.[49]

This probably explains one of the more pernicious stances toward silence—that the absence of dissenting information in the sources is sufficient grounds for treating absence of evidence as evidence of absence. Referring to the use of literary texts as historical sources, A.H. Gardiner wrote: "[i]t appears to me that without undue credulity we may risk a verdict of 'founded upon fact' in these and all similar instances, and that we may use their statements, *in the absence of conflicting testimony*, as the best available evidence with regard to the periods of history to which they relate."[50] Although Gardiner might well have meant otherwise, his qualification swallows his enthusiasm. "In the absence of conflicting testimony" is a parlous state indeed, especially in Egyptology in 1914, when regarding a source as "the best available" was faint praise indeed. Gardiner was right to qualify, but wrong to believe anyway. He saw himself as a pioneer but overlooked the implications of this for his assertion.

XI

The temptation of silence characterizes all disciplines. Before the early nineteenth century, scientists were reluctant to accept that the absence of living counterparts of fossil discoveries indicated extinction. The eminent naturalist Jean-Baptiste Lamarck could not rid himself of his theology: "There are yet so many portions of the surface of the globe where we have not penetrated, so many others that capable observers have crossed only in passing, and so many other still, as the different parts of the depths of the seas, for which we have few means of identifying the animals that live there, that these different places could well be hiding the species with which we are not familiar."[51] Thomas Jefferson, who by his own lights was not fettered by theology, echoed this view in his comments on a Megalonyx fossil he came across: "If this animal then has once existed, it is probable on th[e] general view of the movements of nature that he still exists."[52]

But the continuing detailed analysis of remains and the gradual unfolding of the earth's surface failed to produce living counterparts to the growing fossil record. This eventually forced a grudging recognition that, despite theological opinion to the contrary, extinctions must really have occurred.[53] Theologians, even geologists, resisted this increasing absence of evidence because of the prevailing theological view that extinction was not possible—god did not take away what he had given, but ensured an equilibrium in which species competed on a basis that ensured that none could eliminate the competition. Therefore the number and types of species were fixed, and the absence was perpetually regarded as temporary: was there not always going to be a Patagonian giant or Trachodon out there—somewhere?

Carried to such extremes, such arguments crosscut common sense. The fact that there have been no incontrovertibly attested contacts with extraterrestrial life has led some to infer that no such life exists—that we are a special creation. The further fact that it was announced at the 25th General Assembly of the International Astronomical Union in July 2003 that there are approximately 70 sextillion stars in "the known universe," and that there are over one million known galaxies might seem to strengthen the case. However, when 100,000 of these were measured, they were found to occupy about 13 billion billion cubic light years of space.[54] Since a light year is more than six trillion miles, we are dealing with numbers so large as to be meaningless—except that they tell us that these 100,000 galaxies are spread pretty thin. To assume that any forms of life in them would already have searched us out is more than a little ego-geocentric. Here, total silence is merely a fact of life with no argumentative value either way.

17

MILLIONS OF MOVING PARTS

All my senses suddenly kick in. I feel as though someone has
just plugged me into an electric socket. "You mean," I say,
"that he really didn't have any statistics to back up that percentage?"

Granted, we shall never discover "lost" Roman census data
giving authoritative statistics on the religious composition of
the empire in various periods. Nevertheless, we must quantify—at least in terms of exploring the arithmetic of the possible—if we are to grasp the magnitude of the phenomenon that
is to be explained.

I

In his *Republic* Plato turned to a universal solvent: "I would say that if we can't
locate anything beyond these, we should consider something that applies to all
of them. What? Virtually the first thing everyone has to learn. It is common to all
arts, science, and forms of thought. What? Oh, that trivial business of being able
to identify one, two and three. In sum, I mean number and calculation. Is it not
true that every art and all knowledge must make use of them? Yes, it is."[1]

Two thousand years later, William Maitland, writing a patriotic history of
London, demonstrated the city's primacy by comparing it to Paris in size.
London, he claimed, was "Six Miles, Three Quarters, Two hundred and Ninety-

one Yards" at its shortest length, whereas, according to "the Plan of Paris, publish'd in the Year 1717" that city was "Three *English* Miles, Seventy-seven Yards, Three Inches and a Quarter." Moreover, London was "Ninety-two Yards and Thirty-four Inches broader than *Paris* is in Length."[2] Faced with such precision, who would be so rude as to question whether Maitland really did know the length of Paris to the quarter-inch?

Proponents of large-scale quantification no longer push the moral weight of numbers so palpably, but they do argue that generating and using them is an efficient way to reach solid conclusions and communicate them. My own experience suggests that one of the principal advantages of quantification is its ability to shield claims from falsification by failing to provide requisite information and by creating variables and other assumptions on the basis of evidence not placed in evidence. Intimidation is also ridiculously easy by providing terminological and numerical smokescreens intended to overawe.

T.H. Huxley did not fail to notice the relationship between data and results when quantifying:

> I do not presume to throw the slightest doubt upon the accuracy of any of the calculations. . . On the contrary, it is necessary to my argument to assume that they are all correct. But I desire to point out that this seems to be one of the many cases in which the admitted accuracy of mathematical process is allowed to throw a wholly inadmissible appearance of authority over the results obtained by them. Mathematics may be compared to a mill of exquisite workmanship, which grinds you stuff of any degree of fineness; but, nevertheless, what you get out depends upon what you put in; and as the grandest mill in the world will not extract wheat-flour from peascods, so pages of formulae will not get a definite result out of loose data.[3]

Less long-winded and less fastidious post-Victorians have renamed this principle garbage-in-garbage-out and, while it has a nickname, it does not seem to have much cachet. Two recent books on quantitative historical techniques illustrate this state of mind. Only three of nearly 280 pages in the first work are dedicated to the "reliability of data." The advice offered there is all good, but quickly gets buried in the torrent of ways to amass and manipulate such data.[4] The authors of the second work are even less interested in whether or not garbage goes in, and devote no explicit attention at all to the matter.[5]

II

In 1974 a two-volume study of slavery in the antebellum South appeared, written by two economic historians.[6] Unlike most previous studies of slavery, it was not narrative and anecdotal, but analytical and heavily cliometric. The first volume was devoted to "the economics of American slavery" and the second to "evidence and methods." The message of *Time on the Cross* was that objective statistical analysis demonstrated two unconventional points: slavery was profitable and more efficient than northern capitalism; and slaves were by and large treated humanely, if only for economic reasons. The work aroused an immediate firestorm of protest from those who saw it as whitewash. The critics were unsportsmanlike enough to use Fogel and Engerman's own data against them, arguing that they had committed a number of statistical mortal sins, for example, that their evidence was neither random nor representative, and that too many conclusions were drawn from too few examples.[7] Fogel and Engerman responded, but only to "explain" that their critics underestimated the power and sophistication of their method.[8]

No statistically untrained historian could hope to follow the arguments of either side, but "[o]nce the specialist-practitioners began their task, the peculiar mathematical 'magick' of *Time on the Cross* lost its spell."[9] Why the "once"? Scheiber answered this in part by quoting from bishop John Wilkins' 1648 *Mathematical Magick*: "the ancient Philosophers esteemed it a great part of wisdome to conceale their learning from vulgar apprehension or use."[10] Before historians entered the fray, economists and other social scientists had been impressed and convinced. As one economist giddily put it, sparing no hyperbole, "Fogel and Engerman have with one stroke turned around the whole field of interpretation and exposed the frailty of history done without science."[11] Fogel and Engerman defended themselves with mathematics rather than lucid argument, but there is little evidence that, after a brief honeymoon, they were able to persuade critics that this was enough.

III

The historical record is awash with numbers. We might deplore the exiguousness of the available evidence, but the past has not been niggardly in leaving behind quantifiable data. The earliest written records we have, cuneiform inscriptions from Babylonia, are largely records of commercial transactions, and the cornucopia has continued to pour forth ever since. It was not much later that those who produced the surviving ancient records began to synthesize for themselves. As early as the reign of Khasekhemwy (ca. 2800/2700 BCE) we read that the pharaoh killed 47,209 of the enemy in battle.[12] Later the Assyrian kings aggregated on a heroic level. Sennacherib boasted that he returned from a victorious campaign with 208,000 prisoners, along with "7,200 horses and mules, 11,073 asses, 5,230 camels, 80,050 cattle, [and] 800,100 sheep."[13] Again we have spurious precision combined with absurd exaggeration—what Marco De Odorico calls "high-exact."[14] Some might prefer to believe the plausible numbers, although disagreeing about which these are, and reject the others. The variety of quantifiable evidence continued to increase in kind and number as time passed, intended to impress as much as inform, but which many historians allow to do both. Whether it is Ramesses II casting huge numbers of Hittite casualties at posterity, early historians of the Norman Conquest amazing their readers with the magnitude of it all, or U.S. military authorities attempting to muzzle critics with inflated/deflated body counts, the process has been endless.[15]

IV

Why is history so populated with numbers? Could it be because almost every historical situation can accommodate a range of plausible numbers? Caesar *could have been* assassinated by one man or ten. The attendance at a sporting event *could have been* recorded as any number up to, and even beyond, the seating capacity of the venue. The contact population of Hawaii *could have been* 100,000 or 800,000. Those using historical sources have shown themselves to be hopelessly beguiled by numbers—by their apparent precision and their efficiency in implying much while saying little. No wonder historians count themselves among numbers' greatest admirers. The greater the vacuum, the more passionately numbers are embraced. Critical acumen is discarded, concern about the ways in which these numbers were determined forgotten, worry about numerical disparities in the sources overcome by optimism or by a failure to discover them in the first place.[16]

The difficulties of accepting sources as both consistent and accurate is exemplified in the saga of the number of base hits credited to Cap Anson. Various official sources over the years have credited Anson with 2995, 3000, 3041, 3418, 3423, and 3509 hits. As John Thorn points out, "all these figures are 'right' in that they reflected the best understanding of the encyclopedists and record keepers of a particular time." To exemplify the problem, Thorn quoted a 1896 source: "[a] careful perusal of the tables [box scores] shows that the figures, in several instances, differ from those published last fall. In one case the records give [Bug] Holliday a credit of fifty-seven stolen bases, whereas he stole only a single base."[17] All this is amusing, but also minatory. Because he has made a long and close study of baseball in that era, Thorn knows the statistical vagaries that accompany it, whether outright errors or differing interpretations of existing rules, incomplete box scores, or discrepant information. When plucking numbers from the historical ether, we are unlikely either to have as much information or as close an acquaintance with it.

Although we rely on them heavily, there is nothing more unofficial than "official" statistics. Whether population estimates, production statistics, composition and value of exports, or anything else, like Pearl's counters, no two statistical sources will seem to agree. Whether differences result from differing time periods, differing definitions or calculations, or differing sources hardly matters. Bearing in mind that this situation obtains at the dawn of the third millennium, when data-gathering has never been more proficient, should remind us that drawing on quantitative data from the past can only be risky business.

V

One of the most popular quantitative techniques that historians use is projection. Data that might or might not be reliable are extrapolated back in time or across space to draw conclusions. Half a dozen procedures might be involved, based on assumptions with no known degree of probability. Inevitably, the practice produces effects akin to the numerous attempts to calculate the carrying capacity of the earth, or any part of it—a central tenet in historical demography. Joel Cohen lists 66 efforts between 1679 and 1994, ranging from 500 million to more than one trillion. The latter estimate is more than 2000 times the former, even though the two calculations were made only four years apart.[18] To complicate matters, Cohen also includes 26 definitions of "carrying capacity."[19]

Several historical enterprises have been foregrounded on the reliability of particular sets of numbers, but none so far-reaching, intensive, or extrapolation-ridden as ongoing efforts to determine the population of the Americas at the moment Europeans arrived. With a few ignoble exceptions, no one doubts that, whatever that population was, it declined precipitously—victim of an unequal Columbian Exchange. Beyond that, there have been chronic disputes over the magnitude of the decline, its geographical extent, and its causes. The numbers the early observers advanced were usually high but never provenanced, being intended as metaphors of outrage, and they were largely taken as such by contemporaries attuned to the rhetorical mores of the time.

By the early twentieth century such estimation had passed into the hands of academics. At first it was largely confined to anthropologists who, in harmony with their times about the productive and organizational capabilities of American Indians, thought small. A commonly-held opinion was that about eight million American Indians were living in 1492, based on presumed carrying capacities for peoples who were held to be largely hunter-gatherers needing lots of space. In the 1940s a new school of thought arose, which was entirely different in several ways. It used primary sources more heavily, even more heavily it adopted extrapolative approaches, and it rated the Indians' cultural and reproductive capacities much more favorably. New figures were bruited, with the hemispheric figures exceeding earlier estimates by an order of magnitude or more. A virtual consensus has developed, which puts the population of the Americas as high as 120 million, and hardly ever lower than 50 million.

This range derives from a community of premises: that the numbers of Indians actually cited in the sources were either remnants of a much larger earlier population, were an existing sub-population (e.g., adult males), or were both; that valid extrapolative methods can be applied population decline projected back to 1492; that the sources can construed to say almost anything that moderns want them to. The instrumental premise, however, was that populations declined so much and so rapidly from lethal new European diseases that spread far and wide with great dispatch, killing millions of Indians well before they could even be noticed, let alone counted. Thus means, motive, and opportunity were all identified—the mystery could be solved. Whether the Zeitgeist, the impressive arithmetical procedures, or the confident rhetoric adopted by the new school was most effective, its methods and results have been flattered by constant imitation, whether applied hemispherically, regionally, or somewhere else in the world. Unfortunately, the methods, and therefore the results, were flawed in a number of respects. The remnant premise was advanced repeatedly, but never demonstrated. The arithmetic could be no better than the data that underlay it and that could all too frequently be shown to be inherently defective. The use of sources was corporately sub-standard, often disgracefully so.[20]

VI

An insidious aspect of quantification is that data are legitimized by the very act of being quantified. When a number or set of numbers is multiplied, divided, added, subtracted, or otherwise manipulated, they become part of a larger process that presumes itself to be valid. Once numbers are arrayed—in formulas, in tables, in graphs—they become homogenized, with all incumbents looking very much alike. They have the same typefaces and font sizes. Those with lower probabilities are seldom identified in any way. This is especially true of numbers arranged in lists, where dubious individual entries gather strength in the company of stronger elements.

None of us needs to be told that precision is persuasive. We learn to distrust round numbers and place more faith in those that seem more exact. This makes sense—after all, the proportion of round numbers in the historical record is much greater than it ought randomly to be, and many of us will be far more suspicious of a round number that might be correct than of precise one less likely to be correct. The impulse to grant precision to the past can become addictive. Why else would Nicolas Henrion gauge the decline of man by determining that Adam was "123 pieds [roughly 12 inches each], 9 poulces" in height, and Eve "118 pieds 9 poulces *3/4*"? From what predisposition would he attribute 20 pieds less to Noah and, ever decreasingly, only 6 to Alexander the Great and 5 to Julius Caesar?[21] Why else would William Maitland have done his calculations? Why else would Henry Dobyns suggest that the contact population of central Mexico might have been 58,178,666?[22] Why else would Charles Darwin, whose sensible views on other matters are mentioned elsewhere in this work, succumb to such exercises as calculating that each acre in England produced between 14.58 and 18.12 tons of mould per year or 83.87 pounds per square foot, "assuming the whole surface to be equally productive in castings?"[23]

VII

The increasing ability to manipulate large masses of data to taste has evoked numerous efforts to draw large conclusions from an accumulation of small bits of evidence. Criticisms have usually focused on the aptness of various quantitative techniques, but there is a case to be made about the quality of the small bits of evidence. Cases in point are several ongoing efforts to quantify war—its incidence and patterns, its civilian and combatant casualties, its effects on the societies involved. The sheer magnitude of the enterprise requires a dangerously heavy reliance on secondary sources—or worse.

In *Civilizations, Empires, and Wars: a Quantitative History of War,* William Eckhardt boldly takes his analysis back to 3000 BCE. The sources for anything, even something as memorable as war, are dauntingly exiguous for this period, and for a long time afterward. Eckhardt compounds this problem by relying on a few modern syntheses of the history of warfare rather than seeking out the much larger body of focused studies. It is no surprise then that he manages to locate only fifteen wars in the thirteen centuries after 3000 BCE and that he calculates that only 1.28 percent of deaths in wars occurred before 500 BCE and only 4.2 percent before 1500 CE.[24]

Did humans really become increasingly warlike after 1500 CE? Or did the capacity to inflict casualties increase? All would accept the second premise and some the first, and Eckhardt's data could support both. A better explanation involves correlating his results, not with humanity's will and capacity to fight, but with his unenterprising way of accessing the available historical record. A measure of his failure is his listing of 49 wars during the sixth to third centuries BCE. Although attempting to be global, and alluding to China, Eckhardt did not consult the sources for this time, known as the Spring and Autumn and (aptly) Warring States periods. These speak of incessant warfare in which, they say, millions perished.[25] Eckhardt shows a total of only nineteen wars from the ninth to the seventh centuries BCE, a period when Assyrian kings campaigned almost annually against enemies in every direction.

For the seventh through eleventh centuries CE, Eckhardt lists 158 wars. This seems a large number, but epigraphic record from India alone attests to more wars than this, as the multiplicity of local and regional dynasties contested with each other, and with foreign invaders such as Mahmud of Ghazni, who waged nearly thirty campaigns in India.[26] Eckhardt's definition of war would seem to include these, especially if he believes the grossly exaggerated casualty figures in these records. Even without believing, the death toll in these campaigns greatly exceeded that for the Greco-Persian wars, which are centrally represented in Eckhardt's exposition.[27]

Even though more rigorous use of available sources might create a curve that makes warfare seem a modern pastime, in Eckhardt's case this was exaggerated by his fixation on the western world as traditionally identified. A more serious fixation was the need to produce quantifiable information, clearly indicated by the distillation of his data into over fifty pages of tables. Those using his work will probably consult these first, and perhaps only this, in drawing conclusions about warfare. His frequent—and transparently ingenuous—discussions of his assumptions are not likely to discourage this.[28] Those most likely to rely on Eckhardt's conclusions are proponents of a world-systems approach to studying of the past. Many of these have already shown an alarming propensity to depend on such compendia as Tertius Chandler's thoroughly undigested *Four Thousand Years of Urban History*.[29]

Claudio Cioffi-Revilla's surveys of war resemble Eckhardt's in aims and methodology.[30] He includes a list entitled "the first 101 wars in the hyperwar system, 15th to 1st century B.C." that includes only five from China and one (possibly mythical) from India.[31] Cioffi-Revilla sets his terminus on the grounds that "the first reliably recorded wars are currently dated to c. 1500 B.C."[32] His statement is unprovenanced and patently untrue.[33] Cioffi-Revilla is plugging something he has created and christened "the HYPERWAR system—a purposively designed, microcomputer-based, multi-media information system about all wars for which there is reliable historical evidence." The sample record he displays allows room for numbers, but not for a discussion of their reliability. It indicates as well that his sources are synthetic, modern, and of undetermined value.[34] All the statistics and electronics are accounted for; missing is a critical analysis of the sources for these wars, as well as a large proportion of the wars themselves.

Readers could be daunted by Cioffi-Revilla's electronic panache, with references to the Poisson model, Boolean logic, and "various scenarios of belligerant [sic] force behavior."[35] Nonetheless, a basic question must be asked: is it possible to draw valid inferences about the causes, progress, results, and effects of war in the past on such a grand scale? Ordinarily it would be hard to make such an argument based on so small, unreliable, and tendentious a sample. A party uninitiated in the history of warfare and the problematics of its reporting, however, could be unduly impressed by the sheer complexity of HYPERWAR and be persuaded that its contents present a roughly accurate picture of past warfare.

VIII

A quantitative exercise that has become common is the simulation model, by which a proposition is tested by plugging in a number of assumptions, usually numerical in some way, and carrying out the resulting mathematical logic. Paul Martin developed a simulation model to support an argument that most of the megafauna in the western hemisphere were killed shortly after the arrival of the precursors of the American Indians.[36] By the terms of the model, these were fairly numerous, became more numerous very quickly, and were endowed with well-honed killer instincts. Unaccustomed to humans, the animals learned too late to avoid them and were slaughtered easily and rapidly. Critics immediately disagreed with every assumption of this model, whether the numbers, the killing efficiency, the rate of population expansion, or meat consumption levels.[37] They preferred an alternative multilateral explanation, with environment and climate playing major roles and human predation only a minor culminating one.

Other recent simulation models treat the effects of disease in Mexico in the sixteenth century and the demography of African slavery and the slave trade. Thomas Whitmore develops low, moderate, and high models for Mexico and settles on the moderate.[38] To what degree his choosing and his evidence interrelate is impossible to say, but they could hardly have been entirely independent. As for Patrick Manning's model of the effects of the slave trade, if five historians of the trade were asked to simulate the simulation, five discrepant sets of variables and the numbers put to them would result.[39]

None of Whitmore's three models is outrageously implausible, and none of the five historians' hypothetical models of the slave trade need be either. They would represent less an encounter with the evidence than idiosyncratic interpretations of that evidence repeatedly inserted into the structure of the model. Past reality is ostensibly being simulated, but it is actually the mindset of the modeler.

An unavoidable drawback of quantitative history is that much of the process is beyond the purview of readers. The raw numbers might be available, but they are likely to have been processed before reaching print, or come from so disparate a group of sources as no longer to be traceable. Chances are as great that the manipulations that intervene between the 'raw' numbers and the interpretative phases of the work are also not available. All this leaves readers in a quandary. Are they to accept the results without the data underlying them because they have no practical alternative? Or are they to wonder aimlessly what criteria, definitions, and sources were used, and how? If these are not what we imagine, it might adversely affect our own further calculations without our ever realizing it. In commenting on estimates of coin production in ancient Rome, T.V. Buttrey identified the central dilemma here: "We all yearn for numbers, we would rather have any figures than no figure. But if we lack a number at least we know that we lack it; and no answer is better than the wrong answer."[40]

IX

William Playfair, the apical ancestor of the modern field of graphic display, frequently commented on the ability of pictorial representation to guide and persuade readers.[41] Later, William Taylor was explicit. The new field of statistics had already acquired "the dignity of a science," in no small measure because statistics were able to present diverse material in a "tabular form," which helped promote the appearance of objectivity.[42] Any number of studies have been written on the potent effects of well-executed displays of information. It is no accident that these studies tend to appear in psychology and communications outlets, pointing out the central place that persuasion has in the scheme. Conversely, few studies of graphics as rhetoric have been directed at historians, whether or not of the cliometric ilk.

William Tweed, the corrupt boss of New York City politics in the 1860s and 1870s, knew exactly why he was eventually driven from power. Referring to Thomas Nast's cartoon campaign against him, he raved: "Let's stop them damn pictures. . . . I don't care so much what the papers say about me—my constituents can't read; but damn it, they can see pictures!"[43] Like numbers, the power of graphic presentation lies in its ability to circumscribe the imagination. Several mystery novels featuring Inspector Morse of the Thames Valley police appeared before the TV series was launched, and each reader could form a mental image of the title character, no two of which could have been alike. Along came the TV series and the literary Morse immediately assumed a canonical appearance that was identical to the actor who played him, and it is this image that imprints itself on every reader of the books since then.

X

Many early maps show inhabited earth as a large island with Greece at the center, although by the time China was communicating with Rome, enough was known that they were not regarded as extraterrestrials. For some, the discovery of the new world—hypothesized on some maps but not on most—came as a shock. The biblical categorizing of humanity had not prepared them for unsuspected continental land masses stretching from one pole to the other. As a result, maps had to be redrawn frequently and in haste, as new evidence continued to pour in, and few maps of the known world were reasonably accurate until recent times.[44]

Maps have been with us as long as the written word, possibly longer, and in many areas they preceded literacy by centuries. Most such indigenous "maps" of course were radically different from those we are most familiar with. If there was scale and orientation, it was probably more by accident than design. This hardly means that these maps were impossibly inaccurate, only that they were created by and for individuals with different senses of space and direction than our own. So-called western maps are themselves "indigenous," with well-defined and very visible ideologies of their own.

While we have reached the point where most maps are produced to provide information, that information varies. Like all historical sources, maps must be selective, and therefore subjective. Like numbers, maps are seen to hold out hopes for precision and accuracy—a tiny but true representation of some part of the earth's surface at some point in time. As Brian Harley put it: "[a] map says to you, 'Read me carefully, follow me closely, doubt me not'."[45] Like any other source, no map should be taken at face value, whatever its credentials.

It was only within the last century or so that maps began to measure up to the stresses that historians put on them. Scholars, however, continue an abiding faith in the capacity of these early efforts to answer detailed modern questions. The debate over Columbus's landfall, for example, depends as much on maps as on texts, maps about whose provenance we know almost nothing, and which are demonstrably inaccurate, except, apparently, in whatever the searcher wishes to believe.[46]

Colonialists were bemused when 'natives' declined to be photographed because they feared that the image would capture their souls. But they amused themselves in much the same way, by producing maps that they hoped would capture some portion of the earth's surface for their own use rather than falling to a competing imperial power.[47] At the various international conferences called to parcel out the tropics, each party to the negotiations would fall back on maps that were older or newer or more empirically-based than any others to bolster its case. Maps produced by the colonial administrations are widely used by historians, who must bear in mind that these maps mirror both cartography and politics. Mediatizing entities were often portrayed as larger or more populous than they were in order to legitimize colonial native policy more effctively, and each map bore the imprint of the particular interests of the colonial official who drew it up—sometimes at firsthand, sometimes not.[48] Disputed maps have been the cause of much diplomatic tension, even conflict.[49] Nationalism and irredentism thrive on maps and vice-versa.[50]

Like numbers, maps add verisimilitude to even the most obvious fiction. Mystery novels sometimes contain a map of the village or plan of the stately home in which the crimes were committed, forcing readers to think alike about the environs of the affair since buildings, distances, directions, and logistical possibilities can be interpreted only in the way of the map. Early maps of Africa often showed a large lake in the bull's eye, which was held to be a kind of giant reservoir from which flowed all the rivers in Africa then known—and additional rivers as they became available. There were no sound geographical reasons for this arrangement and no examples of such geophysical marvels from other parts of the world were cited. It was simply an economical way to explain the numerous and often very large rivers that the Europeans learned about during their coastal meanderings.[51]

In many cases cartographers could plead ignorance. In other cases it is harder to understand why so many non-existent places appeared on maps. Henry Stommel illustrated that "[n]ineteenth-century nautical charts contained some two hundred islands that are now known not to exist"—small-scale modern-day Atlantises[52] They sprang into being by way of seamen's reports, fraud, misunderstandings of location, and inadvertent duplication, and their continued cartographic existence owed much to indolence and inertia. The makers of most maps and atlases relied on making changes to earlier products. They revised but seldom questioned. As always, it took more trouble to prove a negative than to accept a positive, and the trouble was not often taken. These phantom islands simply moved from one map or atlas to the next until overwhelming evidence against their existence combined with the requirements of global geopolitics to demand more precision and greater accuracy.[53]

XI

It is impossible to avoid mentioning the new and possibly alarming world of digitization here. Photographic images were once thought to be the equivalent of thousands of words, but the equation has changed for the worse. When we see sports utility vehicles on television perched on the very tops of sheer rock formations or hurtling around sharp curves in defiance of centrifugal force, we suspect that they have been taken there by digitizers rather than by their own unsurpassed qualities. We might realize that we are being gulled for crassly commercial purposes and are content to leave it at that, since it hardly matters unless we are about to buy such a vehicle and are easily tricked

In other cases it does matter. A recent study of iconographic legerdemain in the Soviet Union suggests that optimism would be unwise even for predigital graphics.[54] There David King demonstrates the obsessive distortion of graphic evidence by Stalinists. Individuals out of favor were airbrushed from photographs, huge crowds were added to scenes where Lenin orated, the figure of Stalin was relentlessly positioned in near proximity to Lenin. The expunging was sometimes crudely and palpably done, but other times it was carried out so effectively as to make it imperceptible or, more to the point, to render the need to perceive immaterial.[55] Much to historians' disadvantage, the camera has become less a mechanical eye that can produce unchangeable images on demand, and more a representation of the infinitely mutable human mind.[56]

Under the circumstances, what about published photographs? Are they now to be taken as seriously as previously? Software manufacturers now advertise equipment that includes video editing.[57] With this, users can completely change a visual representation by deleting parts or moving them around. No more mediocre pictures under this regime; no more first-hand unadulterated evidence either. The revolutionizing effects of digital photography are becoming familiar to scholars in almost every field. The specter of digitization now permanently resides between camera and eye.

18

HE SAYS, SHE SAYS

Being angry with one who controverts an opinion which you
value, is a necessary consequence of the uneasiness which you
feel. Every man who attacks my belief, diminishes in some
degree my confidence in it, and thereby makes me uneasy;
and I am angry with him who makes me uneasy.

That much good ensues, and that [geology] is greatly
advanced, by the collision of various theories, cannot be
doubted. Each party is anxious to support opinions by facts . .
. facts come to light that do not suit either party; new theories
spring up; and, in the end, a greater insight into the real structure of the earth's surface is obtained.

I

In his autobiography Charles Darwin recalled his attitude to scholarly colloquy:
"I had, also, during many years followed a golden rule, namely, that whenever
a published fact, a new observation or thought came across me, which was
opposed to my general results, to make a memorandum of it without fail and at
once; for I had found by experience that such facts and thoughts were far more
apt to escape from the memory than favourable ones. Owing to this habit, very
few objections were raised against my views which I had not at least noticed and
attempted to answer."[1]

Not all, perhaps not even most of us, welcome differences of opinion, however. Freud, more typically, wrote that "I have never been able to convince myself of the truth of the maxim that strife is the father of all things. . . It seems to me, on the contrary, that what is known as scientific controversy is on the whole quite unproductive, apart from the fact that it is almost always conducted on highly personal lines." He congratulated himself that until recently he had "only once engaged in a regular scientific dispute."[2]

The progress of argument, and with it, sometimes, knowledge, has a distinct pattern, whether in history or elsewhere. The opening round is little more than mere assertion, often based on evidence to which only one person has access. Experience shows that this is fairly readily taken at face value. But any criticism that results is intrinsically more rigorous because it comes equipped with a context, enjoins specificity, and often results from belated access to the same materials. If competently done, it obliges adherents of the argument being criticized to respond. Moral obligations can weigh lightly, however, and responses seldom come forth.

II

Whenever we think that scholarly communication and politics are not very much alike, we can look at the patterns of colloquy that mark scholarship for reassurance. Those who get their views into the public domain see themselves as incumbents, with all the advantages appertaining thereto. Like sitting officeholders, they are not inclined to risk these advantages in the open field lest they come to grief, preferring instead to tell their audience what they suspect it wishes to hear. They remember that L.Aemilius Paullus died at Cannae, whereas Q. Fabius Pictor did not die on any battlefield.

Drawing inspiration from the activities of a millennial cult, Leon Festinger listed five conditions "under which we would expect to observe increased fervor following the disconfirmation of a belief." One of these is that "the believer is a member of a group of convinced persons who can support one another" in a kind of *laager* complex.[3] There is plenty of evidence to show that historians too are loath to give up disconfirmed beliefs. Although this seldom involves increased proselytizing, it does result in an Olympian detachment that ignores the disconfirmation and its practitioners.

In *Keepers of the Game* Calvin Martin claimed that, before the arrival of Europeans, American Indians had a symbiotic relationship with the fauna of the area. When European diseases arrived, the Indians blamed them on the animals, rather than the Europeans, and abrogated the symbiosis, killing animals, especially beavers, indiscriminately, as much in response to their own loss of faith as to new market opportunities.[4] Martin's hypothesis aroused a storm of protest, culminating in the publication of a collection of essays criticizing *Keepers of the Game*. Each author took a different perspective, but all agreed that Martin had produced no evidence. Martin lamely responded that his was "a book of controlled imagination, well within the usual scholarly bounds." As for treating criticism, he largely declined: "[i]n the final analysis, a book of such a speculative nature either rings true or it does not. For me, not surprisingly, *Keepers of the Game* rings true. . . . Each of the foregoing authors has challenged my interpretation in one way or another, and with one exception I intend to leave it to the reader of my book to decide on the merits of their case versus mine."[5]

In 1999 Christy Turner co-authored a book that claimed that osteological evidence forces us to accept that cannibalism was a major cultural feature in the prehistoric American Southwest. Turner was immediately criticized and promptly, and peremptorily, responded: "I'm satisfied that I've found the answer. Let others test it. This is no longer an interesting problem."[6] In a revised edition of *The Sirius Mystery* published in 1998, Robert Temple is similarly unresponsive, exulting that "[t]he situation regarding *The Sirius Mystery* has changed [in his favor] completely since the initial edition of the book was published in 1976." He refrains from justifying his exultation by, say, addressing the manifold doubts expressed about the book, stating instead that "[m]y collected replies to various critics may be read in a separate pamphlet for reviewers published with this new edition."[7] Neither copy I saw contained or was accompanied by such a defense, nor is it certain that it contained the criticisms, but only Temple's responses.

Protesting much too much, Marcello Lamberti lambasted a critic of a deceased fellow-countryman: "[Harold] Fleming's attack on [Enrico] Cerulli, who is dead and thus cannot defend himself any more, is indicative about the fairness of the author (in order with attacks and insults against living beings who can somehow defend themselves! But on dead persons, who cannot do it anymore, a bit of respect is due!!) and does not need any further comments, especially in consideration of the fact that Cerulli's contribution to Ethiopian studies with his numerous books and articles largely exceeds that of Fleming!"[8]

Turner and Temple represent widely separated points on the professional spectrum—Turner a trained archeologist, Temple a dabbler. Yet both of their works were intensely hypothesis-driven, both argued against the grain of conventional wisdom, both preferred to vacate the field of battle rather than defend it against hostile counterattacks. Temple's self-delusion, Turner's indifference, and Lamberti's *de mortuis* outrage help explain the relative paucity of no-holds-barred debate in historiography. Lamberti's view is particularly repugnant, implying that we can criticize each other only until death confers eternal immunity. Turner, on the other hand, seeks not immunity from being attacked, but from reaffirming his arguments in face of disagreement—just too tiresome. If either case were accepted, colloquy would grind to a halt.

III

Each time a book is published, an opportunity for discussion is created, but this nettle has not been seized with much alacrity.[9] Most scholarly books are reviewed fewer than four times, many not at all, and those that escape this penumbra rarely receive more than ten reviews. Praise is cheap and criticism often quite expensive, and only a tiny percentage of reviews are seriously critical, as many or more are downright fawning, and the great majority are complimentary without knowing why.[10] The impression is that bad books do not get published, and only the best of these get reviewed. Even the small number of reviews is the result of draconian measures. Reviewers are held to word limits, asked not to cite other works, and not to quote liberally.[11] Few journals publish review essays and when they do, it is often of several books, which receive less attention individually than each would have done in a separate review.

It is considered efficient and courteous to produce book reviews as quickly as possible, but a disadvantage of the system is that reviews usually appear almost simultaneously and cannot take advantage of each other. It is demoralizing to see a long point-by-point negative review quickly outgunned by a series of shorter, less critical ones.[12] In these, readers are briefed on the contents of a book and offered a summary evaluation of the author's success, sometimes followed by a few pro forma critical comments about some portion of the work to provide technical balance. Readers will find little comparison and even less sustained criticism, because each is word-intensive. Listing errata and corrigenda as part of a review consumes even more space. This is a pity, since disagreeing with an author's understanding and use of words is very much a legitimate form of debate.

In granting an exception to its rule, the *African Studies Review* reiterated its policy: "[it] does not normally publish responses to book reviews."[13] Such policies are hardly the only culprit, probably not even the most culpable, since they operate as they do for obdurate logistical reasons. The real culprits are attitudes like that of one reviewer, who assured her readers that "[i]n the interest of civility, I have consistently declined to review bad books."[14] Presumably she means bad books in her unsupported opinion, but is anything to be gained, and anything lost, by adopting such a deliberate hands-off policy? Should "civility" be a governing impetus behind book reviewing, and does publicly judging a book bad, and trying to justify the claim, really exhibit bad manners?

More irritating are Alan Gross's and David Lipset's peevish and short-sighted reactions to mixed reviews of their work: "[d]oes the intellectual world need to be protected from the dangers of my book by a long, largely negative review? I contend that there is no danger whatever that our attention will be diverted by a bad academic book if it is simply *not* reviewed."[15] Ironically, the review Gross so disliked afforded him precious space for a directed reply, even though his pique spoiled the opportunity. David Lipset was hardly less offended, and groused that "few reviewers permit themselves or are permitted to express this kind of dudgeon, hostility, etc., either in the pages of *Oceania* or really anywhere else in the world of professional journals."[16] These views are certainly charmingly naïve and egocentric, but hardly of a nature to contribute to improving knowledge through disagreement or—as these authors would no doubt put it—dissent. In these cases the critics were far more specific in making a case than were the authors, whose ruffled *amour-propre* prevented them from defending themselves or their case effectively.

Who is to blame? Authors, for writing books too good to be criticized? Reviewers, for accepting prepayment and then doing as little as possible? Journals, for allocating too little space for reviews? The most refractory problem derives from the growing chasm between the number of books being published and the space available to review them. Cyberspace has stepped in and, although it is too soon to predict the long-term impact of online book reviews, it is reasonable to assume that it will become greater as time passes. H-Net, the major umbrella group for the humanities, comprises nearly 100 separate listserves. By the end of 2004 there were about 8000 reviews archived, all accessible through H-Net Reviews and through Google, and a thousand more are being added each year. A comparison sample of reviews shows that the average online review is more than three times the length of a print review, for fairly self-evident reasons. Access can be attained by entering any one of a number of variables.[17]

Thus the traditional profile of book reviews, which involved waiting as long as several years and then finding reviews of circumscribed length as much by serendipity as system, appears well on its way to being overthrown. Still, however, only a few reviews end up being interactive—so far. Sometimes discussion is spirited, usually there is none at all, but at least a framework is in place.[18] There is no need to limit electronic reviews and they tend to appear months sooner than those in print journals. Finally, electronic reviews are often archived for easy access. All things considered, the online book review has the potential to address many defects of the present system.

The print book review literature falls short for other reasons. Book reviews are not easy to find systematically. They do not feature in most subject bibliographies and indexes, nor are they included in many online table of contents services, with the exception of the Web of Knowledge®, an outgrowth of citation indexes. There are few book review indexes, yet the need for these is obvious, given the random and scattered nature of the review literature. The final nail in this coffin is the esteem with which reviewing is not held in the profession, but it is difficult to distinguish chicken from egg. Five hundred words are less than 10 percent of the typical scholarly article (and maybe .4 to .5 percent of the length of a typical scholarly monograph), so perhaps it is right to judge them lightly. On the other hand, since a review essay of several thousand words is likely to be judged just as lightly, all reviews are tarred by the same brush.

The rampaging proliferation of new journals should encourage colloquy, but the opposite seems to be the case. Many of them are niche or coterie journals designed either to address more and more specialized audiences or to use the journal as a means of promoting a very particular line of thought—to sustain rather than to convert. As fewer and fewer libraries are able to afford more, and more expensive, journals, fewer potential readers will be able to seek out the views these espouse. Now, and for the foreseeable future, much colloquy has been banished to listserves, websites, and other Internet-based locations. As noted, this has the distinct advantages of immediacy and spontaneity, but also, if less and less frequently, the concomitant disadvantages of ephemerality and inaccessibility; unlike formal reviews, these exchanges are not always archived, and when they are, finding them is more of a challenge than for traditional sites. On balance though, more issues are being aired more often and this is likely only to improve in the near future.

IV

An effective means of fostering colloquy, even if in print format, has been a hallmark of *Current Anthropology* for more than forty years. When accepted, most articles are sent to a large number of readers for comment. The responses appear immediately after the original paper, after which the author is allowed a last word. Sometimes the entire package runs to forty or fifty pages of large-format text. To my knowledge no historical journal typically does this. The main reason is probably cost. Few historical journals can publish nearly as many words annually as *Current Anthropology,* and must ration their mote. Just the same, it is likely that any historian who has participated in, or merely read, an example of *Current Anthropology*'s integrative approach has been piqued, even edified.

While such *mano a mano* disputation is likely to achieve the most desirable results, less direct differences of opinion are also beneficial. These occasionally, and accidentally, occur in different contributions to sets of collected essays devoted to a specific topic. Editors of such collections have an obligation to impose stylistic consistency, but a more important obligation not to demand consistency of interpretation. The differences expressed by several authors regarding the utility of the biblical reference to an invasion of the pharaoh "Shishak" to tenth-century BCE Israelite chronology exemplify this. Lowell Handy suggests that a thirteen-year window—937-924 BCE—for dating this event, whereas William Dever alludes to "the raid of Shishak, which can be dated ca. 930-925 BCE."[19] Another contributor to this volume differs from both: "[t]he campaign(s) took place before 929/924 BCE, but how long before is uncertain."[20] Kenneth Kitchen expresses yet another opinion, dating it precisely to 925 BCE.[21] A fifth contributor does not date the raid, but places it one reign earlier than the others.[22] An author writing elsewhere states the obvious, if not the most palatable, conclusion: "[d]epending on one's approach and assumptions, therefore, Solomon could have died at any time between 979 and 922 BCE, [even] assuming the essential accuracy of the biblical figures."[23]

V

It is hardly news that adherents of particular schools quash knowledge of criticism by confining themselves largely to citing one another. When the first edition of *The Vinland Map and the Tartar Relation* appeared in 1965, it consisted entirely of arguments supporting the map's authenticity and reliability.[24] This was appropriate, since there were as yet no dissenting opinions. Controversy over authenticity erupted very quickly, however, ranging from issues of provenance to those of codicology, and in the next thirty years the balance swung remorselessly toward rejecting the map as a forgery. In 1995 a second edition appeared and included five new essays.[25] Rather than welcoming the occasion to strengthen the case by taking critical opinion explicitly into account, these studiously avoided the criticism and any other evidence that might cast doubt on the map's authenticity. It was a case of retrenchment rather than rapprochement—an opportunity not only wasted, but scorned.[26]

Experience—or the lack of it—demonstrates clearly that getting a debate off the ground is yeoman work. More than a century ago, Archibald Geikie, in his capacity as President of a section of the British Association for the Advancement of Science, noted this when he expressed chagrin that "[i]t is difficult satisfactorily to carry on a discussion in which your opponent entirely ignores your arguments, while you have given the fullest attention to his."[27] Still, if to some, public disagreements are embarrassing, they do flare up occasionally. In 1986 Martin Bernal launched the first volume of his *Black Athena* series.[28] Bernal argued on linguistic, archeological, and historical grounds that ancient Greek civilization, and so our own, owed more to Egypt than to "Aryan invaders" from the north. He called his interpretation the "Revised Ancient Model" because, he insisted, the early Greeks themselves accepted this premise, even if they did not elucidate it very clearly. Herodotus, Plato, and others were brought to the witness stand and found to agree with Bernal.

The response was more than Bernal could have hoped for. Besides an unusually large number of standard book reviews and review essays, special issues of journals were dedicated to *Black Athena,* collections of essays on the matter were published, and the public was brought into the discussion through radio and television interviews.[29] The consensus among classicists and Egyptologists was that Bernal—a sinologist by training—was in over his depth. He failed to understand the linguistics and physical anthropology that underlay parts of his argument; he was too credulous in trusting certain ancient sources, while ignoring others entirely; he played the race card remorselessly—and erroneously in many cases.[30]

At this point Bernal had choices: he could, like Haley, ignore the furor, he could engage in selective repartee with his critics, or he could treat much of the criticism as meriting a response. Unlike Haley, he chose the last.[31] Even those who have disagreed most strongly with Bernal's thesis concede that his effort has "already begun to transform classical studies in America" by forcing his critics to defend their arguments—necessarily, at least in part, on his terms rather than theirs.[32] The controversy has begotten a full-scale sociological study of the larger phenomenon, with particular attention to the colloquy between Bernal and his critics. Its author sees weaknesses in Bernal's argument and use of evidence, but considers these less important than the fact that "all scholarly disciplines need a

Bernal or two—though no more than that."[33] Heresy is required to keep orthodoxy on its toes.

As notorious, and certainly more vituperative, is the debate over Margaret Mead's fieldwork in Samoa in the 1920s. Mead herself, and her word, quickly became iconic in the field for those who thought nurture more important than nature. Any reservations by workers who followed her into the field did not surface very prominently, and until her death the work on which Mead's argument and reputation remained virtually inviolate in the public eye. Five years after her death came the publication of Derek Freeman's *Margaret Mead and Samoa*.[34] Freeman spent much more time than Mead in Samoa, and had interviewed many of the same informants. He challenged both Mead's field ethics and her conclusions, and he did so in no uncertain terms. The uproar was immediate. Freeman was accused of being craven for waiting for Mead to die before challenging her, of being wrong himself despite his much more impressive Samoan field experience, of being unnecessarily strident, of being Australian.[35]

To his credit, Freeman, like Bernal, was forever ready to answer his critics. The level of vilification only increased as the discussion continued in well over one hundred publications.[36] So has our knowledge of both Mead's methods and those of Freeman, of Samoan society during and since Mead's research, and of the distorting lenses of fieldwork. One of the most important results of the debate was a work by Martin Orans, who consulted Mead's field notes deposited in the Library of Congress. He concluded that Mead's elucidation of her methodology was insufficient either to verify or falsify her conclusions.

Orans ended his discussion with an interesting *nostra culpa*: "All of us who allowed ourselves to be persuaded by Mead . . . , and especially those of us who disseminated this finding as though it rested upon something solid, ought surely to be faulted. Doubtless many of us did so because we wanted such findings to be correct . . . Those of us who went along with the work did so because, for us, she was on the side of the angels and delivered her message so effectively."[37] Still, Orans found Freeman vulnerable in many of his conclusions, not least from a predisposition to be selective, as well as presuming to criticize without consulting the undenied primary source, Mead's field notes. None of this would have happened had not Derek Freeman dared to criticize Margaret Mead more severely and extensively than any anthropologist had apparently ever considered.

Surveying the reception of Mead's *Coming of Age in Samoa*, Hays was surprised that nearly half the works he looked at did not mention Mead in connection with Samoa. He thought it "tempting to interpret the omissions . . . as indicators of authors' rejection of its validity." However, as he pointed out, "absences are notoriously difficult to account for in any simple way . . ."[38] If every instance of omission could be shown to be oblique criticism, it would be less a reflection on Mead's mystique than on authors who would criticize by omission, thus depriving their impressionable readers (college textbooks were the genre under review) of the chance to learn that Mead's work on Samoa was not universally respected and to show the benefits of true colloquy.

Eventually his colleagues rehabilitated Freeman. As one of them wrote in his obituary, which was allowed to appear in *American Anthropologist*, "Freeman was devoted to Popper's dictum that the method of science is criticism; for the sake of scientific progress, then, no published criticism should go unanswered."[39] This is a fitting epitaph to two decades of rancor and acrimony.[40]

VI

In arguing her unpopular position on the date of first settlement in Iceland, Margrét Hermanns-Audurdóttir closed her reply to a round-table discussion of the matter by claiming that making her case "was worthwhile *despite* the lively criticism on the dating and chronological part of my work."[41] My argument is just the opposite—that the disagreement she aroused and its playing out are likely in the long run to be the most valuable contributions of her work, whether or not her dating, and its implications, eventually become accepted in Iceland.

The case of the Canek Manuscript mentioned earlier provides a condign example of the merits of colloquy. Grant Jones, who edited the document and used it in his own work, failed to use it in his latest work. His comments immediately follow the unmasking and are a straightforward acknowledgment that he had been too quick to accept the text as authentic.[42] He explained that "subsequent close examination of [the Canek] manuscript, comparing it with others with similar characteristics, has led me to agree . . . that the Canek Manuscript is in all probability a forgery." Jones is to be congratulated for his prompt and forthright admission, and for his expressed interest in contributing to "detail[ing] the evidence for this apparent forgery."[43] Jones did more than that, though; he translated Prem's study from German, dealt with his points *seriatim,* and added a few points of his own to strengthen the case against authenticity. If Jones lost the battle for the Canek Manuscript, he won the war against scholarly querulousness and narrow-minded self-interest.

VII

The examples cited here remind us that only when scholars face others' arguments frontally and systematically, and evaluate them on their own terms, will the scholarly world be afforded a genuine basis for choosing among them. Not only do scholarly debates arise less often than desirable, they tend to evolve in fragmented ways, forcing interested parties along tangled bibliographical paths, which do not always lead to all destinations. A desideratum that would alleviate this would be a multi-authored encyclopedia of historiographical disagreements, which would present not only the substance of the disputes, but include complete bibliographies, many of which would run into the hundreds of items.[44] Short of this, those in search of enlightening disputation will find their enterprise increasingly hamstrung.

19

BRINGING TEXTS UP TO CODE

It did not escape my notice that no kind of literary work
brings an author more tedium and less reputation; for while
the reader gets all the benefit, he does not realise what he
owes to the textual critic. And while nothing is more completely thrown away than a kindness done to an ungrateful
person, even more truly wasted is the service rendered to a
man who is unaware of it.

Now the real work awaited: editing.

I

From time to time we observe aging figures in the entertainment world and
wonder how much of the original version has survived multiple liposuctions
and face-lifts. Cosmetic surgery on the grand scale is not confined to this side of
life and not all practitioners have medical degrees. Some call themselves editors.
In 1658 Henry Holden expressed a precocious notion of the printed text:

> . . . it is evident, that the Books of the holy Scripture, especially of the New
> Testament . . . having been written, as it were, accidentally upon several
> occasions . . . a thousand and thousand times copied out by unlearned as well
> as learned Clerks (what a number of faults must there not needs be in these
> pies) printed over and over, God knowes how many times, and in how many

places (how different these Editions must be with various Lections, let any man imagine?) translated into I know not how many tongues by particular and private men (with what security of a faithful expression of the true sense, who dare say?) . . .[1]

Holden was not writing as a text editor, however, but arguing why "tradition" handed down over time—the Roman Catholic way, he averred—was superior to the biblical text, now appropriated by the protestants. Just the same, his notion of the ever-changed, because ever-changing, text remains valid. Unfortunately, many editors have preferred to follow the text at a safe distance. Thus historians must operate at a similarly safe remove when using these texts, and even then cannot be certain, especially when the original text no longer survives. For many sources more than one manuscript version exists, and it is not always clear which is best, and recognizably inferior editions sometimes capture the financial and intellectual marketplace.

II

A well-executed text edition requires a mind that is able to pay close attention to every detail, regards nothing as inherently trivial, learns to spot incongruities and deal with them, has a profound knowledge of the language of the text, seeks out relevant extraneous data and applies them to elucidating the text, becomes conversant with the intellectual outlook of the author of the text as well as his discursive habits, and values and practices persistence and application. These are desirable virtues in the continuing education of any historian, yet, a few fields excepted, textual editing is neither a commonplace of historians' trade nor a means to attract the admiration of their fellows. It is a reasonable guess that outside these fields not one in ten historians has ever undertaken a critical text edition, that even fewer have managed to have their work published, and that still fewer have earned collegial kudos for their efforts.

So it is that much editing of historical sources has fallen into the hands of other disciplines, largely literary critics. This is not entirely a bad thing—literary types often discern problems and opportunities that a historian might overlook. But the reverse is also the case; for literary critics the edition is an end, for historians it is a means, and a historian is likely to provide a more comprehensive editorial apparatus that will benefit a broader range of users. In an ideal world the best critical editions would be collaborative efforts, with at least one historian and one non-historian engaged. Such an edition would be doubly beneficial if points of controversy that arose during the editing process were openly bruited as part of the apparatus rather than compromised behind a façade of unforthcoming unanimity.

III

Referring to texts handed down in Jewish circles over several centuries, Malachi Beit-Arié notes that "[c]opies representing different stages of the text were in circulation. Some of these have survived and are at our disposal; they represent a confusing variety of irreconcilable original readings, in addition to variants caused by physiological and psychological mechanics of copying and the deliberate, critical interference of scribes." Moving on to a particular case, he continues: "I.Z. Feintuch . . . compared the text of the two parallel leaves and analyzed the differences between them [and] found at least fifty disagreements in the seventy-six duplicated lines! In addition to discrepancies in spelling, grammar and the use of abbreviations, changes of names, omissions and additions, there were differences in wording, and some critical interventions which occur in one copy but not in the other."[2]

Emending texts, whether in the interests of ideology, personal preference, or carelessness can only be treated as anathema—but it is an all-too-common activity found in many venues. In Wisconsin, for example, the governor may change the state budget—adding or subtracting a zero, crossing out passages, adding his own—before he signs it, and the legislature is bereft of any further role since it cannot override a veto that never was. This prerogative reminds us of the admission by Samuel Johnson, one of the most influential text editors of all time: "[t]he allurements of emendation are scarcely resistible. Conjecture has all the joy and all the pride of invention, and he that has once started a happy change, is much too delighted to consider what objections may rise against it."[3]

Unlike the governor of Wisconsin, the textual editor has a special responsibility. Entrusted with a text, he must pass it along no worse than he received it. But is "no worse" the most he can aspire to? This is one of the profound questions in textual editing circles. To what degree can—should—a text be changed, even if the changes are palpably appropriate? Any treatment of text editing must begin with its most serious sin, silent emendation, the practice of editors' choosing for themselves unilaterally which text to bring to readers. Simply put, no change should be unannounced. It might be indicated within the main text, relegated to a footnote or even to an endnote, but the change cannot be silent.

John Foxe's *Acts and Monuments* (more commonly, "Book of Martyrs") has suffered about every calamity that can befall a text. When Victorian editors took to reproducing it, they relied on the last of the four editions published during Foxe's lifetime. Using the latest lifetime edition of any text is still de rigueur, but in this case the editors failed to realize how much Foxe had manhandled the four editions—adding and deleting with abandon, repeating stories from one part of the text to another, requoting his sources differently, etc. Later editors added bowdlerism ("buckets of Victorian whitewash"), rearranged matter, rewrote Foxe to meet their own specifications, and cited wrong sources for many of Foxe's passages. Combining Foxe and his later editors produced texts that are "quite literally, worse than useless." But used they are—almost entirely to the exclusion of any efforts to attempt a scholarly text edition incorporating earlier versions.[4]

A further example of an elusive text helps to encapsulate the problems of determining text as warranted by the notion of final authorial intent. Most of us are familiar with the Gettysburg Address, often by being set to memorize it in secondary school. But there are actually several Gettysburg Addresses: the one that Lincoln held in his hand as he delivered the speech at the battle site; the oral text that emanated from his mouth and was recorded—with variations by four onsite stenographers; and some post-delivery texts in Lincoln's hands as he recorded his second, third, and further thoughts on the matter.[5]

By some standards, only one of these variant texts can be considered canonical—the others must be impostors. This sounds straightforward, but which one? Is it the one we all hear today, the one his listeners heard at Gettysburg, or the last text Lincoln himself is known to have written? Our burden in deciding is eased in this case because the competing the texts are quite similar—most of the ringing phrases appear in all versions—but when this is not so, it becomes an onerous chore to choose one and justify the choice—after first carrying out another onerous chore, tracking down as many variants as possible.

As noted above, only two of the many modern editors of Columbus's account of his first voyage have made a sustained effort to bring Columbus rather than themselves to readers.[6] Editors reached Columbus's text only after many failed voyages. Texts that do not merit repeated editing are unlikely to get such second chances. The journal of Marie-Joseph Bonnat detailing his stay in Asante lay unnoticed for more than a century and a formal edition was published only in 1994.[7] Taking advantage of Bonnat's own comments about his "bad writing," the editor extensively rewrote Bonnat's original text to meet her own standards of expression. The new version might get high marks from the Academie Française, but as a text edition it is an abject failure.[8]

Jared Sparks, a busy and generally responsible editor, also felt obliged to save his subject, George Washington, from himself: "[i]t would be an act of unpardonable injustice to any author, after his death, to bring forth compositions, and particularly letters, written with no design to their publication and commit them to the press without previously subjecting them to careful revision."[9] Sparks acted on his principles thousands of times in his twelve-volume edition of Washington's writings.[10]

Editions such as these leave historians in a quandary. Not knowing whether they are reading author, intermediate editor, or latest editor, they have no grounds for choosing how seriously they can trust the text that confronts them. When we read in the Bonnat edition that some event happened in some particular way, and we wish to use that description for further interpretation, what exactly are we risking? If we rely closely on the wording to draw particular conclusions, how are we to know that some other scholar might not consult the original and find that we have been quoting an editor? Knowing the extent of editorial intervention in such cases should not force us into paralysis, but should impel us to seek out the original manuscript if being sure and being exact is crucial. But if we need to do this continually, why have an edition at all?

Although we condemn bowdlerism as a destructive but outmoded pest, it is not hard to find present-day examples.[11] Some recorded versions and scores of Stephen Foster's "My Old Kentucky Home" have replaced Foster's "darkies" with euphemisms like "young ones." The reasons are obvious and not uncongenial, but hardly acceptable either. Whatever else Foster songs are, they are inviolate texts. The urge to improve a text for readers' benefit even infects children's books. *Harry Potter and the Prisoner of Azkaban* and its three predecessors "have been custom-edited for the Yankee audience" in expected ways, and Britishisms became Americanisms so as not to tax the capacity of their western hemisphere readers unduly. In all this the author has colluded, leaving literary critics of the future to fight over the identity of the true Ur-text.[12]

There are many ways to emend that are not silent. The most recognizable way is to use square brackets to indicate editorial insertions. An alternative, although seldom a preferred one, is to consign all changes to the notes. A third approach, whose only advantage is economy, is to announce generic procedures in the preface: all contractions will be expanded, punctuation and capitalization normalized, paragraphing imposed, etc. This apes silence too closely and has the additional handicap that readers will know that changes are occurring without ever knowing exactly what they are. An editor is not an author, although the work can be even more intellectually demanding. and no editor should pretend otherwise by assuming authorial prerogatives when the apparatus allows him to be a co-author in a smaller font.

IV

My argument is simply that, in place of the critical edition's technology of presence, which aims to 'restore' or 'reconstruct' an author's final intentions, we need a technology of difference, by which the reader can create multiple texts. Electronic editing offers the reader a hitherto unavailable opportunity, not only to check an editor's decisions in cases of emendation, but actually to rewrite a whole text or version on the screen of his or her personal computer.[13]

The notion of multiple texts implies that there are as many texts as there are those who engage them. This we might dispute, but variations created by the ravages of time, the indecision of authors, and the pranks of editors do lead to versions that gradually multiply and drift apart.

Should multiple texts be treated as separate entities or as versions of the same original? Lately the issue has assumed substantial importance among the many editors of the Shakespearean corpus. The standard explanation once was that differences between the surviving folio and quarto editions of Shakespeare resulted from deficient transmission or were play texts compiled without Shakespeare's approval. As R.A. Foakes puts it: "that the differences between the two texts [of King Lear, published fifteen years apart] might be the result of authorial revision struck many Shakespeareans with the force of a sudden illumination."[14] This is largely because the popular notion has been that Shakespeare never revised and scarcely even made corrections to his holographs as he proceeded.

To those not in thrall to Shakespeare's preternatural genius, this attitude seems entirely too reverent. After all, which of those who think as much do not themselves edit and tinker, and certainly would want the chance to revise a text written fifteen years or more earlier? Change is even more inevitable in a text intended for repeated oral performance, where actors and audiences have input on performance and content issues. Not surprisingly, a survey of three recent editions of

Shakespeare discloses that "[r]oughly 30,000 lines out of about 100,000 are constructed by the editors in different ways with different rationales." Worse yet, "these changes are almost invariably unexplained."[15]

Many works historians rely on began as multiple texts and in some the various constituent parts still remain. This is particularly true of travel accounts, already noticed above, particularly in the nineteenth century, which saw the zenith of the genre as it affects historians.[16] Hundreds were published, creating definable texts, but whose texts were they? Such sources typically began as scattered notes taken en route, which were then often consolidated—and changed—at various stages during the journey or on returning home. The traveler then consulted a publisher, or was already under contract to one. Publishers were not concerned with dreary accuracy, but wanted excitement to stir up the marketplace. This resulted in still more textual changes, often of real substance, to reshape the work for a hoped-for mass audience. Historians have been too willing to rely on published texts of travel accounts, sometimes even in translation, without seeking out earlier versions that never reached print. In addition to changes along the way to publication, there were numerous differences between editions and, especially, between translations—as determined by the marketplace.

V

Recently the concept of "text" has been enlarged considerably, and is in danger of meaning too much to mean anything at all. Still, it is appropriate to expand the traditional definition of a text as nothing more than an assemblage of words. The Bayeux Tapestry is oddly shaped for something to which the word "text" is normally applied—232 feet by about 20 inches—and while it comes with words, these are distinctly subsidiary to the pictorial depiction of the Norman invasion of England and its prelude. The Tapestry's words and images might once have been self-evident, but no longer, and it has been an object of intensive study—textual criticism in fact—for over a century.[17] Many panels have captions, which are sometimes generic and sometimes cryptic. The result has been a mélange of interpretations that are no less various than an equivalent number of words would have generated.[18] Adding to the complications, the Bayeux Tapestry was "extensively restored [in the nineteenth century] and it is not always possible to distinguish a restored area from an original one, and if it is restored whether it was accurately done."[19]

Differences of opinion afflict both external and internal aspects of the tapes-try.[20] Was it manufactured just after 1066 or as late as the 1080s—or even in 1097? And where—northern France or southern England? And was it the vision of a single artist or many? The consensus for the moment is that the Tapestry was commissioned by Odo of Bayeux, William I's half-brother, and was intended—surprise!—more as propaganda than as a record of events. If produced in England, it is safer to argue that the target audience was largely antipathetic Anglo-Saxon, a point of view supported by the tapestry's incessant moralizing about William's right to the throne and Harold's duplicity.

Questions of content are more numerous, and hardly a panel has escaped con-troversy.[21] There is the apparent depiction of Harold being slain by an arrow through his eye. Although a staple in most descriptions of the battle of Hastings, there is ample reason to doubt. In the first place, not one of the six earliest writ-ten accounts mentions this. David Bernstein's answer is that the depiction was "not intended to be reportorial but rather was an invention by the artist to convey the main theme of the Tapestry," that is, it was a variation on the medieval topos of blinding as divine punishment.[22] Taken alone, this is interesting; taken in con-text it is potentially dangerous as well since, if the depiction of a crucial event is wrenched from history to fantasy, other panels could be subject to the same jour-ney.

Finally, there is the question of the Bayeux Tapestry as historical source, in our time and its own. Eventually, accounts began to appear that did record that an arrow in the eye had killed Harold. Whether these corroborate, or derive from, the Bayeux Tapestry can only be as speculative as the date of composition and degree of public visibility. Since some of these accounts antedate the latest suggested dates for the Tapestry, influence could have been reciprocal. Nor is it impossible that oral tales mentioning an arrow in the eye were sources for both Tapestry and written accounts. None of this allows us to arrive at conclusions that displace all others. As one author put it years ago: "the manner of [Harold's] death will always remain a mystery."[23]

Students of the Bayeux Tapestry treat it as they would a written text, with all its parts scrutinized and re-scrutinized in efforts to understand better its prove-nance and content.[24] The effect has been to come to regard the Tapestry less as straightforward reportage and more as artistic license, less as unalloyed paean to the Normans and more an example of subtle artistic sabotage. Once again the tex-tual critics have managed to muddy the historians' waters.

A second example of a non-verbal text reinforces the point. The most recent exhibition catalog of paintings by J.M.W. Turner captions two paintings as follows: "*The Arrival of Louis-Philippe at Portsmouth, 8 October 1844* . . . (formerly listed as 'Festive Lagoon Scene Venice, c.1845')" and "*The Disembarkation of Louis-Philippe at Portsmouth, 8 October 1844*. . . (formerly listed as 'Procession of Boats, with Distant Smoke, Venice, c.1845)."[25] For a hundred years or more the earlier attributions reigned supreme, surviving thousands of 'readings' primed to accept the attribution without cavil until at last a strong argument was leveled against them. At his murkiest Turner was murky indeed, and these paintings are regarded as even more inchoate than usual. Given his large corpus of paintings of Venetian scenes, the earlier attributions are understandable, but possibly not their prolonged life.

VI

Although it might seem impossibly mundane or arcane, there are times to raise the issue of authorship. Lacking evidence to the contrary, it seems safe to treat a holograph text as the intellectual product of the person who penned it, but sometimes there is evidence to suggest otherwise.[26] The matter was central to a recent difference of opinion about the oeuvre of the early Mormon William Clayton, when an edition of Clayton's writings included a text called "Nauvoo Temple, 1845-1846."[27] Clayton wrote that the dignitary Heber C. Kimball was so ill during the period in question that "he requested me to write his private journal to day [10 December 1845]" and the arrangement continued until 6 January 1846.

A reviewer took exception, arguing that Clayton had merely served as scribe for Kimball, writing that "[n]o responsible historian presumes to publish such journals as part of the papers of the scribes who wrote them . . . Such journals are the journals of those for whom they were written."

Allen asserts that "Clayton never thought of Kimball's journal as his own," but should he not have? Kimball left it to Clayton to read his mind and record the results in his (Kimball's) journal. We can hardly know what Kimball would have written, only what Clayton did write, and he surely did not write exactly what Kimball would have written had he been less preoccupied. At most, we might think of this as a co-written text, but it would be more appropriate to treat it, as Smith did, as written by Clayton, even if inspired in some unknowable way by Kimball.

VII

The Chronicle of Higher Education featured the following text—unpunctuated here: "Dear John I want a man who knows what love is all about you are generous kind thoughtful people who are not like you admit to being useless and inferior you have ruined me for other men I yearn for you I have no feelings whatsoever when we're apart I can be forever happy will you let me be yours Susan"[28] The text was offered twice, each time with a different punctuation set. This manipulation produced texts with diametrically opposite meanings, one a proverbial "Dear John" letter, the other a confession of undying love.

Few historical texts are of such parlor-game quality, but Susan's letter reflects a serious aspect of text editing—more than words are involved. When deciding whether to supply a punctuation mark (clearly noted, of course) the editor of a text is forced to consider not only the author's punctuation habits (as well as his own!), but those of the society in which the original text was composed. Were commas used then to distinguish inclusive and exclusive phrases?[29] Did the dash serve as a period? Did capitalization have any rules (does it yet?)? Did Susan love John—or did she leave him?

The standard version of one of the most important texts in history, the Hebrew bible, was established by introducing one particular form of punctuation. In Semitic languages long vowels are shown, but short vowels are left to the discernment and discretion of readers. Word roots usually consist of three consonants, and various permutations result from the interplay of prefixes, infixes, and suffixes; the doubling of consonants; and of course, the short vowels as they are presumed to exist. By such manipulation, three consonants can end up spawning a large number of words, each with different, if usually related, meanings.

The Hebrew bible had originally been unvocalized; the presumption was that god would not let his half-words be misinterpreted. From the seventh to the ninth centuries CE, a group of scholars known as the Masoretes added the symbols for short vowels, thus removing any pre-existing room for maneuver.[30] The Masoretic text is regarded as canonical, but it can hardly be disregarded that the choices the Masoretes made were ultimately subjective. Martin Luther was one of many who used this circumstance as justification for using the Septuagint—an earlier translation into Greek—to vernacularize the biblical text.

An important question is the degree to which text editing constitutes ideology. In criticizing those who argue that Shakespeare wrote two plays about King Lear, or at least two versions different enough to be treated separately, Paul

Cantor challenges their "destabilizing" of Shakespeare's work as "insidious" because they hide behind "what appears to be an ideologically neutral activity like textual editing."[31] But what is text editing but a series of small and large *choices*? These in turn can be based only on our own propensities and experiences. As noted above, even the best edition of Columbus's journal bears the imprint of the editors' theories about his first landfall. Yet an editor with no knowledge of—and therefore no opinion on—the landfall problem is exceedingly unlikely to know enough to edit the journal well.

VIII

The nineteenth-century text editor Thomas Gaisford recalled that he turned to editing at the advice of one of his teachers that "[y]ou will never be a gentleman, but you may succeed with certainty as a scholar. Take some little known Greek author and throw your knowledge into editing it: that will found your reputation."[32] Times have changed; nowadays the intending editor is likely to receive contrary advice. Most historians have not been exposed to the craft and are in danger of thinking that both textual issues and textual editors are uncomplicated beings. Only by experience can historians be disabused. Graduate students in history should be required to confront a text and try to tame it. Giving the entire class the same text of several thousand words—which could be integral or extracted from a larger text—would instill a usefully competitive spirit. Using a holograph text will further ensure that crucial issues of paleography and calligraphy are dealt with.

The exercise should involve providing an appropriate level of annotation and other apparatus (maps, charts, bibliography, glossary, a discussion of modus operandi). The students would be given a short list of editions of similar works that the instructor deems worthy. Students could collaborate, and adequate time would be allocated for a thorough discussion of what will certainly be a diversity of results. A few in the class will excel, perhaps discover their métier, but is hard to imagine that any students undertaking this exercise would not come to appreciate the intellectual rigors involved in preparing an exemplary text edition.

An impediment to effecting these things is that text editions seldom attract wide audiences. For this we can safely blame human nature, for when esthetics and authenticity clash, the inclination is to prefer the former. It is natural that we should prefer the familiar, hearing Bach or Haydn or Mozart as we learned them rather than as the composers heard their own works. For many, after all,

Shakespeare or Joyce are impenetrable enough without presenting them as actually written.

Familiarity breeding contentment is exemplified by the responses to proposals to refurbish Michelangelo's Sistine Chapel paintings in the 1980s. The ceiling of the chapel suffered from five centuries of gradual encrustation, and it was no longer possible even to be sure what colors Michelangelo had used. Cleaning the ceiling was normal art restoration, but the celebrity of the work polarized both the art world and the general public. One view was that the restoration "rewrites history" and cites the restoration's director that it had "brought to light (and will continue to bring to light) a totally new artist."[33] Others pointed out that what some called "new" was really only a return to the original. Neither side convinced the other; the restoration continued and received rave reviews on its completion.[34]

IX

So John Foxe is not atypical, even if Freeman's careful dissection of the careless work of those relying on his pseudo-texts is. Some hope for such exercises comes from cyberspace, particularly websites, which are natural venues for creating text editions. Websites are also likely venues for storing massive detailed studies too large to publish separately, such as the 80,000-word "appendix" devoted to the borrowing practices of the Elizabethan/Jacobean historian Sir John Hayward.[35] Through its *Documentary Editing*, the Association for Documentary Editing provides an ongoing forum for active and potential editors to become aware of new editions and cutting-edge thoughts and methods. It also fosters the publication of handbooks, bibliographies, and other reference works in the field.[36] Beyond this, there is a need for historical journals to provide space and encouragement for brief discussions of textual cruxes. How many American Historical Association prizes are there, and how many of them for text editing?[37]

20

GAINING AND PROVIDING ACCESS

Let Mr. Macpherson deposit the MS in one of the colleges at
Aberdeen where there are people who can judge, and if the
professors certify the authenticity, then there will be an end of
the controversy.

The literature on the peopling of America is so enormous and
highly specialized that even experts have a hard time keeping
up with the latest research. This book is based on thousands of
different papers, monographs, reviews, and short reports in
many languages. We can cite but a tiny number of them here.

I

Once the thinking has been carried out, doing follows, and this closely
involves the relationship of historian and sources as well as historian and
audience. The scholarly world is being reminded of an old concept—"access"—
which in many cases is what libraries and scholars purchase in lieu of books and
journals, photocopies and microforms. Whether this is a good thing remains to be
seen, although buying access is clearly more risky than buying, and owning, a
product. Too much lies outside scholars' control and in the hands of those who do
not necessarily smile benignly on the idea of the free interchange of ideas. Even
so, as an idea, "access" has a long history in scholarship. Here I group together

discussion of several forms and notions of access, since effective access preordains all progress inside and outside scholarship.

II

Until the nineteenth century little enough was written, or was otherwise available, and the enterprising scholar could learn about materials and come into possession of them without an impossible amount of labor. Nowadays there are far too many primary and secondary sources to consult. As a result, the historian confronts a body of potentially useful information many times greater than that which his grandfather would have faced. Along the way, the word "available" has taken on new and intriguing connotations. Gibbon, Macaulay, Ranke, or Acton had far less to look at, but still had to travel to libraries and archives or pay copyists to act as surrogates. Electronic databases with full-text materials now reside in most research libraries at little or no cost to the user. If a historian wishes to consult a journal issue not physically available in his local library, he can often resort to databases that make available long runs of many hundreds of mainstream scholarly journals. Still, databases should never be mistaken for Ur-texts. A transmission has taken place, with the perils this always involves. Unlike a photocopy, this transmission is from one medium to another. No more than a photograph of an inscription is equivalent to the inscription, or a description of heat to warmth, so users of full-text electronic databases cannot rely entirely on an electronic copy, and should seek out the original if such apparently minor matters as punctuation are at stake.

III

Access to sources has improved steadily in recent years. Finding guides for repositories, online access to hundreds of library catalogs, bibliographic databases galore, keyword searching of the combined contents of hundreds of journals, and many other new opportunities make becoming aware of material, new and old, simpler and more effective than ever. These improvements are not a moment too soon in arriving. Articles of interest to historians have probably tripled in the past twenty years, partly because many historians have become curious about fields they had never noticed before. Historians approaching a new subject of interest must orient themselves more quickly and thoroughly than ever before, not only to grasp the state of the field, but to be sure that they have not been pre-empted.

The traditional method was to cull footnotes, consult colleagues, and, for the most motivated historians, to consult specialized bibliographies systematically.[1] Yet with the decline of the footnote and increasing specialization, the first two alternatives have lost much of their value, while specialized bibliographies now number in the thousands and can be found in print and in electronic formats, and cover even the most exotic fields.

Kenneth Kitchen estimated that the "[E]gyptological output of papers, books, etc. has increased fourfold in 50 years" and that scholars would need to read four items every day of the year to keep pace.[2] In classics, a field some think moribund, "twice as many [classical] scholars now publish 50 percent more material in twice as many journals" than thirty years earlier.[3] Overall, the number of books published today is about four times what it was in 1975. Tabulating even a few major serial bibliographies shows how easily a scrupulous historian could fall victim to cognitive overload. The latest *Année Philologique* has over about 15,000 entries, the *International Medieval Bibliography* has over 11,000, and *Medioevo Latino* nearly 15,000. Meanwhile, the *Bibliographie Annuelle de l'Histoire de la France* has over 13,000, and the *Jahresbericht für deutsche Geschichte* another 17,000, and there are a host of other national historical bibliographies. Even the narrowly-focused historian must blanch at the magnitude of his task, while comparativists might well contemplate changing occupations.

It is possible to search printed bibliographies seriatim in hopes of finding materials about which we knew nothing until we find the citation—that is, serendipity is methodically at work. In contrast, while electronic databases are exceptionally useful for *known* author, title, or keyword searches, they do not foster less specific forms of hunting. The very object of trolling—to learn about new data, especially from sources peripheral to presumed interests—becomes all but impossible. The effect is to circumscribe the historian's ability to work comparatively and interdisciplinarily.

Of particular value are the nearly one thousand serial bibliographies that appear at—mostly—regular intervals.[4] Sometimes these have their own published identity, but more often they are secreted in journals. From all appearances, these bibliographies are an endangered species. For many years such a bibliography appeared in each issue of the *American Historical Review*, but this grew so large that it began to be published separately as *Recently Published Articles*. *Recently Published Articles* varied in quality from one section to another, but it was a brave attempt to canvass the world. For historians interested in currency, comprehensiveness, and the comparative outlook, it was unrivaled. Its real competition proved to be the bottom line, and in 1990 it abruptly ceased publication on the uncongenial grounds that it was a money-loser.[5]

Just thinking about the universe of reference works—past, present, and to come—is overwhelming. It is impossible not to consider the inevitable results of more and more information that is easier and easier to access being funneled into two contumacious bottlenecks: time and the human brain, both far more finite than the production of information. Studies are more and more about less and less, simply to be feasible. Historians of Africa can find more on the numerous aspects of the Atlantic slave trade or on agriculture in colonial Nigeria than their not-so-distant predecessors could on the whole of Africa. As a result, only a few dare write about the continent as a whole, and they must abandon all hope of tying all the argument to all the evidence and opt instead for grand theorizing, for which they have a foolproof excuse. Another response is to bypass more and more evidence by arguing that it is all essentially meaningless anyway. While unfortunate, this response could hardly be called gratuitous, but is almost a justifiable self-defense mechanism for the harried historian.[6]

IV

This proliferation runs against the conventional wisdom of a few decades ago, when print was diagnosed as terminally ill, and no one had yet considered the effects of internetting on the acquisition and dissemination of knowledge. This plenitude often works against us, forcing us to be at once more energetic and more selective. Failing to be either only drops us farther back in the race, yet succeeding at both is no guarantee of success. On the other hand, a number of once standard sources have all but disappeared. How much more difficult it must be to write effectively about events that take place in the days of the telephone and e-mail! While archives continue to bulge at the seams, far less of the influx is as centrally important as the minuted dispatches and memoranda of the past. Ironically, discussion and decision-making is now as much oral as written. The conclusions might still reach paper and posterity, but the arguments that underpin and explain them are more and more frequently lost forever.

Some archives, unfortunately, do not continue to bulge. Many of these are in developing areas, where the costs of maintaining the past must give way to those of easing the present. The National Archives of Ghana offer a stark, but not isolated example. In 1971 they were well-organized and calendared, maintained in a climate-controlled environment, and attended by a staff eager and able to provide prompt and efficient help. Harsh economic conditions in Ghana have since caused a series of untoward events. Materials have been sold for wrapping paper; staff has been reduced to a skeleton force; the air conditioning and dehumidifying have been abandoned; hours of service have been sharply curtailed.[7] As a result, many citations to archives no older than twenty years must now be taken on faith alone. In the heady days of the 1960s and early 1970s the Ghanaian government arranged for materials about the earlier history of the Gold Coast that are held by European archives to be filmed and brought to Ghana, but did little to safeguard their homegrown materials. As a result, history in Ghana for the earlier periods is in danger of reverting to a disproportionately Eurocentric perspective.

V

Many authors appear to agree with Michael Schiffer that "[w]here no authors are cited specifically for the information . . . I have simply made a reasonable guess in the absence of the relevant data."[8] It is not mere pique to argue that users have the obligation to distrust any scholarly work that fails to provide ample and convenient access to the grounds for its arguments. If historians' success in making a case depends on access to required sources, success in propagating it depends on providing effective access to the arguments, including the means to test them. The historian serves as a linchpin in the delicate balance between securing early access and providing later access. No historian should emerge from this process without at least sharing, and preferably enhancing, access to his own arguments and sources. Generally, this is the purpose of footnoting, already briefly discussed.[9]

The historian William Robertson held firm opinions on the need for calculated citing. He criticized Voltaire's historical works on the grounds that "he seldom imitates the example of modern historians in citing the authors from whom they derived their information, [so] I could not with propriety appeal to his authority in confirmation of any doubtful or unknown fact."[10] In turn, he lavished high praise on Gibbon's *History of the Decline and Fall of the Roman Empire*, claiming that he had "traced him in many of his quotations, (for experience has taught me to suspect the accuracy of my brother penmen,) and I find he refers to no passage but what he has seen with his own eyes."[11]

Just the same, in many fields footnotes are rather out of fashion. Publishers are partly at fault for this development. First the move was from the bottom of the page to the end of the book, even when no longer advantageous technologically.

Another gambit has been to retain the footnotes, but aggregate all references in a single paragraph into a portmanteau citation at the end of the paragraph. This is a very unwelcome development, as it becomes impossible for readers to disentangle a string of disparate citations and attach them to the statements they are intended to document. An egregious example is Shepard Krech's *The Ecological Indian*, a scholarly work issued by a commercial press, a burgeoning development. Krech uses notes to advance arguments, but largely to cite relevant literature. All note references are placed at the end of paragraphs, with the result that there are many notes that range from 40 to 65 lines long and contain as many as 25 to 30 references. Lastly, all notes are endnotes, forcing a further needless chore on the already afflicted reader.[12]

The extent to which claims should be documented naturally depends on the intended audience. If historians or other cognoscenti comprise this, the following distinctions seems reasonable if, say, the subject is a reassessment of the performance of general officers in the Confederate army. The causes, general course, and chronology of the Civil War are too well known to require justifying statements about them, although any statements based on unpublished material should be documented. If the historian's case is heterodox—say he intends to make a hero of James Longstreet at the expense of Stonewall Jackson—he must cite literature defending the orthodox position as well as that supporting his own. Although publishers—and many readers—find this irritating, it is far worse to confront a novel argument that documents itself too poorly to convince skeptical readers. Sometimes, it *is* the weight of evidence and not just its quality. If, conversely, the historian's design is to organize commonly-accepted theses into a larger hypothesis, it will be the way he uses his material rather than the material itself that will make or break his case.

If historians have the obligation to seek out the most primary source when quoting, readers have the right to discover this by seeking out the historian's cited sources, checking them, and, if called for, going beyond them. The reasons for this are crystalized in a case where an author misquoted his sources, including himself, about 75 percent of the time.[13] Perhaps this is exceptional, but it underscores the scope for abuse that historians have, and with it the onus to be as scrupulous as possible.

VI

Most handbooks of research method advise us how to render footnotes, but not all preach alike. If anything, there is a tendency to prescribe more information than is ordinarily needed. A good citation should include every element that is necessary to locate a source efficiently, and nothing more. Indispensable elements of footnotes citing a book include author's full name, full title, place and date of publication, and page/s cited. Those citing an article include author's full name and full title, along with the name of the journal, the volume number and date, and specific pages cited. Anything short of this thwarts access.[14] Anything more is usually wasteful.

It is commonplace to see citations to specific information—even to a direct quote—with no page numbers provided. Writing on drought in ancient Egypt Barbara Bell included two quotations. For the first she cited "Frankfort (1951)" and for the second an article by A.H. Gardiner "(*JEA* 1:36)."[15] This is far short of allowing easy tracing and/or interlibrary borrowing. Arguing a case for frequent cometary bombardment of earth, Mike Baillie writes that "Gervase of Canterbury appears to record a more-or-less first-hand account of a major impact on the moon on 25 June AD 1178 which could fit with the existence of the recent Giordano Bruno crater."[16] No one has made just this claim before, and readers will want the evidence, but Baillie offers no argument, cites no edition of Gervase, no secondary source. Are we to take him seriously? In fact, no. Tracking Gervase down shows that he began writing only in 1185, and since he wrote that he was relying on the word of others, questions of misperception, memory, and other distortions arise.[17]

Footnotes can use their very advantages to disadvantage by validating false information. Doubtless this happens more than we imagine, but a very recent, and somewhat odd, example shows the principle at work. In 1999 there appeared what advertised itself as a biography of Ronald Reagan.[18] Its author invented a fictional character to help chronicle Reagan's early years and add immediacy to the story. It is bad enough that he made no explicit mention of this expedient, but far worse that he uses the footnote apparatus to 'document' statements of his fictional source.

Above all, footnotes—even traditional footnotes—need to be accurate. Their consumers will have no way of knowing whether they are until they are unable to locate the materials referenced. At best, moving in the right direction will require unnecessary additional labor—at worst, the source will never be found, perhaps it never existed. No author should published material without conducting at least a random check to be sure that he or she has not made transcriptional or cognitive errors.[19]

VII

Thoughts on the art of clear writing have been sufficiently propagated to need little attention here. The key for the historian is to think carefully about his audience, its needs and abilities. A useful rule of thumb is to presume an audience slightly less well informed than is likely to be the case. Presume much more and readers might feel patronized; presume too little and they will feel bewildered. A recent example of the latter is a book entitled *Chronometric Dating in Archaeology*, which includes chapters on historical issues such as ice cores and other forms of climatostratigraphy, dendrochronology, and thermoluminescence dating.[20] Since historians often show an interest in these matters, they would presumably benefit from up-to-date overviews of the bona fides of these techniques by those who devised them and employ and interpret them routinely in their work.

Unfortunately, it is the rare historian who will find these presentations useful; they are uniformly opaque in presentation, and their bibliographies carry on this infra-dig tradition by making no concessions to outsiders. The authors seem unaware that these techniques interest historians. *Chronometric Dating* was published "in cooperation with the Society for Archaeological Sciences," described as "exist[ing] to encourage interdisciplinary collaboration between archaeologists and colleagues in the natural sciences."[21] Clearly, historians are not among the intended audience, nor is the work likely to be reviewed in organs that historians are apt to consult.

In calculating the population of Peru at contact, N.D. Cook back-projects from later estimates, using a "standard" formula among historical demographers: $P_2 = P_1 e^{rt}$. Daunting enough as it is, this formula becomes useless in Cook's hands, since he does not explain that e is a constant with a value of 2.17828. Cook thereby inoculates himself against attempts to understand or assess his arguments.[22] Did not Cook, or his editors, realize that most of his readers would be historians untrained in the arcana of demography, and that his obligation was to present them with *all* the necessary tools to judge his case?[23]

Lastly, a word about the lowly index. Historians seldom read works in their entirety when pursuing their own research. They are looking for the mot juste, the specific citation, or the reference to matters of common interest, and are apt to consult the index before anything else, in hopes of streamlining their task. In compiling an index, technology is no substitute for the professional indexer, who in turn is seldom an adequate surrogate for the author, to whom indexing might seem an inexpressibly tedious chore after the intellectual challenges of composing the text itself. Compiling an index, however, can uncover repetitions, inconsistencies, and outright errors. Its greatest virtue though is that the author is in the best position to anticipate the needs of others and thus to prepare an index that takes account of the many angles of vision that users might bring to it.

But how about no index at all? Once upon a time this question would only have raised eyebrows, but at present it is all too germane. The authors, editors, and publishers of books in many fields, especially volumes of collected essays (biblical studies comes promptly to mind) seem completely uninterested in providing readers with entrée to the materials they have so laboriously compiled.[24] One can only wonder why an author or publisher would expect a readership for a text that has been rendered impenetrable through indolence or indifference. Authors, editors, and publishers must find common ground that recognizes that the apparatus of a scholarly work is crucial to optimizing the work's impact. Many well-conceived arguments and much well-honed prose go unnoticed and untested by being rendered inaccessible by authors or editors who fail to understand that the most effective access to them is a complex chain of procedures that cannot safely be breached.

VIII

No field presents more problems for broad-gauged access than archeology. For a century or more the standard operating procedure has been to produce one or more volumes which would constitute the official presentation of material and interpretation by members of the excavating team. Site reports feature many photographs and line drawings, are often in large format, tend to be expensive, and were regarded as the final intellectual and moral obligation of those who did the digging.

This is no longer the majority case. Major sites that have been excavated for decades have never produced any site reports.[25] It is estimated, for example, that some 2200 excavations were carried out in Israel between 1989 and 1998, in which "final publications lag far behind." [26] Instead, there is a spate of interpretive overviews, often making outlandish claims that are refuted or retracted as soon as they have been made public. Finally, there are signs of a spirit of possessiveness, in which excavators seek not to disseminate, but to censor, because of professional rivalries or ambitions. The idea is to retain, for as long as possible, exclusive rights to the site, the artifacts, or the texts, and so of their interpretation.

The most notorious recent case of restricting access is that of the so-called Dead Sea Scrolls. After their discovery in the 1940s and 1950s individual rolls or groups of rolls were put into the hands of qualified scholars who were expected to study and edit them, and publish the results with reasonable dispatch. After about thirty years of profound silence, a hue and cry arose from those who wondered why so little material had reached the public domain. The dam finally burst in 1991, as film and computer-generated editions of many of the materials appeared almost simultaneously, followed by numerous editions of particular texts based on these. The most intriguing, if least edifying, aspect of this occasion was the sense of affront that greeted this overdue concern. The new publications were met with cries of resentful anguish from some members of the incumbent cartel, who argued that their careers and those of their anointed graduate students would suffer as a consequence of such "unauthorized" publication.

The carteliers found little sympathy either in the academy or from the public.[27] One scholar identified the real issue when he pointed out that those who produced the 'rogue' editions did so "on the assumption that the need to secure the freedom of access to information outweighs the intellectual property rights" of the carteliers, even though they might be building on work of these members.[28] The troubling words are "property" and "rights." Carteliers can exercise no pre-emptive rights, least of all those they unilaterally took onto themselves. After all, none of the carteliers took part in either the creation or the discovery of the Qumran documents and, in lieu of contractual completion dates, the canons of scholarly business take over, and these cannot be called on to support laggardness of a heroic scale.

IX

To what degree should historians feel obligated to deposit their raw materials where liberal access would be possible, and what should these include? Naturally, scholars have perpetual rights to use materials they have created themselves, but there should be a palpable sense of obligation to share, although this can be confined to materials that would otherwise not become available. Thus photocopies or microforms of archival materials need not be saved, nor such things as preliminary drafts—unless the historian fancies himself the object of future research. Such materials as computational programs, audio or video tapes, and photographs, however, should be preserved. Works in economic history whose conclusions result from amassing and massaging disparate data can be judged only if these data, and their manipulation, are allowed to fall under the gaze of those who might disagree with their content or processing.

Certainly important is the preservation of field tapes, on whose evidence so much history has recently depended.[29] Collecting oral testimonies is a challenging and subtle operation that can go awry without the historian ever realizing it. It is remarkable that consumers of such products are expected to accept not only the bona fides of informants, but also the linguistic capacity of the researcher and/or his interpreters, and finally the appropriate historiographical skills as the researcher turns author. In the forty-odd years since most of this work began to be carried out, many tapes and notebooks that presumably could have provided justification for its collective argumentation have disappeared or become unusable.

As noted above, transcripts are by no means an acceptable substitute. The field tapes themselves must be deposited, preferably with some kind of rough-and-ready index—although the depositing should never be allowed to wait for the indexing. There are several depositories around the world geared to receive, process, publicize, and make available audio and video tapes. One of these, or a comparable alternative site, should be approached long before the tapes begin to dematerialize. Most repositories allow donors to impose an embargo period during which only they have access, allowing them a reasonable opportunity to exploit whatever they have gathered. Otherwise, those who collect and use field materials, but do not share them, usurp some part of the record of the past by suppressing access to it.

X

The sheer magnitude of sources can force its custodians to limit access. Archives have had a century to deal with this, and most well-organized archives do not have serious backlogs of entirely unclassified materials. Despite much doomsaying about the death of the book, however, most research libraries still have sizeable caches of unprocessed materials, some reaching back as far as the 1960s, when library budgets allowed the purchase of practically everything then available, but failed to provide the wherewithal to put these acquisitions on the shelves. Museums seem to be worse off yet. As of 1999, only half of several thousand Babylonian tablets in the British Museum have been cataloged, and only ten percent translated.[30] Such a state of affairs can only make us wonder how it is possible to advance defensible arguments about Babylonian history in full knowledge of the fact that such a substantial portion of the surviving materials have never even been consulted.

Circumstance quite outside the scholarly world often inhibit access to data. If academic politics kept the Qumran scrolls under wraps, politics of a different kind threaten the scholarly study of the American Indian past. The Native American Graves Protection and Repatriation Act (NAGPRA), enacted in 1990, would, if broadly construed, make it virtually impossible for physical and cultural anthropologists to continue the study of Indian skeletal and artifactual remains.

The potential effects became evident with the discovery of the skeleton known as Kennewick Man. Found in 1996 and dated to 9300 years ago, the skeleton appears surprisingly "Caucasoid" to many. If further study were to confirm these first impressions, it could have an incalculable effect on many theories of American prehistory. Pleading NAGPRA, the Army Corps of Engineers took possession of the remains, planning to turn them over to one or more groups of Indians who claim Kennewick Man as their "ancestor" and thus subject to NAGPRA guidelines. Only in 2002 did the courts allow Kennewick Man to be manumitted from the Corps' stifling hammer lock, but this ruling will probably not affect other cases where similar restrictions apply.[31]

XI

A few years ago the *Chronicle of Higher Education* reported that the University of California at Santa Barbara was "experimenting with technology to let faculty members create individual digital-library collections tailored to their teaching and research needs."[32] The appeal is obvious—save steps and time by bringing library resources into home and office. Saving steps might have deleterious effects on health, and saving time is likely to have similar effects on curiosity. The scholar is proactive when he designs his template, but only reactive after that, perhaps thinking that he is repeatedly replicating a visit to the library. But this is hardly so. A historian—or any other scholar—might think he knows what he wants to see, but he cannot possibly anticipate what he might profit from if only he were aware of it. Yet "tailoring" involves decisions about exclusiveness as well as inclusiveness. While it does not foreclose individual initiative, there is a well-recognized tendency by those who use technology to rely increasingly on it, not only for gathering and organizing data, but for making decisions about how to use them.

While cyberspace seems infinite, its boundaries are less permeable than the old-fashioned ways of seeking information, which allowed systematic trolling and serendipity to function. The new databases can search themselves extremely efficiently, and links can be established with other databases which in turn can search themselves just as efficiently. But electronic information is more concerned with efficiency than with expanding horizons, so it can only occasionally offer users ideas other than those that have already been implanted. The lucky find is still possible, but the unexpected one is not, precisely because it was not factored into the ability of bibliographical databases to locate citations for the user who already knows something, and offers the illusion of closure.

The news is not all bad—a lot of it is very good, sometimes in unexpected quarters, and is getting better. In her study of one of the two earliest manuscripts of the Laȝamon *Brut*, which had been damaged by fire, Elizabeth Bryan used "fiber optic backlighting and microscope to examine all 146 folios." These helped to uncover "features of the manuscript no one had guessed were there . . ."[33] Old and new work on digitizing a number of Spanish historical sources provides both enhanced access and improved visual quality for these sources.[34] The Library of Congress is digitizing 83,000 images from its collection of Thomas Jefferson papers, which users will be able to browse by keywords and other methods.[35] The list grows longer—and the sites grow better—every day.[36] The onset of more and more sophisticated digital camera equipment will allow archival research to be streamlined and archeological research to be more thoroughly documented.[37]

Whether one side or the other can claim higher moral ground in these instances is an important issue, but irrelevant to the present discussion. Here the concern is that situations exist that, on balance, are creating diminished access to historical data. Meanwhile, online searching enhances vertical searches but shrinks lateral awareness, and is a special disservice for those whose major interests are comparative.[38] It has become easier to locate references to articles with the word "Cortés" in them, but more difficult to find articles that refer to war reportage generally or collectively. Maybe Pogo had it right—maybe "the enemy is us."

21

HEARING A WHITE HORSE COMING

But the scientific spirit requires a man to be at all times to
ready dump his whole cartload of beliefs, the moment experience is against them.

In this work, it is well that we have an army of eager minds,
each anxious to discover the mistakes of all the others, for
only so can we hope to reach secure results.

I

Gazing both behind and ahead, a historian of science indulged in a moment
of introspection: ". . . in the fullness of time, will future generations of
scholars smile at our methods, at our conclusions, and at our gullibility just as we
smile at what we perceive to have been the geo-chronological absurdities of the
likes of Ussher, Buffon, Kelvin or Joly? Will future generations of scholars have
a far more sophisticated notion of time than that vouchsafed to us and will they
wonder why, in an age of Relativity, we were so naive as to persist with a belief
in time as a simple linear phenomenon?"[1]

The long picture certainly encourages musings along these lines. Ussher
thought the world 6000 years old, Buffon, perhaps as much as 150,000 years but
probably less, Kelvin less than 40,000 years, and Joly about the same. Each used
different scientific methods of their times, and each had a significant short-term
impact on thinking on the matter.[2] Yet, a short century after Kelvin, the age of the

earth was estimated at 4.5 billion years, or more than 100,000 times greater than he had believed.[3]

II

Replying to a reviewer who had thought his work contained "a very great element of fantasy," T.P. Wiseman defended the use of imagination: "[i]magination, controlled by evidence and argument, is the first necessity if our understanding of the past is ever to be improved."[4] Who would quarrel with this, given the qualifying phrase? But imagination should especially be grounded in, and often circumscribed by, the broadest available canvass of recorded human experience. After all, nothing is less imaginative than treating the evidence we encounter as read.

Throughout this work I have tried to emphasize the rich diversity of evidence, argument, and results that have characterized historical inquiry in the past and that continue to do so. Perhaps the most attractive aspect of the study of history is the infiniteness of both the subject matter and its pursuit. Referring to early China, Shaughnessy notes that "the last decade and a half of the twentieth century has brought us an extraordinary wealth of new materials . . . with which to study . . . any number of . . . issues, many of them not even imagined just twenty years ago."[5] Even topics that attract endless attention undergo sea-changes from time to time, as new evidence is gathered or existing evidence subjected to renewed scrutiny that seems to make better sense of it.

A common variable is that historians must avoid absolutes, resisting the temptation to promulgate one version as so wedded to all the available evidence that there is no prospect of overturning it, and therefore no reason to try. Sigmund Freud once pronounced that "[t]he only person who has a right to a conviction is someone who, like me, has worked for many years at the same material and who, in doing so, has himself had the same new and surprising experiences."[6] This looks like a slip of the tongue later named after him. It also sounds much like other numerous protestations on the personal prerogative to be certain.

As Silverstein points out in his discussion of closure fever in the sciences, such claims "assume that the discipline (or field, or science) is bounded by the facts and theories *as they are known at the time.*"[7] The discourse of closure often masks defects in the evidence and arguments based on it. The cases of the contact population of the Americas and the insatiable chronologizing of the ancient Near East are salient, but far from isolated, examples of the pernicious alliance between the weakness of the thing and the strength of the words about it.

III

Assessing new archeological discoveries in Mesopotamia in 1908, the great classical historian Eduard Meyer expressed dismay: "[s]mall wonder that one resisted accepting [this evidence]: how much we had erred, how much above all the Greek information . . . turned out to be historically worthless data, one could not . . . have imagined."[8] Despite his chagrin, Meyer duly accepted the new data and cast aside his reliance on Herodotus and other ancient historians for Mesopotamian matters.

The best, but not always the most successful, historical arguments are those that are presented so objectively and marshal so overwhelming a body of evidence that they convince against best interests and previous experience. Arguments that could persuade a conservative Catholic that many of the saints in the liturgical calendar never existed, a conservative Indian historian that the Mahabharata war never occurred, or an agnostic that certain phenomena cannot be ascribed to 'natural' causes becomes successful because they overcome resistance.

Examples of these are in the nature of things rare enough, and while they must be intensely satisfying, such epiphanic moments should not beguile the historian, nor their absence discourage him. It is not unusual for new ideas to take more than a scholarly lifetime to gain acceptance, and even more common for them not to gain acceptance at all. In 1912 Alfred Wegener first advanced the theory of continental drift to explain the present surface of the earth, and was promptly dubbed a scientific heretic. An opponent clearly enunciated the stakes: "[i]f we are to believe in Wegener's hypothesis we must forget everything that has been learned in the last 70 years and start all over again."[9] For geologists at the time, the prospect was too dire to contemplate, but ultimately (it took another fifty years or so) and with some modifications, Wegener was transformed from pariah to prophet and by the early 1970s the latest revolution in geology was complete: "the plate tectonics version of Drift . . . was firmly entrenched as the new orthodoxy."[10] The lessons are clear. Orthodoxies are easier to establish than to modify or supplant, yet are always subject to overthrow given the right combination of evidence, argument, and timing. It is not only continents that drift; perhaps the new orthodoxy of the 1970s will in turn give way to further variations, although presumably the break will not be as great as between theories before and after Wegener.

IV

In his account of the city of Ebla, whose remains were discovered only about thirty years ago, Giovanni Pettinato included a list of about 80 polities "attested" in the records from there so far examined. Of these we know a bit about a few (Aššur, Emar, Kiš, Mari) and all but nothing beyond these attestations about any of the rest, and there is little reason to think that this will change much.[11] This microcosm should serve as a firm reminder to be diffident in our claims about what our work can accomplish. Paradoxically, Ebla answers questions we never thought to ask while raising many others that we do not know how to answer.

If the past is so infinite, can its study be far behind? The rediscovery of such sites as Ugarit and Ebla have produced cottage industries designed to take advantage of the new evidence. In the past twenty years new sources for Inca history have turned up, with lesser effect, but of substantial value. Scientific advances produce evidence that needs to be interpreted and incorporated into arguments originally developed without them. Challenges that historians now face as to the sheer extent of the evidence can only affect their work adversely. Three examples can make the point. At a slightly more humanly understandable level, a discussion of the promise and problems of new ways of communicating information noted that in 1998 the holdings of the U.S. National Archives and Records Administration were "so huge as to be almost comical," consisting of "four billion pieces of paper; 9.4 million photographs; 338,029 films and videos; 2,648,918 maps and charts; nearly three million engineering and architectural plans; and more than nine million aerial photographs."[12] These holdings are increasing at an increasing rate, and in a variety of formats whose integrity and stability cannot yet be determined.

More dramatically yet, an ongoing effort to estimate the universe of information past and present calculates that, measured in exabytes (10^{18}) the information generated in 1999 alone was equal to 40 percent of "[a]ll words ever spoken by human beings" until then.[13] Of course this figure must be taken with more than the proverbial grain of skepticism, but, even if is accepted as twice as high as it should be, it is a harrowing message to all those interested in the past.

Finally, a new map of a 4° slice—sliver, really—of the universe was recently published and it included 8420 satellites, 14,183 asteroids, and 126,625 galaxies.[14] Undoubtedly each of these numbers will become even greater. There is no hope of coping this kind of near-infinity; we can only try to blind ourselves to the consequences.

V

This forces us to consider what it means to be historians in the Age of Information. As already noted, the electronic world seems to ensure a number of good things. We can learn about more, and learn it more quickly, through bibliographic and other databases. We can gain access to this information without venturing to numerous repositories—our terminals have become repositories in their own right. We can manipulate information faster than ever, and can also write about it more efficiently than we ever could. But we must also recognize that our own synapses and neurons have now become the bottlenecks in the process. Barriers existed before—the costs of travel, the impediment of language, the hardships in tracking down elusive sources—but these were ultimately negotiable. Unfortunately no enhancements have been added to our genetic hard drive and none appear in the offing.

Nonetheless, despair is seldom the answer, even though it can be one of the cards in the deck. A more practical alternative is to concentrate on refining our skills in treating evidence, while at the same time seeking to incorporate as much evidence as possible in our canvass. Individuals will seldom be poised to develop large-scale arguments that are completely defensible. This will be accomplished, if at all, by teams of complementary personnel collectively devising arguments that can withstand foreseeable scrutiny. One way to accomplish this is to ensure that all members of the team routinely act as devil's advocates of their own and their colleagues' use of evidence and argument.

This sounds a bit like the system already in place in the sciences, where articles are sometimes credited to a risible number of authors, often by virtue of status rather than input. But the procedure can work efficiently, as we see in the many text editions that have been achieved recently by two or more editors working in tandem. It does not presume that this approach will become the most common in historiography, only that it is particularly suitable when there is danger that an argument will become estranged from the body of evidence supporting, or not supporting, it.

Many examples discussed here are consequences of ambitions that have outrun the ability or the inclination of historians to assure themselves that they can harness all the data required, not merely those that appear congenial.[15] As Henry Dobyns, a hardened veteran of the contact population wars, put it: "[o]ne either uses such data as may be available and learns something, however inadequate, or abjures such data and learns nothing."[16] Such gauzy definitions of words like "learn" fuel continuing efforts to estimate the contact population of the Americas or determine the exact date of some event, perhaps one not even historical.

VI

There is little hope that an approach that demands better evidence and argument will ever become popular.[17] Writing about ancient Palestine, J.M. Miller and John Hayes were frank: "[i]n the first place, we are cautious about saying anything." In the end they did say a bit, but concluded that "[w]e decline any attempt to reconstruct the earliest history of the Israelites."[18] For William Dever this attitude sprang not from caution, but from a "failure of nerve," based in large part on Miller and Hayes's second putative failure—not using archeological data effectively.[19] Couching the situation in terms of "nerve" suggests that when historians abandon the effort to elucidate some part of the past, it is because they, and not the evidence, are inadequate. It seems easier to push forward, counting on "nerve" to overcome deficiencies in the record.

Also dealing with biblical history, Baruch Halpern and Eben Scheffler took positions not unlike that of Dever. For Halpern, "[t]he question 'what is the minimum we can know?' is a question that impoverishes historical interpretation if it is not followed by the question "what in addition can we reasonably surmise?"[20] Scheffler was slightly more ambivalent, arguing that "[b]oth sides of the debate should rather concede in an anti-positivistic way that we simply do not have absolute and conclusive information for making final judgements." "But," he added, "this is not enough. An agnostic stance is boring."[21]

The challenge of historical research is to work toward the most satisfying answers we can, starting with asking the best questions we can. For many, the emphasis here on the complexities and ambiguities of historical evidence will seem annoyingly inhibiting. As human beings, we crave final answers, and the frustration of historical inquiry is that it provides so few of them. This leads to invidious comments like that of James Barr, who, referring to one of the Biblical minimalists, had this to say: "[i]n comparison with a real historian such as [Gösta] Ahlström, he has many historical ideas and proposals, many of them highly stimulating, but what comes out of it in the end is hardly a history; at times it seems more like a negation of history."[22] No wonder that H.S. Bennett commented in another matter that "[c]ontroversy is not a normal academic method of pursuing Truth, and [G.G.] Coulton had to pay for his unorthodoxy."[23]

Despite their own complexities, all the debates cited here boil down to a single question: is the evidence good enough to support the conclusions? Those who think it is will accept certain things as demonstrable fact and proceed to build on them, while those who do not will proceed to criticize those who do. The historian has several ways of besting the opposition. He can reinterpret the existing evidence in ways that are no worse than other interpretations, or he can seek out new evidence that might suit his purposes better. Or he can distort the evidence to fit his hypotheses or pretend that it doesn't exist. Doubters stimulate progress while believers, content in their position, are less inclined to seek out data that might compromise that contentment. As Arthur Koestler's protagonist put it some sixty years ago: "[t]he ultimate truth is penultimately always a falsehood."[24] To which we might add that it often proves not to be ultimate in its turn either, but merely one moment in a enduring cycle.

VII

It is counterintuitive, almost unimaginable, that a seven-letter word could be misspelled nearly 600 different ways, but the evidence is there for all to ponder.[25] Recognizing such unlikely realities enjoins historians to maintain a modest demeanor and method simply because it is almost always much easier to be wrong than right. On the bright side, those who prefer the chase to the capture might agree that "[s]olving mysteries, or trying to solve them, is wonderful, and if they were all solved that would be rather boring."[26] We can at least ensure that future generations have no chance to marvel at our gullibility, whatever our methods and conclusions.

P.R. Davies, a biblical "minimalist," listed several attributes that, he thought, were useful to historians. The third of these is "to remain sceptical, minimalist, and negative."[27] Davies's juxtaposition is unfortunate, since it suggests that to be skeptical is to destroy rather than to create. When appropriately applied, doubt opens doors, and minds, that are closed; fosters the search for new evidence or lines of reasoning; avoids lockstep adherence to poorly-defined and poorly-defended hypotheses; encourages a flexibility of mind that is commensurate with the exiguousness of the evidence; and stimulates curiosity and the imagination. In this there is nothing "negative" at all.

Speaking of boredom, can it possibly be boring that 44 dates (and counting) have been advocated for the establishment of the Zhou dynasty or 10 dates (and counting) for the accession of Amenemhat II? Is it uninteresting that the Shroud of Turin, perhaps the most studied artifact of all time (1000 tests and 32,000 photographs and counting) continues to elude unanimity or even consensus?[28] This variety is nothing more than the inevitable result of the state of the evidence. It is precisely for this reason that we should accept—and enjoy—the infinite variety of the past as we apprehend it and that makes it the most challenging and rewarding intellectual activity afoot for the particularly inquisitive mind. And, all along the way, it should not be hard to keep in mind the admonition of William Dunning, made in the heyday of Actonian certitude: "[t]he crying need in the study of history to-day is humility."[29]

NOTES

Chapter 1

Galileo to Benedetto Castelli, 21 December 1613, in Galilei, *Lettere*, 105.

Marston, *Wanton Angel*, 238.

[1]See, e.g., Anderson, *Zone of Engagement*, 279-375.

[2]Mill, *History of British India*, 1:xxiv.

[3]Acton, *Lectures*, 315.

[4]Langlois and Seignobos, *Introduction*, 275, emphasis added.

[5]Ibid., 91, emphasis added.

[6]Erichsen, "Tendency," 314. The phrase "the final limit" recurred several times in Erichsen's address.

[7]Maxwell, "Introductory Lecture," 2:244. For the twentieth century see Silverstein, "'End is Near!'"

[8]Michelson, *Light Waves,* 123-24. For the travails of this comment and its variants see Henige, "Mis/adventures," 130-33.

[9]See Badash, "Completeness." That these symptoms pervaded society can be seen from a prediction at the time that "the automobile has practically reached the limit of its development is suggested by the fact that during the past year no improvements of a radical nature have been introduced." *Scientific American* 100/1(January 1909), 6.

[10]Sextus Julius Frontinus, *Stratagems*, 218.

[11]Lemche, "Early Israel," 10.

[12]Leroy, *Interchangeable Course*, 127[V]. For similar thoughts from the time see Henige, "'Truths Yet Unborn'."

Chapter 2

Pawson, *Some By Fire*, 80, emphasis and ellipses in original.

Reade, "Assyrian Eponyms," 261.

[1]For Ramanujan's work and its reception see Kanigel, *Man Who Knew Infinity.*

[2]It is the last that distinguishes "belief" from "ideology."

[3] Forced to choose, I've adopted the male personal pronoun throughout in light of the fact that at the moment only about 30 percent of the procession are women.

[4]If nothing else, this would reduce the number of scholars about whom Joseph Lister wrote: "I remember at an early period of my own life showing to a man of high reputation as a teacher some matters which I happened to have observed. And I was very much struck and grieved to find that, while all the facts lay equally clear before him, only those which squared with his previous theories seemed to affect his organs of vision." Lister, "Graduation Address," 283.

[5]Morison, "Faith of a Historian," 263.

[6]See, e.g., Henige, "Samuel Eliot Morison."

[7]Gilliard, "Apostolicity," provides a convenient summary of the demolition work performed on the French episcopal lists.

[8]Owen, "Socrastical wisdom" (vi.39) in idem., *Latine Epigrams.*

[9]*Art de vérifier les dates,* 1:xxvii-xxxvi. Even more estimates preceded this, for which see Poulouin, *Temps des origines,* 450-51.

[10]Greenway, "Dates in History," 127.

[11]William of Malmesbury, *Gesta,* 1:17.

[12]Leigh, *Foelix Consortium,* 34.

[13]Harvey, *Discoursive Probleme,* 34.

[14]Wiseman, "Forum," 3.

[15]For some criteria determining inclusion and exlusion in the list of officially countenanced popes see Mercati, "New List."

[16]Berkeley, *Three Dialogues,* 48-49.

[17]Narain, *Indo-Greeks,* viii.

[18]For ruminations on how much criticism is acceptable in cases involving non-athletes, see Evans, *Lying About Hitler,* 237-66.

[19]Gleach, "Controlled Speculation," 21.

[20]E.g., Appleby, Hunt, and Jacob, *Telling the Truth,* Evans, *In Defence of History*; Windschuttle, *Killing of History*; McCullagh, *Truth of History.*

[21]Haskell, "Objectivity is not Neutrality," 132.

[22]Bopearachchi, "Indo-Parthians," 391n.

[23]Turnbull, *Fear of Drowning.*

Chapter 3

Barnes, *History of the World,* 245-46.

Plato, *Apology,* 21d.

[1]Goedicke, "Abydene Marriage," 182, emphasis added.

[2]Keightley, "Ping-ti Ho," 409-10.

[3]Thornton, "Historian," 45.

[4]Shakespeare, *Troilus and Cressida*, I.iii.109.

[5]Almost alone among global historians, for instance, Fernández-Armesto, *Civilizations*, treats history as almost entirely contingent.

[6]Lebow, "What's So Different?" 551.

[7]*VHB*, back cover, emphasis added.

[8]Livy, *History,* IX.xvii-xix. For the latest treatment see Morello, "Livy's Alexander Digression."

[9]This is really no different than novels whose protagonists spout views the authors hold while antagonists do not, allowing the novel to present a fictional world more congenial to its author than the real one.

[10]Toynbee, *Some Problems*, 441-86.

[11]Cowley, "Introduction," xiii.

[12]McNeill, "Infectious Alternatives." McNeill's piece exemplifies a game-within-the-game, taking the most obscure, possibly mythical, examples and wringing cataclysmic significance from them.

[13]Hassig, "Immolation of Hernán Cortés," 138. Further collections of examples are *What Might Have Been*/Cowley and *What Ifs?*

[14]Bulhof, "What If?," discusses this, but still argues for carrying the procedure farther.

[15]But popular! In the WorldCat international bibliographic database are more than 400 titles that begin with the words "what if" and undoubtedly many more in other languages. Recent and useful discussions include Lebow, "What's So Different?;" Bunzl, "Counterfactual History;" and Evans et al., "Counterfactual History." Bunzl speaks as a philosopher, but coherently. Of particular interest should be *What Might Have Been*/Rose. www.uchronia.net, contains an extensive bibliography of "alternat[iv]e history."

[16]Hassig, "Counterfactuals," 69.

[17]By this I mean a fixed text to which nothing can be added, a wealth of intimate knowledge about the England in which Holmes 'lived', and a body of data that provides enough precision to cause arguments, but not enough to settle them.

[18]Henige, "Implausibility of Plausibility."

[19]Browne, *Sahagún*, 7.

[20]Millard, "Abraham," 1:40.

[21]"Interview with William H. McNeill," 1.

[22]Appleby, Hunt, and Jacob, *Telling the Truth,* 207.

[23]Dewald, "Narrative Surface," 150-51. See, e.g., Herodotus, *History*, VII.152.3.

[24]Carr, *What is History?*, 5.

[25]Jenkins, *On "What is History?,"* 6.

[26]To compensate, I have established a website (http://minds.wisconsin.edu/handle/1793/180) at which several thousand citations will eventually accrue in order to give greater depth and breadth in support of the arguments laid out here.

[27]Nolte, "Review," 271.

[28]Stigler, *Memoirs*, 201.

[29]For such an argument see Henige, "Deciduous, Perennial, or Evergreen?"

Chapter 4

"Yours Truly, Johnny Dollar," "The Long Shot Matter," broadcast 26 June 1946.

Oscar Wilde, *The Importance of Being Earnest*, Act III.

[1]Episode entitled "Pathetic Fallacy" in the series "Quiet, Please," broadcast 2 February 1948.

[2]Irving, *Life and Voyages,* 1:65.

[3]Simms, *Views and Reviews,* 1:23n.

[4]Cook and Borah, "Credibility," 230.

[5]Hamilton, *Social Misconstruction of Reality,* 217.

[6]Sometimes, however, the opposite occurs. In his earlier years Arthur Conan Doyle asserted that "[n]ever will I accept anything which cannot be proved to me." (Doyle, *Memoirs,* 52). By the end of his life he was publicly believing in fairies.

[7]Discussions of pyrrhonism include Naess, *Scepticism*; Vansina, "Power of Systematic Doubt;" Wlodarczyk, *Pyrrhonian Inquiry.*

[8]For such practical limitations see Ribeiro, "Pyrrhonism."

[9]Sahlins, *How "Natives" Think*, 65.

[10]Hallo, "Limits of Skepticism," 188.

[11]Ibid., all emphases in original.

[12]Ibid., 189.

[13]Oppenheim, *Ancient Mesopotamia.*

[14]Ibid., 190.

[15]Ibid., 191.

[16]Ibid., 192.

[17]Ibid., emphasis added.

[18]Ibid., 199, emphasis added.

[19]Ibid.

[20]See chapter 13 below.

[21]Grabbe, "Of Mice and Dead Men," 139.

[22]Walker, "Jaubertian Chronology," 319, emphasis added.

[23]Smith, "Egypt and C^{14} Dating," 34.

[24]Steggemann, "Qumran," 3.

[25]Cohen, "Masada," 403.

[26]Snyder, "Review," 120.

[27]In this case, for instance, there is a great deal more evidence (not "proof") that the Arthur we know was created by several centuries of successive embellishment, culminating with Geoffrey of Monmouth's farrago of specious history—culminating, but not ending, since Arthurian myth-making continues apace.

[28]Yavetz, "Personality of Augustus," 22.

[29]Montefiore, "Josephus and the New Testament," 141.

[30]Gary Rendsburg, "Down With History, Up With Reading: the Current State of Biblical Studies," at http://www.arts.mcgill.ca/programs/jewish/30yrs (accessed 2 March 2005)

[31]Dever, quoted in Marcus, *View from Nebo,* 122.

[32]McLaren, *Turbulent Times?*, 266n9.

[33]Murnane, "Sed Festival," 369.

[34]Barr, *History and Ideology*, 79.

[35]Unless of course the authors of the historical sources themselves relied on such oracle bones.

[36]Ho, *Cradle of the East*, 240, 288n.

[37]Rafinesque, *American Nations*.

[38]*Walam Olum or Red Score.*

[39]Oestreicher, "Anatomy of the *Walam Olum*."

[40]Sedley, *Brothers of Glastonbury*, 229, emphasis in original, and anachronistically placed in a fifteenth-century context.

[41]Cornell, *Beginnings of Rome*, 217.

[42]Wiseman, "Roman Republic, Year One," 24.

[43]Morley, *Writing of Ancient History*, 93.

[44]Whitelam, "'Israel is Laid Waste'," 10.

[45]As Provan, "Stable," puts it, in disparaging standard forms of verification, it results in "an advance of ignorance."

[46]Charles Darwin to A. Stephen Wilson, 5 March 1879, in Darwin, *More Letters,* 2:422.

[47]Jefferson, *Notes on the State of Virginia*, 33, referring to new geological theories.

Chapter 5

Holt, *Thundering Zeus*, referring to the Diodotid rulers of Bactria, emphasis in original. Skinner, *Fallen Gods,* 233.

[1]Ranke needs no introduction; for Lingard see Jones, *John Lingard.*

[2]There is a further distinction between accidental and purposive sources. Sources that fall into the second category must be judged on their intent as well as their content. Most accidental sources are archeological, although a case could be made that certain kinds of documents—e.g., commercial records—also fall into this category but, even if not intended to influence the future or even much of the present, they need not be reliable. For instance, economic records might have quantities and prices that are too high (to gull one of the parties to the transaction) or too low (to evade taxes).

[3]Sanz, *Diario.*

[4]Henige, *In Search of Columbus.*

[5]Henige, "To Read is to Misread."

[6]Curtin, *Atlantic Slave Trade,* 3-13, and passim.

[7]Henige, "When did Smallpox Reach the New World?"

[8]Isenberg, *Destruction of the Bison,* 23-30.

[9]Henige, "Survival of the Fittest?"

[10]Benediktsson, "*Landnámabók*," 292.

[11]Zumthor, "Intertextualité."

[12]Potter, *Literary Texts*, 79. For eyewitnessing as a measure of authority see Marincola, *Authority and Tradition*, 78-85.

[13]Dictys of Crete in *The Trojan War*, 118. Both works are forgeries dating from the second century CE.

[14]E.g., Henige, "Context, Content, and Credibilty;" Galloway, "Incestuous Soto Narratives;" Dowling, "*La Florida del Inca*;" Henige, "'So Unbelievable it has to be True'."

[15]For this aspect see Henige, "Millennarian Archaeology."

[16]Jacopo d'Ancona, *City of Light*. See Barrett, "Modern History of Asia," and Rachewiltz and Leslie, "Review." For a reply by the putative editor-translator see Jacopo d'Ancona, *City of Light*, ix-xiii, 1-35, 431-95.

[17]Sharlet, "Author's Methods," referring to Earp, *I Married Wyatt Earp*.

[18]*We Saw Lincoln Shot.* A similar set of circumstances is discussed in *Eyewitnesses to Massacre*. For a slightly better performance see Riniolo et al, "Archival Study."

[19]For surveys of recent work see Koriat, Goldsmith, and Pansky, "Toward a Psychology of Memory Accuracy;" and Wells and Olson, "Eyewitness Testimony."

[20]E. g., Banaji and Crowder, "Bankruptcy of Everyday Memory;" Allen and Lindsay, "Amalgamations of Memories;" *Eyewitness Testimony*; Woocher, "Did Your Eyes;" and *Eyewitness Memory.* For a particular species of eyewitness testimony in the Middle Ages see Newman, "What Did It Mean?"

[21]Granger, *Shades of Murder*, 163.

[22]Or even attempt to turn it to advantage, as R.N. Whybray does when he writes: "[t]o regard as useless for the historian's purposes the only account of a nation's history written by its own nationals is, to say the least, extraordinary." Whybray, "What Do We Know," 72.

[23]Earlier, Hughes, *Star of Bethlehem*, and many others had tried to do the same.

[24]Kidger, *Star of Bethlehem*, and Molnar, *Star of Bethlehem.*

[25]E.g., Brown, *Birth of the Messiah*, 36, 52-53, 188-90.

[26]One option would be to adopt Hallo's knew-but-did-not-tell argument discussed above.

[27]Anderson, *Book of Mormon Witnesses*; Sorenson, "'Brass Plates';" Marquardt and Walters, *Inventing Mormonism,* 89-115. A recently published set of essays (*American Apocrypha*) unanimously reject the authenticity of the Book of Mormon.

[28]More than sixty possible geographies have been advanced; for a summary see Sorenson, *Mapping Mormon.*

[29]Josephus, *Contra Apionem*, 1:107-8.

[30]Ibid., 1:122-25; for convenience, dates as in Jidejian, *History of Tyre,* 245-46.

[31]Josephus, *Contra Apionem*, 1:123.

[32]Katzenstein, "Who Were the Parents?;" idem., *History of Tyre*, 129-30.

[33]Ibid., 118.

[34]Safar, "Further Text."

[35]Katzenstein, "Who Were the Parents?"

[36]Lipinski, "Ba'li-ma'zer II."

[37]Peñuela, "Inscripción asíria." Most recently Tetley, *Reconstructing*, 170, rejects the identification and dates Balezor to about 40 years ago to conform to her revised biblical chronology, which forces to her conclude (ibid., 172) that "[t]he entire Tyrian chronology . . . requires reexamination."

[38]Albright, "New Assyro-Tyrian Synchronism," 5.

[39]E.g., *Inscriptions of Tiglath-Pileser III*, 266-68.

[40]Garbini, *History and Ideology*, 23.

[41]E.g., Katzenstein, *History*, 77-128; Jidejian, *History of Tyre*, 39-43, 245-46.

[42]Handy, "Phoenicians," 157, emphasis added.

[43]Barnes, *Studies,* 32.

[44]Or even to Josephus's own time; note his use of a present-tense verb form.

[45]Bloedow, "Siege of Tyre."

[46]Each of these datings has been advanced by one modern writer or another.

[47]Fitzmyer, *Acts of the Apostles*, 126.

[48]Dreyer *et al*, "Umm el-Qaab," 72.

[49]Lerner, *Impact of Seleucid Decline*, 89-113, is a good summary of the issues.

[50]Cribb, "Early Kushan Kings," 177.

[51]Göbl, "Rabatak Inscription;" Alram, "Indo-Parthian and Early Kushan Chronology."

[52]On this prospect see Seldeslachts, "End of the Road."

[53]This popular—because so reassuring—notion has a large web presence; see, among others, www.deanburgonsociety.org and www.lifefebc.com (accessed 4 March 2005)

[54]Thornton, "Kamehameha's Arrow," 4.

[55]Zerjal et al., "Genetic Legacy." In no less startling a parallel, chromosomal evidence shows signs of a strong correlation between Ireland, whose long-derided legendary history claims a migration from Spain, and the Basques; see Hill, Jobling, and Bradley, "Y-Chromosome Variation." As Ó Canann ("Review," 134) points out, this new technique "can potentially revolutionise long-held shibboleths about our understanding of Ireland's past." And then some.

Chapter 6

L. Frank Baum, *The Wizard of Oz.*

Spencer, *Golden Mile of Murder*, 37.

[1]Pearl, *Medical Biometry*, 86-88, emphasis in original.

[2]In counting names in a medieval cartulary, Jarrett ("Power Over Past and Future," 244) came up with 506, others with 476 and 510. He concluded that "I can only say that I count it differently."

[3]Wolters, "History and the Copper Scroll;" Golb, "As the Scrolls Arrive in Chicago."

[4]Wolters, "History and the Copper Scroll," 291.

[5]"Where Was He Born?" *Wisconsin State Journal* (3 June 2000), 1A, 3A, from the *Chicago Tribune*.

[6]Forsythe, *Livy and Early Rome*, esp. 40-73.

[7]Livy, VIII. xviii, 2-4.

[8]Abu-Lughod, "World-System Perspective," 240, contrasting her *Before European Hegemony* with Smith, *Creating a World Economy*.

[9]See Parker, "Columbus Landfall Problem," and Henige, "Guanahaní the Elusive."

[10]Sahlins, *Historical Metaphors*; idem., *Islands of History*.

[11]Obeyesekere, *Apotheosis of Captain Cook*.

[12]Sahlins, *How "Natives" Think*.

[13]Obeyesekere, *Apotheosis of Captain Cook²*, 193-250.

[14]Hammond, *Genius of Alexander the Great*, 201.

[15]Bosworth, *Alexander and the East*, 30.

[16]Cf., for example, Holt, *Alexander the Great*, 21, and passim.

[17]In fact a flurry of Alexander studies appeared in late 2004 in conjunction with a well-publicized movie. Most of these tend to regress to a mean somewhere between the positions of Bosworth and Hammond.

[18]Pearl, *Medical Biometry*, 88-89, all emphases in original. The tallies ranged from 52 to 108, with none being 100, the expected total.

[19]For a host of readings given just eight characters in a Nepalese inscription see Garbini, "Dating." Rollinger, "Stammbaum," arrays no fewer than 21 modern configurations of early Achaemenid genealogy. Etc., etc.

Chapter 7

Spriggs, "Pacific Archaeologies," 121.

An unnamed archaeologist quoted in Säve-Söderbergh, "C[14] Dating," 35.

[1]Hopkins, "Name Change."

[2]Hopkins, "From the Editor;" idem., "From BA to NEA."

[3]Dever, "Archaeology, Ideology."

[4]Mason, "Archaeology," 239.

[5]Deetz, "Archaeological Evidence," 1. For the archeology of non-historical periods we might substitute "cannot" for "already."

[6]Hudson, DePratter, and Smith, "Reply to Henige," 260.

[7]Storey, "Archaeology and Roman Society."

[8]Swedlund and Anderson, "Gordon Creek Woman."

[9]Freedman, "Albright as Historian," 39.

[10]For very sensible comments on a remarkably similar set of circumstances, this time for ancient China, see Bagley, "Shang Archaeology," esp. 124-36, 229-31.

[11]For one exception see the discussion of Martin Bernal's *Black Athena* below.

[12]Hagelia, "First Dissertation." Hagelia provides no specifics, but for an earlier list of about 60 titles see Lemaire, "Tel Dan Stela." For a new interpretation based on rearranging the fragments see Athas, *Tel Dan Inscription*. Hagelia, "First Dissertation," is a mixed assessment of Athas's arguments. Between 1976 and 1979 nearly ninety articles on Ebla appeared in the scholarly and popular press, most addressing the alleged mention of

Sodom and Gomorrah in the texts found there: Freedman, "Ebla and the Old Testament," 331-35.

[13]Edwards, "In Search of Himiko," 77, citing a conversation between the two.

[14] Wiener, "Time Out," 393.

[15]Kendall, "Origin of the Napatan State;" idem., "Response."

[16]Henige, *Chronology of Oral Tradition*, 71-75.

[17]Kendall, "Response," 166. Morkot, *Black Pharaohs*, 138-44, prefers the short chronology but accepts the matter as open.

[18]E.g., Acsádi and Nemeskéri, "Recommendations."

[19]Molleson and Cox, *Spitalfields Project*, 2:9-10, 167-72.

[20]Ibid., 2:169.

[21]This brings up the issue of who owns what, which is taken up, among others, in Nicholas and Bannister, "Copyrighting the Past."

[22]Gitin, "Formulating a Ceramic Corpus," 75-77.

[23]The interpretation of mass graves illustrates archeology's dilemma, since these are often attached to events in recorded history retroactively. Recent remains in central France have been confidently identified as those of victims of the battle of Gergovia between Caesar's forces and the Gauls in 52 BCE. Yet the site of the battle does not command consensus, nor do we know anything about the particular history of the area during the many centuries since, when there could have been numerous unrecorded occasions that left large numbers of dead in their wake.

[24]Benerjee, "Some Problems," estimates that there are 90,000 inscriptions are known from south Asia alone.

[25]E.g., *Afterlife of Inscriptions*.

[26]For postmodernist studies of early Indian epigraphs and literary texts, see the essays in *Querying the Medieval*, and for an enlightening case of the results of close textual analysis, see Cohen, "Problems."

[27]Henige, "Phantom Dynasties."

[28]Hasel, "Israel in the Merneptah Stela;" Yurco, "Merenptah's Canaanite Campaign."

[29]Dever, "What Did the Biblical Writers Know," 248, emphases added.

[30]Any scholarly concerns were quickly squashed by marketing, irredentism, and similar concerns; Fowler, *Iceman*.

[31]Hodder, *Archaeological Process*, 138-44. In retrospect at least, this seems especially imprudent since, despite all this attention, it took ten years to discover that an arrowhead was embedded in Ötzi's chest cavity and another two years to decide how he died. This belated discovery brought new and unevidenced, but still circumstantial, revised scenarios of his last moments: Cullen, "Testimony From the Iceman."

[32]*Nationalism, Politics, and the Practice of Archaeology*; *Archaeology and Nationalism*; *Archaeology Under Fire*; *Nationalism and Archaeology in Europe*; Han Xiaorong, "Present Echoes;" Hyung Il Pai, *Constructing 'Korean' Origins*, 237-87. Kohl, "Nationalism and Archaeology," lists about 100 recent studies, while ten essays on contemporary states are included in *Journal of Contemporary History* 39 (2003), 5-162.

[33]Feldman, "Masada," 218.

[34]As I write, newspapers and websites are bursting with claims that both the cave where John the Baptist operated and the site of the biblical miracle at Cana have been reliably identified, while the discovery of an apparent palace in Rome has instigated claims that the traditional details about Rome's foundation are essentially correct.

[35]Dunlop and Sigurdsson, "Interdisciplinary Investigation."

[36]Albarella, "'Mystery of Husbandry'," 874. Recent colloquies are Vansina, "Historians, Are Archeologists Your Siblings?," answered by Robertshaw, "Sibling Rivalry?" See, as well, *Archaeology and Ancient History*.

[37]Salmon, "Philosophy of Archaeology," 331. See as well, idem., *Philosophy and Archaeology*, esp. 31-56.

[38]Takashi, "Japan and the Continent," 286, emphasis added.

[39]Adam Zertal, in response to claims that archeology has not corroborated the biblical accounts of the Exodus and conquest, quoted in *USA Today* (3 November 1999), 11D, emphasis added.

Chapter 8

H.R. Schoolcraft, quoted in *Schoolcraft's Expedition*, 5.

Miles, *Saint's Rest,* 67-68.

[1]Berkowitz, "Reporting an Experiment," 237.

[2]For the general ambiance see, e.g., Tavard, *Seventeenth-Century Tradition*; Southgate, "Blackloism and Tradition."

[3]Cressy, *Exomologesis*, 174, 182, emphasis in original.

[4]Digby, *Discourse,* 185, 215.

[5]John Dryden, *Religio Laici, ll.* 270-75, in *John Dryden*, 234.

[6]Beckman, *Hittite Diplomatic Texts*, 20.

[7]For varying earlier views see Dorson, "Debate."

[8]Translated as Vansina, *Oral Tradition.*

[9]Among them, *African Past Speaks*; Henige, *Oral Historiography*; and Vansina, *Oral Tradition as History*.

[10]Hicks, "Skepticism in Ethnohistory," for instance, recommends explicitly seeking out apparent skeptics as informants.

[11]For an amusing example of such entrepreneurship see Vansina, "Kuba Chronology."

[12]For one such case see Whiteley, "Anthropology."

[13]*In Pursuit of History* addresses a variety of personal and intellectual challenges that can accompany collecting oral data in other societies.

[14]Halpert and Widdowson, *Folktales of Newfoundland,* 1:liv-lxviii passim.

[15]Ibid., lv, emphasis added.

[16]This is not to say that much has not been done along these lines. In fact, an ongoing commercial venture (www.alexanderstreet2.com/orhilive) comprises—as of early 2005—finding guides to some 2500 English-language oral history collections from throughout the world and permits users to search more than 250,000 pages of full-text interviews ranging

from 1930 to 2004. It includes as well nearly 2000 audio and video files and 13,500 bibliographic records. Access will be through subscription, presumably by academic research libraries. This is a quantum leap forward in gaining intelligence about and access to these notoriously fugitive materials. At the same time it is a tocsin to potential beneficiaries to become even more efficient.

[17]For several essays on the tangled web of 'ownership' of materials collected in the field see *Protection of Intellectual.*

[18]Brannigan and Zwerman, "Real 'Hawthorne Effect'," 56.

[19]Among others, see Gillespie, *Manufacturing Knowledge*; Sundstrom, "Work Groups."

[20]The Hawthorne Effect is hardly limited to oral productions of information. Those writing with an eye to posterity will present a case different from those who do not. Those who write under patronage offer a different narrative than others. Those writing with a particular audience in mind will tend to that audience rather than future historians.

[21]Quintilian V.vii.32.

[22]Vincent, *Intelligent Person's Guide*, 1.

[23]See, for instance, several essays in *Historian's Craft in the Age of Herodotus* that treat his work as oral to written. See as well *Spoken Word*; Melve, "Literacy-Aurality-Orality;" and *Orality and Literacy in the Middle Ages*; but these are only a sampling.

[24]See, e.g., Scheub, *Poem in the Story.*

[25]McHardy, "The Wee Dark Fowk o' Scotland," 109.

[26]Roberton, "Significance," 41, 43.

[27]The song known as "Wildwood Flower," first published in 1860, became popular in folk circles, where it was handed down orally from one musical generation to the next. Such a text would seem to be a good candidate for a "fixed text," but neither the combined requirements for rhyme or rhythm or melody were able to keep the text honest. A century later the oral text, constrained as it was, had degenerated into partial gibberish, which retained some of the sounds, along with the rhythm and melody, etc. Data obtained by searching "Wildwood Flower" on the Internet, October 2003.

[28]Niditch, *Oral World and Written Word.*

[29]Henige, "Survival of the Fittest?"

[30]Another bleak aspect—or at least a dilemma for skeptics—is that it has become commonplace to mask the identity of informants for their safety and for other reasons; see, e.g., Makley, "'Speaking Bitterness'." While this probably increases the probabilities of eliciting more interesting information, it also shields fieldworkers as much as it does informants.

[31]Henige, "Truths Yet Unborn?"

[32]Blake, "Wiowurrung, the Melbourne Language," 4:34.

[33]*Words of Our Country*, 41-42.

[34]E.g., Lankford, "Pleistocene Animals;" Best, "Here Be Dragons;" Burney and Ramilisonina, "*Kilopilopitsofy.*"

[35]Echo-Hawk, "Ancient History," 274.

[36]Moodie and Catchpole, "Northern Athapaskan Oral Traditions," 165, referring to a volcanic eruption possibly dated to 720 CE.

[37]Thomas, *Skull Wars,* 206, emphasis added. For recent view that oral tradition is "real history" and collecting ands interpreting it is "akin to scientific method" see Anyon et al, "Native American Oral Tradition."
[38]Roberts, "Possibilities," 164-65.
[39]Krinov, *Giant Meteorites.*
[40]Stille, "Man Who Remembers," quoting Scoditti.

Chapter 9

Brown, "Assyriology," 27-28.
Perry, *Bedford Square*, 235.
[1]Huizinga, "Definition," 6.
[2]Holmes, "Scientific Writing," 225. For another, more recent, example see Pugh, *Growth.* Literary works are far more likely to survive in multiple drafts than historiographical works, but the lessons are transferable.
[3]Among many, Driver, "Abbreviations," and Wenham, "Large Numbers." Willis, *Latin Textual Criticism*, 47-188, is a systematic discussion of reasons for and responses to textual corruption. An assortment of ways to mistranscribe is discussed in Castellani, "Transcription Errors."
[4]The extent and variety of emendation in one major historical text is studied in Brown, *Textual Transmission.* The literature for and against emendation is of course enormous. A couple of recent studies with specific, but widely separated, focuses are Gassmann, "To Emend or not to Emend?" and Clunies Ross, "Conjectural Emendation."
[5]Purdy, "Sinuhe."
[6]E.g., Barnes, "Sinuhe's Message to the King," thinks it is "a real autobiography" but declines to assess its reliability. Baines, "Interpreting Sinuhe," approaches it as literature rather than reportage.
[7]Greig, "*SDM = F* and *SDM.N = F*," 341.
[8]E.g., Helly, *Livingstone's Legacy*; Dawson, "Many Minds;" Lockhart, "In the Raw;" Finkelstein, "Unraveling Speke's Africa."
[9]Grove, *Imaginary Voyage*, 181-402, listed 215 accounts of such voyages in the eighteenth century alone.
[10]For an extended discussion of frontispieces as "counterfeit authority" see Barchas, *Graphic Design,* 19-59.
[11]Adams, *Travelers and Travel Liars*; idem., *Travel Literature.* For a recent skimming overview see Roberts, *Great Exploration Hoaxes.*
[12]Douville, *Voyage au Congo.*
[13]Cooley, "Review;" Lacordaire, "Review."
[14]Stamm, "Jean-Baptiste Douville," 36.
[15]Miller, "Note on Jean-Baptiste Douville." Now see Vansina, "Many Uses."
[16]Johnson, "News from Nowhere," 64.
[17]Drury, *Madagascar*, iv.

[18]Parker Pearson, "Reassessing *Robert Drury's Journal*," 251.

[19]Bruce, *Travels.*

[20]Reid, *Traveller Extraordinary,* 305-06; Bredin, *Pale Abyssinian.*

[21]Salt, *Voyage to Abyssinia,* 325-44 passim.

[22]See, e.g., Hall, *Perilous Vision.*

[23]Kawai, "*Mokusatsu;*" Coughlin, "Great *mokusatsu* Mistake;" Mee, *Meeting*, 235-48.

[24]*Journals and Other Documents,* 68; Dunn and Kelley, Diario, 75; *Journal of the First Voyage,* 33.

[25]Morison, *Admiral of the Ocean Sea*, 1:367.

[26]Dunn and Kelley, Diario, 100-01, 204-05, 208-11, 246-47, 324-25.

[27]Henige, *Numbers From Nowhere,* 170-72, 368-69.

[28]Henige, "Primary Source," 296.

[29]Denhardt, "Truth about Cortés's Horses." Since then more translations have provided further variation.

[30]Watson, "The *Shih chi* and I," 199.

[31]*Journals and Other Documents,* passim.

[32]Dunn and Kelley, Diario.

[33]Van Dantzig, "Willem Bosman;" idem., "English Bosman and Dutch Bosman."

[34]Two recent collections of essays address these issues in some detail; *Bible Translation on the Threshold* and *Bible Translation: Frames of Reference.*

[35]Furuli, *Role of Theology*, addresses differences in translation of several recent editions.

[36]Schindler, "Johannine Comma," 164.

[37]Solms, "Controversies," is a cautionary tale about a major corpus.

Chapter 10

Jane Austen, *Northanger Abbey.*

Maxwell, *So Long, See You Tomorrow*, 27.

[1]Holway, *Last .400 Hitter,* 295; Linn, *Hitter*, 173.

[2]Linn, *Hitter*, 263-64; *Total Baseball*, 941, 1546; cf. ibid., 849.

[3]Hiatt, *Making*, xi.

[4]Henige, "Finding Columbus," 153.

[5]Martire de Anghiera, *Opera*, 50.

[6]Millard, "Abraham," 39.

[7]Groneman, "Controversial Alleged Account," 136-37.

[8]See, e.g., Shrimpton, *History and Memory,* 80-227.

[9]Poovey, *History of the Modern Fact*, discusses the matter of accuracy in this respect.

[10]For an argument against anachronistic homogenization see Voight, "Fie on Figure Filberts."

[11]True even before the drug issue, now center stage, ever arose.

[12]*Arrian*, preface.

[13]Including artifacts; for a denunciation of the "forgery culture," that allows fake antiquities to repose unidentified and unstudied in museum collections see Muscarella, *Lie Became Great,* 1-29 and passim. For a number of essays dealing with late medieval/early modern examples of scholarly fraud see *Shell Games.* For 45 studies, mostly of French literature, see *Topos du manuscrit trouvé.* Of course any number of other studies could also be cited, but none so wide-ranging or demoralizing as the studies in *Fälschungen im Mittelalter,* which address more than 150 cases.

[14]E.g., Merkle, "Telling the True Story;" idem., "Truth."

[15]For a bibliography to the early twentieth century see Leclercq, "Filumena," 1604-6. A case similar in time and motivation, though of much greater magnitude even if of less effect, is discussed in Boutry, "Saints."

[16]Butler, Thurston, and Attwater, *Butler's Lives of the Saints*, 8:131-32.

[17]Perry, *Chronicles of Eri*; Leerssen, *Remembrance and Imagination*, 83-84.

[18]Jones, "Canek Manuscript," 243; idem., *Manuscrito Can Ek.*

[19]Prem, "'Canek Manuscript'."

[20]The Canek manuscript retains admonitory value. Jones, "Revisiting the Canek Manuscript," 315, closed his comment on Prem's case by noting that in hindsight "we should all have been suspicious from the outset, and I have no doubt that when next a new and exciting, but odd and uncharacteristic, 'colonial document' appears, we will exercise skepticism and carry out far more rigorous background analysis."

[21]Barrett, "Historicity of Acts," 524-27.

[22]For a study of several attempts at verisimilitude in modern novels see *Novel History.*

[23]Burlingame, "New Light on the Bixby Letter."

[24]Thomson, *Diversions,* 304n.

[25]Temple, *Sirius Mystery.*

[26]For instance, Temple regarded the work of Germaine Dieterlen, Griaule's acolyte, as "definitive." Temple to Editor, *The Observatory* 95 (1975), 52-54. For background on the belief see Davis, "Review."

[27]Brecher, "Sirius Enigmas," 109-11.

[28]Beek, "Dogon Restudied," with replies and response. One of the respondents (ibid., 158), lamented that "fault-finding and blame fixing a posteriori are not the same as substantively increasing the breadth, scope, and depth of extant ethnographies." Griaule's daughter and one of his disciples soon sprang to his defense as well: Calame-Griaule, "On the Dogon Revisited," and Luc de Heusch, "On Griaule on Trial." In "Haunting Griaule" van Beek chronicles the academic obloquy he endured for his revelations.

[29]Henige, "Truths Yet Unborn?"

[30]See, e.g., *Amarna Diplomacy.*

[31]Henige, "Problem of Feedback."

[32]Zuidema, Ceque *System.* Zuidema took a more historical approach in his *Inca Civilization in Cuzco.* For an extended critique of Zuidema's work, see Nowack, Ceque *and More.*

[33]Duviols, "Dinastía de los Incas." For critiques of Duviols see Grou, "Empereurs incas," and Gose, "Past is a Lower Moiety."

[34]Rostworowski Díez de Canseco, *Inca Realm*, 29.

[35]Ibid., 102, 258.

[36]Ibid., 102, emphasis added.

[37]For this see Henige, *Chronology of Oral Tradition,* 71-94.

[38]Rostworowski, *Inca Realm*, 177-81. In particular, she agrees (ibid., 179) that "in principle we can accept that the two Inca moieties functioned simultaneously, [but] this does not help us re-create an adjusted chronology of Inca rulers" because the rulers in the two moieties did not rule in lockstep, as structural chronology would prefer.

[39]Rowe, "Absolute Chronology."

[40]For a good start see Urton, *History of a Myth.*

[41]Another form of forgery is not new, but has been newly dubbed with the oxymoronic "invented tradition." It has been applied to sundry efforts across history to flog newly-devised ideas as hoary tradition, giving them a past when they barely have a present. Numerous recent studies of "invented traditions" illustrate how easy it has been to manufacture stories of the past and get them accepted as "tradition/s" in both their times and ours. The term was first used, or at least first noticed, in *Invention of Tradition.*

Chapter 11

Doniger, "Female Bandits?" 19.

Renan, "Que'est-ce qu'une nation?" 1:891.

[1]E.g., Vlasich, *Legend for the Legendary.* In very similar fashion the origins of rugby football have wrongly been credited to a single epiphanic moment and a single inventor; see van der Merwe, *William Webb Ellis.*

[2]Quoted in Mehl, *History and the State*, 1. Cf. Brownlee, *Japanese Historians,* for the aftermath.

[3]Josephus, *Jewish War*, vii. 252-406.

[4]Schwartz, Zerubavel, and Barnett, "Recovery of Masada," 47.

[5]For details on this early period see Paine, "Masada;" Ben-Yehuda, *Masada Myth,* 71-146; and Zerubavel, *Recovered Roots,* 60-76, 119-33.

[6]Feldman, *Josephus*, 883; cf. Syrkin, "Paradox of Masada."

[7]Yadin's excavations and their influence on the myth are thoroughly dealt with in Ben-Yehuda, *Sacrificing Truth.*

[8]Yadin, *Masada,* 15.

[9]Ibid., 201.

[10]Ben-Yehuda, *Masada Myth*, 179-205; Zerubavel, *Recovered Roots*, 133-37.

[11]For this generally, see Silberman, *Between Past and Present,* 87-101; idem., *Prophet From Amongst You,* 288-93.

[12]Trude Weiss-Rosmarin wrote two stinging reviews of Yadin, *Masada*, but evoked little response. See Weiss-Rosmarin, "Masada and Yavneh;" and idem., "Masada, Josephus, and Yadin." Ben-Yehuda, *Masada Myth*, lists nearly 500 items published between 1949 and the mid-1990s.

[13]Alter, "Masada Complex;" Paine, "Masada," 386-96; Zerubavel, *Recovered Roots*, 193-97, 207-13. For a Masada-replacement myth see Terrill, "Political Mythology."

[14]Ben-Yehuda, *Masada Myth*, 14 and passim.

[15]Shargel, "Evolution of the Masada Myth," 360.

[16]E.g., Schwartz and Kaplan, "Judaism, Masada, and Suicide."

[17]Hoenig, "Sicarii in Masada;" Zerubavel, *Recovered Roots*, 203-7.

[18]Cohen, "Masada;" Newall, "Forms."

[19]Cohen, "Masada," 396; Ladouceur, "Masada," 260; "Newall, "Forms," 290.

[20]Josephus, *Jewish War* vii. 323-88.

[21]Ibid., vii. 404-5.

[22]Feldman's argument (*Josephus*, 776) that since "memories were highly cultivated in antiquity, especially among Jews, [the informant] might have retained much of the speeches. Moreover, the acoustics in these underground sewers is excellent" is risible, and fails to speak to problems of multilingual transmission after this.

[23]For ten examples see ibid., 777-79.

[24]As Smallwood, *Jews Under Roman Rule,* 338.

[25]Feldman, *Josephus*, 764, summarizes some discussions in Hebrew on the matter.

[26]Ibid., 769-72.

[27]Cohen, "Masada," 394-95, has a good discussion of the improbabilities of Yadin's forced explanations.

[28]E.g., Hoenig, "Sicarii in Masada," 22-23.

[29]Josephus, *Jewish War*, v. 567-69, vi. 420.

[30]Cohen, "Masada," 399, 401.

[31]As both Ben-Yehuda, *Masada Myth*, and Zerubavel, *Recovered Roots,* make clear when discussing their interviews.

[32]See Zerubavel, *Recovered Roots*, 130, 136.

[33]The belief that every defender died before surrendering is contradicted by several contemporary accounts—some of the Texans even tried to hide! See Williams, "Critical Study;" *In the Shadow of History*, 9-58; McWilliams, "Alamo From Fact to Fable;" Crisp, *Sleuthing the Alamo*.

[34]The value of the untouched myth as commemoration is treated in Brear, *Inherit the Alamo*, and Flores, *Remembering the Alamo*.

[35]E.g., Slotkin, *Gunfighter Nation.*

[36]Barra, *Inventing Wyatt Earp.*

[37]Ehret, *Civilizations*, 15, 91.

[38]E.g., FitzGerald, *America Revised*; Loewen, *Lies My Teachers Told Me.*

[39]For a currently evolving mythicizing process see Ranger, "Nationalist Historiography."

[40]Thoms, *Human Longevity*, xii.

Chapter 12

Theodórsson, "Norse Settlement," 35.

Hopkins, *Conquerors and Slaves,* 19-20.

[1]Cf. Matthew 1:20–2:15; Luke 1:5–2:39.

[2]Shanks, "Exodus."

[3]Lewis, "review of *HSE.*"

[4]Frame, "Inscription of Sargon II."

[5]Redford, "Note on the Chronology." Using the same evidence, Kahn, "Inscription of Sargon II," further disagreed and argued that Shebiktu succeeded Shabaka in 707/06 BCE, without a co-regency.

[6]Narasimha Murthy, *Sevunas of Devagiri*, 34, 206-7.

[7]Yadav, *Yadavas*, 274, 320.

[8]For a similar case of imagining gaps, only for the purpose of filling them, see Thaplyal, "Govindragupta."

[9]Xu, "Cemetery," 199, 225-28.

[10]More recently see Li Boqian, "Sumptuary System." Li is more optimistic, but fails to cite Xu's article. Nivison and Shaughnessy, "Jin Hou Su Bells," make a case for identifying the names on the tombs with specific Jin rulers by positing strategic errors in the sources.

[11]Forsyth, *Thera in the Bronze Age*, 106-16, 150-56, provides a balanced summary of the issues as they then stood.

[12]The latest study of the problem suggests a fairly wide window for the eruption; see Bronk Ramsey, Manning, and Galimberti, "Dating."

[13]Fridriksson, *Sagas and Popular Antiquarianism*, 28-40.

[14]Theodórsson, "Norse Settlement," 29. Olsson, "Experiences."

[15]Nordahl, *Reykjavík*.

[16]Hermanns-Audardóttir, "Early Settlement."

[17]Vilhjálmsson, "Early Settlement," 174-75; idem., "Dating Problems."

[18]Fridriksson, *Saga and Popular Antiquarianism,* 40-44.

[19]Theodórsson, "Norse Settlement;" idem., "Aldur landnáms."

[20]For an earlier cautionary discussion of the *Landnámabók* see Benediktsson, "*Landnámabók.*" Benediktsson did not address the dating issue, it not having yet arisen.

[21]Theodórsson, "Norse Settlement," 36-37.

[22]See, e.g., Einarsson, *Settlement of Iceland*, 41-46.

[23]Vilhjálmsson, "Early Settlement," 167-81. Recently, Olsson, "Geophysical Aspects," has tried to bring archeological and documentary sources into closer harmony, largely at the expense of the first.

[24]Byock, *Medieval Iceland*; Durrenberger, "Text and Transaction;" and Hastrup, *Island of Anthropology*, 69-82, 98-100.

[25]The authors of the latest study argue that the dating of barley grain samples tends to uphold the traditional date even if that for wood remains does not; see Sveinbjörnsdóttir et al., "Dating." On the other hand, Karlsson, *History of Iceland*, 9-15, while adopting the traditional view, also feels obliged to defend it, thus introducing his readers to the disputed state of affairs, an encouraging departure from past histories of the island.

[26]Marwick, *New Nature of History.*

[27]Hoffer, *Past Imperfect*, 209-10.

Chapter 13

A.W. Schlegel (ca. 1803), quoted in Jolles, "German Romantic Chronology," 51.

Pallis, *Chronology*, 310, in constructing his version of Mesopotamian chronology discussed below.

[1]Locke, *Some Thoughts Concerning Education*, 237-38.

[2]I borrow this chapter's title from an ad for pickup trucks, which seems to imply that those unfortunates who had purchased previous models had made a bad deal.

[3]Manning, *Absolute Chronology*, 117.

[4]For summaries of the earlier historiography see Goossens, "Révision" and especially Pallis, *Chronology*, 235-434, which treats the first half of the enterprise in exhausting, but convenient, detail.

[5]Beinlich-Seeber, *Bibliographie Altägypten*, 3:114-17, 165-69, lists more than 150 works devoted to astronomy and another 200+ to chronology. In only 13 years between 1822 and 1946 was nothing published directly on these subjects.

[6]Poole, *Horae Aegyptiacae*, 79-92.

[7]For brief histories of Egyptian chronologizing see Ridley, "Auguste Mariette," and Lasken, "Towards a New Chronology."

[8]Well over a century ago, A.H.M.J. Stokvis asked: "[m]ust we regard the 31 dynasties of Manetho as all succeeding one after another, or must we admit that some of them ruled jointly?" Stokvis then listed 14 contemporary opinions of the accession date of Menes, ranging from 5867 BCE to 2691 BCE. Stokvis, *Manuel*, 1:396. He concluded that "[i]t is not possible to resolve this issue in a satisfactory manner," and chose 4372 BCE—not one of the 14 dates but based on a "new system" combining Manetho and the Turin Canon.

[9]Drower, *Flinders Petrie*, 313-16, 471.

[10]Petrie, *History of Egypt*, ix-x.

[11]Ricci, "Table de Palermo," 108.

[12]Wilkinson, *Royal Annals*, 77.

[13]Kitchen, "Basics of Egyptian Chronology," 37.

[14]Jürgen von Beckerath alone published three disparate versions of New Kingdom chronology between 1984 and 1997: Beckerath, *Handbuch*, 160-61; idem., *Neuen Reiches*, 35-47, 118, 124; idem., *Pharaonischen Agypten*, 103-23, 189-90.

[15]For a study of III Dynasty chronological and genealogical problems see Baud, *Djéser.*

[16]O'Mara, "Multi-Modeled Chronology," 43, 44.

[17]Most recently, Hasel, *Domination and Resistance*, 118-19, 150-52, 178.

[18]Rawlinson, "Assyrian History," 724. For the whirligig of late-nineteenth-century conjecture see Holloway, "Quest."

[19]See King, "Babylonia and Assyria," 3:109; idem., *Chronicles*, 1:83.

[20]King, *Chronicles*, 1:9.

[21]Ibid.

[22]It is now taken for granted that between ca. 2120 BCE and ca. 1450 BCE (middle chronology), Mesopotamia (Assyria excepted) was never entirely ruled by a single dynasty.

[23]Langdon, "Early Chronology," 123.

[24]Olmstead, "Assyrian Chronology," 225, reviewing a work which brought forward new evidence that "antiquated the whole" of Olmstead's own chronology published just two years earlier.

[25]Cook, "Chronology," 1:155.

[26]Weidner, *Assyrologie.*

[27]Böhl, *King Hammurabi,* 7.

[28]For the history of early attempts at astronomical dating see Langdon and Fotheringham, *Venus Tablets of Ammizaduga*, 28-44.

[29]E.g., ibid., 60-68, 82-83, 87.

[30]E.g., Rowton, "Date of Hammurabi."

[31]The astronomical data and their early convolutions were summed up by Sidersky, "Nouvelle étude," who added his own newly-calculated date.

[32]Cryer, "Chronology," 2:658. Eclipse dating has a long, if not entirely honorable, history; see, e.g., Grafton, "Some Uses."

[33]*HML?*

[34]A recent analysis of the tablets argues that only certain of the data are authentic; if true, this would allow more possible dates within the same time period. See Reiner and Pingree, *Venus Tablets of Ammisaduqa.* Several papers in *Under the Sky* argue that ancient Near East astronomical data are not capable of providing incontrovertible chronological information. For a discussion of several failed attempts to correlate astronomical and terrestrial events throughout history see Henige, "'Day'," and idem., "Myth."

[35]Weidner, *Könige von Assyrien.* Here Aššur-bil-nišešu became the forty-third ruler.

[36]E.g., Postgate, "Chronology of Assyria."

[37]Brinkman, "Comments," 310.

[38]Poebel, "Khorsabad King List," 479n.

[39]Poole, *Horae Aegyptiacae,* 131.

[40]Langdon, "Early Chronology," 133, 134, 136.

[41]Thureau-Dangin, "Chronologie," 196-97.

[42]Breasted, "Predynastic Union," 709.

[43]Böhl, *King Hammurabi,* 8n.

[44]Goossens, "Révision," 25n, emphasis added.

[45]Pallis, *Chronology,* 302-8.

[46]Ibid., 308-24.

[47]Later Pallis adopted the middle chronology in his *Antiquity of Iraq.*

[48]Albright, "Revolution," 18, 21.

[49]Albright, "New Light," 26.

[50]Ibid., 30.

[51]Albright, "Third Revision."

[52]Ibid., 33, emphasis in original.

[53]Albright, "Revision," 83.

[54]Albright, "Readjustment," 52.

[55]Ibid. 53, exclamation point in original.

[56]Ibid., 54.

[57]For Albright's lifelong propensity for speaking ex cathedra see Long, *Planting and Reaping Albright.*

[58]Gasche et al., *Dating the Fall of Babylon*, 48.

[59]Ibid., 49-65.

[60]Some results of this are discussed in Warburton, "Eclipses," who concludes that "neither the 'Middle' nor the 'Low Chronology' can be saved," both being too high.

[61]Gasche et al., *Dating the Fall of Babylon*, 45.

[62]Ibid., 92.

[63]A case of explicit devil's advocacy that would lower the beginning of XXI Dynasty about 100 years is presented in Hagens, "Critical Review;" and idem., "Ultra-Low Chronology."

[64]Cooper, *Pre-Sargonic Inscriptions*, 3.

[65]Pallis, *Chronology,* 324-400, 430-34.

[66]Manning, *Absolute Chronology*, 112.

[67]In fact the ancient Near East is only the most elaborate example of the curious concoction of repeated assured discourse and constant changes of mind. The chronology of ancient and medieval India has an even longer history, and there are also the numerous—and so far unsuccessful—attempts to bring chronological closure to precontact Mesoamerica.

[68]Obviously yes; K.A. Kitchen, one of the more ardent chronologizers, ends a recent article with "Solomon's dates are secure." Kitchen, "How We know When Solomon Ruled," 58. In contrast, see above for the range of current opinion.

[69]Ancient Near Eastern chronology now depends in part on data collected as far away as Sardinia, Ireland, even the western United States.

[70]Or maybe not; a set of nineteen papers recently published argue on a number of grounds for pushing archaic Egyptian chronology back 200 to 300 years; see *Radiocarbon* 43 (2001), 1147-1390. Even more recently, in their attempt to date the Thera eruption, Bronk Ramsey, Manning, and Galimberti, "Dating," 337, observe that "new evidence is now beginning to suggest that the historical-numerical chronology of Egypt in this period [early Middle kingdom] may not be as secure as has been supposed."

Chapter 14

Huber, "Astronomical Evidence," 5, arguing against the great bulk of other evidence. Walpole, *Works,* 2:106.

[1]Fomenko, *Empirico-Statistical Analysis*, 2:xiii.

[2]Ibid., 2:29-31, 335.

[3]Ibid., 2:xiii.

[4]Whiston, *Memoirs*, 1:240.

[5]Blinzler, *Prozess Jesu,* 101-02.

[6]Olmstead, "Chronology," 6.

[7]Humphreys and Waddington, "Dating the Crucifixion,"

[8]Ibid., 746. They fail to explain how a lunar eclipse could cause discernible darkening.
[9]A conspectus of competing interpretations is in Brown, *Death of the Messiah*, 2:1350-78.
[10]Humphreys and Waddington, "Dating the Crucifixion," 746.
[11]Brown, *Death of the Messiah*, 2:1350.
[12]Ibid., 2:1361n.
[13]Nivison, *Key.*
[14]Ssu-ma Ch'ien, *Grand Scribe's Records,* xxviii.
[15]Needham, *Science and Civilisation,* 3:173-74.
[16]Saussure, "Chronologie chinoise."
[17]Bishop, "Chronology of Ancient China."
[18]Yetts, "Shang-Yin Dynasty," 683-85.
[19]Karlgren, "Weapons and Tools," 114-16; Yetts in Moule, *Rulers,* xv-xvi.
[20]Karlgren, "Weapons and Tools," 120.
[21]Ong," Date of the Chou Conquest," 157-59.
[22]Ho, *Cradle,* 5.
[23]Keightley, *"Bamboo Annals,"* 425.
[24]Ibid., 425-26.
[25]Ibid., 438.
[26]Shaughnessy, "'New' Evidence."
[27]Pankenier, "Astronomical Dates," 3.
[28]Ibid., 3, 26n11.
[29]Ibid., 4.
[30]Ibid., 13-16.
[31]Ibid., 17-21.
[32]Ibid., 7, 22.
[33]Nivison, "Dates of Western Chou," 535-46.
[34]Ibid., 565, emphasis in original.
[35]Nivison, "1040," 76-78.
[36]Ibid., 77.
[37]Pankenier, *"Mozi,"* 176-80.
[38]Ibid., 180.
[39]Nivison and Pang, "Astronomical Evidence."
[40]Huang, "Study," 97-98.
[41]Ibid., 111.
[42]Nivison, "Response," 167.
[43]Pankenier, "Forum."
[44]Zhang Peiyu, "Forum," 133.
[45]Ibid., 133-50.
[46]Ibid., 147-49.
[47]Pang, "Extraordinary Floods," 153.
[48]Shaughnessy, *Sources,* 217.
[49]Ibid., 221-35.
[50]Ibid., 286-87.

[51]Allan, "Review."

[52]Barnard, "Astronomical Data," 50n3.

[53]As he notes, Barnard here follows Keightley, *"Bamboo Annals,"* 423-38.

[54]Barnard, "Astronomical Data," 70-71.

[55]Editorial introduction to Ssu-ma Ch'ien, *Grand Scribe's Records,* 85.

[56]Huang, "Study," 98; Zhang, "Forum," 147.

[57]As did W.F. Albright, noted above.

[58]Pankenier, "Lunar Aspect," 67.

[59]Baillie, *Slice Through Time,* 156.

[60]Ibid., 149-58 and passim.

[61]Ibid., 90-95.

[62]Ibid., 149.

[63]Ibid., 158, emphasis in original.

[64]Baillie, *Exodus to Arthur,* 230, 236.

[65]Diamond, *Guns, Germs, and Steel,* 408.

Chapter 15

Green, *Fatal Cut,* 181.

Carroll, "Stage and Spirit of Reverence," 288, emphasis in original.

[1]Boyle, "Proemial Essay" in Boyle, *Works of the Honourable Robert Boyle,* 1:307, written in 1661, italics in original.

[2]For a case study of audience-specific discourse see Fahnestock, "Arguing."

[3]Prevas, *Hannibal,* 152.

[4]E.g., Gransden, "Prologues."

[5]Dever, "Postmodern Malarkey."

[6]Ibid., 28.

[7]Ibid. For a counterpoint on who has the most votes see Zwelling, "Fictions of the Bible."

[8]Dever, "Postmodern Malarkey," 68n5.

[9]Ibid., 30; idem., "Identity of Ancient Israel," 19, emphasis added.

[10]Newson, "Old World Diseases," 17.

[11]Ibid., emphasis added.

[12]Finlay, "How Not to (Re)Write World History," 242, commenting on Menzies, *1421,* quoting Menzies.

[13]Flight, "Bantu Expansion."

[14]Granger, *Keeping Bad Company,* 18.

[15]Wright, "Accidental Creationist," 59.

[16]Hornblower, "Story of Greek Historiography," 27, emphasis in original.

[17]Oakley, *Commentary,* 1:77n204, 1:77n206.

[18]For another case from Classical Antiquity see Scodel, *Credible Impossibilities.*

[19]Henige, "Implausibility of Plausibility."

[20]Bowersock, "Art of the Footnote;" Henige, "What Price Economy?;" Grafton, *Footnote.*

For a survey of the philosophy and practice of annotating since the Renaissance see Connors, "Rhetoric of Citation Systems."

[21]In this vein, the website I mentioned earlier can be considered to be an electronic footnote designed to strengthen the cases made here.

[22]Newson, "Population of the Amazon Basin."

[23]Vésteinsson, "Patterns of Settlement," 2-4, 26.

[24]Dever, "Archaeology and the 'Age of Solomon'," 221.

[25]Mallory, *In Search of the Indo-Europeans*, 143. No references to Sayce's works are given.

[26]Bordi, *Foundations of Latin*, 40, has nine maps covering theories of Indo-Aryan homelands ranging from Sinai to Sweden.

[27]For caution in scientific writing see Hyland, *Hedging*.

[28]Chang, "Search for Shang," 67.

[29]Rainey, "Review," 159.

[30]Becking, *Fall of Samaria*, 52, also credits the Old Testament with providing "dates."

[31]Aling, "Historical Synchronisms," 19.

[32]Noting that for Hittite chronology, there are "no year-names, no eponyms, no counting of regnal years, no era, no kinglist," Wilhelm, "Generation Count," 74, 76, places the ordinal numbers of several Hittite rulers, including this one, in quotation marks.

[33]Brown, " Battle of Hastings," 8.

[34]Hassan, "Population Dynamics," 698-99. The article is riddled with outsized claims.

[35]A generous estimate based on the frontispiece map in Davies, *Incas*.

[36]Allardyce, "Toward a World History," 67.

Chapter 16

Carroll, *Through the Looking-Glass*, chapter 7, emphasis in original.

Williams, *Aldgate Mystery*, 189-90.

[1]Mark Twain, *Is Shakespeare Dead?*, 49.

[2]Anderson, "Scientists Probe for Earth's Biggest Beast," 24.

[3]Gillette, *Seismosaurus*.

[4]Ibid., 157.

[5]Chang, "China on the Eve of the Historical Period," 59-65, 72.

[6]For incremental gains in our knowledge about a somewhat later peripheral state see Pang Bangben, "In Search of Shu."

[7]For an archeological interpretation of the phase see Demattè, "Longshan Era Urbanism."

[8]*Japan in the Chinese Dynastic Histories*, 9-27.

[9]Steggemann, "Qumran," 13.

[10]For example, a recent estimate (Strasburger, "Umblick") is that about one-fortieth of Greek historical writing has survived. According to Schoville, *Biblical Archaeology*, 157, only "about thirty" of "over five thousand ancient ruins" in Israel and Jordan have been "the scenes of major excavations," although no doubt this figure is somewhat higher now.

[11]Reichel, "Modern Crime," 355.

[12]Fischer, *Historians' Fallacies*, 62.

[13]For an argument that negative results have value, for instance, in setting limits, see Collins, "Lead into Gold."

[14]For extended disagreements with Wood see Rachewiltz, "Marco Polo," and Larner, *Marco Polo*, 60-63. Later, Wood, "Did Marco Polo?" reiterated her position, but retreated a bit from her reliance on the argument from silence.

[15]Poole, *Our Lady of Guadalupe,* 105-26.

[16]The Vatican apparently was not impressed by the silence, nor by the fact that recent scientific analysis (Vera, "Manos humanas") has dated the tincture on the cloak to the twentieth century, since it canonized Juan Diego, the peasant in question, in August of 2002. The article by Vera produced an immediate outpouring of commentary on the Internet; see, e.g., www.forocristiano.com (accessed 25 January 2005)

[17]In late 2002 an ossuary was publicized that contained wording about a James who was the son of a Joseph and brother of a Jesus. To some this provides needed corroboration, and within a month after the first announcement there were 200 websites indexed by google.com. Others, among them the Israel Antiquities Authority, see it as a coincidence (all three were very common names in the period) or a partial forgery.

[18]Josephus, *Antiquities of the Jews*, xviii.63-64.

[19]Meier, "Jesus in Josephus," 77.

[20]Feldman, "*Testimonium Flavianum*," 181-85; Hardwick, *Josephus*, 84-86, 122. Olson, "Eusebius," 306, regards "the entire passage [as] spurious," while Whealey, *Josephus on Jesus*, suspends judgment.

[21]E.g., Vermes, "Jesus Notice." The latest is Bardet, Testimonium Flavianum, 79-88.

[22]Wells, *Jesus Myth*, 196-223; Harris, "References to Jesus."

[23]In a recent exposition of the issue, Paget adopts a limited goal: "[i]t has in part been the aim of this article to show up something of th[e] complexity [of the evidence] without necessarily arriving at some new solution." He continues that he himself is "in favour of retaining the passage in some emended form," while conceding that "I am as clear as anyone about the weaknesses of such a position." See Paget, "Josephus and Christianity," 603.

[24]For details see Henige, "'Disease of Writing'."

[25]Utley, "One Hundred and Three Names."

[26]Metzger, "Names for the Nameless," 98.

[27]Ibarra Rojas, "Epidemias," 593, emphasis added.

[28]Ibid.

[29]Dobyns, *Their Number Become Thin*, 8-32 and passim.

[30]Martin, "Deep History," 278-79.

[31]For Haley's misadventures in the Gambia see Wright, "Uprooting Kunta Kinte."

[32]Haley, *Roots*, 685.

[33]Mills and Mills, "*Roots* and the New Faction," emphasis in original.

[34]E.g., Dillehay, *Monte Verde,* and *First Americans*.

[35]For the most recent set of essays addressing the revived and expanded issues, see *Entering America.*

[36]Fiedel, "Older than We Thought," 110.

[37]Murray, "Thirteenth Address of the President," 516.

[38]Schäfer, *Documentation,* 4, emphasis added. See as well Russell, "Shakespearean Coinages."

[39]Sperling, *Original Torah*, 3-4.

[40]Shanks, "Meaning of Unhistory," 6.

[41]Such arguments usually impute functional illiteracy to the Israelites to explain this lack of epigraphic evidence, but never explain why this should have been so when the Israelites were surrounded by states that did produce inscriptions.

[42]Mossiker, *Pocahontas*, 84-86; Lemay, *Pocahontas,* esp. 58-97.

[43]The author of the latest study argues that the entire episode was a myth created by Smith for his own purposes; Townsend, *Pocahontas,* 52-56.

[44]Martin, *Plague?,* 204, 205. Martin, ibid., 25-26, admits that many letters were destroyed on receipt as possibly infectious, but this has little effect on his argument, unless we believe that coincidently all letters mentioning rats happened to be among them.

[45]Martin's work is only one of several recent studies that question that rat-driven bubonic plague was the only, or even the principal, disease that was called "plague." For the context see Eamon, "Plagues, Healers, and Patients," and on a much larger scale, Cohn, *Black Death Transformed,* who begins his introduction (ibid., 1) with the assertion that "[t]he Black Death in Europe . . . was any disease other than the rat-based bubonic plague." Susan Scott and Christopher Duncan, *Biology of Plague*, rediagnose the cause of the Black Death as a hemorrhagic fiolovirus—one reason, no rats. They have updated this work for a more general audience in Scott and Duncan, *Return*. However, some recent thinking—in part stimulated by the missing rats—is that the fleas that spread the plague could have lived on any member of the rodent family, thus negating the significance of rats in particular, whether or not absent.

[46]Davis, "Scarcity of Rats," 467, 470.

[47]Martin, *Plague?*, 7-20.

[48]Davis, "Scarcity of Rats," 462n16.

[49]Some (e.g., McCormick, "Rats") believe that the silence has been overtaken by new evidence.

[50]Gardiner, "New Literary Works," 36, emphasis added.

[51]Lamarck. *Philosophie zoologique*, 1:75-76, quoted in Burkhardt, *Spirit of System,* 134.

[52]Jefferson, "Discovery of Certain Bones," 256; Boyd, "Megalonyx."

[53]E.g., Rudwick, *Meaning of Fossils.*

[54]See msowww.anu.edu.au/2dFGRS/Public/Pics/2dFzcone.gif (accessed 2 March 2005).

Chapter 17

Glenn, *Reading Athena's Dance Card*, 135, quoting a source for S.L.A. Marshall's influential "ratio of fire" argument.

Stark, *Rise of Christianity*, 14, emphasis in original.

[1]Plato, *Republic*, 216 (vii.522).

[2]Maitland, *History of London*, 548, emphasis in original.

[3]Huxley, "Geological Reform," xlix, discussing recent calculations of the retardation of the earth's rotation.

[4]Hudson, *History by Numbers*, 13-16.

[5]Feinstein and Thomas, *Making History Count*. For a critique of Annaliste quantifying see Carrard, *Poetics of the New History*, esp. 166-89.

[6]Fogel and Engerman, *Time on the Cross*.

[7]The *Book Review Index* listed nearly sixty reviews in the first year, a phenomenal number. Among the major critiques were Sutch, "Treatment;" Scheiber, "Black is Computable;" Gutman, *Slavery and the Numbers Game*; and Ratcliffe, "*Das Kapital*."

[8]Fogel and Engerman, "Explaining;" eadem, "Explaining: Reply."

[9]Scheiber, "Black is Computable," 673.

[10]Ibid., 672.

[11]Passell, "Review," 4.

[12]Baines, "Origins," 142-43.

[13]De Odorico, *Use of Numbers*, 58, 173-74, 204.

[14]Ibid., 171-73.

[15]Henige, *Numbers From Nowhere*.

[16]A recent example of quantification run amok is Chase-Dunn and Manning, "City Systems." The authors believe that they can identify the seven largest cities in 2000 BCE, enact a demographic Bode's Law for the size of cities, and assert that urban centers in all times and places arose and fall "synchronously." For their data they rely entirely on Chandler, *Urban Growth*.

[17]John Thorn (jthorn@totalsports.net) to SABR-L@apple.ease.lsoft.com, 18 August 1999.

[18]Thus the remarkable difference cannot be attributed to differing notions about technology, productivity, and the like.

[19]Cohen, *How Many People*, 402-18.

[20]For details see Henige, *Numbers From Nowhere*, 23-213, 321-82.

[21]Gros de Boze, "Eloge de M. Henrion," 382, emphasis added.

[22]Dobyns, "Reassessing," 9.

[23]Darwin, *Formation*, 154-65 passim. He also cited approvingly an estimate that 53,767 worms per acre would be needed to produce all this mould.

[24]Eckhardt, *Civilizations,* 272-73.

[25]E.g., *Chinese Ways in Warfare*; Sima Qian, *Records*, esp. 22-45; and Sun Pin, *Sun Pin Military Methods*, 13-75, 246-63.

[26]Bosworth, *Ghaznavids*, 98-128.

[27]Based on the testimony of Korean chronicles, Bong Kang, "Reconsideration," calculates that there were 198 "warfare" episodes in Korea between the first century BCE and the eighth century CE These are hardly very reliable sources, but they could, just possibly, roughly reflect the level of Korean warfare during this period. Neither Eckhardt and Cioffi-Revilla include Korea in their surveys.

[28]E.g., Eckhardt, *Civilizations*, 97-124, 173-77; cf. idem., "War-Related Deaths."

[29]Chandler, *Urban Growth.*

[30]Cioffi-Revilla, "Long Range Analysis."

[31]Ibid., 628-29. Eckhardt and, at this point, Cioffi-Revilla, rely heavily on Dupuy and Dupuy, *Harper Encyclopedia of Military History*, a work that devotes just one page to China before 400 BCE.

[32]Cioffi-Revilla, "Long Range Analysis," 606.

[33]Later Cioffi-Revilla, "Chinese Warfare and Politics," went to the opposite extreme, accepting and counting 104 wars in ancient China from 2697 BCE to 722 BCE, that is, even before the Spring and Autumn Period began.

[34]Cioffi-Revilla, "Long Range Analysis," 613-14.

[35]Ibid., 621-27.

[36]Mosimann and Martin, "Simulating Overkill."

[37]See the numerous essays in *Mass-Extinction Debate* for point and counterpoint.

[38]Whitmore, *Disease and Death.*

[39]Manning, *Slavery and African Life.*

[40]Buttrey, "Calculating Ancient Coin Production," 351.

[41]Playfair, *Commercial and Political Atlas.*

[42]Taylor "Objects and Advantages."

[43]Tweed, quoted in Vinson, *Thomas Nast,* 19.

[44]E.g., Mignolo, "Misunderstanding and Colonization."

[45]Harley, "Deconstructing the Map," 1.

[46]E.g., Gainer, "Cartographic Evidence."

[47]There is no lack of examples; a recent one is MacMillan, "Sovereignty 'More Plainly Described'."

[48]E.g., Stone, "District Map."

[49]Closer to home, Toledo is now in Ohio and the Upper Peninsula is in Michigan as a result of the settlement of the tempest in a teapot known at the Toledo War, which flared in the 1830s over the mapping of disputed boundary lines between Michigan and Ohio.

[50]Ramaswamy, "Catastrophic Cartographies;" Henige, "Power of Pink."

[51]For an Australian analog see Johnson, *Search for the Inland Sea.* For other examples of long-held beliefs in nonexistent physical features that appeared on countless maps, see Bassett and Porter, "'From the Best Authorities';" Mitchell, "Science, Giants, and Gold."

[52]Stommel, *Lost Islands*, xv.

[53]While most inaccurate maps became that way by accident or ignorance, atlases and maps produced in the Soviet Union as early as 1937 were replete with deliberate falsifications. Cities, rivers, and other features were moved or deleted, apparently in an attempt to confuse potential enemies, even though more accurate earlier editions could be consulted by these same potential enemies. "Soviet Cartographic Falsification."

[54]King, *Commissar Vanishes.*

[55]For a pessimistic diagnosis, but optimistic prognosis, of the problem see Farid, "Picture Tells a Thousand Lies."

[56]Of course even pre-digital photographs need to be contextualized and scrutinized, but at least most of them stand as taken. Many studies have appeared recently on the need to

understand photographers, subjects, and situations if we are to understand photographs themselves. In fact, photography had hardly been invented before its practitioners began to fool their audiences by, e.g., casting European models and European scenes as oriental. See, among others, Ackerman, *Origins*; Baldwin, *Roger Fenton*; Daniel, "'More Than Mere Photographs';" Orvell, *Real Thing*.

[57]Recently a nationwide chain selling electronic products advertised a "photo & print production studio all in one machine" that can "[p]rint, scan, copy, fax and edit digital photos with included hardware." To today's user this is a very appealing proposition. For tomorrow's historians it might seem to have one capability too many, since it renders every digital image suspect of being

Chapter 18

James Boswell, quoting Samuel Johnson, 3 April 1776, in *Boswell's Life of Johnson*, 3:10-11

Beche, *Sections and Views*, iii.

[1]Darwin, *Life and Letters,* 1:87.

[2]Freud, "Psycho-analysis and Psychiatry," 16:244-45.

[3]Festinger, Riecken, and Schachter, *When Prophecy Fails*, 3-4.

[4]Martin, *Keepers of the Game.*

[5]Martin, "Comment," 191.

[6]Christy Turner III, quoted in Kiefer, "Indian Stew."

[7]Temple, *Sirius Mystery²*, 1, 16.

[8]Lamberti, "Omotic and Cushitic," 556.

[9]For a set of essays on reviewing, past and present, see *Storiografia* 1 (1997), a special issue entitled "La recensione: origini, splendori e declino della critica storiografica."

[10]Blackey, "Words to the Whys;" Runnels, "Place of Book Reviews;" Jajko, "Comments;" Greene and Spornick, "Favorable and Unfavorable Book Reviews;" Henige, "Reviewing Reviewing."

[11]For an insider's view of pragmatic and philosophical issues in book reviewing, see Spall, "Book Reviews."

[12]E.g., Gates, "James Belich."

[13]*African Studies Review* 42 (1999), 201.

[14]Hall, "Letter," 712. For civility and its consequences, see Snider, "Stifling the Naysayer."

[15]Gross, "Science Wars," 449.

[16]Lipset, "Response," 67.

[17]McGrath, Metz, and Rutledge, "H-Net Book Reviews."

[18]Baird, "Confessions." McGrath, Metz, and Rutledge, "H-Net Book Reviews," do not consider this aspect at all.

[19]Handy, "Dating," 100-01; Dever, "'Age of Solomon'," 239.

[20]Niemann, "Socio-Political Shadow," 296.

[21]Kitchen, "Egypt and East Africa," 117-20.

[22]Knauf, "Roi est mort," 93-95.

[23]Ash, *David,* 26.

[24]*Vinland Map[1].*

[25]*Vinland Map[2].* For a discussion see McNaughton, "What's New?"

[26]Seaver, *Maps, Myths, and Men*, offers a rather unedifying account of the controversy, arguing that the Vinland Map not only is a forgery, but that this should have been recognized from the beginning.

[27]Geikie, "Presidential Address," 724, referring to Lord Kelvin and his theories on the age of the earth noted above.

[28]Bernal, *Black Athena*. A second volume appeared in 1991 and two more are promised.

[29]A recent listing of major contributions is Fagan, "Bibliography."

[30]Berlinerblau, *Heresy in the University*, 6, calculated that negative reviews have outnumbered favorable ones by over two to one, even more heavily in relevant scholarly journals.

[31]Ibid., 245-47, lists over fifty contributions by Bernal to the debate. Sixteen extended responses have been gathered together in Black Athena *Writes Back*.

[32]Levine, "Bernal and the Athenians," 2. Others, e.g., Lefkowitz, "*Black Athena*," give no credit to Bernal as a catalyst.

[33]Berlinerblau, *Heresy*, 179; cf. ibid., 19, 41.

[34]Freeman, *Margaret Mead and Samoa.*

[35]Freeman, who died in 2001, refuted the first charge several times, most recently in his *Fateful Hoaxing*, 203-6, while admitting to the last.

[36]For a recent overview of the debate see Shankman, "Samoan Sexual Conduct."

[37]Orans, *Not Even Wrong,* 155-56.

[38]Hays, "Sacred Texts," 93.

[39]Tuzin, "Derek Freeman," 1013.

[40]For a petulant, but not very convincing, defense of Mead's right not to be challenged see Caldararo, "War, Mead, and Nature."

[41]Hermanns-Audurdóttir, "Reply to Comments," 31, emphasis added.

[42]Jones, "Revisiting the Canek Manuscript."

[43]Jones, *Conquest,* 426n5.

[44]E.g., Mead and Freeman, *Roots*, Martin Bernal's theories, and the recent very bitter, and very unresolved, discussion of Daniel Goldhagen's *Hitler's Willing Executioners*, for which see, among many already, *Unwilling Germans?*; "*The Goldhagen Effect*;" and Fred Kautz, *German Historians*. More recently yet, the debate over Polish participation in the Jedwabne massacre can be studied at http://www.pogranicze.sejny.pl/jedwabne/index.html (accessed 12 February 2005), as well as in *Thou Shalt Not Kill* and *Neighbors Respond*.

Chapter 19

Desiderius Erasmus to Thomas Ruthall, 7 March 1515, in *Correspondence of Erasmus*, 3:64-68, referring to his textual criticism of the Septuagint.

Draper, *Daniel Boone*, 20.

[1]Holden, *Analysis of Divine Faith,* 73-74.

[2]Beit-Arié, "Publication and Reproduction," 226, 232.

[3]*Johnson on Shakespeare*, 60.

[4]Freeman, "Texts, Lies, and Microfilm." Freeman cites numerous modern misconceptions of Foxe from failing to recognize how dynamic and indeterminate his texts are.

[5]These issues are discussed in, among others, Wills, *Lincoln at Gettysburg*, 191-203. See as well Peters, "Lincoln's Gettysburg Address," for textual criticism.

[6]Henige, *In Search of Columbus*, 65-101.

[7]Bonnat, *Marie-Joseph Bonnat et les Ashanti.*

[8]Henige, "Barbed-Wire Bonnat?"

[9]Washington, *Writings*, 2:xv.

[10]E.g., Knollenberg, *Washington,* 151-55.

[11]For the bowdlerization of folktales in the nineteenth century see Schacker, *National Dreams.*

[12]Radosh, "American Kids."

[13]Ross, "Electronic Text," 226. This view might help account for the decline in quality text-editing discussed in Hunter, "Whither Editing?"

[14]Foakes, "Shakespeare Editing," 434.

[15]Heller, "Minutes," 73.

[16]For the abundance of one group of nineteenth-century travel accounts see Fage, *Guide.*

[17]Over 500 items are listed in Brown, *Bayeux Tapestry*, and much more has appeared since.

[18]Even the numbers of panels comprising the Tapestry is in doubt; a recent surfing of the Internet yielded numbers from 54 to 79. Presumably it is a matter of definition, but a useful window on the complexities involved.

[19]Bernstein, "Blinding of Harold," 40; cf. idem., *Mystery of the Bayeux Tapestry*, 144-59.

[20]For a useful, though dated, orientation to some of these see Werckmeister, "Political Ideology."

[21]For instance, in the panel entitled "Here a cleric and Aelfgyva," which seems to be a flashback, as the plot of the Tapestry is presently understood, Aelfgyva has variously been identified as "a young girl, a married woman, a widow, an abbess and a death symbol"— and an embroidery teacher; Grape, *Bayeux Tapestry*, 40. See further McNulty, "Lady," and Campbell, "Aelfgyva."

[22]Bernstein, "Blinding of Harold," 64.

[23]"Battle of Hastings and the Death of Harold," 47.

[24]Thus works like Grape, *Bayeux Tapestry*, which includes all the panels in color together with transcriptions and translations of the captions and suitable commentary are genuine text editions in their own right.

[25]Warrell, *Turner and Venice*, 255-57. Perhaps made cautious by the new order, the catalog lists the new titles only as "most appropriate" in the state of the evidence.

[26]As in the case of the Bixby letter noted above.

[27]Allen and Smith, "Editing William Clayton," 134.

[28]*Chronicle of Higher Education* (22 January 1999), A6.

[29]Peters, "Lincoln's Gettysburg Address," makes much of such a case.

[30]E.g., Tov, *Textual Criticism.*

[31]Cantor, "On Sitting Down," 454. Performing a third choice—a happy ending—was common practice in the eighteenth century.

[32]Quoted in Annan, *Dons*, 32.

[33]Alexander Eliot, "Cleansing," responding to Pope-Hennessey, "Storm."

[34]See, e.g., Cast, "Finishing the Sistine;" Brandt, "Grime of the Centuries."

[35]Collinson, "One of Us?" 148.

[36]E.g., Kline, *Guide*, and Luey, *Editing Documents and Texts.*

[37]Nor is editing as a skill, a goal, or a livelihood mentioned in Bender et al., *Education.* For one defense against claims of intellectual inferiority see Stevens, "'Most Important Work'."

Chapter 20

Boswell, *Journey*, 67, sub 23 August 1773. Despite widespread doubt about the authenticity of Macpherson's "Ossianic" poems, he never did submit any originals to public scrutiny, and they have long since been dismissed as frauds.

Fagan, *Great Journey*, 263.

[1]By historians' own admission, the last expedient was the least utilized; see Stieg, "Information Needs of Historians."

[2]Kitchen, "Curse of Publication," 625.

[3]Hanson and Heath, *"Who Killed Homer?*, 2.

[4]Henige, *Serial Bibliographies.*

[5]For details see *Bibliographic Services of the American Historical Association: Recently Published Articles (RPA), Writings on American History (WAH)*, submitted by the ABH/AHA Task Force to the Research Division of AHA, Spring 1989.

[6]Henige, "Coping With Evidence."

[7]Jones, "Neglected Heritage;" more generally, Henige, "Half Life of African Archives."

[8]Schiffer, *Behavioral Archaeology*, 49.

[9]For some other purposes see Heintze, "Referencing in the Humanities."

[10]Robertson, *Charles the Fifth,* 1:290.

[11]William Robertson to William Strahan, 15 March 1776, in Gibbon, *Miscellaneous Works,* 2:159-60.

[12]Krech, *Ecological Indian*, 231-308.

[13]Henige, "Omphaloskepsis," reviewing Cohen, *Combing of History.*

[14]Kochen, "How Well Do We Acknowledge Intellectual Debts?," proposed a system in which referees and editors would collaborate to test the bibliographies of submitted papers. Nothing seems to have come of it.

[15]Bell, "Dark Ages," 2, 8.

[16]Baillie, *Exodus to Arthur,* 129.

[17]Gervase of Canterbury, *Historical Works,* 1:xv, 276. See as well Cragoe, "Reading and Rereading."

[18]Morris, *Dutch.*

[19]Studies on incorrect citing and its effects include Hernon and Metoyer-Duran, "Literature Reviews," and Benning, "Incorrect Citations." Of special interest is a study of citations in journals in librarianship that found that error rates ran from 19 percent to 60 percent: Pope, "Accuracy of References."

[20]*Chronometric Dating in Archaeology.*

[21]Ibid., title page, xi.

[22]Cook, *Demographic Collapse*, 90. Whitmore, *Disease and Death,* 15, does the same.

[23]Another example, even though expressly written for the informed, but non-specialist, reader, is Stephenson, *Historical Eclipses.*

[24]For a discussion of several examples, see Henige, "Indexing."

[25]Among many others, see Karageorghis, "It's Publish or Perish;" *Archaeology's Publication Problem*; and Kingsnorth, "Whither the Site Report?" The problem is hardly confined to the Near East; only 130 of the 698 sites excavated in India between 1953 and 1995 produced full site reports; Chakrabarti, *Archaeology*, 27-31, 47-50, 91-96, 119-24, 149-58.

[26]Kletter and De-Groot, "Excavating to Excess?" 76. Ottaway, "Publish or be Damned," lists more sites with publication problems.

[27]For a collective discussion of this aspect of the matter, including comments by several insiders of both persuasions, see "Ethics of Publication of the Dead Sea Scrolls."

[28]Lawrence Schiffman in ibid., 464-65; Shanks, "Blood on the Floor."

[29]Henige, "'In Possession of the Author'."

[30]Peter Davies to Editor, *NS* 2175 (27 February 1999), 55-56.

[31]For the Kennewick Man decision: Watkins, "Beyond the Margin," and www.kennewick-man.com. NAGPRA-like restrictions are hardly unique; see, e.g., Rudelson, "Xinjiang Mummies."

[32]Olsen, "Researchers."

[33]Bryan, *Collaborative Meaning*, xiv.

[34]Faulhaber, "Digital Scriptorium;" González García, *Informatización*. http://www.kb.dk/elib/mss/poma/ (accessed 27 November 2004) has digital facsimiles much superior to print versions, partial English translations, and several unpublished papers dealing with the ongoing controversy over the authorship of the *Nueva Corónica*, mentioned above. For more see Adorno, "Archive."

[35]See http://memory.loc.gov/ammem/mtjhtml/mtjhome.html (accessed 1 March 2005). It is unclear whether this will update, supplement, duplicate, or render obsolete the ongoing (for fifty years) printed edition of Jeffersoniana.

[36]E.g., the ongoing electronic edition of Pepys's famous diary at www.pepysdiary.com (accessed 12 February 2005).

[37]Whatever disadvantages we might glean from a too-swift transition to electronic formats, it is easy to see the value of such productions as the *History of Parliament* on CD-ROM. Here 13 million words, already published, are gathered on a single disk, and all of

them can be searched as a single process, enabling the kinds of broad comparisons and contrasts that are all but impossible by plowing through the 23 large-format volumes that are available: Hoppit, "Embarrassment of Riches;" and Daunton, "Virtual Presentation." [38]The promise and perils of the new age are discussed in Rosenzweig, "Scarcity or Abundance?"

Chapter 21

Peirce, *Collected Papers*, 1:24.
Barton, "'Higher' Archaeology," 260.
[1]Davies, "On the Nature of Geo-History," 9.
[2]Dalrymple, *Age of the Earth*, 12-78. See as well Burchfield, *Lord Kelvin*, 45-53, 96-108, 163-201. Huxley, "Evidence," noted that all these arguments were "based on the premise that the whole of physics was already known and that it was safe to ignore the possibility that there might exist other sources . . . that had not been identified in the laboratories."
[3]For nineteen essays on the development of the age-of-the-earth controversies see *Age of the Earth*.
[4]Wiseman, *Historiography*, xiii.
[5]Shaughnessy, "New Sources," 98.
[6]Freud, "Psycho-analysis and Psychiatry," 243-44.
[7]Silverstein, "End is Near," 418, emphasis in original.
[8]Meyer, "Eberhard Schrader," 158-59.
[9]Chamberlin, "Objections," 87.
[10]LeGrand, *Drifting Continents,* 2-3. See as well *Plate Tectonics.*
[11]Pettinato, *Città sepolta,* 352-54.
[12]Stille, "Overload," 42-43. For similar comments see Galison, "Removing Knowledge." An initiative by the Abraham Lincoln Association has turned up—so far—more than 100,000 documents "pertaining to Lincoln's law practice" alone. Davis, "Now He Belongs to the Sages," 5.
[13]See http://www.sims.berkeley.edu/research/projects/how-much-info-2003/execsum. htm, "Summary of Findings" and Table 1.1 (accessed 19 January 2005). The study further estimates that this is the equivalent of 500,000 Libraries of Congress.
[14]Jamieson, "From Here to Eternity."
[15]The title of this chapter is based on a fluffed line in a radio script of "The Lone Ranger," quoted in Harmon, *Great Radio Heroes*, 171, and serves as a microcosm of the facility with which we all keep going even when the evidence stops.
[16]Dobyns, *Native American Historical Demography,* 7.
[17]For two very different, yet similar, demonstrations of this see Epstein, "Confirmational Response Bias," and Cargill, "Ancient Israel."
[18]Miller and Hayes, *History,* 78, 79.
[19]Dever, "Current Crisis," 21*.
[20]Halpern, "State of Israelite History," 545.

[21]Scheffler, "Late-Dating," 527.

[22]Barr, *History and Ideology,* 70-71, referring to P.R. Davies.

[23]Bennett, "George Gordon Coulton," 278. Because of his inclination to engage in public disputes, Coulton was denied the status and perquisites normally accruing a British academic of his attainments. Cf. Gunson, "Robert Langdon" for another example.

[24]Koestler, *Darkness at Noon*, 97.

[25]At www.google.com/jobs/britney.html (accessed 29 December 2004).

[26]Mathematician-physicist Roger Penrose, quoted in Horgan, "Quantum Consciousness," 33.

[27]Davies, "Whose History?" 122.

[28]For the latest twist here see Rogers, "Studies."

[29]Dunning, "Truth in History," 229. I suppose I have in mind here the kinds of unexpected results that such techniques as DNA analysis, mentioned briefly in chapter 5, are producing with increasing frequency and impact. Perhaps a rough-and-ready way to measure humility, or the lack of it, in a particular author might be to judge works with titles that begin with "A History" somewhat more generously than those that begin with "The History."

BIBLIOGRAPHY

AA   *American Anthropologist*
AAy   *American Antiquity*
AHB   *Ancient History Bulletin*
AHR   *American Historical Review*
AICRJ   *American Indian Culture and Research Journal*
AM   *Ancient Mesoamerica*
AS   *The Age of Solomon: Scholarship at the Turn of the Millennium.* Ed. Lowell K.
         Handy. Leiden, 1997
ATR   *Anglican Theological Review*
BA   *Biblical Archaeologist*
BAR   *Biblical Archaeology Review*
BASOR   *Bulletin of the American Schools of Oriental Research*
BSOAS   *Bulletin of the School of Oriental and African Studies*
CA   *Current Anthropology*
CAC   *Coins, Art, and Chronology: Essays on the Pre-Islamic History of the Indo-
         Iranian Borderlands.* Ed. Michael Alram and Deborah E. Klimberg-Salter.
         Vienna, 1999
CBQ   *Catholic Biblical Quarterly*
CEA   *Cahiers d'Études Africaines*
CJAS   *Canadian Journal of African Studies*
EC   *Early China*
HA   *History in Africa*
HJAS   *Harvard Journal of Asiatic Studies*
HML?   *High, Middle, or Low?* Ed. Paul Aström. 3 vols. Gothenburg, 1987-89
HS   *History of Science*
HSE   *The Hernando de Soto Expedition: History, Historiography and "Discovery"
         in the Southeast.* Ed. Patricia K. Galloway. Lincoln, 1997
HT   *History and Theory*
IJAHS   *International Journal of African Historical Studies*
ISR   *Interdisciplinary Science Reviews*

279

280 ❖ Bibliography

JAH   *Journal of African History*
JAOS   *Journal of the American Oriental Society*
JARCE   *Journal of the American Research Center in Egypt*
JBL   *Journal of Biblical Literature*
JEA   *Journal of Egyptian Archaeology*
JHI   *Journal of the History of Ideas*
JIH   *Journal of Interdisciplinary History*
JJS   *Journal of Jewish Studies*
JPS   *Journal of the Polynesian Society*
JSOT   *Journal for the Study of the Old Testament*
JSP   *Journal of Scholarly Publishing*
JTS   *Journal of Theological Studies*
MDAIK   *Mitteilungen der deutschen Archäologische Instituts, Kairo*
NAR   *Norwegian Archaeological Review*
NS   *New Scientist*
NT   *Novum Testamentum*
PP   *Past and Present*
RA   *Revue d'Assyrologie et d'Archéologie Orientale*
TI   *Terrae Incognitae*
TP   *T'oung Pao*
VHB   *Virtual History and the Bible.* Ed. J. Cheryl Exum. Leiden, 2000
What If? *What If? The World's Foremost Military Historians Imagine What Might Have Been.* Ed. Robert Cowley. New York, 1999
ZAS   *Zeitschrift für ägyptische Sprache und Altertumskunde*

Abu-Lughod, Janet. *Before European Hegemony: the World System, A.D. 1250-1350.* New York, 1989.
—. "The World-System Perspective in the Construction of Economic History." In *World History: Ideologies, Structure, and Identities.* Ed. Philip Pomper, Richard Elphick, and Richard Vann. Oxford, 1989, 69-80, 240-44.
Ackerman, James. *Origins, Imitation, Conventions: Representation in the Visual Arts.* Cambridge, Mass., 2002.
Acsádi, G.F. and J. Nemeskéri. "Recommendations for Age and Sex Diagnoses of Skeletons." *Journal of Human Evolution* 9 (1980), 517-49.
Acton, John Dahlberg, Baron. *Lectures in Modern History.* London, 1906.
Adams, Percy G. *Travel Literature and the Evolution of the Novel.* Lexington, Ky., 1983.
—. *Travelers and Travel Liars, 1660-1800.* Berkeley, 1962.
Adorno, Rolena. "The Archive and the Internet." *The Americas* 61 (2004), 1-18.
The African Past Speaks. Ed. Joseph C. Miller. Folkestone, 1980.
The Afterlife of Inscriptions: Reusing, Rediscovering, Reinventing, and Revitalizing Ancient Inscriptions. Ed. Alison E. Cooley. London, 2000.
The Age of the Earth from 4004 BC to AD 2002. Ed. C.L.E. Lewis and S.J. Knell. London, 2001.

Albarella, Umberto. "'The Mystery of Husbandry:' Medieval Animals and the Problem of Integrating Historical and Archaeological Evidence." *Antiquity* 73 (1999), 867-75.

Albright, W.F. "The New Assyro-Tyrian Synchronism and the Chronology of Tyre." *Annuaire de l'Institut de Philologie et d'Histoire Orientales* 13 (1953), 1-9.

——. "New Light on the History of Western Asia in the Second Millennium B.C." *BASOR* 77 (February 1940), 20-30.

——. "The Readjustment of Assyro-Babylonian Chronology by the Elimination of False Synchronisms." *Journal of the Society of Oriental Research* 8 (1924), 51-59.

——. "A Revision of Early Assyrian and Middle Babylonian Chronology." *RA* 18 (1921), 83-94.

——. "A Revolution in the Chronology of Ancient Western Asia." *BASOR* 69 (February 1938), 18-21.

——. "A Third Revision of the Early Chronology of Western Asia." *BASOR* 88 (December 1942), 30-31.

Aling, Charles F. "Historical Synchronisms and the Date of the Exodus." *Artifax* 17/2 (2002), 19.

All the Mighty World: the Photographs of Roger Fenton, 1852-1860. Ed. Gordon Baldwin, Malcolm Daniel, and Sarah Greenough. New Haven, 2004.

Allan, Sarah. "Review of Shaughnessy, *Sources.*" *BSOAS* 55 (1992), 585-87.

Allardyce, Gilbert. "Toward World History: American Historians and the Coming of the World History Course." *Journal of World History* 1 (1990), 23-76.

Allen, Bem P. and D. Stephen Lindsay. "Amalgamations of Memories: Intrusion of Information from One Event into Reports of Another." *Applied Cognitive Psychology* 12 (1998), 277-85.

Allen, James and George Smith. "Editing William Clayton and the Politics of Mormon History." *Dialogue* 30/2 (Summer 1997), 129-56.

Alram, Michael. "Indo-Parthian and Early Kushan Chronology: the Numismatic Evidence." In *CAC*, 19-48.

Alter, Robert. "The Masada Complex." *Commentary* 56 (July 1973), 19-24.

Amarna Diplomacy: the Beginnings of International Relations. Ed. Raymond Cohen and Raymond Westbrook. Baltimore, 2000.

American Apocrypha. Ed. Dan Vogel and Brent Metcalfe. Salt Lake City, 2002.

Anderson, Ian. "Scientists Probe for the Earth's Biggest Beast." *NS* 114 (23 April 1987), 24.

Anderson, Perry. *A Zone of Engagement.* London, 1992.

Anderson, Richard. *Investigating the Book of Mormon Witnesses.* Salt Lake City, 1989.

Annan, Noel. *The Dons: Mentors, Eccentrics, and Geniuses.* Chicago, 1999.

Anyon, Roger et al. "Native American Oral Tradition and Archaeology: Issues of Structure, Relevance, and Respect." In *Native Americans and Archaeologists: Stepping Stones to Common Ground.* Ed. Nina Swidler et al. Walnut Creek, Calif., 1997, 77-87.

Appleby, Joyce, Lynn Hunt, and Margaret Jacob. *Telling the Truth About History.* New York, 1994.

Archaeology and Ancient History: Breaking Down the Boundaries. Ed. Eberhard W. Sauer. London, 2004.

Archaeology and Nationalism. Ed. John A. Atkinson, Iain Banks, and Jerry O'Sullivan. Glasgow, 1996.

Archaeology Under Fire: Nationalism, Politics, and Heritage in the Eastern Mediterranean and Middle East. Ed. Lynn Meskell. New York, 1998.

Archaeology's Publication Problem. Ed. Hershel Shanks. Washington, 1996.

Arrian. *Arrian.* Trans. P.A. Brunt. 2 vols. London, 1976-83.

Art de vérifier les dates. 18 vols. Paris, 1821-44.

Ash, Paul. *David, Solomon, and Egypt: a Reassessment.* Sheffield, 1999.

Athas, George. *The Tel Dan Inscription: a Reappraisal and a New Interpretation.* Sheffield, 2003.

Badash, Lawrence. "The Completeness of Nineteenth-Century Science." *Isis* 63 (1972), 48-58.

Bagley, Robert. "Shang Archaeology." In *Cambridge History of Ancient China.* Ed. Edward L. Shaughnessy and Michael Loewe. Cambridge, 1999, 124-231.

Baillie, Mike. *Exodus to Arthur: Catastrophic Encounters with Comets.* London, 1999.

—. *A Slice through time: Dendrochronology and Precision Dating.* London, 1995.

Baines, John. "Interpreting Sinuhe." *JEA* 68 (1982), 31-44.

—. "Origins of Egyptian Kingship." In *Ancient Egyptian Kingship.* Ed. David O'Connor and David Silverman. Leiden, 1995, 95-156.

Baird, Bruce. "Confessions of an Electronic Book Review Editor." *Editing History* 15/2 (Spring/Summer 1999), 1, 4, 7-9.

Baldwin, Gordon. *Roger Fenton: Pasha and Bayadère.* Los Angeles, 1996.

Banaji, M.R. and R.G. Crowder. "The Bankruptcy of Everyday Memory." *American Psychologist* 44 (1989), 1185-93.

Barchas, Janine. *Graphic Design, Print Culture, and the Eighteenth-Century Novel.* New York, 2003.

Bardet, Serge. *Le* Testimonium Flavianum: *examen historique, considérations historiographiques.* Paris, 2002.

Barnard, Noel. "Astronomical Data from Ancient Chinese Records: the Requirements of Historical Research Methodology." *East Asian History* 6 (1993), 47-74.

Barnes, J.W.B. "Sinuhe's Message to the King." *JEA* 53 (1967), 6-14.

Barnes, Julian. *A History of the World in 10 ¹/₂ Chapters.* London, 1989.

Barnes, William. *Studies in the Chronology of the Divided Monarchy of Israel.* Atlanta, 1991.

Barr, James. *History and Ideology in the Old Testament.* London, 2000.

Barra, Allen. *Inventing Wyatt Earp: His Life and Many Legends.* New York, 1998.

Barrett, C.K. "The Historicity of Acts." *JTS* 50 (1999), 515-34.

Barrett, T.H. "The Modern History of Asia and the Faking of 'The City of Light'." *Modern Asian Studies* 32 (1998), 1017-23.

Barton, George. "'Higher' Archaeology and the Verdict of Criticism." *JBL* 32 (1913), 244-60.

Bassett, Thomas and Philip Porter. "'From the Best Authorities': the Mountains of Kong in the Cartography of West Africa." *JAH* 32 (1991), 367-413.

"The Battle of Hastings and the Death of Harold." In *Complete Peerage*. Ed. Vicary Gibbs. 13 vols. London, 1910-59, 12/1, Appendices, 35-48.

Baud, Michel. *Djéser et la III dynastie*. Paris, 2002.

Beche, Henry de la. *Sections and Views Illustrative of Geological Phaenomena*. London, 1830.

Beckerath, Jürgen von. *Chronologie des ägyptischen Neuen Reiches*. Hildesheim, 1994.

—. *Chronologie des pharaonischen Ägypten*. Mainz, 1997.

—. *Handbuch der ägyptischen Königsnamen*. Munich, 1984.

Becking, Bob. *The Fall of Samaria: an Historical and Archaeological Study*. Leiden, 1992.

Beckman, Gary. *Hittite Diplomatic Texts*. Ed. Harry A. Hoffner. Atlanta, 1996.

Beek, Walter E.A. van. "Dogon Restudied: a Field Evaluation of the Work of Marcel Griaule." *CA* 32 (1991), 139-67.

—. "Haunting Griaule: Experiences from the Restudy of the Dogon." *HA* 31 (2004), 43-68.

Beinlich-Seeber, Christine. *Bibliographie Altägypten, 1822-1946*. 3 vols. Wiesbaden, 1998.

Bell, Barbara. "The Dark Ages in Ancient History." *American Journal of Archaeology* 75 (1971), 1-26.

Ben-Yehuda, Nachman. *The Masada Myth: Collective Memory and Mythmaking in Israel*. Madison, 1995.

—. *Sacrificing Truth: Archaeology and the Myth of Masada*. Amherst, N.Y., 2002.

Bender, Thomas et al. *The Education of Historians for the Twenty-First Century*. Urbana, 2004.

Benediktsson, Jakob. "*Landnámabók*: Some Remarks on Its Value as a Historical Source." *Saga-Book of the Viking Society* 17 (1966/69), 275-92.

Benerjee, Manabendu. "Some Problems of Editing Sanskrit Inscriptions." In *Problems of Editing Ancient Texts*. Ed. V.N. Jha. New Delhi, 1993, 63-73.

Bennett, H.S. "George Gordon Coulton, 1858-1947." *Proceedings of the British Academy* 23 (1947), 267-81.

Benning, S.P. et al. "Incorrect Citations: a Comparison of Library Literature with Medical Literature." *Bulletin of the Medical Library Association* 81 (1993), 56-58.

Berkeley, George. *Three Dialogues Between Hylas and Philonous*. Chicago, 1935 [1713].

Berkowitz, Leonard. "Reporting an Experiment: a Case Study in Leveling, Sharpening, and Assimilation." *Journal of Experimental Social Psychology* 7 (1971), 237-43.

Berlinerblau, Jacques. *Heresy in the University: the Black Athena Controversy and the Responsibilities of American Intellectuals*. New Brunswick N.J., 1999.

Bernal, Martin. *Black Athena: the Afroasiatic Roots of Classical Civilization, I, The Fabrication of Ancient Greece, 1785-1985*. New Brunswick, N.J., 1987.

Bernstein, David. "The Blinding of Harold and the Meaning of the Bayeux Tapestry." *Anglo-Norman Studies* 5 (1983), 40-64.

—. *The Mystery of the Bayeux Tapestry*. Chicago, 1986.

Best, Simon. "Here Be Dragons." *JPS* 97 (1988), 239-59.

Bible Translation: Frames of Reference. Ed. Timothy Wilt. Manchester, 2003.

Bible Translation on the Threshold of the Twenty-First Century: Authority, Reception, Culture, and Religion. Ed. Athalya Brenner and Jan Willem van Henten. London, 2002.

Bishop, C.W. "The Chronology of Ancient China." *JAOS* 52 (1932), 232-43.

Black Athena Writes Back: Martin Bernal Responds to His Critics. Ed. David C. Moore. Durham, N.C., 2001.

Blackey, Robert. "Words to the Whys: Crafting Critical Book Reviews." *History Teacher* 27 (1993/94), 159-66.

Blake, Barry. "Wiowurrung, the Melbourne Language." In *The Handbook of Australian Languages*. Ed. R.M.W. Dixon and Barry Blake. 4 vols. Melbourne, 1977-91, 4:31-122.

Blinzler, Josef. *Der Prozess Jesu*. 4th ed. Regenburg, 1969.

Bloedow, Edmund. "The Siege of Tyre in 332 B.C.: Alexander at the Crossroads of His Career." *Parola del Passato* 301 (1998), 255-93.

Böhl, F.M.T. *King Hammurabi of Babylonia in the Setting of His Time (About 1700 B.C.)*. Amsterdam, 1946.

Bonnat, Marie-Joseph. *Marie-Joseph Bonnat et les Ashanti. Journal, 1869-1874*. Ed. Claude-Hélène Perrot and Albert Van Dantzig. Paris, 1994.

Bopearachchi, Osmund. "Indo-Parthians." In *Das Partherreich und seine Zeugnisse*. Ed. Josef Wiesehöfer. Stuttgart, 1998, 389-404.

Bordi, Philip. *The Foundations of Latin*. Berlin, 1999.

Boswell, James. *Boswell's Journal of a Tour to the Hebrides with Samuel Johnson LL.D., 1773*. Ed. Frederick Pottle and Charles Bennett. New Haven, 1961.

—. *Boswell's Life of Johnson*. Ed. George B. Hill. Rev ed. 6 vols. Oxford, 1934.

Bosworth, A.B. *Alexander and the East: the Tragedy of Triumph*. London, 1996.

Bosworth, C.E. *The Ghaznavids*. Edinburgh, 1963.

Boutry, Philippe. "Les saints des catacombes; Itinéraires français d'une piété ultramontaine, 1800-1881." *Mélanges de l'École Française de Rome: Moyen-Âge/Temps Modernes* 91 (1979), 875-930.

Bowersock, G.W. "The Art of the Footnote," *American Scholar* 53 (1983/84), 54-62.

Boyd, Julian. "The Megalonyx, the Megatherium, and Thomas Jefferson's Lapse of Memory," *Proceedings of the American Philosophical Society* 102 (1958), 420-35.

Boyle, Robert. "Proemial Essay." In *Works of the Honourable Robert Boyle*. 6 vols. London, 1772, 1:299-318.

Brandt, Kathleen. "The Grime of the Centuries is a Pigment of the Imagination: Michelangelo's Sistine Ceiling." In *Palimpsest: Editorial Theory in the Humanities*. Ed. George Bornstein and Ralph Williams. Ann Arbor, 1993, 257-69.

Brannigan, Augustine and William Zwerman. "The Real 'Hawthorne Effect'." *Society* 38/2 (January/February 2001), 55-60.

Brear, Holly. *Inherit the Alamo: Myth and Ritual at an American Shrine*. Austin, 1995.

Breasted, J.H. "The Predynastic Union of Egypt." *Bulletin de l'Institut Français d'Archéologie Orientale* 30 (1931), 709-24.

Brecher, Kenneth. "Sirius Enigmas." In *Astronomy of the Ancients*. Ed. Kenneth Brecher and Michael Feirtag. Cambridge, 1979, 91-115.

Bredin, Miles. *The Pale Abyssinian: the Life of James Bruce, African Explorer and Adventurer*. London, 2000.

Brinkman, J.A. "Comments of the Nassouhi Kinglist and the Assyrian Kinglist Tradition." *Orientalia* 42 (1973), 306-19.

Bronk Ramsey, Christopher, Sturt W. Manning, and Mariagrazia Galimberti. "Dating the Volcanic Eruption at Thera." *Radiocarbon* 46 (2004), 325-44.

Brooks, N.P. and H.E. Walker. "The Authority and Interpretation of the Bayeux Tapestry." *Anglo-Norman Studies* 1 (1979), 1-34.

Brown, Francis. *Assyriology: Its Use and Abuse in Old Testament Study*. New York, 1885.

Brown, R. Allen. "The Battle of Hastings." *Anglo-Norman Studies* 3 (1980), 1-21.

Brown, Raymond. *The Birth of the Messiah*. New York, 1993.

—. *The Death of the Messiah*. 2 vols. New York, 1994.

Brown, S.A. *The Bayeux Tapestry: History and Bibliography*. Woodbridge, 1988.

Brown, Virginia. *The Textual Transmission of Caesar's Civil War*. Leiden, 1972.

Browne, Walden. *Sahagún and the Transition to Modernity*. Norman, 2000.

Brownlee, John. *Japanese Historians and National Myths, 1600-1945*. Vancouver, 1997.

Bruce, James. *Travels to Discover the Source of the Nile in the Years 1768, 1769, 1770, 1771, 1772 & 1773*. 5 vols. Edinburgh, 1790.

Bryan, Elizabeth. *Collaborative Meaning in Medieval Scribal Culture: the Otho Laȝamon*. Ann Arbor, 1999.

Bulhof, Johannes. "What If? Modality and Its History." *HT* 38 (1999), 145-68.

Bunzl, Martin. "Counterfactual History: a User's Guide." *AHR* 109 (2004), 845-58.

Burchfield, Joe. *Lord Kelvin and the Age of the Earth*. New York, 1975.

Burkhardt, Richard. *The Spirit of System: Lamarck and Evolutionary Biology*. Cambridge, 1995.

Burlingame, Michael. "New Light on the Bixby Letter." *Journal of the Abraham Lincoln Association* 16/1 (1995), 59-71.

Burney, David and Ramilisonina. "The *Kilopilopitsofy*, *Kidoky*, and *Bokyboky*: Accounts of Strange Animals from Belo-sur-mer, Madagascar, and the Megafaunal 'Extinction Window'." *AA* 100 (1998), 957-66.

Butler, Alban, Herbert Thurston, and Donald Attwater. *Butler's Lives of the Saints*. 12 vols. London, 1926-38.

Buttrey, T.V. "Calculating Ancient Coin Production." *Numismatic Chronicle* 153 (1993), 344-51.

Byock, Jesse. *Medieval Iceland: Society, Sagas, and Power*. Berkeley, 1988.

Calame-Griaule, Geneviève. "On the Dogon Revisited." *CA* 32 (1991), 575-77.

Caldararo, Niccolo. "War, Mead, and Nature of Criticism in Anthropology." *Anthropological Quarterly* 77 (2004), 311-22.

Campbell, M.W. "Aelfgyva: the Mystery Lady in the Bayeux Tapestry." *Annales de*

Normandie 34 (1984), 127-45.

Cantor, Paul. "On Sitting Down to Read *King Lear* Once More: the Textual Deconstruction of Shakespeare." In *The Flight from Science and Reason*. Ed. Paul Gross et al. Albany, 1996, 445-58.

Cargill, Jack. "Ancient Israel in Western Civ Textbooks." *History Teacher* 34 (2001), 297-326.

Carr, E.H. *What is History?* London, 1961.

Carrard, Philippe. *Poetics of the New History: French Historical Discourse from Braudel to Chartier*. Baltimore, 1992.

Carroll, Lewis. "The Stage and the Spirit of Reverence." *The Theatre* n.s. 11 (1888), 275-84.

Carson, Cindy. "Raiders of the Lost Scrolls: the Right of Scholarly Access to the Contents of Historical Documents." *Michigan Journal of International Law* 16 (1995), 299-348.

Cast, David. "Finishing the Sistine." *Art Bulletin* 173 (1991), 669-84.

Castellani, Arrigo. "Transcription Errors." In *Medieval Manuscripts and Textual Criticism*. Ed. Christopher Kleinhenz. Chapel Hill, 1976.

Chakrabarti, Dilip K. *Archaeology in the Third World: a History of Indian Archaeology since 1947*. New Delhi, 2003.

Chamberlin, R.T. "Some of the Objections to Wegener's Theory." In *Theory of Continental Drift: a Symposium*. Ed. W.A.J.M. van der Gracht. Tulsa, 1928, 83-87.

Chandler, Tertius. *Four Thousand Years of Urban Growth: an Historical Census*. 2d ed. Lewiston, 1987.

Chang, K.C. "China on the Eve of the Historical Period." In *Cambridge History of Ancient China*. Ed. Edward L. Shaughnessy and Michael Loewe. Cambridge, 1999, 37-73.

—. "The Search for Shang." *Archaeology* 52/2 (March-April 1999), 66-69.

Chase-Dunn, Christopher and E.S. Manning. "City Systems and World Systems: Four Millennia of City Growth and Decline." *Cross-Cultural Research* 36 (2002), 379-98.

Chinese Ways of Warfare. Ed. Frank Kiernan and John Fairbank. Cambridge, 1984.

Chronometric Dating in Archaeology. Ed. R.E. Taylor and Martin Aitken. New York, 1997.

Cioffi-Revilla, Claudio. "Chinese Warfare and Politics in the Ancient East Asian International System, ca. 2700 B.C. to 722 B.C." *International Interactions* 26 (2001), 347-78.

—. "The Long-Range Analysis of War." *JIH* 21 (1990/91), 603-29.

Clunies Ross, Margaret. "Conjectural Emendation in Skaldic Editing Practice, with Reference to *Egils saga*." *Journal of English and Germanic Philology* 104 (2005), 12-30.

Cohen, David. *The Combing of History*. Chicago, 1994.

Cohen, Joel. *How Many People Can the Earth Support?* New York, 1995.

Cohen, Richard S. "Problems in the Writing of Ajanta's History: the Epigraphic Evidence." *Indo-Iranian Journal* 40 (1997), 125-48.

Cohen, Shaye J.D. "Masada: Literary Tradition, Archaeological Remains, and the Credibility of Josephus." *JJS* 33 (1982), 385-405.

Cohn, Samuel. *The Black Death Transformed: Disease and Culture in Early Renaissance Europe.* New York, 2002.

Collins, H.M. "Lead into Gold: the Science of Finding Nothing," *Studies in the History and Philosophy of Science* 34 (2003), 1-25.

Collinson, Patrick. "One of Us? William Camden and the Making of History." *Transactions of the Royal Historical Society* 6th ser. 8 (1998), 139-63.

Connors, Robert. "The Rhetoric of Citation Systems." *Rhetoric Review* 17 (1998/99), 6-48, 219-47.

Cook, N.D. *Demographic Collapse: Indian Peru, 1520-1620.* Cambridge, 1981.

Cook, Sherburne and Woodrow Borah. "On the Credibility of Contemporary Testimony on the Population of Mexico in the Sixteenth Century." In *Summa Anthropologica en homenaje a Robert J. Weitlaner.* Mexico City, 1966, 229-39.

Cook, Stanley. "Chronology: Mesopotamia." *Cambridge Ancient History.* Cambridge, 1923, 1:145-56.

Cooley, W.D. "Review." *Foreign Quarterly Review* 10 (August 1832), 163-206.

Cooper, Jerrold. *Presargonic Inscriptions.* New Haven, 1986.

Cornell, T.J. *The Beginnings of Rome.* London, 1995.

Coughlin, William. "The Great *mokusatsu* Mistake: Was This the Deadliest Error of Our Time?" *Harper's Magazine* 206 (March 1953), 31-40.

Cowley, Robert. "Introduction." In *What If?*, i-xv.

Cragoe, Carol D. "Reading and Rereading Gervase of Canterbury.*" Journal of the British Archaeological Association* 154 (2001), 40-53.

Cressy, Serenus. *Exomologesis.* Paris, 1647.

Cribb, Joe. "The Early Kushan Kings: New Evidence for Chronology: Evidence from the Rabatak Inscription of Kanishka I." In *CAC,* 177-204.

Crisp, James E. *Sleuthing the Alamo.* New York, 2004.

Cryer, Frederick. "Chronology: Issues and Problems." In *Civilizations of the Ancient Near East.* 4 vols. New York, 1995, 2:658-63.

Cullen, Bob. "Testimony from the Iceman." *Smithsonian* 33/12 (February 2003), 42-50.

Curtin, P.D. *The Atlantic Slave Trade: a Census.* Madison, 1969.

Dalrymple, G. Brent. *The Age of the Earth.* Stanford, 1991.

Daniel, Malcolm. "'More Than Mere Photographs:' the Art of Roger Fenton." *Metropolitan Museum of Art Bulletin* 61/4 (Spring 1999), 24-31.

Darwin, Charles. *The Formation of Vegetable Mould Through the Action of Worms, with Observations on Their Habits.* London, 1881.

—. *The Life and Letters of Charles Darwin.* Ed. Francis Darwin. 3 vols. London, 1888.

—. *More Letters of Charles Darwin.* Ed. Francis Darwin. 2 vols. New York, 1903.

Daunton, M.J. "Virtual Presentation: the *History of Parliament* on CD-ROM." *Past and Present* 167 (May 2000), 238-61.

Davies, G.L.H. "On the Nature of Geo-History, with Reflections on the Historiography of Geomorphology." In *History of Geomorphology.* Ed. K.J. Tinkler. Boston, 1989, 1-10.

Davies, Nigel. *The Incas.* Niwot, 1995.

Davies, P.R. "Whose History? Whose Israel? Whose Bible? Biblical Histories, Ancient and Modern." In *Can a 'History of Israel' Be Written?* Ed. Lester Grabbe. Sheffield, 1997, 104-22.

Davis, Cullom. "Now He Belongs to the Sages: Lincoln and the Academy." *Documentary Editing* 21/1 (March 1999), 1-8.

Davis, David. "The Scarcity of Rats and the Black Death: an Ecological History." *JIH* 16 (1986), 455-70.

Davis, Ronald. "Review of Temple, *Sirius Mystery." IJAHS* 10 (1977), 655-67.

Dawson, Marc. "The Many Minds of Sir Halford J. Mackinder: Dilemmas of Historical Editing." *HA* 14 (1985), 27-42.

De Odorico, Marco. *The Use of Numbers and Quantification in the Assyrian Royal Inscriptions.* Helsinki, 1995.

Deetz, James. "Archaeological Evidence of Sixteenth- and Seventeenth-Century Encounters." In *Historical Archaeology in Global Perspective.* Ed. Lisa Falk. Washington, 1991, 1-8.

Demattè, Paola. "Longshan-Era Urbanism: the Role of Cities in Predynastic China," *Asian Perspectives* 38 (1999), 119-50.

Denhardt, Robert. "The Truth about Cortés's Horses." *Hispanic American Historical Review* 17 (1937), 525-32.

Dever, William. "Archaeology and the 'Age of Solomon:' a Case-Study in Archaeology and Historiography." In *AS,* 217-51.

—. "Archaeology and the Current Crisis in Israelite Historiography." *Eretz-Israel* 25(1996), 18*-27*.

—. "Archaeology, Ideology, and the Quest for an 'Ancient' or 'Biblical' Israel." *Near Eastern Archaeology* 61/1 (March 1998), 39-52.

—. "Identity of Ancient Israel: a Rejoinder to Keith W. Whitelam." *JSOT* 72 (1996), 3-24.

—. "Save Us from Postmodern Malarkey." *BAR* 26/2 (March-April 2000), 28-35, 68-69.

—. "What Did the Biblical Writers Know, and When Did They Know It?" In *Hesed ve-Emet: Studies in Honor of Ernest S. Frerichs.* Ed. Jodi Magness and Seymour Gitin. Providence, 1998, 241-57.

Dewald, Carolyn. "Narrative Surface and Authorial Voice in Herodotus' *Histories.*" Arethusa 20 (1987), 147-70.

Diamond, Jared. *Guns, Germs, and Steel.* New York, 1997.

Digby, Kenelm. *A Discourse Concerning Infallibility in Religion.* Paris, 1652.

Dillehay, Tom. *Monte Verde: a Late Pleistocene Settlement in Chile.* Washington, 1990.

Dine, Jeffrey. "Authors' Moral Rights in Non-European Nations: International Agreements, Economics, Mannu Bhandari, and the Dead Sea Scrolls." *Michigan Journal of International Law* 16 (1995), 545-82.

Dobyns, Henry. *Native American Historical Demography: a Critical Bibliography.*

Bloomington, 1976.

——. "Reassessing New World Population at the Time of Contact." *Encuentro* 4/4 (Winter 1988), 8-9.

——. *Their Number Become Thinned: Native American Population Dynamics in Eastern North America.* Knoxville, 1983.

Doniger, Wendy. "Females Bandits! What Next?" *London Review of Books* 26/14 (22 July 2004), 19-20.

Dorson, Richard. "The Debate over the Trustworthiness of Oral Traditional History." In idem., *Folklore: Selected Essays.* Bloomington, 1972, 199-224.

Douville, Jean-Baptiste. *Voyage au Congo et dans l'intérieur de l'Afrique équinoxiale.* 3 vols. Paris, 1832.

Dowling, Lee. "*La Florida del Inca*: Garcilaso's Literary Sources." In *HSE*, 98-154.

Doyle, Arthur Conan. *Memoirs and Adventures.* London, 1924.

Draper, Lyman. *The Life of Daniel Boone.* Ed. Ted Belue. Mechanicsburg, Pa., 1998.

Dreyer, G. et al. "Umm el-Qaab. Nachuntersuchungen im Frühzeitlichen Königsfriedhof." *MDAIK* 52 (1996), 11-81.

Driver, G.R. "Abbreviations in the Massoretic Text." *Textus* 1 (1960), 126-30.

Drower, Margaret. *Flinders Petrie: a Life in Archaeology.* Madison, 1995.

Drury, Robert. *Madagascar, or Robert Drury's Journal of Fifteen Years' Captivity on that Island.* London, 1729.

Dunlop, Rory and Jón Vidar Sigurdsson. "An Interdisciplinary Investigation of Bergen's Forgotten Fire: Confrontation and Reconciliation." *NAR* 28 (1995), 73-92.

Dunn, Oliver and James E. Kelley, jr. *The* Diario *of Christopher Columbus's First Voyage to America, 1492-1493.* Norman, 1989.

Dunning, William A. "Truth in History." *AHR* 19 (1915), 219-30.

Dupuy, R. Ernest and Trevor Dupuy. *The Harper Encyclopedia of Military History.* 4th ed. New York, 1993.

Durrenberger, E. Paul. "Text and Transactions in Commonwealth Iceland." *Ethnos* 55 (1990), 74-91.

Duviols, Pierre. "La dinastía de los Incas ¿Monarquía o diarquía? Argumentos heurísticos a favor de una tesis estructuralista." *Journal de la Société des Américanistes* 66 (1979), 67-83.

Eamon, William. "Plagues, Healers, and Patients in Early Modern Europe." *Renaissance Quarterly* 52 (1999), 474-86.

Earp, Josephine. *I Married Wyatt Earp.* Tucson, 1976.

Echo-Hawk, Roger. "Ancient History in the New World: Integrating Oral Traditions and the Archaeological Record in Deep Time." *AAy* 65 (2000), 267-90.

Eckhardt, William. *Civilizations, Empires, and Wars: a Quantitative History of War.* Jefferson N.C., 1992.

——. "War-Related Deaths Since 3000 BC," *Bulletin of Peace Proposals* 22 (1991), 437-43.

Edwards, Walter. "In Search of Himiko: Postwar Archaeology and the Location of Yamatai." *Monumenta Nipponica* 51 (1996), 53-79.

Ehret, Christopher. *The Civilizations of Africa: a History to 1800.* Oxford, 2002.

Einarsson, Bjarni. *The Settlement of Iceland: a Critical Approach*. Reykjavík, 1995.

Eliot, Alexander. "Cleansing the Sistine Chapel." *New York Review of Books* (3 December 1987).

Entering America: Northeast Asia and Beringia Before the Last Glacial Maximum. Ed. D.B. Madsen. Salt Lake City, 2004.

Epstein, William M. "Confirmation Response Bias and the Quality of the Editorial Processes among American Social Work Journals." *Research on Social Work Practice* 14 (2004), 45-58.

Erasmus, Desiderius. *The Correspondence of Erasmus*. Trans. R.A.B. Mynors and D.F.S. Thomson. Ed. James McConica. 12 vols. Toronto, 1974 to date.

Erichsen, John. "The Tendency of Modern Surgery," *British Medical Journal* (1886), 314-17.

"Ethics of Publication of the Dead Sea Scrolls: a Panel Discussion." In *Methods of Investigation of the Dead Sea Scrolls and the Khirbet Qumran Site: Present Realities and Future Prospects*. Ed. Michael. Wise et al. New York, 1994, 455-97.

Evans, Richard. *In Defence of History*. London, 1997.

—. *Lying About Hitler: History, Holocaust, and the David Irving Trial*. New York, 2001.

— et al. "Counterfactual History: a Forum." *Historically Speaking* 5/4 (March 2004), 11-32.

Eyewitness Memory: Applied and Theoretical Perspectives. Ed. Charles Thompson et al. Mahwah, N.J., 1998.

Eyewitness Testimony: Psychological Perspectives. Ed. Gary Wells and Elizabeth Loftus. Cambridge, 1984.

Eyewitnesses to Massacre: American Missionaries Bear Witness to Japanese Atrocities in Nanjing. Ed. Zhang Kaiyuan. Armonk, N.Y., 2001.

Fagan, Brian. *The Great Journey: the Peopling of Ancient America*. London, 1987.

Fagan, Jody C. "The *Black Athena* Debate: an Annotated Bibliography." *Behavioral and Social Sciences Librarian* 23 (2004), 11-48.

Fage, J.D. *A Guide to Original Sources for Precolonial Western Africa Published in European Languages*. 2d. ed. Madison, 1994.

Fahnestock, Jeanne. "Arguing in Different Forums: the Bering Crossover Controversy." *Science, Technology, and Human Values* 14 (1989), 26-42.

Fälschungen im Mittlelalter. 5 vols. Hannover, 1988.

Farid, Hamid. "A Picture Tells a Thousand Lies." *NS* 180 (6 September 2003), 38-41.

Faulhaber, Charles. "The Digital Scriptorium: a New Way to Study Medieval Iberian Manuscripts." In *Multicultural Iberia: Language, Literature, and Music*. Ed. Dru Dougherty and Milton Azevedo. Berkeley, 1999, 9-21.

Feinstein, Charles H. and Mark Thomas, *Making History Count*. Cambridge, 2002.

Feldman, Louis H. *Josephus and Modern Scholarship, 1937-1980*. Berlin, 1984.

—. "Masada: a Critique of Recent Scholarship." In *Christianity, Judaism, and Greco-Roman Cults*. Ed. Jacob Neusner. 4 vols. Leiden, 1975, 3:218-48.

—. "The *Testimonum Flavianum*: the State of the Question." In *Christological Perspectives*. Ed. Robert Berkey and Sarah Edwards. New York, 1982, 179-99.

Fernández-Armesto, Felipe. *Civilizations*. London, 2000.

Festinger, Leon, Henry Riecken, and Stanley Schachter. *When Prophecy Fails.* New York, 1956.

Fiedel, Stuart. "Older Than We Thought: Implications of Corrected Dates for Paleoindians." *AAy* 64 (1999), 95-115.

Finkelstein, David. "Unraveling Speke's Africa: the Unknown Revision of a Victorian Exploration Classic." *HA* 30 (2003), 117-32.

Finlay, Robert. "How not to (Re)Write World history: Gavin Menzies and the Chinese Discovery of America." *Journal of World History* 15 (2004), 229-42.

Fischer, David Hackett. *Historians' Fallacies.* New York, 1970.

FitzGerald, Frances. *America Revised: History Textbooks in the Twentieth Century.* Boston, 1979.

Fitzmyer, Joseph. *Acts of the Apostles.* New York, 1998.

Flight, Colin. "Bantu Expansion and the SOAS Network," *HA* 15 (1988), 261-301.

Flores, Richard. *Remembering the Alamo: Memory, Modernity, and the Master Symbol.* Austin, 2002.

Foakes, R.A. "Shakespeare Editing and Textual Theory: a Rough Guide." *Huntington Library Quarterly* 60 (1998), 425-42.

Fogel, Robert and Stanley Engerman. "Explaining the Relative Efficiency of Slave Agriculture in the Antebellum South." *American Economic Review* 67 (1977), 275-96, with replies, *American Economic Review* 70 (1980), 672-90.

——. *Time on the Cross.* 2 vols. Boston, 1974.

Fomenko, A.T. *Empirico-Statistical Analysis of Narrative Material and Its Application to Historical Dating.* 2 vols. Dordrecht, 1994.

Forsyth, Phyllis. *Thera in the Bronze Age.* New York, 1997.

Forsythe, Gary. *Livy and Early Rome: a Study in Historical Method and Judgment.* Stuttgart, 1999.

Fowler, Brenda. *Iceman.* New York, 2000.

Frame, Grant. "The Inscription of Sargon II at Tang-i Var." *Orientalia* 68 (1999), 31-57.

Freedman, D.N. "Ebla and the Bible." In *Studies in the Period of David and Solomon and Other Essays.* Tokyo, 1979, 309-35.

——. "W.F. Albright as an Historian." In *The Scholarship of William Foxwell Albright: an Appraisal.* Ed. Gus van Beek. Atlanta, 1989, 33-43.

Freeman, Derek. *The Fateful Hoaxing of Margaret Mead: a Historical Analysis of Her Samoan Research.* Boulder, 1999.

——. *Margaret Mead and Samoa: the Making and Unmaking of an Anthropological Myth.* Cambridge, Mass., 1983.

Freeman, Thomas. "Texts, Lies, and Microfilm: Misreading Foxe's 'Book of Martyrs'." *Sixteenth-Century Journal* 30 (1999), 23-46.

Freud, Sigmund. "Psycho-analysis and Psychiatry." In *The Standard Edition of the Complete Psychological Works of Sigmund Freud.* Trans. and ed. James Strachey. 24 vols. London, 1952-74, 16:243-56.

Fridriksson, Adolf. *Sagas and Popular Antiquarianism in Iceland Archaeology.* Aldershot, 1994.

Frontinus, Sextus Julius. *The Stratagems and the Aqueducts of Rome.* Trans. Charles

Bennett. London, 1950.

Furuli, Rolf. *The Role of Theology and Bias in Bible Translation.* Huntington Beach, 1999.

Gainer, Kim. "The Cartographic Evidence for the Columbus Landfall." *TI* 20 (1988), 43-68.

Galilei, Galileo. *Lettere.* Ed. Fernando Flora. Milam, 1978.

Galison, Peter. "Removing Knowledge." *Critical Inquiry* 31 (2004), 229-43.

Galloway, Patricia. "The Incestuous Soto Narratives." In *HSE*, 11-44.

Gans, J.S. and G.B. Shepherd. "How are the Mighty Fallen: Rejected Classic Articles by Leading Economists." *Journal of Economic Perspectives* 8 (1994), 165-80.

Garbini, Giovanni. *History and Ideology in Ancient Israel.* New York, 1988.

Garbini, Riccardo. "On Dating the Jayavarman Inscription." *East and West* 52 (2002), 421-25.

Gardiner, Alan. "New Literary Works from Ancient Egypt." *JEA* 1 (1914), 20-36, 100-06.

Gasche, H. et al. *Dating the Fall of Babylon: a Reappraisal of Second-Millennium Chronology.* Ghent, 1999.

Gassmann, Robert H. "To Emend or not to Emend? On Determining the Integrity of Some Ancient Chinese Texts." *Asiatische Studien* 56 (2002), 533-48.

Gates, John. "James Belich and the Modern Maori *Pa*: Revisionist History Revised." *War and Society* 19 (2001), 47-68.

Geikie, Archibald. "Presidential Address—Section C, Geology." *Report of the British Association for the Advancement of Science* 69 (1899), 718-30.

Gervase of Canterbury. *The Historical Works of Gervase of Canterbury.* Ed. William Stubbs. 2 vols. London, 1879.

Gibbon, Edward. *The Miscellaneous Works of Edward Gibbon, Esq.* Ed. John, Lord Sheffield. 5 vols. London, 1814.

Gillespie, Richard. *Manufacturing Knowledge: a History of the Hawthorne Experiments.* New York, 1991.

Gillette, David. *Seismosaurus, the Earth Shaker.* New York, 1994.

Gilliard, Frank D. "The Apostolicity of the Gallic Churches." *Harvard Theological Review* 68 (1975), 17-33.

Gitin, Seymour. "Formulating a Ceramic Corpus: The Late Iron II, Persian, and Hellenistic Pottery at Tell Gezer." In *Retrieving the Past: Essays on Archaeological Research and Methodology in Honor of Gus W. Van Beek.* Ed Joe D. Seger. Winona Lake, Ind., 1995, 75-101.

Gleach, Fredric. "Controlled Speculation: Interpreting the Saga of Pocahontas and Captain John Smith." In *Reading Beyond Words: Contexts for Native History.* Ed. Jennifer Brown and Elizabeth Vibert. Peterborough, Ont., 1996, 21-42.

Glenn, Russell W. *Reading Athena's Dance Card: Men Against Fire in Vietnam.* Annapolis, 2000.

Göbl, Robert. "The Rabatak Inscription and the Date of Kanishka." In *CAC*, 151-70.

Goedicke, Hans. "The Abydene Marriage of Pepi I." *JAOS* 75 (1955), 180-83.

Golb, Norman. "As the Scrolls Arrive in Chicago. . ." *Oriental Institute News and Notes* 165 (Spring 2000), 1-4.

Goldhagen, Daniel J. *Hitler's Willing Executioners: Ordinary Germans and the Holocaust.* New York, 1996.

The "Goldhagen Effect." Ed. Geoff Eley. Ann Arbor, 2000.

González García, Pedro. *Informatización del Archivo de Indias: estrategias y resultados.* Madrid, 1999.

Goossens, G. "La révision de la chronologie mésopotamienne et ses conséquences pour l'histoire orientale." *Muséon* 61 (1948), 1-29.

Gose, Peter. "The Past is a Lower Moiety: Diarchy, History, and Divine Kingship in the Inka Empire." *History and Anthropology* 9 (1996), 383-414.

Grafton, Anthony. *The Footnote: a Curious History.* Cambridge, 1997.

—. "Some Uses of Eclipses in Early Modern Chronology." *JHI* 64 (2003), 213-29.

Granger, Ann. *Keeping Bad Company.* London, 1999.

—. *Shades of Murder.* London, 2000.

Gransden, Antonia. "Prologues in the Historiography of Twelfth-Century England." In *England in the Twelfth Century.* Ed. Daniel Williams. Woodbridge, 1990, 55-82.

Grape, Wolfgang. *The Bayeux Tapestry: Monument to a Norman Triumph.* Munich, 1994.

Green, Christine. *Fatal Cut.* Sutton, 1999.

Greene, Robert. and Charles Spornick. "Favorable and Unfavorable Book Reviews: a Quantitative Study." *Journal of Academic Librarianship* 21 (1995), 449-53.

Greenway, Diana. "Dates in History: Chronology and Memory." *Historical Research* 72 (1999), 127-39.

Greig, Gary. "*SDM = F* and *SDM.N = F* in Sinuhe." In *Studies in Egyptology Presented to Miriam Lichtheim.* Ed. Sarah Israelit-Groll. 2 vols. Jerusalem, 1990, 1:264-343.

Groneman, William. "The Controversial Alleged Account of José Enrique de la Peña." *Military History of the West* 25 (1995), 130-65.

Gros de Boze, Claude. "Eloge de M. Henrion." *Histoire de l'Académie Royale des Inscriptions et Belles-Lettres* 5 (1729), 379-84.

Gross, Alan. "The Science Wars and the Ethics of Book Reviewing." *Philosophy of the Social Sciences* 30 (2000), 445-50.

Grou, Gilbert. "Les empereurs incas: critique du modèle diarchique selon Duviols." *Recherches Amérindiennes au Québec* 19/4 (1989), 53-59.

Grove, Philip. *The Imaginary Voyage in Prose Fiction.* New York, 1941.

Gunson, Niel. "Robert Langdon: 'the Fervour for Truth Burned Strong'." *Journal of Pacific History* 39 (2004), 123-32.

Gutman, Herbert. *Slavery and the Numbers Game.* Urbana, 1975.

Hagelia, Hällvard. "The First Dissertation on the Ten Dan inscription." *Scandinavian Journal of the Old Testament* 18 (2004), 134-46.

Hagens, Graham. "A Critical Review of Dead-Reckoning from the 21st Dynasty." *JARCE* 33 (1996), 153-63.

—. "An Ultra-Low Chronology of Iron Age Palestine." *Antiquity* 73 (1999), 431-39.

Haley, Alex. *Roots*. Garden City, 1976.

Hall, Gwendolyn Midlo. "Letter." *AHR* 104 (1999), 712-13.

Hall, Louis. *The Perilous Vision of John Wyclif*. Chicago, 1983.

Hallo, W.W. "The Limits of Skepticism." *JAOS* 110 (1990), 187-99.

Halpern, Baruch. "The State of Israelite History." In *Reconsidering Israel and Judah: Recent Studies on the Deuteronomistic History*. Ed. Gary Knoppers and J. Gordon McConville. Winona Lake, Ind., 2000, 540-65.

Halpert, Herbert and J.D.A. Widdowson. *Folktales of Newfoundland: the Resilience of the Oral Tradition*. 2 vols. New York, 1996.

Hamilton, Richard. *The Social Misconstruction of Reality: Validity and Verification in the Scholarly Community*. New Haven, 1996.

Hammond, N.G.L. *The Genius of Alexander the Great*. Chapel Hill, 1997.

Han Xiaorong. "The Present Echoes of the Ancient Bronze Drum: Nationalism and Archeology in Modern Vietnam and China." *Explorations in Southeast Asian Studies* 2/2 (Fall 1998), 27-46.

Handy, Lowell. "On the Dating and Dates of Solomon's Reign." In *AS*, 96-105.

—. "Phoenicians in the Tenth Century BCE." In *AS*, 154-66.

Hanson, Victor and John Heath. "*Who Killed Homer*? the Prequel." In *Bonfire of the Humanities: Rescuing the Classics in an Impoverished Age*. Ed. Victor Hanson et al. Wilmington, Del., 2001, 239-97.

Hardwick, Michael. *Josephus as a Historical Source in Patristic Literature through Eusebius*. Atlanta, 1989.

Harley, J.B. "Deconstructing the Map." *Cartographica* 26/2 (Summer 1989), 1-20.

Harmon, Jim. *The Great Radio Heroes*. Jefferson, N.C.

Harris, Murray. "References to Jesus in the Early Classical Authors." In *The Jesus Tradition Outside the Gospels*. Sheffield, 1984. 343-68.

Harvey, John. *A Discoursive Probleme Concerning Prophecies*. London, 1588.

Hasel, Michael. *Domination and Resistance: Egyptian Military Activity in the Southern Levant, ca. 1300-1185 B.C.* Leiden, 1998.

—. "Israel in the Merneptah Stela." *BASOR* 296 (1994), 45-61.

Haskell, Thomas. "Objectivity is not Neutrality: Rhetoric vs. Practice in Peter Novick's *That Noble Dream*." *HT* 29 (1990) 129-57.

Hassan, Fekr. "Population Dynamics." In *Companion Encyclopedia of Archaeology*. Ed. Graeme Barker. 2 vols. London, 1999, 2:672-713.

Hassig, Ross. "Counterfactuals and Revisionism in Historical Explanation." *Anthropological Theory* 1 (2001), 57-72.

—. "The Immolation of Hernán Cortés: Tenochtitlán, June 30, 1521." In *What If?*, 123-38.

Hastrup, Kirsten. *Island of Anthropology*. Odense, 1990.

Hays, Terence. "Sacred Texts and Introductory Texts: the Case of Mead's Samoa." *Pacific Studies* 20 (1997), 81-103.

Heintze, Beatrix. "Referencing in the Humanities: Strategies of Being Open, Being Obscure, and Being Misleading." *HA* 27 (2000), 437-42.

Heller, Samantha. "Minutes of the Columbia University Seminar on Shakespeare."

Shakespeare Newsletter 238 (February 1998), 73.

Helly, Dorothy. *Livingstone's Legacy: Horace Waller and Victorian Mythmaking.* Athens, Ohio, 1987.

Henige, David. "Barbed-Wire Bonnat? the Case of the Clueless Text." *HA* 23 (1996), 439-51.

——. "Can a Myth Be Astronomically Dated?" *AICRJ* 23/4 (1999), 127-57.

——. *The Chronology of Oral Tradition: Quest for a Chimera.* Oxford, 1974.

——. "The Content, Context, and Credibility of *La Florida del Ynca.*" *The Americas* 43 (1986), 1-23.

——. "Coping With Evidence in the Study of the African Past." In *Rethinking African History.* Ed. K.L. King et al. Edinburgh, 1997, 293-310.

——. "'Day was of Sudden Turned into Night:' the Use of Eclipses in Dating Oral History." *Comparative Studies in Society and History* 18 (1976), 576-601.

——. "Deciduous, Perennial, or Evergreen: the Choices in the Debate Over 'Early Israel'." *JSOT* 27 (2003), 387-412.

——. "'The Disease of Writing:' Ganda and Nyoro Kinglists in a Newly-Literate World." In *The African Past Speaks.* Ed. Joseph C. Miller. Folkestone, 1980, 240-61.

——. "Finding Columbus: Implications of a Newly-Discovered Text." In *The European Outthrust and Encounter.* Ed. Cecil. Clough and P.E.H. Hair. Liverpool, 1994, 141-65.

——. "Guanahaní the Elusive: the Columbus Landfall Debate in Historical Perspective." *Mariner's Mirror* 78 (1992), 449-67.

——. "The Half Life of African Archives." In *African Resources and Collections.* Ed. Julian Witherell. Metuchen, N.J., 1989, 198-212.

——. "The Implausibility of Plausibility/The Plausibility of Implausibility." *Historical Reflections/Réflexions Historiques* 30 (2004), 311-35.

——. "'In Possession of the Author:' the Problem of Source Monopoly in Oral Historiography." *International Journal of Oral History* 1 (1980), 181-94.

——. *In Search of Columbus: the Sources for the First Voyage.* Tucson, 1991.

——. "Indexing: a Users' Perspective." *JSP* 33 (2002), 230-47.

——. "Millennarian Archaeology, Double Discourse, and the Unending Quest for de Soto." *Midcontinental Journal of Archaeology* 21 (1996), 191-216.

——. "Mis/adventures in Mis/quoting," *JSP* 32 (2001), 123-36.

——. *Numbers from Nowhere: the American Indian Contact Population Debate.* Norman, 1998.

——. "Omphaloskepsis and the Infantilizing of History." *JAH* 36 (1995), 311-18.

——. *Oral Historiography.* London, 1982.

——. "Oral Tradition as a Means of Reconstructing the Past." In *Writing African History.* Ed. John E. Philips. Rochester, 2005, 169-90.

——. "The Power of Pink: Graphics as Imposed Epistemology." *JSP* 34 (2003), 83-100.

——. "Primary Source by Primary Source? On the Role of Epidemics in New World Depopulation." *Ethnohistory* 33 (1986), 293-312.

——. "The Problem of Feedback in Oral Tradition: Four Examples from the Fante

Coastlands." *JAH* 14 (1973), 223-35.

——. "Reviewing Reviewing." *JSP* 33 (2001/02), 23-36.

——. "Samuel Eliot Morison as Translator and Interpreter of Columbus' *diario de a bordo.*" *TI* 20 (1988), 69-88.

——. *Serial Bibliographies and Abstracts: an Annotated Guide.* Westport, Ct., 1986.

——. "'So Unbelievable It Has to be True:' Garcilaso in Two Worlds." In *HSE*, 155-77.

——. "Some Phantom Dynasties of Early and Medieval India: Epigraphic Evidence and the Abhorrence of a Vacuum." *BSOAS* 38 (1975), 325-49.

——. "Survival of the Fittest? Darwinian Adaptation and the Transmission of Information." *HA* 30 (2003), 157-77.

——. "To Read is to Misread, to Write is to Miswrite: Las Casas as Transcriber." In *Amerindian Images and the Legacy of Columbus.* Ed. Nicholas Spadaccini and René Jara. Minneapolis, 1992, 198-229.

——. "Truths Yet Unborn? Oral Tradition as a Casualty of Culture Contact." *JAH* 23 (1982), 395-412.

——. "What Price Economy? the Decline of the Footnote in Historical Scholarship." *Editing History* 4/1 (Spring 1987), 13-16.

——. "When Did Smallpox Reach the New World (and Why Does it Matter)?" In *Africans in Bondage: Studies in Slavery and the Slave Trade.* Ed. Paul E. Lovejoy, Madison, 1986, 11-26.

Hermanns-Audurdóttir, Margrét. "The Early Settlement of Iceland," *NAR* 34 (1991), 1-9, with comments and reply, 10-33.

Hernon, Peter and Cheryl Metoyer-Duran. "Literature Reviews and Inaccurate Referencing: an Exploratory Study of Academic Librarians." *College and Research Libraries* 53 (1992), 499-512.

Heusch, Luc de. "On Griaule on Trial." *CA* 32 (1991), 434-37.

Hiatt, Alfred. *The Making of Medieval Forgeries: False Documents in Fifteenth-Century England.* London, 2004.

Hicks, Frederic. "Skepticism in Ethnohistory." *Ethnohistory* 45 (1998), 611-20.

Hill, Emmeline W., Mark A. Jobling, and Daniel G. Bradley. "Y-Chromosome Variation and Irish Origins." *Nature* 404 (23 March 2000), 351-52.

The Historian's Craft in the Age of Herodotus. Ed. Nino Luraghi. London, 2002.

Ho, Ping-ti, *The Cradle of the East.* Chicago, 1975.

Hodder, Ian. *The Archaeological Process: an Introduction.* Oxford, 1999.

Hoenig, Sidney. "The Sicarii in Masada—Glory or Infamy?" *Tradition* 11/1 (Spring 1970), 5-30.

Hoffer, Peter C. *Past Imperfect: Facts, Fictions, Fraud.* New York, 2004.

Holden, Henry. *The Analysis of Divine Faith; or the Resolution of Christian Belief.* Paris, 1658.

Holloway, Steven W. "The Quest for Sargon, Pul, and Tiglath-Pileser in the Nineteenth Century." In *Mesopotamia and the Bible: Comparative Explorations.* Ed. Mark W. Chavalas and K. Lawson Younger, jr. Sheffield, 2002, 68-87.

Holmes, Frederic. "Scientific Writing and Scientific Discovery." *Isis* 78 (1987), 220-35.

Holt, F.L. *Alexander the Great and the Mystery of the Elephant Medallions*. Berkeley, 2003.

—. *Thundering Zeus: the Making of Hellenistic Bactria*. Berkeley, 1999.

Holway, John. *The Last .400 Hitter*. Dubuque, 1992.

Hopkins, David. "From *BA* to *NEA*: the Editor's Thanksgiving." *Near Eastern Archaeology* 61/4 (December 1998), 186-87.

—. "From the Editor." *BA* 60/1 (March 1997), ii.

—. "Name Change Voted for *Biblical Archaeologist*." *Newsletter of the American Schools of Oriental Research* 46/4 (Winter 1996), 7.

Hopkins, Keith. *Conquerors and Slaves*. Cambridge, 1978.

Hoppit, Julian. "An Embarrassment of Riches." *Parliamentary History* 18 (1999), 189-205.

Horgan, John. "Quantum Consciousness." *Scientific American* 261/5 (November 1989), 30-33.

Hornblower, Simon. "The Story of Greek Historiography: Intertextuality and the Greek Historians." In *Greek Historiography*. Ed. Simon Hornblower. Oxford, 1994, 1-72.

Huang, Yi-long. "A Study of Five-Planet Conjunctions in Chinese History." *EC* 15 (1990), 97-112.

Huber, Peter J. "Astronomical Evidence for the Long and Against the Middle and Short Chronologies." In *HML?*, 5-17.

Hudson, Charles, Chester DePratter, and Marvin Smith. "Reply to Henige." In *The Expedition of Hernando de Soto West of the Mississippi, 1541-1543*. Ed. Gloria Young and Michael Hoffman. Fayetteville, Ark., 1993, 255-69.

Hudson, Pat. *History by Numbers: an Introduction to Quantitative Approaches*. London, 2000.

Hughes, David. *The Star of Bethlehem: an Astronomer's Confirmation*. New York, 1979.

Huizinga, Jan. "A Definition of the Concept of History." In *Philosophy and History: Essays Presented to Ernst Cassirer*. Ed. Raymond Klibansky and H.J. Paton. Oxford, 1936, 1-10.

Humphreys, Colin J. and W.G. Waddington. "Dating the Crucifixion." *Nature* 306 (22/29 December 1983), 743-46.

Hunter, Michael. "Whither Editing?" *Studies in the History and Philosophy of Science* 34 (2003), 805-20.

Huxley, Andrew. "Evidence, Clues, and Motive in Science." Presidential Address to the British Association for the Advancement of Science, Aston University, Birmingham, 1977.

Huxley, T.H. "Geological Reform." *Quarterly Journal of the Geological Society of London* 25 (1869), xxxviii-liii.

Hyland, Ken. *Hedging in Scientific Research Articles*. Philadelphia, 1998.

Ibarra Rojas, Eugenia. "Las epidemías del Viejo Mundo entre los indígenes de Costa Rica antes de la conquista española: ¿mito o realidad? (1501-1561)." *Mesoamérica* 36 (1998), 593-618.

Ife, B.W. *Journal of the First Voyage/Diario del primer viaje*. Warminster, 1990.

In Pursuit of History: Fieldwork in Africa. Ed. Carolyn K. Adenaike and Jan Vansina. Portsmouth N.H., 1996.

In the Shadow of History. Ed. J. Frank Dobie et al. Austin, 1939.

The Inscriptions of Tiglath-Pileser III, King of Assyria. Ed. Hayim Tadmor. Jerusalem, 1994.

"Interview with William H. McNeill." *Historian* 53 (1990/91), 1-16.

The Invention of Tradition. Ed. Eric Hobsbawm and T.O. Ranger. Cambridge, 1983.

Irving, Washington. *A History of the Life and Voyages of Christopher Columbus*. 4 vols. Paris, 1828.

Isenberg, Andrew. *The Destruction of the Bison: an Environmental History, 1750-1920*. New York, 2000.

Jacopo d'Ancona. *The City of Light*. Ed. and trans. David Selbourne. New York, 2000.

Jajko, Edward. "Comments on MELA Reviewing, Middle East Librararianship, and Four Book Reviews." *MELA Notes* 60 (Spring 1994), 27-31.

Jamieson, Valerie. "From Here to Eternity." *New Scientist* (22 November 2003), 36-39.

Japan in the Chinese Dynastic Histories. Ed. and trans. Ryusaku Tsunoda and L. H. Goodrich. Kyoto, 1968.

Jarrett, Jonathan. "Power Over Past and Future: Abbess Emma and the Nunnery of Saint Joan de las Abadesses." *Early Medieval Europe* 12 (2003), 229-58.

Jefferson, Thomas. *Notes on the State of Virginia*. Williamsburg, 1955.

—. "On the Discovery of Certain Bones of an Animal of the Clawed Kind in the Western Parts of Virginia." *Transactions of the American Philosophical Society* 4 (1799), 246-60.

Jenkins, Keith. *On "What is History?" from Carr and Elton to Rorty and White*. London, 1995.

Jidejian, Nina. *Tyre Through the Ages*. Beirut, 1969.

John Dryden. Ed. Keith Walker. Oxford, 1987.

Johnson, Marion. "News From Nowhere: Duncan and 'Adofoodia'." *HA* 1 (1974), 55-66.

Johnson, Richard. *The Search for the Inland Sea*. Melbourne, 2002.

Johnson, Samuel. *Johnson on Shakespeare*. Ed. Walter Raleigh. New York, 1931.

Johnston, Mark. "E-Journals for Medieval Studies." *La Corónica* 27 (1998/99), 155-70.

Jolles, Frank. "German Romantic Chronology and Its Impact on the Interpretation of Prehistory." In *Time and Archaeology*. Ed. Tim Murray. London, 1999, 49-60.

Jones, Adam. "Neglected Heritage." *West Africa* (6 July 1987), 1298-1300.

Jones, Edwin. *John Lingard and the Pursuit of Historical Truth*. Brighton, 2001.

Jones, Grant. "The Canek Manuscript in Ethnohistorical Perspective." *AM* 3 (1992), 243-68.

—. *The Conquest of the Last Maya Kingdom*. Stanford, 1998.

—. *El Manuscrito Can Ek. Descubrimiento de una visita secreta del siglo XVII a Tah Itzá (Tayazal) última capital de los mayas itzáes*. Mexico City, 1991.

—. "Revisiting the Canek Manuscript." *AM* 10 (1999), 313-16.

Josephus, Flavius. *Josephus*. 10 vols. Cambridge, Mass., 1926-81.

Journals and Other Documents on the Life and Voyages of Christopher Columbus. Ed. S.E. Morison. New York, 1963.

Kahn, Dan'el. "The Inscription of Sargon II at Tang-i Var and the Chronology of Dynasty 25." *Orientalia* 71 (2001), 1-18.

Kang, Bong. "A Reconsideration of Population Pressure and Warfare: a Protohistoric Korean Case." *CA* 41 (2000), 873-81.

Kanigel, Robert. *The Man Who Knew Infinity.* New York, 1991.

Karageorghis, Vassos. "It's Publish or Perish. . ." *Eretz-Israel* 25 (1996), 28*-30*.

Karlgren, Bernhard. "Some Weapons and Tools of the Yin Dynasty." *Bulletin of the Museum of Far Eastern Antiquities* 17 (1945), 101-44.

Karlsson, Gunnar. *The History of Iceland.* Minneapolis, 2000.

Katzenstein, H.J. *The History of Tyre.* Jerusalem, 1983.

—. "Who Were the Parents of Athaliah?" *Israel Exploration Journal* 5 (1954), 194-97.

Kautz, Fred. *The German Historians:* Hitler's Willing Executioners, *and Daniel Goldhagen.* Montreal, 2003.

Kawai, Kazuo. "*Mokusatsu*, Japan's Response to the Potsdam Declaration." *Pacific Historical Review* 19 (1950), 409-13.

Keightley, David N. "The *Bamboo Annals* and Shang-Chou Chronology." *HJAS* 38 (1978), 423-38.

—. "Ping-ti Ho and the Origins of Chinese Civilization" *HJAS* 37 (1977), 381-411.

Kendall, Timothy. "The Origin of the Napatan State: El Kurru and the Evidence for the Royal Ancestors." In *Studien zum antiken Sudan.* Ed. Steffen Wenig. Wiesbaden, 1999, 3-117.

—. "A Response to László Török's 'Long Chronology of el Kurru'." In *Studien zum antiken Sudan.* Ed. Steffen Wenig. Wiesbaden, 1999, 164-76.

Kidger, Mark. *The Star of Bethlehem: an Astronomer's View.* Princeton, 1999.

Kiefer, Michael. "Indian Stew." *Phoenix New Times* (4-10 February 1999). www.phoenixnewtimes.com.

King, David. *The Commissar Vanishes: the Falsification of Photographs and Art in Stalin's Russia.* Edinburgh, 1997.

King, L.W. "Babylonia and Assyria." *Encyclopaedia Britannica.* 11th ed. London, 1910-11, 3:99-112.

—. *Chronicles Concerning Early Babylonian Kings.* 2 vols. London, 1907

Kingsnorth, Alice. "Whither the Site Report? an Exemplary Contemporary Compromise." *BASOR* 318 (May 2000), 59-71.

Kitchen, Kenneth. "The Basics of Egyptian Chronology in Relation to the Bronze Age." In *HML?*, 37-55.

—. "The Curse of Publication and the Blight of Novelty." In *Proceedings of the Seventh International Congress of Egyptologists (Cambridge 1995).* Ed. C.J. Eyre. Leuven, 1998, 625-30.

—. "Egypt and East Africa." In *AS*, 107-25.

—. "How Do We Know When Solomon Ruled?" *BAR* 27/5 (September-October 2001), 32-37, 58.

Kletter, Raz and Alon De-Groot. "Excavating to Excess? Implications of the Past Decade of Archaeology in Israel." *Journal of Mediterranean Archaeology* 14 (2001), 76-109.

Kline, Mary-Jo. *A Guide to Documentary Editing.* Baltimore, 1987.

Knauf, Ernst. "Le roi est mort, vive le roi!" a Biblical Argument for the Historicity of Solomon." In *AS*, 81-95.

Knollenberg, Bernard. *Washington and the Revolution: a Reappraisal.* New York, 1940.

"Knowledge Discovery in Bibliographic Databases." *Library Trends* 48 (1999), 1-281.

Kochen, Manfred. "How Well Do We Acknowledge Intellectual Debts?" *Journal of Documentation* 43 (1987), 54-64.

Koestler, Arthur. *Darkness at Noon.* New York, 1941.

Kohl, Philip. "Nationalism and Archaeology: on the Constructions of Nations and the Reconstruction of the Remote Past." *Annual Review of Anthropology* 27 (1998), 223-46.

Koriat, Asher, Morris Goldsmith, and Ainat Pansky. "Toward a Psychology of Memory Accuracy." *Annual Review of Psychology* 51 (2000), 481-537.

Krech, Shepard. *The Ecological Indian: Myth and History.* New York, 1999.

Krinov, E.L. *Giant Meteorites.* Oxford, 1966.

Lacordaire, Théodore. "Review." *Revue des Deux Mondes* 8 (November 1832), 245-67.

Ladouceur, David. "Masada: a Consideration of the Literary Evidence." *Greek, Roman, and Byzantine Studies* 21 (1980), 245-60.

Lamarck, Jean-Baptiste. *Philosophie zoologique.* 2 vols. Paris, 1809.

Lamberti, Marcello. "Omotic and Cushitic: a Reply to Fleming." *Anthropos* 88 (1993), 555-57.

Langdon, Stephen. "The Early Chronology of Sumer and Egypt and the Similarities in Their Culture." *JEA* 7 (1921), 133-53.

— and J.K. Fotheringham. *The Venus Tablets of Ammizaduga.* London, 1928.

Langlois, C.V. and C. Seignobos. *Introduction aux études historiques.* Paris, 1898.

Lankford, George E. "Pleistocene Animals in Folk Memory." *Journal of American Folklore* 93 (1980), 293-304.

Larner, John. *Marco Polo and the Discovery of the New World.* New Haven, 1999.

Lasken, Jesse. "Towards a New Chronology of Ancient Egypt." *Discussions in Egyptology* 17 (1990), 102-15.

Lebow, Richard. "What's So Different About a Counterfactual?" *World Politics* 52 (1999/2000), 550-85.

Leclercq, H. "Filumena." In *Dictionnaire d'Archéologie Chrétienne et de Liturgie.* Ed. Fernand Cabrol et al. 15 vols. in 30. Paris, 1907-53, 5/2: 1600-06.

Leerssen, J.T. *Remembrance and Imagination: Patterns in the Historical and Literary Representation of Ireland in the Nineteenth Century.* South Bend, 1997.

LeGrand, H.E. *Drifting Continents and Shifting Theories.* New York, 1988.

Leigh, Edward. *Foelix Consortium.* London, 1663.

Lemaire, André. "The Tel Dan Stela as a Piece of Royal Historiography." *JSOT* 81 (1998), 3-14.

Lemay, J.A.L. *Did Pocahontas Save Captain John Smith?* Athens, Ohio, 1992.

Lemche, N.P. "Early Israel Revisited." *Currents in Research: Biblical Studies* 4 (1996), 9-34.

Lerner, Jeffrey. *The Impact of Seleucid Decline on the Eastern Iranian Plateau.* Stuttgart, 1999.

Le Roy Ladurie, Emmanuel. *The Territory of the Historian.* Chicago, 1979.

Levine, Molly. "Bernal and the Athenians in the Multicultural World of the Ancient Mediterranean." In *Classical Studies in Honor of David Sohlberg.* Ed. R. Katzoff. Ramat Gan, 1996, 1-56.

Lewis, James. "Review of *The Hernando de Soto Expedition.*" *AICRJ* 23 (1999), 234-36.

Li Boqian. "The Sumptuary System Governing Western Zhou Rulers' Cemeteries, Viewed From a Jin Rulers' Cemetery." *Journal of East Asian Archaeology* 1 (1999), 251-76.

Linn, Ed. *Hitter: the Life and Turmoils of Ted Williams.* New York, 1993.

Lipinski, Eduard. "Ba'li-ma'zer II and the Chronology of Tyre." *Revista degli Studi Orientali* 45 (1970), 59-65.

Lipset, David. "Response to Jadran Mimica's Review of *Mangrove Men.*" *Oceania* 70 (2000), 67-68.

Lister, Joseph. "Graduation Address." *Edinburgh Medical Journal* 22 (1876), 380-84.

Liverani, Mario. "2084: Ancient Propaganda and Historical Criticism." In *The Study of the Ancient Near East in the Twenty-First Century.* Ed. Jerrold Cooper and Glenn Schwartz. Winona Lake, Ind., 1996, 283-89.

Livy. *Livy.* trans. B.O. Foster. 14 vols. Cambridge, Mass., 1951-63.

Locke, John. *Some Thoughts Concerning Education.* Ed. John W. Yolton and Jean S. Yolton. Oxford, 1989 [1693].

Lockhart, Jamie Bruce. "In the Raw: Some Reflections on Transcribing and Editing Lieutenant Hugh Clapperton's Writings of the Borno Mission of 1822-1825." *HA* 26 (1999), 157-95.

Loewen, James. *Lies My Teachers Told Me: Everything Your American History Textbook Got Wrong.* New York, 1996.

Long, Burke. *Planting and Reaping Albright: Politics, Ideology, and Interpreting the Bible.* University Park, Pa., 1997.

Luey, Beth. *Editing Documents and Texts: an Annotated Bibliography.* Madison, 1990.

MacMillan, Ken. "Sovereignty 'More Plainly Described:' Early English Maps of North America, 1580-1625." *Journal of British Studies* 42 (2003), 413-47.

Maitland, William. *History of London from Its Foundation to the Present Time.* London, 1739.

Makley, Charlene. "'Speaking Bitterness:' Autobiography, History, and Mnemonic Politics on the Sino-Tibetan Frontier." *Comparative Studies in Society and History* 47 (2005), 40-78.

Mallory, J.P. *In Search of the Indo-Europeans: Language, Archaeology, and Myth.* London, 1989.

Manning, Patrick. *Slavery and African Life: Occidental, Oriental, and African Slave Trades.* Cambridge, 1990.

Manning, Sturt. *The Absolute Chronology of the Aegean Early Bronze Age: Archaeology,*

Radiocarbon, and History. Sheffield, 1995.

Marcus, Amy. *The View from Nebo: How Archaeology is Rewriting the Bible and Reshaping the Middle East.* Boston, 2000.

Marincola, John. *Authority and Tradition in Ancient Historiography.* Cambridge, 1997.

Marquardt, H. Michael and Wesley Walters. *Inventing Mormonism: Tradition and the Historical Record.* Salt Lake City, 1994.

Marston, Edward. *The Wanton Angel.* New York, 1999.

Martin, A. Lynn. *Plague? Jesuit Accounts of Epidemic Disease in the Sixteenth Century.* Kirksville, 1996.

Martin, Calvin. "Comment" in *Indians, Animals, and the Fur Trade: a Critique of* Keepers of the Game. Ed. Shepard Krech III, Athens, 1981, 189-97.

—. *Keepers of the Game: Indian-Animal Relationships and the Fur Trade.* Berkeley, 1978.

Martin, Paul. "Deep History and a Wilder West." In *Ecology of Sonora Desert Plants.* Ed. R.H. Robichaux. Tucson, 1999, 256-90.

Martire de Anghiera, Pietro. *Opera.* Graz, 1966.

Marwick, Arthur. *The New Nature of History: Knowledge, Evidence, Language.* London, 2001.

Mason, Ronald. "Archaeology and Native American Oral Traditions." *AAy* 65 (2000), 239-66.

The Mass-Extinction Debates: How Science Works in a Crisis. Ed. William Glen. Stanford, 1991.

Maxwell, James. "Introductory Lecture on Experimental Physics." In *The Scientific Papers of James Clerk Maxwell.* Ed. W.D. Niven. 2 vols. Cambridge, 1890, 2:241-55.

Maxwell, William. *So Long, See You Tomorrow.* New York, 1980.

McCormick, Michael. "Rats, Communications and Plague: Toward an Ecological History," *JIH* 34 (2003), 1-25.

McCullagh, C. Behan. *The Truth of History.* London, 1998.

McGrath, Eileen L., Winifred F. Metz, and John B. Rutledge. "H-Net Book Reviews: Enhancing Scholarly Communication with Technology." *College and Research Libraries* 66 (2005), 8-19.

McHardy, Stuart. "The Wee Dark Fowk o' Scotland: the Role of Oral Transmission in Pictish Studies." In *The Worm, the Germ, and the Thorn: Pictish and Related Studies Presented to Isabel Henderson.* Woodbridge, 1997, 106-12.

McLaren, James. *Turbulent Times? Josephus and the Scholarship on Judaea in the First Century CE.* Sheffield, 1998.

McNeill, William. "Infectious Alternatives: the Plague That Saved Jerusalem, 701 B.C." In *What If?*, 1-12.

McNulty, J. Bard. "The Lady Aelfgyva in the Bayeux Tapestry." *Speculum* 55 (1980), 659-68.

McWilliams, Percy. "The Alamo from Fact to Fable." *Journal of the Folklore Institute* 15 (1978), 221-33.

Mee, Charles L., jr. *Meeting at Potsdam.* New York, 1975.

Mehl, Margaret. *History and the State in Nineteenth-Century Japan*. New York, 1998.

Meier, John. "Jesus in Josephus: a Modest Proposal." *CBQ* 52 (1990), 76-103.

Melve, Leidulf. "Literacy-Aurality-Orality: a Survey of Recent Research into the Orality/Literacy Complex of the Latin Middle Ages, 600-1500." *Symbolae Osloenses* 78 (2003), 43-97.

Menzies, Gavin. *1421: the Year China Discovered the World*. London, 2002.

Mercati, Angelo. "The New List of Popes." *Medieval Studies* 9 (1947), 71-80.

Merkle, Stefan. "Telling the True Story of the Trojan War: the Eyewitness Account of Dictys of Crete." In *The Search for the Ancient Novel*. Ed. James Tatum. Baltimore, 1994, 183-96.

—. "The Truth, and Nothing But the Truth." In *The Novel in the Ancient World*. Ed. Gareth Schmeling. Leiden, 1996, 563-80.

Metzger, Bruce. "Names for the Nameless in the New Testament: a Study in the Growth of Christian Tradition." In *Kyriakon: Festschrift Johannes Quasten*. Ed. Patrick Granfield and Josef Jungmann. 2 vols. Münster, 1970, 2:79-99.

Meyer, Eduard. "Eberhard Schrader," *Biographisches Jahrbuch und Deutscher Nekrolog* 13 (1908), 156-73.

Michelson, A.A., *Light Waves and Their Uses*, Chicago, 1903.

Mignolo, Walter. "Misunderstanding and Colonization: the Reconfiguration of Space and Memory." *South Atlantic Quarterly* 92 (1993), 209-60.

Miles, Keith. *Saint's Rest*. New York, 1999.

Mill, James. *The History of British India*. 3d ed. 6 vols. London, 1826.

Millard, A.R. "Abraham," *Anchor Bible Dictionary*. 6 vols. New York, 1992, 1:35-41.

Miller, J. Maxwell and John Hayes. *A History of Ancient Israel and Judah*. Philadelphia, 1986.

Miller, Joseph C. "A Note on Jean-Baptiste Douville." *CEA* 49 (1973), 150-53.

Mills, Gary and Elizabeth. "*Roots* and the New Faction: a Legitimate Tool for Clio?" *Virginia Magazine of History and Biography* 89 (1981), 3-26.

Mitchell, Ken. "Science, Giants, and Gold: Juan de la Cruz Cano y Olmedilla's Map." *TI* 31 (1999), 25-41.

Molleson, Theya and Margaret Cox. *The Spitalfields Project, II, the Anthropology*. London, 1993.

Molnar, Michael. *The Star of Bethlehem: the Legacy of the Magi*. New Brunswick, N.J., 1999.

Montefiore, H.W. "Josephus and the New Testament." *NT* 4 (1960), 139-60.

Moodie, D. Wayne and A.J.W. Catchpole. "Northern Athapaskan Oral Traditions and the White River Volcano." *Ethnohistory* 39 (1992), 148-71.

Morello, Ruth. "Livy's Alexander Digression (9.17-19): Counterfactuals and Apologetics." *Journal of Roman Studies* 92 (2002), 62-85.

Morison, S.E. *Admiral of the Ocean Sea*. 2 vols. Boston, 1942.

—. "Faith of a Historian." *AHR* 56 (1950/51), 261-75.

Morkot, R.G. *The Black Pharaohs: Egypt's Nubian Rulers*. London, 2000.

Morley, Neville. *The Writing of Ancient History*. Ithaca, 1999.

Morris, Edmund. *Dutch: a Memoir of Ronald Reagan*. New York, 1999.

Mosimann, James and Paul Martin. "Simulating Overkill by Paleoindians." *American Scientist* 63 (1975), 304-13.

Mossiker, Frances. *Pocahontas: the Life and the Legend*. New York, 1976.

Moule, A.C. *The Rulers of China*. New York, 1957.

Murnane, William. "The Sed Festival: a Problem in Historical Method." *MDAIK* 37 (1981), 369-76.

Murray, J.A.H. "Thirteenth Address of the President." *Transactions of the Philological Society* (1882/84), 501-31.

Muscarella, O.W. *The Lie Became Great: the Forgery of Ancient Near Eastern Cultures*. Groningen, 2000.

Naess, Arne. *Scepticism*. London, 1968.

The Napoleonic Options: Alternate Decisions of the Napoleonic Wars. Ed. Jonathan North. London, 2000.

Narain, A.K. *The Indo-Greeks*. Oxford, 1957.

Narasimha Murthy, A.V. *The Sevunas of Devagiri*. Mysore, 1971.

Nationalism and Archaeology in Europe. Ed. Margarita D'az-Andreu and Timothy Champion. Boulder, 1996.

Nationalism, Politics, and the Practice of Archaeology. Ed. Philip Kohl and Clare Fawcett. Cambridge, 1995.

Needham, Joseph. *Science and Civilization in China*. 3 vols. Cambridge, 1959.

The Neighbors Respond: the Controversy over the Jedwabne Massacre in Poland. Ed. Antony Polonsky and Joanna Michlic. Princeton, 2004.

Newall, Raymond. "The Forms and Historical Value of Josephus' Suicide Accounts." In *Josephus, the Bible, and History*. Ed. Louis Feldman and Gohei Hata. Detroit, 1987, 278-94.

Newman, Barbara. "What Did It Mean to Say 'I Saw?' the Clash Between Theory and Practice in Medieval Visionary Culture." *Speculum* 80 (2005), 1-43.

Newson, Linda. "Old World Diseases in the Early Colonial Philippines and Spanish America." In *Population and History: the Demographic Origins of the Modern Philippines*. Ed. Daniel Doeppers and Peter Xenos. Madison, 1998, 17-36.

—. "The Population of the Amazon Basin in 1492: a View From the Ecuadorian Headwaters." *Transactions of the Institute of British Geographers* 21 (1996), 5-26.

Newton, Robert R. *Medieval Chronicles and the Rotation of the Earth*. Baltimore, 1972.

Nicholas, George P. and Kelly P. Bannister. "Copyrighting the Past? Emerging Intellectual Property Rights Issues in Archaeology." *CA* 45 (2004), 327-42, with comments and response, 342-50.

Niditch, Susan. *Oral World and Written Word: Ancient Israelite Literature*. Louisville, 1996.

Niemann, Hermann. "The Socio-Political Shadow Cast by the Biblical Solomon." In *AS*, 252-99.

Nivison, David S. "1040: the Date of the Chou Conquest." *EC* 8 (1982/83), 76-78.

—. "The Dates of Western Chou." *HJAS* 43 (1983), 545-56.

—. *The Key to the Chronology of the Three Dynasties: the "Modern Text"* Bamboo Annals. Philadelphia, 1999.

—. "Response." *EC* 15 (1990), 151-72.

— and Kevin D. Pang. "Astronomical Evidence for the *Bamboo Annals*' Chronicle of Early Xia." *EC* 15 (1990), 87-95.

— and E.L. Shaughnessy. "The Jin Hou Bells Inscription and Its Implications for the Chronology of Early China." *EC* 25 (2000), 29-48.

Nolte, Nancy. "Review of Jones, *The End of Roman Britain*," *Albion* 29 (1997), 269-71.

Nordahl, Else. *Reykjavík from the Archaeological Point of View*. Uppsala, 1988.

Novel History. Ed. Mark C. Carnes. New York, 2001.

Nowack, Kirsten. Ceque *and More: a Critical Assessment of R. Tom Zuidema's Studies on the Inca*. Bonn, 1998.

Oakley, S.P. *A Commentary on Livy, Books VI-X*. 2 vols. Oxford, 1997.

Obeyesekere, Gananath. *The Apotheosis of Captain Cook: European Mythmaking in the Pacific*. Princeton, 1992.

—. *The Apotheosis of Captain Cook: European Mythmaking in the Pacific*. 2d. ed. Princeton, 1997.

Ó Canann, Tomás G. "Review of *Leabhar Mór na nGenealach: the Great Book of Irish Genealogies*." *Journal of the Royal Society of Antiquaries of Ireland* 132 (2002), 127-37.

Oestreicher, David. "The Anatomy of the Walam Olum: the Dissection of a Nineteenth-Century Anthropological Hoax." PhD. dissertation, Rutgers, 1995.

Olmstead, A.T. "Assyrian Chronology." *American Journal of Semitic Languages* 38 (1921/22), 225-28.

—. "The Chronology of Jesus' Life." *ATR* 24 (1942), 1-26.

Olsen, Florence. "Researchers Seek to Build Data 'Landscapes' for Classroom and Lab." *CHE* (24 September 1999), A39.

Olson, K.A. "Eusebius and the *Testimonium Flavianum*." *CBQ* 61 (1999), 305-22.

Olsson, Ingrid. "Experiences of ^{14}C Dating of Samples From Volcanic Areas." *Pact* 29 (1991), 213-23.

—. "Geophysical Aspects of Problems of Interpretations of Icelandic Radiocarbon Dates of Archaeological Samples." *NAR* 32 (1999), 95-110.

O'Mara, Patrick. "Toward a Multi-Modeled Chronology of the 18th Dynasty." *Discussions in Egyptology* 17 (1990), 29-44.

Ong Tee-wah. "On the Date of the Chou Conquest of the Shang." *Journal of Nanyang University* 2 (1968), 157-59.

Oppenheim, A. Leo. *Ancient Mesopotamia: Portrait of a Dead Civilization*. Chicago, 1977.

Orality and Literacy in the Middle Ages: Symbioses, Performances, Fictions. Ed. Mark Chinca and C. Young. Turnhout, 2005.

Orans, Martin. *Not Even Wrong: Margaret Mead, Derek Freeman, and the Samoans*. Novato, Calif., 1996.

Orvell, Miles. *The Real Thing: Imitation and Authenticity in American Culture, 1880-*

1940. Chapel Hill, 1989.

Ottaway, James. "Publish or be Damned: Problems in Archaeological Publication." In *Mauerschau: Festschrift für Manfred Korfmann.* 3 vols.: Remshalden-Grumbach, 2002, 3:1141-51.

Owen, John. *The Latine Epigrams of John Owen.* Trans. Thomas Harvey. London, 1677.

Paget, J. Carleton. "Josephus and Christianity." *JTS* 52 (2001), 535-624.

Pai, Hyung Il. *Constructing 'Korean' Origins: a Critical Review of Archaeological, Historical, and Racial Myths in Korean State-Formation Theories.* Cambridge, 2000.

Paine, Robert. "Masada: a History of a Memory." *History and Anthropology* 6 (1994), 371-409.

Pallis, S.A. *The Antiquity of Iraq.* Copenhagen, 1956.

—. *Chronology of the Shub-ad Culture.* Copenhagen, 1941.

Pang, Kevin D. "Extraordinary Floods in Early Chinese History: Their Absolute Dating." *Journal of Hydrology* 96 (1987), 139-55.

Pang Bangben. "In Search of the Shu Kingdom: Ancient Legends and New Archaeological Discoveries in Sichuan." *Journal of East Asian Archaeology* 4 (2002), 75-99.

Pankenier, David W. "Astronomical Dates in Shang and Western Zhou." *EC* (1981/82), 3-37.

—. "Forum." *EC* 15 (1990), 117-32.

—. "*Mozi* and the Dates of Xia, Shang, and Zhou." *EC* 10 (1983/85), 175-83.

—. "Reflections of the Lunar Aspect on Western Chou Chronology." *TP* 78 (1992), 33-76.

Parker, John. "The Columbus Landfall Problem: a Historical Perspective." *TI* 15 (1983), 85-103.

Parker Pearson, Mike. "Reassessing *Robert Drury's Journal* as a Historical Source for Southern Madagascar." *HA* 23 (1996), 233-56.

Passell, Peter. "Review of Fogel and Engerman, *Time on the Cross.*" *New York Times Book Review* (28 April 1974), 4.

Pawson, Stuart. *Some by Fire.* London, 1999.

Pearl, Raymond. *Introduction to Medical Biometry and Statistics.* 3d. rev. ed. Philadelphia, 1940.

Peirce, C.S. *Collected Papers of Charles Sanders Peirce.* Ed. Charles Hartshorne and Paul Weiss. 6 vols. Cambridge, Mass., 1960.

Peñuela, Joaquín María. "La inscripción asíria IM 55644 y la cronología de los reyes de Tiro." *Sefarad* 13 (1953), 217-37; 14 (1954), 3-42.

Perry, Anne. *Bedford Square.* New York, 1999.

Perry, F.T. *The Chronicles of Eri.* London, 1939.

Peters, John U. "Lincoln's Gettysburg Address," *Explicator* 60 (2001/02), 22-24.

Petrie, W.M. Flinders. *History of Egypt From the Earliest Kings to the XVIth Dynasty.* London, 1924.

Pettinato, Giovanni. *La città sepolta. I misteri di Ebla.* Rome, 1999.

Pine, Lisa. "The Dissemination of Nazi Ideology and Family Values Through

Textbooks." *History of Education* 25 (1996), 91-109.

Plate Tectonics: an Insider's Story of the Modern Theory of the Earth. Ed. Naomi Oreskes. Boulder, 2001.

Plato. *The Republic*. Trans. Richard Sterling and William Scott. New York, 1985.

Playfair, William. *The Commercial and Political Atlas*. London, 1786.

Poebel, Arno. "The Khorsabad King List." *JNES* 1 (1942), 247-306, 2 (1943), 56-90, 460-92.

Poole, R.S. *Horae Egyptiacae: the Chronology of Ancient Egypt*. London, 1851.

Poole, Stafford. *Our Lady of Guadalupe: the Origins and Sources of a Mexican National Symbol, 1531-1797*. Tucson, 1995.

Poovey, Mary. *A History of the Modern Fact: Problems of Knowledge in the Sciences of Wealth and Society*. Chicago, 1998.

Pope, Nancy. "Accuracy of References in Ten Library Science Journals." *Reference Quarterly* 32 (1992), 240-43.

Pope-Hennessey, John. "Storm Over the Sistine Ceiling." *New York Review of Books* (8 October 1987), 17-19.

Postgate, Nicholas. "The Chronology of Assyria: an Insurmountable Obstacle." *Cambridge Archaeological Journal* 1 (1991), 244-46.

Potter, David. *Literary Texts and the Roman Historian*. London, 1999.

Poulouin, Claudine. *Le temps des origines*. Paris, 1998.

Prem, Hanns. "The 'Canek Manuscript' and Other Faked Documents." *AM* 10 (1999), 297-311.

Prevas, John. *Hannibal Crosses the Alps: the Enigma Re-examined*. Rockville Center, N.Y., 1998.

Protection of Intellectual, Biological, and Cultural Property in Papua New Guinea. Ed. Kathy Whimp and Mark Busse. Canberra, 2000.

Provan, Iain. "In the Stable of the Dwarves: Testimony, Interpretation, Faith, and the History of Israel." In *IOSOT Congress Volume 1998*. Leiden, 2000, 281-319.

Pugh, Anthony R. *The Growth of* A la recherche du temps perdu*: a Chronological Examination of Proust's Manuscripts from 1909 to 1914*. 2 vols. Toronto, 2004.

Purdy, Strother. "Sinuhe and the Question of Literary types." *ZÄS* 104 (1977), 112-27.

Querying the Medieval: Text and the History of Practices in South Asia. Ed. Ronald Inden. Oxford, 2000.

Rachewitz, Igor de. "Marco Polo Did Go to China." *Zentralasiatische Studien*. 27 (1997), 34-92.

— and Donald Leslie. "Review of *City of Light*." *Journal of Asian History* 32 (1998), 180-85

Radosh, Daniel. "Why American Kids Don't Consider Harry Potter an Insufferable Prig." *New Yorker* 75 (20 September 1999), 54-55.

Rafinesque, Constantine. *The American Nations*. Philadelphia, 1836.

Rainey, Anson. "Review of T.L. Thompson, *Early History of the Israelite People*." *AJS Review* 20 (1995), 156-60.

Ramaswamy, Sumathi. "Catastrophic Cartographies: Mapping the Lost Continent of

Lemuria." *Representations* 67 (Summer 1999), 92-129.

Ranger, Terence. "Nationalist Historiography, Patriotic History, and the History of the Nation: the Struggle over the Past in Zimbabwe." *Journal of Southern African Studies* 30 (2004), 215-34.

Ratcliffe, Donald. "The *Das Kapital* of American Negro Slavery? *Time on the Cross* After Two Years." *Durham University Journal* 69 (1976/77), 103-30.

Rawlinson, G.W. "Assyrian History," *Athenaeum* 1805 (31 May 1862), 724-25.

Reade, J.E. "Assyrian Eponyms, Kings, and Pretenders, 648-605 BC." *Orientalia* 67 (1998), 255-65.

Redford, Donald. "A Note on the Chronology of Dynasty 25 and the Inscription of Sargon II at Tang-i Var." *Orientalia* 68 (1999), 58-60.

Reichel, Clemens. "A Modern Crime and an Ancient Mystery: the Seal of Bilalama." In *Festschrift für Burkhart Kienast*. Ed. Gebhard Selz. Münster, 2003, 355-89.

Reid, J.M. *Traveller Extraordinary: the Life of James Bruce of Kinnaird.* London, 1968.

Reiner, Erica and David Pingree. *The Venus Tablets of Ammisaduqa.* Malibu, 1975.

Renan, Ernest. "Qu'est-ce qu'une nation?" In idem., *Oeuvres Complètes*. Ed. Henriette Psichari. 10 vols. Paris, 1947-61 [1882], 1:887-906.

Ribeiro, Brian. "Is Pyrrhonism Psychologically Possible?" *Ancient Philosophy* 22 (2002), 319-31.

Ricci, Seymour de. "La table de Palermo." *Comptes-Rendus de l'Académie des Inscriptions et Belles-Lettres* (1917), 107-15.

Ridley, Ronald. "Auguste Mariette: One Hundred Years After." *Abr-Nahrain* 22 (1983/84), 118-58.

Riniolo, Todd et al. "An Archival Study of Eyewitness Memory of the *Titanic*'s Final Plunge." *Journal of General Psychology* 130 (2003), 89-95.

Roberton, J.B.W. "The Significance of New Zealand Tribal Tradition." *JPS* 67 (1958), 39-57.

Roberts, David. *Great Exploration Hoaxes*. New York, 2001.

Roberts, Richard. "The Possibilities of Precolonial West African History." *CJAS* 32 (1998), 162-73.

Robertshaw, Peter. "Sibling Rivalry? The Intersections of Archeology and History." *HA* 27 (2000), 261-86.

Robertson, William. *History of the Reign of Charles the Fifth.* 2 vols. London, 1856 [1769].

Rogers, Raymond N. "Studies on the Radiocarbon Sample from the Shroud of Turin." *Thermochimica Acta* 425 (2005), 189-94.

Rollinger, Robert. "Der Stammbaum des achaimenidischen Könighauses oder die Frage der Legitimität der Herrschaft des Dareios." *Archäologisches Mitteilungen aus Iran* 30 (1998), 155-209.

Ross, Charles. "The Electronic Text and the Death of the Critical Edition." In *The Literary Text in the Digital Age.* Ed. Richard Finneran. Ann Arbor, 1996, 225-31.

Rostworowski Díez de Canseco, María. *History of the Inca Realm.* New York, 1999.

Rowe, J.H. "Absolute Chronology in the Andean Region." *AAy* 10 (1944/45), 265-84.

Rowton, M.B. "The Date of Hammurabi." *JNES* 17 (1958), 97-111.

Rudelson, Justin. "The Xinjiang Mummies and Foreign Angels: Art, Archaeology, and Uyghur Nationalism in Chinese Central Asia." In *Cultural Contact, History, and Ethnicity in Inner Asia*. Ed. Michael Gervers and Wayne Schlepp. Toronto, 1996, 168-83.

Rudwick, Martin. *The Meaning of Fossils*. New York, 1976.

Runnels, Curtis. "The Place of Book Reviews in the Professional Literature." *Journal of Field Archaeology* 21 (1994), 357-60.

Russell, Thomas. "Shakespearean Coinages: Fewer Than Supposed?" *English Language Notes* 16/3 (March 1989), 8-18.

Safar, Fuad. "A Further Text of Shalmaneser III from Assur." *Sumer* 7 (1951), 3-21.

Sahlins, Marshall. *Historical Metaphors and Mythical Realities: Structure in the Early History of the Sandwich Islands Kingdom*. Ann Arbor, 1981.

—. *How "Natives" Think: About Captain Cook, for Example*. Chicago, 1995.

—. *Islands of History*. Chicago, 1985.

Salmon, Merrilee. *Philosophy and Archaeology*. New York, 1982.

—. "Philosophy of Archaeology: Current Issues." *Journal of Archaeological Research* 1 (1993), 323-43.

Salt, Henry. *A Voyage to Abyssinia and Travels into the Interior of that Country.* London, 1814.

Sanz, Carlos, ed. *Diario de Colón: libro de primera navegación de las Indias*. Madrid, 1962.

Saussure, Léopold de. "La chronologie chinoise et l'avènement des Tcheou." *TP* (1924), 287-346; 29 (1932), 276-386.

Säve-Söderbergh, T. and I.U. Olsson. "C^{14} Dating and Egyptian Chronology." In *Radiocarbon Variations and Absolute Chronology*. Ed. Ingrid Olsson. Stockholm, 1969, 35-55.

Schacker, Jennifer. *National Dreams: the Remaking of Fairy Tales in the Nineteenth Century.* Philadelphia, 2003.

Schäfer, Jürgen. *Documentation in the O.E.D.: Shakespeare and Nashe as Test Cases*. Oxford, 1980.

Scheffler, Eben. "Debating the Late-Dating of the Old Testament." *Old Testament Essays* 11 (1998), 522-33.

Scheiber, Harry. "Black is Computable: the Controversy over *Time on the Cross* and the History of American Slavery." *American Scholar* 44 (1974/75), 656-73.

Scheub, Harold. *The Poem in the Story: Music, Poetry, and Narrative*. Madison, 2002.

Schiffer, Michael. *Behavioral Archaeology*. New York, 1976.

Schindler, Marc. "The Johannine Comma: Bad Translation, Bad Theology." *Dialogue* 29 (Fall 1996), 157-64.

Schoolcraft's Expedition to Lake Itasca: the Discovery of the Source of the Mississippi. Ed. Philip Mason. East Lansing, 1958.

Schoville, Keith. *Biblical Archaeology in Focus*. Grand Rapids, 1978.

Schwartz, Barry, Yael Zerubavel, and Bernice Barnett. "The Recovery of Masada: a Study in Collective Memory." *Sociological Quarterly* 27 (1986), 147-64.

Schwartz, Matthew and Kalman Kaplan. "Judaism, Masada, and Suicide." *Omega* 25

(1992), 127-32.

Scodel, Ruth. *Credible Impossibilities: Conventions and Strategies of Verisimilitude in Homer and Greek Tragedy*, Stuttgart, 1999.

Scott, Susan and Christopher Duncan. *Biology of Plagues: Evidence from Historical Populations*. Cambridge, 2001.

—. *Return of the Black Death*. Chichester, 2004.

Seaver, Kirsten A. *Maps, Myths, and Men: the Story of the Vinland Map*. Stanford, 2004.

Sedley, Kate. *The Brothers of Glastonbury.* London, 1997.

Seldeslachts, Erik. "The End of the Road for the Indo-Greeks?" *Iranica Antiqua* 39 (2004), 249-95.

Shankman, Paul. "The History of Samoan Sexual Conduct and the Mead-Freeman Controversy." *AA* 98 (1996), 555-67.

Shanks, Hershel. "Blood on the Floor at New York Dead Sea Scroll Conference." *BAR* 19/2 (March-April 1993), 63-72.

—. "The Exodus and the Crossing of the Red Sea According to Hans Goedicke." *BAR* 6/5 (September-October 1981), 42-50.

—. "The Meaning of Unhistory: Not Everyone Shows Up in the Written Record." *BAR* 25/3 (May-June 1999), 6, 59.

Shargel, Baila. "The Evolution of the Masada Myth." *Judaism* 28 (1979), 357-71.

Sharlet, Jeff. "Author's Methods Lead to Showdown Over Much-Admired Book on Old West." *CHE* (11 June 1999), A19-A20.

Shaughnessy, Edward L. "'New' Evidence of the Zhou Conquest." *EC* 6 (1980/81), 57-79.

—. "New Sources of Western Zhou History: Recent Discoveries of Inscribed Bronze Vessels." *Early China* 26/27 (2001/02), 73-98.

—. *Sources of Western Zhou History: Inscribed Bronze Vessels*. Berkeley, 1991.

Shell Games: Studies in Scams, Frauds, and Deceits, 1399-1650. Ed. Mark Crane, Richard Raiswell, and Margaret Reeves. Toronto, 2004.

Shrimpton, Gordon. *History and Memory in Ancient Greece*. Montreal, 1997.

Sidersky, D. "Nouvelle étude sur la chronologie de la dynastie Hamurapienne." *RA* 37 (1940/41), 45-54.

Silberman, Neil. *Between Past and Present: Archaeology, Ideology, and Nationalism in the Modern Middle East*. New York, 1989.

—. *A Prophet From Amongst You: the Life of Yigael Yadin, Soldier, Scholar, and Mythmaker of Modern Israel*. New York, 1994.

Silverstein, Arthur. "'The End is Near!' the Phenomenon of the Declaration of Closure in a Discipline." *HS* 37 (1999), 407-25.

Sima Qian. *The Great Scribe's Records*. Ed. William Nienhauser and Robert Reynolds. Trans. Tsai-fa Cheng, Zongli Lu, and William H. Nienhauser. Bloomington, 1994 to date.

—. *Records of the Grand Historian: Qin Dynasty*. Trans. Burton Watson. New York, 1993.

Simms, William Gilmore. *Views and Reviews in American Literature, History, and*

Fiction. 2 vols. New York, 1845.

Skinner, Quintin. *Fallen Gods*. London, 2003.

Slotkin, Richard. *Gunfighter Nation: the Myth of the Frontier in Twentieth-Century America*. New York, 1992.

Smallwood, E. Mary. *The Jews Under Roman Rule from Pompey to Diocletian*. Leiden, 1976.

Smith, Alan K. *Creating a World Economy: Merchant Capital, Colonialism, and World Trade, 1400-1825*. Boulder, 1991.

Smith, H.S. "Egypt and C^{14} Dating." *Antiquity* 38 (1964), 32-37.

Snider, Alvin. "Stifling the Naysayer in the Age of Compulsory Niceness." *CHE* (7 May 1999), A64.

Snyder, Christopher. "Review of N.J. Higham, *King Arthur: Myth-Making and History*." *Arthuriana* 13/2 (2003), 119-20.

Solms, Mark. "Controversies in Freud Translation." *Psychoanalysis and History* 1 (1998), 28-43.

Sorenson, John. "The 'Brass Plates' and Biblical Scholarship." *Dialogue* 10/3 (Fall 1977), 31-39.

—. *Mapping Mormon*. Provo, 2000.

Southgate, Beverly. "Blackloism and Tradition: from Theological Certainty to Historiographical Doubt." *JHI* 61 (2000), 97-114.

"Soviet Cartographic Falsification." *Military Engineer* no. 410 (Nov-Dec 1970), 389-91.

Spall, Richard. "Book Reviews: Some Basics for Authors and Reviewers." *Editing History* 14/2 (Fall 1998), 3-6.

Spencer, Sally. *The Golden Mile of Murder*. Sutton, 2001.

Sperling, S. David. *The Original Torah*. New York, 1998.

The Spoken Word: Oral Culture in Britain, 1500-1850. Ed. Adam Fox and Daniel Wolff. Manchester, 2002.

Spriggs, Matthew. "Pacific Archaeologies: Contested Ground in the Construction of Pacific History." *Journal of Pacific History* 34 (1999), 109-21.

Ssu-ma Ch'ien. *The Grand Scribe's Records, I, the Basic Annals of Pre-Han China*. Ed. William H. Nienhauser, jr. Bloomington, 1994.

Stamm, Anne. "Jean-Baptiste Douville: voyage au Congo (1827-1830)." *CEA* 37 (1970), 5-39.

Stark, Rodney. *The Rise of Christianity*. Princeton, 1996.

Steggemann, Hartmut. "Qumran, Founded for Scripture: the Background and Significance of the Dead Sea Scrolls." *Proceedings of the British Academy* 97 (1998), 1-14.

Stephenson, F.R. *Historical Eclipses and Earth's Rotation.* Cambridge, 1997.

Stevens, Michael E. "'The Most Important Scholarly Work:' Reflections on Twenty Years of Change in Historical Editing." *Documentary Editing* 20 (1998), 81-84, 97.

Stieg, Margaret. "The Information Needs of Historians." *College and Research Libraries* 42 (1981), 549-60.

Stigler, George J. *Memoirs of an Unregulated Economist*. Chicago, 2003.

Stille, Alexander. "The Man Who Remembers." *New Yorker* 74 (15 February 1999), 50-63.

—. "Overload." *New Yorker* 74 (8 March 1999), 38-44.

Stokvis, A.M.H.J. *Manuel d'histoire, de généalogie et de chronologie de tous les états du globe.* 4 vols. Leiden, 1888-93.

Stommel, Henry. *Lost Islands.* Vancouver, 1984.

Stone, Jeffrey. "The District Map: an Episode in British Colonial Cartography in Africa, with Particular Relation to Northern Rhodesia." *Cartographic Journal* 19 (1982), 104-12.

Storey, Glenn. "Archaeology and Roman Society: Integrating Textual and Archaeological Data." *Journal of Archaeological Research* 7 (1999), 203-45.

Strasburger, H. "Umblick im Trümmerfeld der griechischen Geschichtsschreibung." In *Historiographia Antiqua.* Louvain, 1977, 3-52.

Sun Pin. *Sun Pin Military Methods.* Trans. and ed. Ralph Sawyer and Mei-chün Sawyer. Boulder, 1995.

Sutch, Richard. "The Treatment Received by American Slaves: a Critical Review of Evidence Presented in *Time on the Cross,*" *Explorations in Economic History* 12 (1975), 335-438.

Sveinbjörnsdóttir, Arny et al. "^{14}C Dating of the Settlement of Iceland." *Radiocarbon* 46 (2004), 387-94.

Swedlund, Alan and Duane Anderson. "Gordon Creek Woman Meets Kennewick Man: New Interpretations and Protocols Regarding the Peopling of the Americas." *AAy* 64 (1999), 569-76.

Syrkin, Marie. "The Paradox of Masada." *Midstream* 19 (October 1973), 66-70.

Takashi, Okazaki. "Japan and the Continent." In *The Cambridge History of Japan. I. Ancient Japan.* Cambridge, 1993, 268-316.

Tavard, George. *The Seventeenth-Century Tradition: a Study in Recusant Thought.* Leiden, 1978.

Taylor, William. "Objects and Advantages of Statistical Science." *Foreign Quarterly Review* 16 (1835), 103-16.

Temple, Robert. *The Sirius Mystery.* London, 1975.

—. *The Sirius Mystery: New Scientific Evidence of Alien Contact 5,000 Years Ago.* Rochester Vt., 1998.

Terrill, W. Andrew. "The Political Mythology of the Battle of Karameh." *Middle East Journal* 55 (2001), 91-111.

Tetley, M. Christine. *The Reconstructed Chronology of the Divided Kingdom.* Winona Lake, Ind., 2005.

Thaplyal, K.K. "Situating Govindragupta in History." *Indian Historical Review* 27 (2000), 41-60.

Theodársson, Páll. "Aldur landnáms og geislakolsgreiningar." *Skírnir* 17 (1997), 92-110.

—. "Norse Settlement in Iceland—Close to AD 700?" *NAR* 31 (1998), 29-38.

Thomas, David Hurst. *Skull Wars: Kennewick Man, Archaeology, and the Battle for Native American Identity.* New York, 2000.

Thoms, W.J. *Human Longevity: Its Facts and Fictions.* London, 1879.

Thomson, Basil. *The Diversions of a Prime Minister.* Edinburgh, 1894.

Thornton, Cliff. "Kamehameha's Arrow." *Cook's Log* 27/3 (2004), 4.

Thornton, John. "The Historian and the Precolonial African Economy." *African Economic History* 19 (1990/91), 45-54.

Thou Shalt Not Kill: Poles on Jedwabne. Warsaw, 2002.

Thureau-Dangin, François. "La chronologie des trois premières dynasties babyloniennes." *RA* 24 (1927), 181-98.

Le topos du manuscrit trouvé: hommages à Christian Angelet. Ed. Jan Herman and Fernand Hallyn. Louvain, 1999.

Total Baseball. Ed. John Thorn and Pete Palmer. New York, 1989.

Tov, Emmanuel. *Textual Criticism of the Hebrew Bible.* Minneapolis, 1992.

Toynbee, Arnold. *Some Problems of Greek History.* London, 1969.

The Trojan War: the Chronicles of Dictys of Crete and Dares the Phrygian. Ed. and trans. R.M. Frazer, jr. Bloomington, 1966.

Turnbull, Peter. *Fear of Drowning.* London, 1999.

Tuzin, Donald. "Derek Freeman, 1916-2001." *AA* 104 (2002), 1013-15.

Twain, Mark. *Is Shakespeare Dead?* New York, 1909.

Under the Sky: Astronomy and Mathematics in the Ancient Near East. Ed. John Steele and Annette Imhausen. Münster, 2002.

Unwilling Germans? the Goldhagen Debate. Ed. R.R. Shandley. Minneapolis, 1998.

Urton, Gary. *The History of a Myth. Pacariqtambo and the Origin of the Inkas.* Austin, 1990.

Utley, Francis. "The One Hundred and Three Names of Noah's Wife." *Speculum* 15 (1941), 426-52.

Van Dantzig, Albert. "English Bosman and Dutch Bosman: a Comparison of Texts." *HA* 2 (1975), 185-216; 3 (1976), 91-126; 4 (1977), 247-73; 5 (1978), 225-56; 6 (1979), 265-85; 7 (1980), 281-91; 9 (1982), 285-302; 11 (1984), 307-29.

—. "Willem Bosman's *New and Accurate Description of the Coast of Guinea*: How Accurate is It?" *HA* 1 (1974), 101-08.

Van der Merwe, F.S.G. *William Webb Ellis: fiksie of feite?* Stellenbosch, 1999.

Vansina, Jan. "Historians, Are Archeologists Your Siblings?" *HA* 22 (1995), 369-408.

—. "Kuba Chronology Revisited." *Paideuma* 21 (1975), 134-50.

—. "The Many Uses of Forgeries: the Case of Douville's *Voyage au Congo*," *HA* 31 (2004), 369-87.

—. *Oral Tradition: a Study in Historical Methodology.* Chicago, 1965.

—. *Oral Tradition as History.* Madison, 1985.

—. "The Power of Systematic Doubt in Historical Enquiry." *HA* 1 (1974), 109-27.

Vera, Rodrigo. "Manos humanas pintaron la Guadalupana." *Proceso* (Mexico City) (12 May 2002), 25-31.

Vermes, Géza. "The Jesus Notice Re-Examined." *JJS* 38 (1987), 1-10.

Vésteinsson, Orri. "Patterns of Settlement in Iceland: a Study in Prehistory." *Saga-Book of the Viking Society* 22 (1998), 1-29.

Vilhjálmsson, Vilhjálmur Orn. "Dating Problems in Icelandic Archaeology." *NAR* 23

(1990), 43-53.

—. "The Early Settlement of Iceland: Wishful Thinking or an Archaeological Innovation?" *Acta Archaeologica* 62 (1991), 167-81.

Vincent, John. *An Intelligent Person's Guide to History.* London, 1996.

The Vinland Map and the Tartar Relation. Ed. R.A. Skelton, Thomas Marston, and George Painter. New Haven, 1965.

The Vinland Map and the Tartar Relation. Ed. R.A. Skelton, Thomas Marston, and George Painter. 2d ed. New Haven, 1995.

Vinson, J. Chal. *Thomas Nast: Political Cartoonist.* Athens, Ga., 1967.

Vlasich, James. *A Legend for the Legendary: the Origins of the Baseball Hall of Fame.* Bowling Green, 1990.

Voight, David. "Fie on Figure Filberts: Some Crimes Against Clio." *Baseball Research Journal* 10 (1983), 32-38.

Walam Olum or Red Score: the Migration Legend of the Lenni Lenape or Delaware Indians. Indianapolis, 1954.

Walker, Norman. "Concerning the Jaubertian Chronology of the Passion." *NT* 3 (1959), 317-20.

Walpole, Horace. *The Works of Horatio Walpole.* 5 vols. London, 1798.

Warburton, David. "Eclipses, Venus-Cycles, and Chronology." *Akkadica* 123 (2002), 108-14.

Warrell, Ian. *Turner and Venice.* London, 2003.

Washington, George. *Writings of George Washington.* Ed. Jared Sparks. 12 vols. Boston, 1838-39.

Watkins, Joe E. "Beyond the Margin: First Nations and Archaeology in North America," *AAy* 68 (2003), 273-85.

Watson, Burton. "The *Shih chi* and I." *Chinese Literature: Essays, Articles, Reviews* 17 (1995), 199-206.

We Saw Lincoln Shot: One Hundred Eyewitness Accounts. Ed. Timothy Good. Jackson, 1995.

Weidner, E.F. *Der Assyrologie, 1914-1922.* Leipzig, 1922.

—. *Die Könige von Assyrien.* Leipzig, 1921.

Weinstein, Lisa. "Ancient Works, Modern Dilemmas: the Dead Sea Scrolls Copyright Case." *American University Law Review* 43 (1994), 1637-71.

Weiss-Rosmarin, Trude. "Masada and Yavneh." *Jewish Spectator* 31 (November 1966), 4-7.

—. "Masada, Josephus, and Yadin." *Jewish Spectator* 32 (October 1967), 2-8, 30-32.

Wells, G.A. *The Jesus Myth.* Chicago, 1999.

Wells, Gary and Elizabeth Olson. "Eyewitness Testimony," *Annual Review of Psychology* 54 (2003), 277-95.

Wenham, J.W. "Large Numbers in the Old Testament." *Tyndale Bulletin* 18 (1967), 19-53.

Werckmeister, O.K. "The Political Ideology of the Bayeux Tapestry." *Studi Medievali* 17 (1976), 535-95.

What Ifs? of American History: Eminent Historians Imagine What Might Have Been. Ed.

Robert Cowley. New York, 2003.

What Might Have Been: Leading Historians on Twelve What Ifs of History. Ed. Andrew Roberts. London, 2004.

What Might Have Been: the Social Psychology of Counterfactual Thinking. Ed. Neal J. Rose and James M. Olson. Mahwah, N.J., 2005.

Whealey, Alice. *Josephus on Jesus: the* Testimonium Flavianum *Controversy from Late Antiquity to Modern Times.* New York, 2003.

Whiston, William. *Memoirs of the Life and Writings of Mr. William Whiston.* 3 vols. London, 1749.

Whitelam, Keith. "'Israel is Laid Waste: His Seed is No More:' What if Merneptah's Scribes Were Telling the Truth?" In *VHB*, 8-22.

Whiteley, Peter M. "Why Anthropology Needs More History." *Journal of Anthropological Research* 60 (2004), 487-514.

Whitmore, Thomas. *Disease and Death in Early Colonial Mexico: Simulating Amerindian Depopulation.* Boulder, 1992.

Whybray, R. N. "What Do We Know About Ancient Israel?" *Expository Times* 108 (1996), 71-74.

Wiener, M.H. "Time Out: the Current Impasse in Bronze Age Archaeological Dating." In *Metron: Measuring the Aegean Bronze Age.* Ed. Karen P. Foster and Robert Laffineur. Liège, 2003, 363-98.

Wilhelm, Gernot. "Generation Count in Hittite Chronology." In *Mesopotamian Dark Age Revisited.* Ed. Hermann Hunger and Regine Pruzsinszky. Vienna, 2004, 71-79.

Wilkinson, Toby. *Royal Annals of Ancient Egypt: the Palermo Stone and Its Associated Fragments.* London, 2000.

William of Malmesbury. *Gesta Regum Anglorum/The History of the English Kings.* Ed. and trans. R.A.B. Mynors, R.M. Thomson, and M. Winterbottom. Oxford, 1998.

Williams, Amelia. "A Critical Study of the Siege of the Alamo and of the Personnel of Its Defenders." *Southwestern Historical Quarterly* 36 (1932/33), 251-87; 37 (1933/34), 1-44, 79-115, 157-84, 237-312.

Williams, Gerard. *Dr. Mortimer and the Aldgate Mystery.* London, 2000.

Willis, James. *Latin Textual Criticism.* Urbana, 1972.

Wills, Garry. *Lincoln at Gettysburg: the Words that Remade America.* New York, 1992.

Windschuttle, Keith. *The Killing of History.* New York, 1997.

Wiseman, T.P. "Forum." *History Today* 34 (July 1984), 3.

—. *Historiography and Imagination.* Exeter, 1994.

—. "Roman Republic, Year One." *Greece and Rome* 45 (1998), 19-26.

Wlodarczyk, Marta. *Pyrrhonian Inquiry.* Cambridge, 2000.

Wolters, Al. "History and the Copper Scroll." In *Methods of Investigation of the Dead Sea Scrolls and the Khirbet Qumran Site.* Ed. Michael Wise et al. New York, 1994, 285-98.

Woocher, Fredric. "Did Your Eyes Deceive You? Expert Psychological Testimony on the Unreliability of Eyewitness Identification." *Stanford Law Review* 29 (1977), 969-1030.

Wood, Frances. *Did Marco Polo Go to China?* London, 1995.

—. "Did Marco Polo Go to China?" *Asian Affairs* 83 (1996), 296-304.

Words of Our Country. Ed. R.M.W. Dixon. St. Lucia, 1991.

Wright, Donald. "Uprooting Kunta Kinte: On the Perils of Relying on Encyclopedic Informants." *HA* 8 (1981), 205-17.

Wright, Robert. "The Accidental Creationist." *New Yorker* 75 (13 December 1999), 56-65.

Xu, Jay. "The Cemetery of the Western Zhou Lords of Jin." *Artibus Asiae* 56 (1996), 193-231.

Yadav, J.N. Singh. *Yadavas Through the Ages*. Delhi, 1992.

Yadin, Yigael. *Masada: Herod's Fortress and the Zealots' Last Stand*. New York, 1966.

Yavetz, Zvi. "The Personality of Augustus: Reflections on Syme's *Roman Revolution*." In *Between Republic and Empire: Interpretations of Augustus and His Principate*. Ed. G.W. Bowersock et al. Berkeley, 1990, 21-41.

Yetts, W. Perceval. "The Shang-Yin Dynasty and the An-yang Finds." *Journal of the Royal Asiatic Society* (1933), 657-85.

Yurco, F.J. "Merenptah's Canaanite Campaign." *JARCE* 23 (1986), 189-215.

Zerjal, Tatiana et al. "The Genetic Legacy of the Mongols." *American Journal of Human Genetics* 72 (2003), 717-21.

Zerubavel, Yael. *Recovered Roots: Collective Memory and the Making of Israeli National Tradition*. Chicago, 1995.

Zhang Peiyu. "Forum." *EC* 15 (1990), 133-50.

Zuidema, R.T. *The Ceque System of Cuzco: the Social Organization of the Capital of the Inca*. Leiden, 1964.

—. *Inca Civilization in Cuzco*. Trans. Jean-Jacques Decoster. Austin, 1990.

Zumthor, Paul. "Intertextualité et mouvance." *Littérature* 41 (1981), 8-16.

Zwelling, Jeremy. "The Fictions of the Bible." *HT* 39 (2000), 117-41.

INDEX

Abraham, historicity of, 22, 104
Abu-Lughod, Janet, 61
Achaemenid dynasty, 173, 252n19
Acton, John Dahlberg, Baron, 2, 6, 224, 243
Acts of the Apostles, 54, 109
Adam, height of, 192
Aelfgyva, 274n21
African Studies Review, 203
age of the earth, 10, 236-37
Ahlström, Gösta, 241
Akhenaten, 137
Alalakh, 182
Alamo, myth of the, 122-23, 260n33
Albarella, Umberto, 75
Albright, W.F., 52, 68, 137, 142-44, 170, 264n57
Aling, Charles, 171
Allan, Sarah, 156
Allen, James, 219
alternative histories, 20-22
Amenemhat II, 135, 242
Ammisaduqa, 138-39
anachronisms: in baseball rules, 107-8; in bible, 104-5 in meanings of words, 105; in succession practices, 105-6
Anderson, Duane, 67
Angkor Wat, 74
angla, meaning of, 99
Année Philologique, 2, 225
annotation, 168-69, 267n20
anonyms: in bible, 179
Anson, A.C., 189
Antandroy, 96
Antietam, 21
Appleby, Joyce et al: on postmodernism, 25
archeologists: and Masada, 119-20
archeology: access issues, 231-32; and bible, 67-68, 72; epistemology of, 75-76; high

costs of, 74; and nationalism, 73-74; preservation issues, 70-71; and public, 67-68; and written record, 75
archives: in Ghana, 226-27; in Tyre, 52-53; in U.S., 239
argument from silence, 37-38, 173-85
Arnason, Ingólfr, 133
Arrian, 53, 108, 167
Art de vérifier les dates, 10
Arthur, king, 40, 57, 248n27
Asante, 214-15
Aššur-bil-nišešu, 139
Assyria, 139-41 143, 189, 239
authorship, concept of, 110, 219
Avesta, 126
Avila, Roberto, 102
Aztecs: and counterfactual history, 21

Babylon, First Dynasty of, 137, 138-39, 142, 144, 145
Bactria, 249
Baillie, M.G.L., 158-59, 160, 229
Balezor, ruler of Tyre, 51-52
Ba'limanzer, ruler of Tyre, 51-52
Bamboo Annals, 151-57, 171
Bantu expansion, 167
Barnard, Noel, 157
Barnes, William, 52, 241
Barrett, C.K., 54, 109
baseball, effects of changes in, 107-8; myth of origins, 117; records of, 102-3, 107, 189-90
Basque-Irish connection, 251n55
Bayeux Tapestry, 217-18
Beckerath, Jürgen von, 262n14
Beek, Walter van, 111-12
Beinlich-Seeber, Christine, 262n5

Turner, J.M.W., 219
Tuthmosis I, 145
Twain, Mark, 173
Tweed, William, 196
Tyre, chronology of, 51-55

cUbar, 67
Ugarit, 182, 239
universe, size of, 185, 239
Ur III dynasty, 141
Ussher, James, 236
Utley, Francis, 179

Van Dantzig, Albert, 101
Vansina, Jan, 79
Velikovsky, Immanuel, 126
Velleius Paterculus, P., 216
Venus Tablets, 138-39, 142, 143, 145, 146, 148, 263n34
Vera, Rodrigo, 268n16
verisimilitude in fiction, 258n22
Vésteinsson, Orri, 169-70
Vianney, Jean-Baptiste, 108
Vilhjálmsson, V.O., 132
Vincent, John, 85
Vinland map, 206-7, 273n26
volcanic eruptions: in oral tradition, 88-89; Thera, 126, 130-31, 261n12
Voltaire, 227
Vratakhanda, 128-29

Wa, 174
Waddington, W.G., 150
Walam Olum, 38-39
Walker, Norman, 35
Walpole, Horace, 96
wan-guo period in ancient China, 174
warfare: quantifying, 192-94, 271n33
Washington, George, 57, 215
Watson, Burton, 100
Wegener, Alfred, 238
Wei zhi, 174

Weidner, Ernst, 138, 139, 143
Weiss-Rosmartin, Trude, 122, 259n12
Wells, G.A., 178
Wen Wang, 154
Whiston, William, 149
Whitelam, Keith, 48
Whitmore, Thomas, 195
Whybray, R.N., 250n22
Widdowson, J.D.A., 83
"Wildwood Flower," 255n27
Wilkins, John, 188
William I, king of England, 218
William of Jumièges, 171
William of Malmesbury, 10
William of Poitiers, 171
Williams, Ted, 21, 102-3
Wiseman, T.P., 11, 39, 237
Wolters, Al, 59
Wood, Frances, 176, 268n14
Wright, Frank Lloyd, 60
Wright, Robert, 167
Wyclif, John, 97

Xia dynasty, 38, 151-57
Xian, 74
Xu, Jay, 130

Yadav, J.N.S., 129
Yadin, Yigael, 119-20, 122, 259n7
Yamatai, 174
Yavetz, Zvi, 36
Yersinia pestis, 183-84
Yetts, W.P., 152
Yizhoushu, 153
Yü, 154

Zealots, 119-22
Zertal, Adam, 254n39
Zhang Peiyu, 155, 157
Zhou dynasty, 43, 129-30, 151-57, 242
Zuidema, R.T., 114-15, 258n32
Zumthor, Paul, 46